Seeing the
FOREST
Despite the
TREE

The Meaning and Purpose for Life on Earth

RICK SCHRAMM

WESTBOW·
PRESS
A DIVISION OF THOMAS NELSON
& ZONDERVAN

WestBow Press books may be ordered through booksellers or by contacting:

WestBow Press
A Division of Thomas Nelson & Zondervan
1663 Liberty Drive
Bloomington, IN 47403
www.westbowpress.com
1 (866) 928-1240

Scripture taken from the New King James Version®. Copyright © 1982 by Thomas Nelson, Inc. Used by permission.

Any people depicted in stock imagery provided by Thinkstock are models, and such images are being used for illustrative purposes only. Certain stock imagery © Thinkstock.

ISBN: 978-1-4908-1746-0 (sc)
ISBN: 978-1-4908-1745-3 (hc)
ISBN: 978-1-4908-1747-7 (e)

Library of Congress Control Number: 2013921144

Printed in the United States of America.

WestBow Press rev. date: 02/06/14

CONTENTS

PREFACE

My name is Rick Schramm, and I am a sinner.

In high school I had a passion for math and science. I graduated from the University of Minnesota as a math and physics double major with the intent of getting a good education so that I could launch a career as a scientist or an engineer and land a well-paying job to pay for a big house, a fancy car, a lake home, and all the things of this world that people think will make them happy. I continued to make my way toward that end: I married my soul mate, and God blessed us with a precious and miraculous son; my wife and I had our dream home built for us; we had two cats looking out the french windows; and our future looked bright.

Then my world came crashing down on me in the spring of 1992. My father died as a result of a series of small heart attacks over the previous few years. Within a month of his death, while I was still grieving that loss, I started to have strange symptoms regarding my vision that were eventually diagnosed as being caused by a brain tumor. After that, a neurosurgeon told me that I was going to first go blind and then die. God saved my life with an eight-hour brain surgery, but then I experienced hydrocephalus and almost died again, and then I underwent a second brain surgery, during which I had a near-death experience. After all of this occurred, when I was so sick that I did not know if I would live and did not know if I wanted to live, God called me to write this book about my experience and how it explains the meaning and purpose for life on this planet earth with words that are found in the pages of the Bible.

So I wondered why God would call me, who had never read the Bible, to do this rather than some skilled theologian who was already familiar with the Bible. Then I remembered that Jesus did not call the religious leaders and scholars of His day to be His disciples; He chose uneducated fishermen and tax collectors. And I ran across this passage in the Bible: "For you see **your calling**, brethren, that **not many wise according to the flesh, not many mighty, not many noble,** *are called.* [27] But God has **chosen** the **foolish things** of the **world** to **put to shame** the **wise**, and God has chosen **the weak things** of the world to **put to shame** the things **which are mighty;** [28] and the **base things** of the world and the things **which are despised** God has **chosen**, and the things **which are not**, to bring to nothing the things **that are,** [29] that **no flesh should glory in His presence**" (**1Corinthians 1:26–29 NKJV**). "Weak," "not mighty," "not noble," and "someone who is not" all pretty much describe my calling and the broken physical, mental, emotional, and spiritual state I was in at that time.

Then I wondered, *If God wanted me to write a book, why did He leave me with such a bad memory?* And God led me to this passage: "But the Helper, the Holy Spirit, whom the Father will send in My name, He will **teach you all things**, and **bring to your remembrance all things that I said to you.** [27] Peace I leave with you, My peace I give to you; not as the world gives do I give to you. **Let not your heart be troubled,** neither **let it be afraid**" (**John 14:26–27 NKJV**).

And finally I wondered, *If God wanted me to write this book, why did He leave me in such poor health and with such physical weakness?* Then I discovered that the apostle Paul had an experience that left him with what he called *a thorn in the flesh*: "And lest I should be exalted above measure by the **abundance of the revelations**, a **thorn in the flesh** was given to me, a messenger of Satan to buffet me, lest I be exalted above measure. [8] Concerning this thing I pleaded with the Lord three times that it **might depart from me.** [9] And He said to me, '**My grace is sufficient for you,** for **My strength is made perfect in weakness.**' Therefore most gladly I will rather **boast in my infirmities**, that the **power of Christ may rest upon me.** [10] Therefore **I take pleasure in infirmities**, in **reproaches**, in **needs**, in **persecutions**, in **distresses**, for Christ's sake. For **when I am weak, then I am strong**" (2 Corinthians 12:8–10 NKJV). While I am most certainly no Paul, all of us who are suffering for Christ's sake would do well to use Paul as our role model, because God has a reason and a purpose for our suffering.

In all this, God wanted me to know that this book about the knowledge and understanding of the meaning and purpose of this temporary life on this temporary earth was not from me but from Him, that I should not try to take any credit for it as if I were someone special, but that I acknowledge that this is a gift from God for the benefit of all. I believe the timing of this revelation of truth is all part of God's plan for the end times, which I believe we are in and which we will see evidence of in a prophecy of Jesus Himself that we will examine in the chapter "The Third Age of the Church."

And I have come to know why God allows us to suffer:

> "*My son,* **do not despise the chastening of the LORD,** *Nor be discouraged when you are* **rebuked by Him**; *⁶ For* **whom the LORD loves He chastens, And scourges every son whom He receives**." *⁷* If you **endure chastening**, God deals with you as with sons; for what son is there whom a father does not chasten? ⁸ But if you are without chastening, of which all have become partakers, then you are illegitimate and not sons … Now **no chastening seems to be joyful for the present**, but **painful**; nevertheless, afterward it yields the **peaceable fruit of righteousness** to those who have been trained by it. (**Hebrews 12:5–8, 11**)

Suffering is the tough love of God that lets us, His children, know that we are going down a path that is harmful and will lead to our death. As we have all experienced, suffering causes us to stop and consider what we are doing, and turns us back to God, who loves us and cares for us. It gives us an opportunity to consider a better way. God has a better way for all of us if we will only stop long enough to consider the truth that He wants us to know. It will change our hearts and minds and make us free. I can tell you that I consider the suffering that I went through in my cancer wake-up call as the best thing that ever happened to me!

To anyone who may be suffering and going through the kind of things I went through, I want you to know that when you cannot see a way out, there is a hope you never dreamed of hoping for. I have dedicated my life to share the truth that God shared with me, for it is a gift of priceless worth that I would not trade for the whole world!

INTRODUCTION

AFTER MY CANCER wake-up call and near-death experience, when I was not even sure if I was going to live, God called me to write a book and even gave me the title of the book I was to write; it was to be called something like *Seeing the Forest despite the Tree*. It was to be the big picture of the truth that we cannot see because we are too close to and too focused on one tree. I used the words "something like" above because when God called me to write this book, He did not communicate to me orally with words that I could hear; rather, an idea came to mind with a strong feeling that it was from God, and I had to struggle to put it into words.

Later in the early years after my experience, a neighbor invited me to talk about my near-death experience at her church. In my talk, I recalled my experience of being before what I called "All Knowledge"; I described it as being like a tree and a like a library—not that it looked like a tree, but knowledge and understanding were arranged in "branches" of knowledge that I could understand as I went "down through." Later when I asked for questions, someone in the audience asked if I had ever connected that Tree of All Knowledge with the Tree of Life. I said I had not, but that was a good idea.

Even though I did not recall "seeing" God in my experience, I knew that it came from God and was about God. While I had a passion for math and science and had gone to college that I might have a career as an engineer or a scientist, this near-death experience convinced me that there was something much more important than that. And God put a hunger for the Word of God on my heart that I cannot explain.

I had memorized some verses from the Bible when I was confirmed in the Christian faith, but I had never read the Bible, let alone studied it, but now that was all I wanted to do. This book is the result of over twenty years of intensely studying the Bible; attending multiple Bible studies; reading and acquiring a small library's worth of Christian books; listening to and watching Christian audio and video tapes, CDs, and DVDs; watching Bible teaching sermons on TV; and attending multiple Christian churches that teach the Bible—as many as three or four on a Sunday—to re-create the incredible knowledge and understanding I had been shown in my experience.

My intent is to let the words of God written in the Bible tell the story. I do not want to say anything that is not found in the Bible, because then it would only be my opinion, and there are already many opinions about what the Bible says. We will examine the ancient Hebrew and Greek when necessary to help us understand the choices the translators made when they chose English words for the ancient Hebrew and Greek words from the original writings, and we will see how the meaning changes and the message becomes clearer and makes more sense if another word is used in translation. Words are not precise; they often can have multiple meanings. As anyone who has learned another language knows, a person can write some ridiculous and hilarious things by creating a word-for-word translation into another language.

Even though we are sometimes confused and befuddled by what the Bible says in English, I am convinced that the disciples who were taught directly by Jesus knew and understood what they wrote and were teaching, and they were willing to die for sharing what they knew with others! I will be using the New King James Version of the Bible unless otherwise noted. I have not changed the text of the Bible verses I quote in any way. The words in italics are those of the original translation. The Bibles that I use do not contain any boldface, so that is what I used to emphasize ideas that I think are important in the Bible text.

I use the NKJV translation of God's Word because it correctly renders some Hebrew words that reveal important concepts in the Bible and it references Old Testament verses quoted in the New Testament. It also works well with *Strong's Exhaustive Concordance of the Bible,* which presents the King James Version with numbers next to the English words and phrases (numbers preceded by an *H* for Hebrew words, such as H120, and a *G* for Greek words, such as G25); this allows us to quickly find the actual Hebrew and Greek words in the original writings and locate their definitions. I use an electronic version of this, which makes finding the ancient definitions even faster.

In this book, I make logical and reasonable interpretations of the meanings of these verses for your consideration. I base my interpretations not on one verse each, but on a number of verses. One property of truth helps us identify the right interpretation: All truths are consistent; one truth never contradicts other truths. When a new interpretation clears up previous confusion and makes sense and has that ring of truth to it, we know that we are on the right track and that understanding will be exciting and may even fill us with "Holy Ghost bumps"!

Winston Churchill once said that to learn a new language is to become a new person. We will experience becoming a new person when we understand what God is trying to say to us, which will happen if we will only listen. There are some amazing things in the Bible that many people, including me, never knew were there. Be prepared to be amazed at how your knowledge and understanding of the Bible change, as mine did. There is hope, peace, love, and unspeakable joy in knowing and understanding the truth of God found in the Bible! In this book I repeat important verses in the Bible because, just as with learning a new language, repetition helps us connect individual ideas together to form a larger framework of understanding that will help us to become a new person. If you are already very familiar with these verses, please be patient because I am also writing this book for people who have never read the Bible or heard of God's Word.

In this book I first describe my cancer wake-up call and my near-death experience—the events that changed my life. I then present an in-depth, focused Bible study examining passages in the Bible that speak of truth, love, connectedness or oneness, and the Tree of Life—the subjects that I can distinctly remember from my experience. With that basic knowledge of the Word of God, we will understand the ways of God and why they alone lead to peace, prosperity, indescribable joy, and eternal life.

From there we will put together verses from all over in the Bible in a timeline fashion to show what the purpose and meaning of this temporary life on this temporary earth is all about. We will learn that this life on earth is not all there is. There is another spiritual reality where God is. When we are done, we will know the answers to questions that people have asked about the Bible through the ages. I think that the reason God has chosen this time to reveal these truths to us is that we are in the end times. A lot of Bible scholars also think that. In this book I will support this view with verses from the Bible.

Below are some examples of questions people have asked in the many Bible studies I have participated in, which we will seek to answer in this book.

- If God is all-powerful and He is a God of love, why is there so much evil on the earth? Either He is not all-powerful or He is not a God of love.
- Why does God seem so harsh in the Old Testament— killing whole nations, children and all—and so much more gentle and kind in the New Testament? Did God change?
- Was God the Father calling the shots in the Old Testament and the kinder and gentler Jesus given that authority in the New Testament?
- Did God learn as He went from the Old Testament to the New Testament?
- Where does the Original Sin doctrine come from, and why were we guilty of Adam's sin before we were even born?
- Why did God hate Esau and love Jacob before they were born and before they even had a chance to do anything good or bad, as described in Romans chapter 9? Is God unrighteous?

- What did Jesus mean when He said of the bread and wine at the Last Supper, "This is My body" and "This is My blood"?
- We are taught that Jesus died to save us, but exactly why did He have to die on the cross?
- Why did God give us the law if He knew it would not and could not save us?
- If God is to separate the believers that are His in the rapture and by the end of the tribulation, what purpose does the millennium serve? Why doesn't He take us right to heaven?
- If God promised the land in the Middle East to the Jews, why don't they possess all the land now?
- How come all the Jews are not saved? God promised Abraham that his descendants would be saved.
- How can those who are not Jews be saved?
- Why is the Bible so mysterious, written in parables and symbolic language? Why doesn't God just come out and tell us the truth that will save us?
- How come God said, "Let there be light," and there was light in the first day of creation, but God did not create the sun, the moon, and the stars for light until the fourth day?
- Is the invisible hand doctrine of capitalism and free trade the best economy for a nation, and is it biblical?
- If Eve sinned first, why is Adam blamed for the fall of man?
- What kind of fruit is the fruit of the Tree of Knowledge of Good and Evil? Is it an apple?
- Why was the way to the Tree of Life blocked so that Adam and Eve could not eat of it and live forever?
- If God's almighty power cannot rescue us from bondage to Satan, how can faith rescue us?
- What is predestination all about?
- Who are the elect of God and when and why were they elected?
- When does the rapture occur—pretribulation, midtribulation, or posttribulation?
- What is the great mystery of oneness—Unio Mystica?

- What is the correct baptism, and what is it for?
- What does it mean to be born again, born of the Spirit, born of God?
- Why did God create man on earth, where Satan and his fallen angels (called demons) are, instead of in heaven?
- What does it mean to be in the Spirit?
- Why, when Christ was raised, did He first descend into hell?
- How is it that God created man in His own image but the Bible says that Seth, the third child born to Adam and Eve, was born in the image of fallen Adam?
- Why was man created male and female in the sixth day of creation in Genesis chapter 1 and then created again in the second chapter?
- Why does God harden Pharaoh's heart? Is God arbitrarily choosing whom He loves and whom He shows wrath?
- Who is the Holy Spirit?
- Who is Satan, and how did he become our adversary and the enemy of our souls?

By the end of this book, we will know and understand the answers to these questions and a lot more. So get out your copy of the NKJV of the Bible and *Strong's Greek and Hebrew Dictionary of the Bible* and discover with me the answers to these questions that will change your life!

MY CANCER EXPERIENCE

THE SPRING OF 1992 was not a good time for me or my family. My father, who had suffered a number of heart attacks over recent years, passed on to be with the Lord April 9, 1992. Within a month of his death, while I was still just beginning to grieve, I started experiencing some very strange sensations. One day in a meeting at work, an eerie, dizzy, light-headed feeling came over me. It didn't last too long, but because I had never felt anything quite like that before, it struck me as being so odd that it startled me.

After that first occurrence, that strange sensation seemed to steadily increase in frequency and intensity. At the age of thirty-five, I was the only member of my family of seven that did not need glasses, but now my eyesight seemed to rapidly degenerate. I went from having 20/10 vision to the point of needing to get fitted with my first pair of glasses in a span of a month or so. I remember telling my wife that I always expected I would need glasses someday, but I didn't think it would happen so fast.

One weekend I was helping my older brother construct the framing and roof on a cabin he was building. I was already having a bit of trouble because I had recently broken a small bone in my left foot and was hobbling around. I remember standing on the roof, trying to measure some plywood that needed to be cut, and I noticed that I was having a hard time lining up the little lines on the tape measure. Finally my vertigo got so bad that, along with my broken foot, I was afraid I would fall off the roof, and so I was relegated to ground work only.

I started to have trouble with depth perception and being able to look up, a condition that I later discovered is called Parinaud's syndrome. I also began to experience increasing difficulty in tracking movement with my eyes. One day while golfing with my wife and my father-in-law, I said to my wife after teeing up a golf ball to drive, "Sweetheart, I definitely see two golf balls!" Soon the symptoms had advanced to include outright double vision, especially when it involved moving my eyes by turning my head quickly. I went from doctor to doctor to try to find out what was going on.

I first went to a general practitioner, who decided that I must be under stress, having just started a new job and being in the middle of building a new house with my wife and all. She said I just needed to get a few good nights of sleep, and she prescribed some sleeping pills. I suppose I was under some stress, but I knew I had been under much greater stress at other times in my life without experiencing anything like this. I never even had the sleeping pill prescription filled.

Someone suggested that I should see an optometrist since my vision was getting bad anyway, and have the doctor check for tumors in or behind the eye, which could account for the eye symptoms. This is when I got that first pair of glasses, but there was no evidence of any tumor. Next I went to see an ear, nose, and throat specialist to see if I had some kind of severe sinus problem that could be causing these symptoms.

An X-ray of my head didn't show anything conclusive with my sinuses, but I remember asking about a peanut-shaped white spot that stood out on the X-ray. I was told that that was my pineal gland. The fact that it was white indicated that it had calcified, which was not unusual except that it usually didn't happen to people until they were in their sixties or seventies, while I was only thirty-six at the time. I was told that if I really wanted to get to the bottom of what was going on, I should go to a neurologist and have an MRI of my entire head performed.

So I took off a few hours from a very busy schedule both at work and at home to undergo an MRI scan. Before the scan, I was to meet with a neurologist to discuss what the MRI scan would show. So I had my first MRI, with and without contrast, and I was expecting to leave and return to work after the MRI, but when I asked if I was free to go, they said that I should wait in the waiting room.

I waited impatiently in the waiting room for what seemed like a long time, not thinking anything about my health condition but being more concerned about what I had to do when I got back to work. I probably should have suspected something was wrong, especially when they told me that I should come on back because a doctor wanted to talk to me, but a serious health condition was not in my mind's realm of possibilities.

Instead of the usual poking and prodding, the doctor had me follow his finger with my eyes as he moved it back and forth and asked me if watching a tennis match as a spectator from the sidelines would have been difficult for me. I said it would. He had me follow his finger as he raised it up, and as I did, I felt my eyes quiver as I tried with considerable difficulty to look up. He said that the condition of having difficulty with upward gaze was called Parinaud's syndrome.

All of a sudden he seemed to know a lot about the symptoms I had, and then from out of the blue came the words that I will never forget: "You have a brain tumor." It is hard for me to describe the intensity of the shock those words were to me. In my mind, at that time at least, receiving a diagnosis of a brain tumor was like being given a death sentence with no possibility of a pardon. After a while, when I could finally get my mouth to form words again, I said to him, "Doctor, I feel like you just dropped a load of bricks on me!"

The neurologist said that he believed that it was best to always come right out with the facts and not sugar coat them, but the way I was feeling right then, I was not convinced he was right. He showed me the tumor on a set of the MRI scans they had just taken. There it was—a ¾" × 1" oval-shaped tumor, almost dead center in my brain, in what he called the pineal region, just above the brain stem!

This neurologist told me that because of the difficulty presented by the location of this tumor, most surgeons would not even attempt to perform this surgery. He said that I needed to have the very best surgeon available. He said that the reason I had had to wait so long after the MRI to see him was that he had already been on the phone and had scheduled the best neurosurgeon in the state of Minnesota, Dr. Nagib, for a presurgery appointment.

My world had just come crashing down around me. I remember that I called my wife at work and tearfully told her this incredibly bad news, and we both just cried on the phone together. I was so shaken up by what had just transpired that I had to wait at the doctor's office a while to regain my composure enough to be sure it was safe for me to drive home.

As my wife and I were preparing for the first meeting with the neurosurgeon, we ran across a number of people who knew of Dr. Nagib, and they all praised him as a wonderful, talented, caring, and surgically skillful and successful surgeon and told us how fortunate we were to even get him. So we finally went to that presurgery appointment with Dr. Nagib and his assistant, Therese O'Fallon, to discuss my brain surgery. They talked about what my options were, and the neurosurgeon discussed with us how each surgery he did was reviewed by a team of neurosurgeons as to what his best approach would be.

Dr. Nagib and Therese were very nice and kind as they talked with us to let us know what we could expect, and they answered all the questions we had. They took a lot of time to counsel us and to encourage us so that we would be better prepared for the ordeal we were about to go through. When we told Dr. Nagib about all the glowing remarks we had received from everyone we talked to, he humbly said, "I just take my time and do the very best job I can, and then I just put it in God's hands."

We asked if the tumor could be benign, and he told us that chances were that it was malignant. He said that it didn't really matter anyway, because even a benign tumor would continue growing and needed to be removed. He told us about the different kinds of cancer that are typically found in this region of the brain and the chances of my having each one. He said his approach would be to do a "cranial surgery" and remove as much of the tumor as possible.

Dr. Nagib said that the surgery would be performed with me in the sitting position and that he would go in through the back of my head. He said that he expected the surgery to last about eight hours. Because of this unusual position, my heart would have difficulty keeping my blood circulating into my legs. To help with this, my legs would be wrapped with a device that would inflate and deflate periodically to keep the blood flowing through them to prevent serious complications.

He told us that when he "sawed out" a triangular piece of skull from the back of a patient's head, sometimes the piece taken out would be too small to be put back in. He said that when the size of the entry was small in surgeries, he would just leave the removed piece of skull out. He said that in my case, the portion of the skull that would need to be removed was large enough that if the piece couldn't be put back in, my skull would have to be patched with a synthetic product.

He showed me an example of this product on a mock-up of a human skull. There it was, a plastic mesh with a grey plastic compound spread over it. I was suddenly struck with a flashback to earlier years when I used to fix up old, rusted-out cars. To repair a rusted-out hole in the body of an old car, I would cut and grind out the rusted-out metal and then repair it. I used an auto body repair kit containing plastic mesh and a can of plastic goop. I would place the mesh in the hole where metal used to be. I had to mix the goop with a catalyst to harden it. I remember how many hard hours of work I put into repairing these cars and painting them, just for them to start rusting out again in a short time. This synthetic skull repair looked just like the repairs I made on these old cars! I said to Dr. Nagib, "If there is absolutely any way possible, unless it is needed to save my life, please use the piece of skull!" I didn't want my skull repair to end up in total failure like my '68 Dodge Charger!

As it turned out, my experience with bodywork on cars may have been some sort of forewarning, because some time later, when we talked to my sister-in-law, Carol, who is a nurse that has assisted in brain surgeries, she said that some patients that had been patched with that

5

synthetic product had to go through another brain surgery to it have removed later because of allergic reactions!

The neurosurgeon said he would use a set of microscopic glasses and would remove the tumor layer by layer and stop when he saw the gray color of brain matter. He said that he would not remove any brain matter unless the tumor had invaded the brain. During the surgery, a sample of the tumor would be sent to the lab for analysis. The way he would proceed in the surgery would be determined by what kind of tumor it was. I am still amazed at the preparation, planning, and coordination that has to go into performing a surgery like this. I mean, surgeons can't be on their feet doing surgery for eight hours straight. They have to take breaks to eat, go to the bathroom, etc. These brain surgeons are certainly extremely gifted, talented, and dedicated people.

My wife and I were really impressed with how kind and caring the neurosurgeon and his assistant both were and how much time they spent just encouraging us and giving us reason to hope. They were just as concerned about the emotional side of what we were going through as the medical side. They seemed to know that the positive attitude of the patient was important for a successful outcome, and I owe them a huge debt of gratitude for all their kindness and caring, which I will probably never be able to repay. The two of them seemed to work together as complementary parts of a perfect whole. We left that meeting with our hopes high and our spirits raised.

My wife and I wanted to be as informed as we could be about this kind of tumor and what our options were. We started our research by going to the University of Minnesota's medical library to check out some books about tumors in the pineal region of the brain. As we started reading these books, our spirits sank and our hope of a good outcome looked bleak. These books were written *by* doctors *for* doctors, and they were very frank; they were not meant to lift the spirits of patients. There was no sugar coating for the encouragement of the patient going on here. It appeared that surgery in this region, almost dead center in the brain, was not even considered possible just a few years before.

The pictures in these books were ghastly! The back of the skull was literally sawn off, and the two lobes of the brain were separated halfway back and laid to the side. The cerebellum below was pulled down and out of the way, and there, exposed for the first time to the light of day and the eye of a camera, would be the center of a human brain. The sight wrenched me to my very soul. This is what I had to go through; this is what I had to recover from. We read about the chances of success and the survival rates, which were very dismal. The graphic language and pictures seemed to suck the hope and spirit right out of us. We became so depressed and sickened from reading these books that we had to stop.

We discussed our dreadful experience with Dr. Nagib and Therese. They reminded us that these books were a few years old and didn't reflect medical advances made more recently. They reminded us that this was technical talk between doctors and not intended for interpretation by patients with limited medical knowledge. They recommended that we stop getting ourselves all worked up and worried. They said it was important to go into this with a positive attitude and outlook. Again they were very kind and concerned about what we were going through emotionally. They were very encouraging again, and they lifted up our spirits. We closed the books up and took them right back to the library we had gotten them from.

As we continued to prepare ourselves for what we had never imagined we would have to go through, we decided it would be prudent to get a second opinion for any surgery, but especially important for one that was a matter of life and death and could easily end up destroying our family. I made a call to schedule an appointment to get a second opinion from the Mayo Clinic, thinking this was a place we could get state-of-the-art medical advice. It turned out that the first available appointment was some time in the future, and my rapidly increasing symptoms told me that I dare not miss the surgery already scheduled with Dr. Nagib.

Our other thought for a second opinion was a neurosurgeon who reportedly had performed the most brain surgeries in the state of Minnesota. We showed up at our appointment with this doctor with

MRIs and medical records in hand. His office was incredibly beautiful and well furnished. It was what I would call opulent. He obviously was very successful at what he did. I liked the idea that he had done so many surgeries, thinking that practice surely must make perfect. Well, we didn't have to wait long for his diagnosis. Within a half an hour or so, he came back to us with his plan for attack. He would first do a needle biopsy by drilling a hole in the skull and then guiding the needle by fluoroscope through the brain. He would avoid important areas of the brain (I thought they were all important) and retrieve a sample of the tumor for analysis.

After analysis, they would only do a tumor resection (removal by surgery) if another better treatment wasn't available. At one point I asked him what his "gut feeling" was about what my likely outcome would be, based on all his experience in this type of situation. He paused and got a very serious, almost spooky, look on his face and told me that he thought I would likely first go blind and then "succumb," which was his euphemism for "die." Wow, back into the depths of depression! At home my wife and I just held each other and sobbed.

At yet another appointment with Dr. Nagib, we told him about this second opinion we had received. He said that he and his group of surgeons *had* considered doing a needle biopsy before the surgery but had rejected the idea. He said there are numerous blood vessels in the brain that could be hit, with a fatal result. He said that this had happened with even very prestigious surgeons and hospitals. He further said that even if all goes well in a needle biopsy, the size of the sample from the tip of the needle is so small that it is difficult to get an accurate analysis. He said that sometimes tumors are of a mixed variety (gleoblastoma) that is very deadly, and that a small sample may lead to a false favorable analysis. He advised against this approach because it was too risky and uncertain. I asked him what he thought my chances of having a favorable outcome were. I said I wasn't asking about a life without any side effects, but rather a life worth living. He said I had about a 50/50 chance. Although I suspected he may have been a little optimistic with the odds in order to encourage us and give me hope and a will to live, I was very encouraged that he wasn't giving up on me.

So there I was, faced with a decision between two different doctors and two different ways of thinking. One doctor had a warm, moderate, and humble office, and the other a cold, glitzy, and extravagant office. One doctor had spent much time being kind and encouraging and genuinely cared about our emotional state; the other barely spent a half hour with us, including diagnosis time, and was very straightforward and businesslike. One doctor had told me I had chance to live, and the other had not. One put his faith in the hands of God; one did not seem to care about my emotional or spiritual health. I know I didn't want to put my life into the hands of someone who thought I was going to die. To me the choice was a no-brainer. I chose to put my life into the hands of the surgeon who would put my surgery into the hands of God.

And so I was putting my life into the hands of God. In addition to my feeble prayers, I had many people praying for me. My wife and my three-year-old son Nick, along with our church, were praying for me. My extended family and the four churches they attended were praying for me. After returning to work, a dear friend told me he had a prayer chain at his church praying for me. I had many friends and even acquaintances praying for me that I didn't even realize were doing so.

Just the other day at a graduation party of a friend of my wife, almost ten years after my first brain surgery, I met a person I didn't recognize, and she excitedly asked me how I was doing. She tearfully said she had been praying for me and hugged me warmly. It is moments like these that make me forget all the pain and suffering and make me want to give something back to those who prayed for me and to all who are now, or will be, going through what I went through. I want to find and talk to people who are at the end of their rope, to lift them up and show them that life can be better than they ever hoped possible.

After settling our medical plan of action, there were only a handful of days left before the surgery. Ironically, now with the possibility of having only a few days of my life left, I finally had time to really reflect on what life was all about. A lot of the things that I had thought were so important to me now seemed so trivial. I now tell people that I know

9

from experience that a man on his deathbed does not wish he had spent more time in the office.

I thought about my wife, the love of my life, my soul mate who literally waltzed into my life as I met her in a ballroom dance class when I was at the end of another rope—a broken relationship with a girlfriend I cared about very much. I thought about my one and only three-year-old son, my "miracle child" that God had given us when it looked like we might never have children. Now I considered the all-too-real possibility, maybe probability, that I would never get to see him grow up and play baseball in Little League, never get to see him graduate from high school and college, never get to see the girl he chose to marry, never get the chance to just be his dad.

I thought about my wife having to raise Nick without a husband. I thought about Nick having to grow up without his father. I thought about how my death would affect my brothers and sisters and my mom, and those thoughts broke my heart. Could my life be coming to an end? What lay ahead for me after death? Was I about to find out? There was nothing I had always wanted to see, nowhere I had always wanted to travel to, and nothing I had always wanted to do that mattered now. I only wanted to spend time with my family and friends. I went on picnics with my wife and young son; we went on a paddleboat ride at a local park. My family threw a victory party for me before I went in for surgery. What a great experience that was!

All my friends and family were there giving me strength and encouragement. This loving, caring, and sharing with friends and family is what life *should* be about, but sadly, this isn't what life is about until some crisis happens. Some close friends of mine told me that they were worried about what I had to go through. I told them I was not worried about me. I said, "I am worried about what you will have to go through, waiting and wondering how it is going, worrying about how things will turn out during the eight long hours of the surgery. I will be unconscious through the whole deal and won't know what is going on." I was worried about poor Dr. Nagib and all his staff, who would be on their feet for eight hours. How would they make time for lunch, coffee breaks, bathroom breaks? What a grueling day at work they would have just working that all out. All that work and effort, just to help me.

Well, the surgery was a success in that I was still alive afterward. But, as it would turn out, my battle with cancer had only just begun. Lab analysis had indicated that the tumor was malignant with a type of cancer called a germinoma. Apparently I was fortunate, if it is possible to use that word in the same sentence that contains the word "cancer." This type of cancer is readily destroyed by radiation therapy (I didn't respond particularly well to the radiation either). An oncologist told me that chemotherapy would have been difficult because of the blood–brain barrier. I would have had to receive a spinal tap each time treatment was administered to get past that barrier. Well, it sounded like I got a huge break on the type of tumor it turned out to be; some of the other kinds sounded awfully grim. I was willing to take all the good news I could get!

I spent a number of days in the intensive care unit. I was so weak I couldn't do much of anything for myself. I had hoses and wires connected to so many different parts of my body that I looked like a Frankenstein experiment gone bad. People were sticking me with so many needles so often that I thought that I must surely be part of some kind of nurse training program.

I remembered being so modest during a previous stay in the hospital for some minor surgery that I insisted on not using the bedpan and taking care all of my needs alone in the bathroom. Now I needed help just turning over in bed. I had a tube going up my urethra to allow me to urinate without assistance, and I wasn't worried about it in the least. I was in survival mode. I was just happy I didn't have to get out of bed. All the notions of modesty, dignity, privacy, and embarrassment were thrown right out the window. I had nurses putting catheters in my urethra and taking them out, taking my clothes off, giving me sponge baths, and dressing me. Later, when I could get out of bed with help, I had nurses assisting me in the bathroom and wiping and washing my bottom.

I remember later reading the book *Tuesday with Morley*, which is about a man with Lou Gehrig's disease who was progressively losing control of his muscles and needing more and more assistance from nurses. He lamented to a friend about having to face the day when he would need to have someone to wipe his butt. I remember thinking that I had used to feel that way, but after all I had been through, I now thought, *Morley, in the scheme of things, it's not a big deal!*

At some point in intensive care, I woke up and could hardly feel my legs. I had this awful, panicky feeling that if I didn't get up and walk right away and get the blood flowing in my legs, I was going to lose them. Apparently the bloodflow in my legs had not recovered adequately from the "sitting position" surgery. In a panic, I called the nurse, and with her assistance and all the strength I could muster, I started walking the halls. I was so afraid of losing my legs that I just kept walking and walking and walking.

Looking back, it kind of reminded me a little of Forrest Gump when he was so happy to be free of his leg braces that he couldn't quit running. I walked so much that the nurses would have to take turns walking with me. I wore them out, or maybe it was so boring for them to walk with me that long that they couldn't take it anymore. Eventually I became strong enough to be trusted to walk alone, first with a walker and later with a cane. Wow, now I could really put on some miles. I shuffled through the halls with my hospital-issue slippers so much that dust bunnies started building up on my feet. Nurses started calling me the Duster and joked that I should be getting paid for dusting all the halls.

After I recovered enough to go home, I began a six-week course of radiation treatment. The surgery had removed all the cancer that could be seen, and the radiation would kill all the microscopic cancer cells that might be left. This treatment would expose my entire brain to six thousand rads of X-ray radiation. My friends and family took turns driving me to and from radiation treatment on a daily basis for the next six weeks. It is a tribute to the support I received from many others that one therapist remarked that I received rides from a larger number of different people than any other patient she knew of.

As I was preparing for my first radiation treatment, one of the radiation therapists told me something that I found incredible about the difference between diagnostic amount of radiation used in typical X-rays and the therapeutic amount of radiation I was going to receive: the total amount of radiation my brain was to receive, by the end of the course of treatment, was roughly equivalent to a half million chest X-rays' worth of radiation! I found that just amazing. I thought you were supposed to stay away from radiation because it *caused* cancer, but now I was being given a megadose of radiation to fight cancer! How contrary to my way of thinking and reasoning that treatment seemed to be, but it worked, and it was the state of the art for cancer treatment.

I contemplated all I had just been through. I had survived an eight-hour brain surgery during which as much of the tumor was removed as possible. I had received the good news that mine was a favorable type of cancer, and the radiation treatment to eliminate all the microscopic bits that might be left was well underway. I did have that little complication with my legs in intensive care that required me to use a cane, but I was almost wearing a path in the carpet walking many laps around the house with that cane, and my legs were getting stronger. I was optimistic, thinking things were finally returning to normal, and I was getting anxious to get back to work.

I told my wife and my mom that I was concerned about using up all my "sick time" and thought I could go back to work in a week or so. My mom and my wife both tried to discourage me from doing that, telling me that it required at least six weeks for the body to recover from any major surgery. But my mind-set was that I was going to get back to work and do the best I could to forget that this "thing" ever happened. Little did I know that this "thing" was far from being over and would never be forgotten.

Well, that initial optimism I had quickly turned south. Somewhere in the last half of the six-week course of radiation treatment, I started to notice that I was becoming sicker and sicker, and it was a real struggle to get through the last few trips for radiation treatment. I began to feel very ill and began throwing up—something I hadn't done in over twenty years. I reported this to my radiologist, and he put me on a medication called Compazine to reduce nausea. This helped for a while, but soon the vomiting continued. The dosage of Compazine was increased, but that didn't help for long and the vomiting worsened.

I now felt extremely ill and miserable and had a very hard time mustering up the energy and enthusiasm required to journey to the hospital for my daily radiation treatment, even though this only required getting showered and dressed, on my part. I was still relying on family and friends to transport me to the hospital and back on a rotating basis; I would end up being incapable of driving for almost a year.

It is kind of amazing how some things around me during that time imprinted on my mind so that even years later they still remind me of how ill I felt then. Certain commercials and sounds that played on TV then still make me feel queasy today. There was a magnetic-block game that the kids played with in the waiting room at the place where I received radiation treatments. My wife, Jenny, ended up buying one like it for Nick because he and the other kids liked it so much, but I never liked to even see it because it reminded me of how sick I had been.

The vomiting continued even after I finished the radiation treatments. I now had seriously painful headaches, and I became very lethargic, sleeping twelve, fourteen, sixteen, and more hours a day. Besides feeling like death warmed over, I am told that I was very forgetful. I kept asking the same questions over and over again. Apparently I was starting to act very goofy, even for me. I was singing songs and telling off-color jokes in the wrong company. I have some faint recollections of wearing an old high school baseball cap and singing the old high school pep rouser song, and I am definitely not a singer. Anyone who has heard me sing knows what a painful thing that is to the ears around me.

I remember being taken to my wife's office, a place I had been many times before. Somehow it now looked very different, all twisted around and distorted. As my wife led me to the front door, I remember remarking that we were going the wrong way, that we had never gone in through (what I perceived to be) the side door before. Of course there was no side door, but in my mind that was how I saw things, all twisted around. I vaguely remember trying to sleep in one of her dental chairs.

Most of the events of the last week before my eventual second brain surgery are gone from my memory. It was only with great difficulty that I was able to recall some of these pre-second-surgery events with the help of friends and family. The rest of my recollections of this time are the result of piecing together what people have told me happened. I later learned that I was suffering from hydrocephalus, a condition that results from the increase of pressure of the fluid surrounding the brain.

I was told that cerebral spinal fluid (CSF) is made in the head and that this fluid normally flows through the ventricles and into the spine. A doctor told me that the human brain "doesn't like to be messed with." Apparently the trauma of surgery and the six weeks of radiation therapy had caused the ventricles in my head to swell shut. This in turn resulted in increasing pressure in my head because of the constant production of CSF with nowhere to go. This increasing pressure is what caused the symptoms I experienced, and this condition, if left unchecked, ultimately would have led to death.

In that last week before my second brain surgery, I was so incapable of seeking medical attention for myself that if I had been living alone, I would have surely died. It is only by the grace of God and the persistence of my dear wife that I am alive today. My wife's recognition that my symptoms were not normal and her determination to make sure that I received timely and appropriate medical attention saved my life. When I finally got in to see a doctor and they recognized the condition I was in, they rushed me into an emergency brain surgery at 8:00 on a Friday night to install a shunt in my head to relieve the pressure on my brain.

This surgery, though only lasting about two hours and less complicated than the original eight-hour surgery to remove the brain tumor, was a lot harder on me. It left me feeling much worse and was much more difficult for me to recover from. I overheard a nurse talking to a patient who shared a hospital room with me. I was only separated from him by a drawn curtain partition. She told my roommate that his surgery was scheduled for a certain time but that, because his surgery was not critical, it might be "bumped" for someone requiring emergency surgery. She gave my surgery as an example of a life-threatening emergency surgery that might "bump" his. She said that my surgery that Friday night was not optional, and that if I had not been operated on immediately, my heart and lungs would have stopped.

I remember waking up a number of times in the presence of different people and in different rooms after the surgery, in intensive care. I could tell because of the different colors of paint on the walls. I was asked some questions that I initially did not want to answer. I remember having the impression that something had gone wrong for me and that they weren't telling me something. I had the impression that many years had passed. The feeling was so strong that I surely thought all my friends and family must have passed away. Strangely, I had this feeling that if they were not going to tell me what happened to me, I wasn't going to tell them anything either. I remember then having a "softening of the heart" during one of the periods when the lights were off. I decided that I would cooperate with them and start answering questions.

It was at some point during this second brain surgery that I had my "experience."

MY NEAR-DEATH EXPERIENCE

THIS IS WHAT I wrote after my surgery when I was not sure how long I would live:

> Nick, my dear son, I had an experience while I was in my life-and-death battle with cancer, when you were only three, that I want you to know about so that someday you can understand it. It was the most incredible experience I have ever had by a long shot, and it is part of my life story. I had an experience during the time of my second brain surgery that I don't know exactly how to describe. This experience has changed my life, and because of it, I will never be the same. At the time this happened, I had never heard of anyone experiencing anything quite like it. It was not exactly clear to me what it was that I had experienced, what its purpose was, or what it meant. Some may think it could have been a dream, but I certainly have never had a dream anything like this before.
>
> I call it a near-death experience, but I don't know if I crossed some boundary between life and death or not. I don't remember how I got to the surgery or even the last week or so before I had this second brain surgery. If it wasn't for your mom's recognition that something was seriously wrong and her persistence in getting me in to see a doctor, I would not be here today. I was at a point where I was totally incapable to seek help by myself. Your mom saved my life.

What I do know is that when I came out of surgery and was in intensive care, a nurse was talking to another patient behind a curtain in the same room who was also scheduled for a brain surgery. She told him that his surgery was not urgent and could be "bumped" if an emergency came up. "Like Rick," she said, "who, if he had not had immediate brain surgery to relieve the pressure on his brain from hydrocephalus, his heart and lungs would have stopped." So whether I had technically crossed some line between life and death I cannot say, but I was near death.

At some point before surgery, in surgery, or after surgery in intensive care, I don't know which, I felt as though I were drifting to a place that I can maybe best describe by stating what I did not see. I did not see a bright light or a tunnel. I do not recall seeing the image of another person, and I did not even see myself; nor did I physically, audibly hear anyone speak. I did, though, have the sensation that I had gone somewhere. Whatever this was, it was more of a mental experience than a physical experience. Wherever it was that I had gone, I knew that I was before the presence of what I call "All Knowledge." I describe it as being like a tree and like a library. Not that it looked like a tree, but it had branches of knowledge, and when one went down a branch, he would understand the knowledge contained in that branch.

I do not remember receiving a verbal invitation from anyone, but I knew that I was free to receive and to experience that knowledge. The knowledge did not just come to me all at once. It was more like it was divided into different areas of knowledge, as in a library that was spread out or organized like a tree, and I had to "go down" a certain branch in order to experience its knowledge.

As I look back over my life, I guess I have always been a seeker of the truth. This is something that I have come to realize now, since my cancer experiences. I had given up the path for a more traditional career in engineering for a more uncertain but more exciting one in physics and math. It seems that I was not satisfied in simply knowing enough to solve problems; my heart's desire was always to know why things worked the way they did.

I had changed my major in college from civil engineering to physics after Jeff Stifter, a good friend of mine, suggested that I watch a series on public television in celebration of Albert Einstein's one hundredth birthday. I added a second major of mathematics when I took an advanced math class that cleared up some misunderstanding I had about linear algebra. That eye-opening (or "I-opening") experience gave me the hunger to understand more about mathematics.

Further evidence of my nature to be a seeker of the truth is revealed in my fascination with the second JFK assassination investigation by the US Senate. I read several books on different theories of what really happened. It is not that I wanted to find out who did it so they could be punished, although I think that should have happened; I mainly wanted to know if people inside the US government might have been involved. If that had been the case, it would have changed my whole perception of what the country I lived in was like. In my mind, the assassination of the president by a conspiracy of people inside the government, to overthrow the government, like some third-world coup; I felt it could not happen here. If this could happen in the United States, that would mean it was not the place I thought it was and that mattered to me.

And now this incredible knowledge that would change my perception about this world I live in was being revealed to me! I recall that I was free to explore and choose what areas of understanding I wanted to "go into." I distinctly remember being absolutely overwhelmed with, and in awe of, what I was now able to understand as I went down that first branch. It was so far above what we know and understand that I kept on thinking, *Oh, now I see.* As I went deeper into different branches of understanding, the knowledge and understanding from each branch started connecting with the knowledge of other branches. and I remember that I kept on thinking, "*Oh, now I see, Oh, now I see.*"

It was such an incredibly joyful thing, being able to learn and understand all of this awesome knowledge, that it reminded me of a story I heard about Archimedes, who was a king's royal scientist. As I remember the story, the king had a new crown of gold made for him and felt that he had been cheated. He thought the goldsmith had mixed silver in with the gold. He went to Archimedes and asked him to find out if his crown was pure gold or not. This was a pretty tough assignment, and he Archimedes pondered for a long time how he might be able to do this.

Then one day, while Archimedes was climbing into the bathtub, he noticed that the water rose in the bathtub as he climbed in. All of a sudden, the light went on in his head and he discovered how he was going to determine if the king's crown was solid gold or not. He would weigh the crown and determine the volume of the crown by measuring how much water it displaced. He would then displace water with a mass of solid gold equal in weight to the crown and compare the two volumes of displaced water.

As the legend goes, Archimedes was so excited about his discovery that he ran through the streets naked yelling, "Eureka, I have found it! Eureka I have found it." I surely can relate to the intense joy he had in the discovery of something he did not know before. Well, what I was being shown was far greater than discovering how to find the density of irregularly shaped objects. The joy I experienced is hard to describe with words. Maybe the best phrase I can think of is "pure euphoria." Anyway, after choosing a number of different branches and gaining the knowledge and understanding that all those branches contained, I just sort of became aware that I needed to leave wherever I was and return, or go back, whatever that means.

I remember being incredibly amazed and incredulous about what I had just come to understand, and I remember thinking that I just had to hang on to this somehow so I could remember what I learned and share this understanding with others when I "got back." It felt a little bit like when I was in college. Even though I now have a very bad memory as one of the consequences of my battle with a cancerous brain tumor, I am coming to believe that I never really had a very good memory to begin with. This brings to mind a quote I heard: "All people have a photographic memory; it is just that some do not have any film." That is the way I think I am. I didn't have much film to begin with, and what film I had has been exposed to radiation.

As an example of my lack of memory, whenever I had to prepare for a physics final exam in which I was not allowed to use notes, I wouldn't try to actually memorize the whole list of formulas that I might need for the test. I would instead memorize a few basic formulas and then derive the rest of the formulas quickly from them during the test. I guess the tradeoff here was that I spent less time memorizing formulas at the expense of taking more time to thoroughly understand the principles needed to derive them. Assuming that the brain is going to take the path of least resistance, I guess this means that it is easier for my brain to perform additional logical calculations than to do additional memorization.

During my experience, in order to help me remember what I had learned, I started making a mental outline of what I needed to remember so that I would be able to re-create this knowledge when I got back. But as I slowly departed, I realized that I was losing some of the intricate fringe details of the mental outline I had made to remember the knowledge I had been shown, and I had to make my mental outline smaller. This kept happening, and I kept making my mental outline smaller and smaller, and I was getting really frustrated. Finally I was left with only two words. I distinctly remember thinking, *Boy, I don't know if this is going to be enough of a clue to help me re-create all the knowledge and understanding that I was shown, but these two words are the best I can do.* I then became concerned about whether I would even be able to remember those two words.

Finally I woke up and returned to a normal state of consciousness, and I remember thinking, *What are those two words?* There was pause as I struggled to recall, and then it came to me. I did remember, or was allowed to remember, those two words that I chose or that were given to me to summarize all the knowledge that was shown to me. Those two words were "truth" and "love!" Even though they were the only specific things I could recall, I was very thankful that I could indeed remember them. I felt that they were proof to me that this amazing experience really happened.

I recall thinking that of all the pairs of words that could possibly be used to summarize all knowledge and understanding, "truth" and "love" would probably be one of my last choices. I was completely dumbfounded. I mean, "truth" and "love" are very powerful words, but I could not understand how they could be the keys to all knowledge and understanding. Even so, the awesome power of this experience is the foundational event that has radically changed how I view life and the world around me.

At the time of my cancer and this second brain surgery, I had a bachelor's degree in physics and was within one course of a bachelor's degree in mathematics and was at the level of knowing basic quantum mechanics, special relativity, and an overview of general relativity. The theory that was the holy grail of theories in physics, which I knew almost nothing about other than that it existed, was the unified field theory. Albert Einstein had been working on this theory to unify the four known physical forces in the universe—gravity, electromagnetism, and the strong and weak nuclear forces—into one theory. In science, these four basic forces describe how the universe works and explain what "makes it tick."

To me, being able to tie these forces together into one grand theory would be the ultimate understanding of the universe. It would be what I would have thought "All Knowledge" was about. Einstein worked on this theory, without success, until the day he died, and physicists work on it still. With my physics and math background and my scientific way of thinking, I previously thought that the understanding of how these four forces are connected was the limit of what we can possibly know. But what was revealed to me was so far beyond that level of knowledge that I was in total, fall-down-on-your-knees, indescribable awe. There is a lot of knowledge, truth, and understanding that we have yet to learn.

This whole situation of my limited thinking being shattered and overwhelmed with a much greater understanding reminded me of what one of my professors said about the state of physics at the end of the nineteenth century. He told the story about Lord Kelvin, who in an address to the leading scientists of his time, said that just about all there is to know about science and the laws that determine how the universe works have already been discovered. Kelvin went on to say that there is only a little bit left to be "cleaned up" in two areas. One area concerned experiments involving the speed of light, from which later grew Einstein's theory of relativity. The other area concerned the dual nature of light and matter as being both a particle and a wave, out of which grew quantum mechanics. My professor, with tongue in cheek, calmly remarked that out of these two areas exploded a can of worms of scientific inquiry and research.

The history of fallen man shows that we have always been quick to believe we know everything there is to know. Man has always thought that he has it all figured out. There was a time in our history when people were killed for saying that the world was round when it was obvious to everyone that the world was flat. Galileo announced his scientific discoveries by writing children's books that talked about them, out of fear of persecution by authorities.

One of my physics professors remarked that many physicists refused to accept Einstein's theory of relativity no matter how much experimental evidence supported it. He said that eventually they all died and every new student who is schooled in the science of physics has no problem accepting Einstein's theories. It seems that as people grow from their youth and develop into adults, their thinking is formed by their culture and the knowledge they are exposed to. Eventually what they think and believe becomes their whole nature, their personality, who they are, and how they live. It becomes their identity.

For people to change their thinking after a certain point is like them becoming new, different people. For them to change their thinking in even a small way becomes a very hard thing to do, because when they add something new and different to their current framework of thinking, it would contradict some of their other currently held beliefs. When this happens, they have to work to make all of their thinking and reasoning consistent; otherwise, they would suffer from cognitive dissonance.

Cognitive dissonance occurs when something we believe to be true contradicts something else that we believe to be true. This dissonance in our mind is a powerful phenomenon, and it can lead us to do strange things. The human mind is fascinating! It seems that Cognitive dissonance is similar to the feeling of guilt, but it is not necessarily about doing something wrong. It is the uneasy feeling you get about believing contradictory things to be true. Because contradictory truths can reach deep down into our belief system, people are often more comfortable with denying the truth than living with pangs of cognitive dissonance or performing the work required to make all their understanding consistent.

I still remember a story about Benjamin Franklin that I heard in my first psychology class. As I recall, Benjamin Franklin loved books and was kind of a librarian. In his political life, there was a man who was his political adversary and personal enemy. Benjamin won this man over to be his friend and ally by using the power of cognitive dissonance. As the story goes, Ben found out that this man was trying to find a certain rare book. Well, with Ben's connections to booksellers and such, he found this book and gave it to his enemy as a gift. The fact that this man's enemy gave him a very precious gift sent his mind into a mental tizzy because it contradicted everything he had believed about Benjamin. The easiest way to relieve this cognitive dissonance was for him to become Benjamin Franklin's friend, and that is exactly what happened!

Amazingly, the Bible speaks of this phenomenon in **Romans 12:20–21**: "Therefore *'If your enemy is hungry, feed him; If he is thirsty, give him a drink; For **in so doing you will heap coals of fire on his head**.'* [21] Do not be overcome

25

by evil, but overcome evil with good." When we return love and kindness for evil, it can change what others think and believe to be true. The burning fire is the metaphor for what is going on in the minds of others as they struggle with this cognitive dissonance. And love is how Jesus gets us who rejected and rebelled against Him to change our hearts and minds. "But God demonstrates His own love toward us, in that **while we were still sinners, Christ died for us**" (**Romans 5:8**).

What I experienced, though, was not a small change in my belief system; it showed me that we are not even close to knowing everything there is to know. This experience has opened the eyes of one who thought that he pretty much knew it all, but thankfully it happened before my thinking became set in stone. This experience humbled me, as I realized how much I didn't know.

Anyway, here I was having experienced such awesome knowledge and understanding, and only having the words "truth" and "love" as clues to re-create this experience. Besides those two specific words, though, I did have some general feelings and impressions of this experience that I vividly recall. I remember being incredibly amazed at how everything was interconnected and related in ways that I never would have believed possible. I remember having the feeling that all fields of knowledge and learning are connected together in ways we don't yet understand. It is pretty easy for me to understand how science and math are connected, but history, psychology, sociology, economics, etc., are connected in some way that we don't yet understand.

Not only are knowledge and education connected, but people are connected as well, in ways that we don't yet understand. I had the understanding that people are connected in such a way that if I were to hurt someone else, it would be like hurting myself. I have always described this to people by saying, "It would be like if I cut off your hand, it would be like cutting off my own hand; we are that connected." And not only are people connected with each other, but we are also connected with animals in some way we do not yet understand. And not only that, but we are connected with rocks and trees and plants in some way that we do not know. I cannot understand or explain this yet, as of the time of my experience anyway, but I will try to describe all of this in a way that will make sense.

I also distinctly remember that when I was learning and understanding the branches of knowledge, "truth" came before "love." I remember that I was kind of reveling in the understanding of how good and necessary truth was, and then, all of a sudden, I felt an ill-boding feeling that "truth" had for me. Then I went through the branch of "love," and again I was just reveling and thoroughly enjoying learning about love and how good it was, and I remember that somehow "love" took away the ill-boding feeling that I had felt as I learned about truth. I also had a strong feeling that this experience was related to God and provided to me by God.

To help explain this experience to others, I use the metaphor of a treasure hunter. I feel a bit like a treasure hunter who has always been searching for a hidden treasure that legend says is buried somewhere on some tropical island. Then one day this treasure hunter was blindfolded and taken somewhere, the blindfold was taken off, and there was the treasure chest he had sought for so long, filled with diamonds and rubies, gold and silver. Then the blindfold was put back on him and he was taken right back to where he had been. After all that, he is still only a treasure hunter, not a treasure finder, but now there is a big difference. He has seen the treasure and knows for certain that it exists and that the legend is true. Whereas before he may have had the thought that the legend may not be real and he may have been wasting his time, now he knows that he is not wasting his time, because he has seen it with his own eyes!

I feel like I have been shown some knowledge and understanding that transcends my present limited thinking. I have been given a strong desire and a passion to seek the truth and to re-create and again understand what I was shown. I know that this knowledge and understanding of the truth exists because I saw it, I experienced it, I understood it, and I reveled in the joy of it. My concept of what is possible, what is real, and what is true has been forever changed.

I know that this is the work that God has called me to do and that it is the reason He saved my life and allowed me to have cancer in the first place. God needed to get my attention so that I would stop and seek the truth that leads to eternal life. After this experience, God has given me an incredible hunger, thirst, and passion for the Word of God that never ceases to amaze and astound me and that I cannot even begin to explain to others. I may have memorized some verses from the Bible in confirmation classes when I was younger, but I never actually read the Bible before, let alone studied the Bible, but now that is all I want to do.

And so I began and continue the work of discovering the pieces of truth I need to put together to see the big-picture truth in my quest to understand what my truth-and-love experience means. After facing death, I need to discover what the meaning of life is, and I seek to answer the three basic questions of life that I have thought about a lot: Where am I going? Where did I come from? Why am I here?

MY WAKE-UP CALL

I BELIEVE THAT my cancer was a wake-up call from God. Many people know the day that they first believed and were saved, or born again, but I am not really sure when exactly that happened. I think that I might have been saved when I was younger, around the time I was confirmed when I had an awakening faith in God and a fairly strong spiritual feeling. Nobody I knew in those days used the term "born again." In fact, I remember one day when I was a youngster, my family drove by a church that had a sign that said, "Ye must be born again," and my parents reasoned that it must be "one of those churches" that believed in reincarnation. Maybe that explains why later, when I heard people say they were "born again," it kind of bugged me, as though they were something special that I was not. That feeling changed when I actually read the Bible and found out that Jesus himself said to Nicodemus, "You must be born again."

Obviously, my faith was not very deep in understanding, and that might explain why I had become what I call a "back-burner Christian," putting my faith on hold during the late part of high school and throughout college as I became more concerned about the things of this world: going to college and getting a good education, launching a good career, getting married, and having a big house, a fancy car, a cabin on a lake, and all of the things that many people think will make them happy.

As I look back on my life, I believe that God tried to get my attention by sending me a series of increasing crisis events in my life that would cause me to stop for a while and reassess what I was doing. But when I at last got over the impact of each event, God would send a somewhat bigger crisis, trying to get my attention with as little pain as He could.

In hindsight, I can see how things in the past, such as severe illness, a broken jaw, and a broken relationship with a girlfriend that devastated me at the time, were actually God's attempts to get me to focus on something much more important—the meaning of life on earth. Though they caused me to stop and think about life and drew me back to God for a season, I returned to my old ways of focusing on me and my plans for my life. I managed to spiritually sleep right through these earlier wake-up calls.

I must be a slow learner, because even after having a neurosurgeon tell me I was going to first go blind and die from a brain tumor, and then having God miraculously save me in that first brain surgery, I still didn't get it. I tried to hit the snooze bar on God's wake-up call again. My attitude after that first brain surgery was to try to get back to work as soon as I could, try to forget that this whole thing ever happened, and get my life back to normal.

Thankfully, God did not give up on me. He had tried to get my attention as gently as He could, but I had been too thickheaded to get it. But God patiently, lovingly tried again, a little more firmly, to get my attention with the complication of hydrocephalus, emergency brain surgery, and an incredible near-death experience. Now He finally had my full attention. The experiences of the next few months left me completely broken, on my knees, and humbled, with any remaining traces of pride removed. In this broken state, barely alive and not able to function on my own, God started calling me. Ironically, it was only after a neurosurgeon had cut several holes in my head to install the shunt that God was able to get my attention. Metaphorically speaking, it was like God had to do this to get through my thick skull to let the light of truth shine into a dark place.

Having been faced with my own mortality *has* changed my life. It is hard to explain, but when you are forced to consider that your days on earth are most likely at an end, that your loved ones will have to continue on without you, and that you know your death will bring suffering and hurt to those you love, it does something to you. It causes you to realize how precious and fragile life is. At any instant, any one of us, healthy or not, can be struck down without warning by a massive heart attack or a fatal car accident or by just being in the wrong place at the wrong time. It happens all the time; just watch the evening news.

In a way, I am very lucky to not have died instantly, as so many do, and to have received the opportunity to think about what life is really about before it is gone. I have been given the chance to reexamine my priorities in life and to reconsider what is really important. There are fundamental questions about life that are critical in deciding how we should live our lives, yet we become so busy just living this modern life that we do not even have time to consider if the way we are living our life makes any sense. There are three such questions that I have thought a lot about lately; they are simply (1) where am I going?, (2) where did I come from?, and 3) why am I here? The way people live this temporary life should at least be consistent with their answers to these three questions.

My priorities in life have changed. Besides just trying to stay alive, I began to see things in a different light. The things that I thought were important before cancer just seemed to fade away. What became important to me after cancer were relationships—a loving relationship with God above all, and a loving relationship with others. It is only when we love God that we can truly love others. The words of the song "Turn Your Eyes upon Jesus," by Helen H. Hemmel, describes this feeling I had: "The things of this world grow strangely dim in the light of His beauty and grace."

I started to notice that strange little things that seemed to be coincidences started happening all the time; I realized they were not really coincidences at all but signs from God letting me know that He was working in my life. For example, the three questions about life above were thoughts that popped into my mind a few months prior, one by one, in the order above while I was thinking about big-picture issues. Then I heard Dr. James Dobson use those same three questions in a radio program, worded almost exactly the same except that questions two and three were reversed in order.

One evening Oprah just happened to be on when I turned on the TV, and she described this "calling from God" as God dropping increasingly bigger pebbles our heads to get our attention. After a while, He will drop a stone, and then a slightly bigger stone, until finally He drops a brick. That's how I felt. God had been giving me wake-up calls all along, and I just kept hitting the snooze bar. The God who created the universe and everyone and everything in it had called me, and I finally recognized and accepted His call. I believe that He saved my life for a reason. God used these little miracles to help me remember that He was near and that He was in control. God has sent me many, many, examples of His divine providence in my life ever since.

I didn't know then what His purpose for me was, but I believed that He would supply me with everything I needed to do whatever purpose He had for my life, large or small. I haven't gone through all that God had to do to get my attention to turn away now, nor do I want to. I have discovered that following Jesus is not the difficult burden that some may think it is. It may be work, as some would say, but it is a labor of love.

It is like having a career that you really love, such as playing baseball or painting or playing music, and knowing that you would be doing this even if it wasn't your job. God has taken me from a miserable, helpless, completely broken state, in the depths of depression and total despair, when I had no hope for a future and I couldn't see any way out of my predicament; and He has lifted me up. He has filled my heart with a peace and joy and a feeling of purpose for my life.

A friend and coworker of mine, Jim Bossert, once took me aside, and we talked about "life" and "things." He told me a story about someone he knew who went on a mountain-climbing expedition with some others. When they got near the top of the mountain, the weather suddenly turned ugly and a blizzard set in. They abandoned their goal of getting to the mountaintop and made a hasty retreat back down the mountain. Their only goal now was to get back down alive. One of the climbers developed such a severe case of frostbite and was so weak from hypothermia and exhaustion that he was unable to continue. The other climbers weren't able to carry him down, so they bundled him up as best they could, covered him with snow to insulate him from the bitter cold, and continued on without him. They basically left him for dead. Anyway, he miraculously survived the blizzard and eventually made it back down the mountain, though he lost some toes and maybe a finger or two to severe frostbite. Jim upon hear about this "near-death experience," said his whole personality and outlook on life changed. He said that his whole demeanor had changed for the better. Jim went on to say that he saw some of those same changes in me.

Recently, I talked with a contractor who services our autoclaves on the St. Paul campus. He told me about his quadruple heart bypass surgery, which he went through during the Halloween blizzard back in 1991, less than a year before my brain surgeries. He told me how his faith in God had grown and how emotional he had become. He told me that he often cried while watching movies now. He explained that he looked at life differently since then.

Having had those same experiences, I asked him, "Have you ever watched the show *Rescue 911?*" He said that he used to but that he couldn't stand to watch it anymore, as it always made him cry now. I told him that I experienced the very same thing. I said that this was a good show to watch because it could help you prevent or respond to emergency situations, but I also said that I couldn't stand to see the people on the show, especially children, get hurt anymore; I now had to get up and walk away from it.

Now, years later, I have run across many people who have suffered like I have. Some have had near-death experiences, and all have had their lives change for the better. We will understand why all people, even good people, have to suffer later in this book.

ROCKY ROAD TO RECOVERY

AFTER SOME ADDITIONAL recovery in the hospital, I was released and had a very shaky return home only to immediately feel as if I were going to die from an allergic reaction to Decadron, a drug to help prevent swelling that I had been taking since even before my first surgery. I discovered later that I had been given a large intravenous dose just before I left the hospital. I actually felt *indescribably miserable* during the wheelchair ride to my wife's car and on the way home, and I felt as though I needed to return to the hospital.

An incredible night of bizarre symptoms followed. Besides feeling incredibly bad, a roar, like the sound of a freight train, was going through my head, and everyone's voice was eerily distorted, sounding like the voice of a witness whose identity is being protected. Amazingly enough, through all the pain and strange sensations that I had been through, and all the slim chances of living I had been given, I had never really felt as though I were going to die, but all of a sudden I felt as if death may be a real possibility. I felt incredibly ill in a way that I could only describe to nurse practitioner Therese O'Fallon as feeling "like a hangover you might get from drinking a cup of gasoline." I have never done that, of course, but it felt as though I had just drank some chemical poison.

I tried to call Dr. Nagib, and I reported these symptoms as I had been told to do, but he was busy in another surgery. I felt as though I needed medical attention or I was going to die, and that I had nowhere to turn. I was afraid to go to sleep for fear I would not wake up again. Eventually

Dr. Nagib talked to another doctor who said that he had a patient who had experienced a severe reaction to Decadron, the medicine I had been taking; his patient had to be physically restrained because he kept trying to pull the IV tubes out, thinking they were snakes.

Dr. Nagib called me back and told me not to take any more Decadron under any circumstances (Decadron is a drug that you aren't supposed to stop taking cold turkey, but to slowly taper off of its use). He told me to stop taking the pills, to "throw them out the window" (which I didn't), and to drink cranberry juice to flush the poison from my system. He said that cranberry juice is a known antitoxin.

I have never been a cranberry juice fan, but oddly enough we had recently tried some cranberry juice blended with other juices, such as grape, raspberry, blueberry, etc., and just happened to have four jugs on hand. I remember staying up all night drinking glass after glass and jug after jug of cranberry juice. I remember being afraid to go to sleep out of fear that I would never wake up again. After what seemed to be a long while, I noticed a slight improvement in my symptoms. Step by step and glass by glass, the roaring in my head began to diminish and the other symptoms started to gradually subside, and toward morning I finally felt that it was safe to go to sleep. It was a night that I will never forget, and it left me physically and emotionally devastated.

As bad as those experiences were, my battle wasn't over yet; it was only beginning. I was having a very difficult time recovering from this second of two brain surgeries that had occurred just a few weeks apart. Even though this brain surgery had only been two hours long, as compared to the eight-hour length of my first brain surgery, it left me in a much worse condition. I still had severe eye problems with double vision that required me to wear an eye patch on one eye in order to focus on a single image. The shunt that had been installed in my head to relieve cerebral spinal fluid pressure buildup left my head so painfully sensitive that I often had to walk on tiptoe to cushion the jarring shock incurred just by walking.

I had great difficulty sleeping, partly due to the discomfort of the shunt penetrating through a hole in my skull on the top of my head and a hose that ran from my brain, under the scalp on the right side of my head, and down my neck, where it drained in the parietal area where my stomach and other organs are. During the first surgery, I'd had a large triangular chunk of skull permanently removed from the back of my head. And the other part of my difficulty in sleeping was due to the removal of my pineal gland. This gland in the center of the brain produces a hormone called melatonin that many doctors believe controls the body's "clock" and regulates sleep. I certainly believe it does, because after this gland was removed, my sleeping went down the drain. I had a hard time sleeping more than a couple hours at a time and had to take afternoon naps to survive.

I still felt incredibly ill. There was no noticeable improvement in my condition from day to day or week to week, or even month to month. Dr. Nagib and his assistant Therese talked about a "window of opportunity" for healing to take place, but as time passed by, I felt that the opportunity for improvement was passing me by, that the window was closing. As the weeks went by, I became afraid that I would never get much better. I began to doubt that I would ever be capable of living a life anywhere close to normal or a life worth living.

To make matters worse, I had no long-term disability insurance and I totally blamed myself for the situation I was in. I felt as though I had really let my family down by allowing myself to get into this situation. If I couldn't return to a meaningful job, I would become a great burden to my family. The guilt overwhelmed me, and it grieved my heart greatly. Ironically, a friend of mine was in a situation that prevented him from being able to continue working as a doctor, but he had great disability insurance, which enabled his family to carry on normally, at least financially. The stark difference between our states of preparedness poured salt into my wounds. I was haunted by the thought, *If only I had taken the time to be better prepared with insurance in case my life did not work out the way I planned.*

I remember thinking that if I did not regain my health, I would lose my job. And if I lost my job, I would lose my health insurance. And if I lost my health insurance, because of the many huge medical bills, I would lose the house my wife and I had just built. I sank into a deep depression; it seemed as though my whole world was crashing in on me. I wasn't making any noticeable improvement, and I couldn't see any way out of the predicament I was in. I couldn't even imagine a possible way life could ever get better.

This was far and away the lowest point of my life. I began to pray to God very humbly and very desperately. I remember lying in bed beside my wife with tears silently rolling down my cheeks night after night, and my silent prayers would end with "Father, if this is all that I have left to live for, take me home; take me home." I remember telling people that out of all the pain I suffered, and it was considerable, by far the worst thing was this deep depression. I remember times when I was recovering at home alone when I would be sitting in a chair and I didn't even have enough energy or enthusiasm to get up and turn on the TV. I describe the deep depression I was in as a total loss of all hope. Hope was gone from my life, and what a wretched, tormented feeling it was.

My spirit was totally broken, and I had little will to live. Over and over again I prayed the daily prayer from July 19 on my Heart Warmers flip calendar that my brother Al and his wife Cres had given me: *"When my world is at its darkest, Father, I need to feel Thy loving hand on my shoulder and Thy blessed assurance 'that this too shall pass'. Amen."* I prayed that prayer as if it were a lifeline. At that point I could feel that the Lord began answering my prayers. I noticed a very small, almost imperceptible, improvement in my physical health and a more substantial improvement in my emotional health, but I still had a long way to go. Because I had now used up more than three months of accumulated sick and vacation time, I returned to work probably a couple of months earlier than I really should have. But it was important to me now, because of the burden I felt I had become to my family, that I not lose even an hour's pay from my paycheck. And so I returned to work with no sick time and only a few hours of vacation time left on the books.

I was in no condition to drive myself, because of the damage to my eyesight, but the good Lord provided me with a guardian angel in the form of a coworker named Jim Bossert, who drove me to and from work on an almost daily basis during this time of crisis, for which I will be eternally grateful. It was the only practical way I could have returned to work at that time. Thankfully, my boss, Ken Martin, was very supportive of my condition and assigned another supervisor, Tim Norton, to assist me with my duties; Tim virtually held my hand for several months after I returned. These were two more gifts from God that allowed me to survive.

Even with all this help, work was exceedingly difficult for me. At first my memory was so poor that I would literally not remember things that I had talked about with someone only five or ten minutes earlier. Because of what cancer did to the visual cortex of my brain, I had great difficulty keeping my sight from breaking up into double vision, and tracking from word to word and line to line was very difficult. Reading became so slow and difficult that I had time to attempt to read only the most urgent short memos. The rest I tried to make up for by talking to others in the office.

Even the smallest of decisions were hard to make, partly because I worried so much and partly because it didn't take much to totally overwhelm me. Our department had just gone through a major shakeup in organization, and it was a very tense time between management and staff. A few of the less sensitive individuals I supervised, unaware of what I was personally going through, took every opportunity to make me painfully aware of my shortcomings. But most others were very supportive.

I was still bald at the time, having lost all my hair after radiation treatments, with a scalp that looked like a lunar landscape after the two surgeries. I am sure everyone there must have thought I was a real "dough head," yet everyone was very kind. It was a very humbling experience, as was everything else in my life lately. Life after cancer was often embarrassing, but the term "embarrassment" was taking on a whole new meaning for me. When I was focused on just surviving, just trying to make it through another day, things that would have embarrassed me before seemed to be unimportant.

In my depression, I wasn't thinking very clearly. I often thought about the burden I was becoming on my family. I felt that my whole life was a failure, and I often dwelled on the idea that I was worth more to my family dead than alive. I really punished myself for letting my family down. Then I remembered that I had a $100,000 life insurance policy—not through any foresight of my own, but because in order for my wife to buy a $100,000 life insurance that she wanted, the University of Minnesota required me to carry that same amount of coverage for myself. What a break this was; at least my family would have something to help them survive in the event that I didn't.

One of the responsibilities of an operations supervisor—my position at the time of my cancer recovery—is to check on jobs and projects in buildings all over a very large campus. I had worked on the Minneapolis campus for some fifteen years as a student and later as a full-time welder, but I had only been on the St. Paul campus a couple of months before my cancer diagnosis, and so everything was new to me. Because of my seeing difficulties—double vision, difficulty tracking moving objects, Parinaud's syndrome, incredibly slow adjustment to changes in light levels, loss of depth perception, etc.—I was left with a sensation similar to that of tunnel vision. I can only attempt to describe this feeling as being like looking through two toilet paper tubes. It's not that my field of vision was surrounded by dark circles or anything, but I had a very narrow field of focused vision with my peripheral vision breaking up into double vision, especially when I moved my head or turned my head to an extreme angle, as when backing up a car. It was now painfully apparent to me that healthy eyes do an incredible amount of things to make normal vision happen that we take for granted. I never realized all that my eyes were doing for me until they weren't able to do it anymore. What an incredible creation the human eyes are.

When walking, since I could only keep a small area in focus, I chose that area to be in front of my feet, which I needed to do to avoid tripping over obstacles or twisting an ankle by stepping into a pothole or something. My eyes were incapable of looking up, down, side to side, and around rapidly while still keeping things in focus. Because of these problems, ***I could never get the "big picture" of where I was*** and so couldn't learn the layout of the campus or even retrace my steps. When crossing busy streets, I could not look left, right, left, in front of me, and down in front of my feet anywhere near fast enough to avoid getting run over by a car, so I had to rely on the person walking next to me.

I would scan the area in front of my feet so that I wouldn't stumble, and I would look at the feet of people walking next to me and use the sound of them walking to let me know when I could cross the street safely. This was a workable solution that allowed me to have some dignity of not having to hold someone's sleeve to cross the street, but it was a little dicey, and embarrassing, until I learned what I needed to do. I remember trying to explain this to my wife, Jenny, when we were shopping at Ridgedale Mall, where we had shopped many times before. I said to her, "Don't get too far away from me, or I'll get lost!" I described myself as being "directionally challenged."

Because my eyes were incredibly slow at adapting to light, when I would go into a dimly lit mechanical room on campus from the bright light outdoors, especially when there was bright sun on white snow outside, the room inside would appear to be totally jet black for five or ten minutes. A mechanical room is a very dangerous place to be if you can't see. It contains high-temperature steam pipes with areas of exposed pipes and valves that can scald and burn you instantly. There are exposed belts, motors, and pulleys that can catch hands, fingers, ties, and loose clothing and take off fingers, hands, and arms in the process.

There are pipes that you have to duck under and step over, and unprotected drop-offs that, in this case, went down up to twenty feet! Needless to say, I had to remain at the entrance for the five to ten minutes it took for me to be able to see adequately enough to be safe. The reverse would happen when I would go back outside. The outside light was so intensely bright that everything would go to a "whiteout" situation or to totally blue, as though I were looking through blue-colored lenses, or even an occasional "greenout" that I think had to do with the difference in intensity of the light levels. Again, I would have to wait the five or more minutes it took for my eyes to adjust before I could move.

I'll never forget one day that a friend and coworker, Tim Norton, and I went with some other people into a large control room that was a maze of pipes, ductwork, control panels, and other HVAC equipment. I had to wait a while at the door for my eyes to adjust enough so I could walk safely, and in the meantime the others went ahead and I got left behind. I wandered around for a while trying to find them, and because of my tunnel vision and my being directionally challenged, I got lost. I didn't have the faintest idea where I was. I needed a ride back to the office from them, and I began to panic. I ended up having to call out to Tim to come and get me. I was totally embarrassed, humiliated, and humbled, but looking back, I think this is just what God wanted to happen.

Many evenings, after what was now always a grueling day at work, when Jim Bossert would drive me home in the dark, tears would silently roll down my cheeks. On the days when my wife had to pick me up because Jim could not, I felt even worse because I knew what a burden it was on her to have to come all the way to St. Paul from St. Louis Park after her busy day to pick me up and take me home, and I openly wept. It was still very difficult for me to even imagine a time when I would be happy again.

Daily, I waged a battle in my mind. Improvements, if they were coming, were so slow as to be barely noticeable. I worried about that window of time in which I could expect improvements, and how much function I would regain after all was said and done. I wondered if my time for recovery had already run out. I was worried sick that this was as much as I could ever hope to recover! I was worried about how my boss viewed my performance. I was just barely making it even with Tim's assistance, and I had no idea how long that arrangement would last. I was still far from being able to drive myself anywhere. How long would Jim be willing or able to provide transportation back and forth to work for me? I was totally dependent on him to get to work.

At that time, if I had lost my job, I could only have maintained my health insurance by paying for it myself; that option would only last for a few months, and then it wouldn't be available to me at all. I desperately needed to keep my insurance, because in my health condition, no one else would be willing to give me insurance—with the possible exception of Lloyd's of London. I hoped and reasoned that if my boss determined I was unable to perform my current duties, university civil service rules would allow me to perhaps move to a vacant position elsewhere on campus that I was qualified for, but what would I be qualified to do? I began to consider positions as a parking attendant or custodian that would allow me to keep a job and my health benefits, but I didn't know if I could take the physical demands of those jobs.

The passing of time was my only hope for a better existence. I tried to take it one day at a time. I tightly held onto that promise of God that ***"this too shall pass."*** I remember one time when my dear wife kind of scolded me, saying, "Why can't you at least put a smile on your face?" She was certainly under a lot of stress because of me and my cancer. I remember being a little surprised, because I thought I was doing a fairly good job of hiding how I felt, but I guess it's true that what you feel inside shows on your face. I remember trying very hard then to smile, but I ***couldn't*** make my muscles produce any facial gesture that would pass for even an unenthusiastic smile. I couldn't even force a smile, and it really scared me.

MY CALLING

I WAS BORN, raised, and confirmed in the Lutheran faith, but as I said before, I put my faith on the back burner while seeking the things this world had to offer. I married a Catholic girl, and God gave us our miraculous son. After my life-and-death battle with cancer started, I had a whole different outlook on life. I was starting to see God in a whole new light, and I began to see that all the petty bickering between denominations in the same Christian faith was a little ridiculous and a lot harmful. And so I, a Lutheran, started attending a Catholic church near our home for family unity.

As I was recovering from cancer, my family and I were going to "a little white church on the hill," a little wooden church painted white that looked as if it had been built in the late 1800s. It had a tall steeple and sat on the top of a green grass hill. As the weeks went by, I began to get the feeling that God was calling me. The feeling was particularly strong whenever they played that beautiful song "Here I am, Lord."

At that time I thought that when God called someone, it meant that He wanted them to be a missionary in some third-world country or something. I remember thinking, as this feeling of being called kept happening, "God, what can I do? I am just barely alive and not sure how long I am going to live." I wasn't sure what I could do for Him, as I was not able to drive and could not walk or see well, and was mainly concerned with surviving and keeping my job. Nevertheless, that feeling that God was calling me kept happening to me week after week at church. It was not an audible calling but a strong feeling in my heart and mind. Finally I said to God in my mind, *Okay, I will answer Your call if I hear the song "Here I am, Lord" played before we leave church, the song that had been touching my heart lately.*

It may sound pretty crazy, but that's what I did. I figured that the church service was almost over, and I felt that there was very little chance of that song being played. You see, I was trying to get a "no-go" answer. Well, lo and behold, the next song that was played was, you guessed it, "Here I Am, Lord." I felt as if God were speaking to me personally and intimately through those words, and I answered His call by singing the chorus:

> Here I am, Lord. Is it I Lord? I have heard You calling in the night
>
> (and I really had heard Him calling, waking me up with inspirational messages to me in the night).
>
> I will go Lord, if You lead me, I will hold Your people in my heart.

All of a sudden I felt a warmth come down over me, and I was tingling from head to toe. I was so filled with awe and so overwhelmed with the feeling of God's presence that I had the shivers all over my body, and tears of joy were welling up in my eyes. This feeling, I now believe, was caused by the Holy Spirit indwelling me; what some call the **Holy Ghost bumps.** I had a feeling that God had a purpose for my life or whatever was left of it. This song, "Here I Am, Lord," became "my song," **the song that the Lord used to call me,** and I still get **Holy Ghost bumps** all over whenever I hear it.

It was after that call by God that things started to turn around in my life in a big way. My health improved, and soon I was able to drive to work. I remember one day when I was driving my pickup truck to work and I felt a tingle in the back of my neck. I felt excited, and I suddenly felt a hope for my life that I had not felt for a long time.

God also put a hunger on my heart for the Word of God that I cannot explain. I had memorized some Bible verses when I went through confirmation, but I never actually read the Bible, let alone studied it.

But now that was all I wanted to do. I started reading books about near-death experiences and spiritual stories by Christian writers. I bought my first Bible and started reading it whenever I had time.

My neighbor, Jay Sather, invited me to Bible Study Fellowship, where I spent fourteen years in a very intense study of the Bible. It was in Bible Study Fellowship that a seasoned Bible scholar taught me to begin every Bible study session by praying on my knees for the Holy Spirit to help me understand. That was the best advice I have ever received. The Bible started coming alive to me, and my understanding exploded. I sought out Bible-teaching churches, and I attended two or three different Bible-teaching churches a week. I finally felt that God was calling me to Calvary Lutheran Church, where I attended programs like Alpha, the Truth Project, Faith Search, etc., and was constantly in a Bible study there.

I had stumbled across the Bible teaching ministry of Charles Stanley on TV while I was in recovery at home, and I watched it as though it were a spiritual lifeline. Every word from the Bible that Pastor Stanley taught was like food to a starving man. I now started to tape his sermons every Sunday which led to listening and taping three Christian programs before going to Church on Sunday. Then I discovered Northwestern Book Store, a Christian bookstore, where I was like a kid in a candy store. I purchased so many Christian books and audio and video tapes that I now have a small library of Christian material. Such was my passion for the Word of God and the truth.

I started to recognize how God was working in my life with amazing "coincidences" that were not coincidences at all but God's hand working all things together for my good that I might grow in faith. God connected me with other Christians so that I could hear what they had to say or for me to say what they needed to hear. And God gave me little miracles that only I would recognize as miracles; these came in the form of answers to things I was thinking about, as though God knew what I was thinking. Whenever the Holy Spirit revealed an idea from the Bible that I had never heard before and that made me wonder if it was from God or just something from me, God would have me hear the same idea from two, three, or sometimes four different Christian sources in rapid succession so that by miraculous "coincidence" I would know that my thoughts were true and divinely inspired.

God began to answer my prayers for little things and big things. He even answered some of my prayers for the healing of others, but not always. I think God wanted me to know that sometimes my prayers for healing were in conflict with His greater plan to humble someone through suffering so that he or she might be open to listening to Him for a greater purpose, just as God allowed me to suffer with cancer to get my attention for the work He called me to do, something that I now recognize as the best thing that ever happened to me. And not only did I see how God was working in my life now, but I also started to see how God has always been working in my life, preparing me for the work He has called me to do. I began to realize that this life on earth is not a bunch of random events, but that God is in control and has a plan for all of our lives. King David recognized this when he said, "Your eyes saw my substance, being **yet unformed**. And in Your book they all were written, The **days fashioned for me, When as yet there were none of them**" (**Psalm 139:16**).

And the work that God called me to do is to write a book and to teach. And He even gave me the name that the book should be called, which is *something like* "Seeing the Forest Despite the Trees. Now when God gave me that name, it was not that God spoke to me with words that I could audibly hear, but rather an intense thought or idea in my mind that I had to struggle to put into words. And that is why I say *something like* because I originally I called the book *Seeing the Forest despite the Trees*, but when I learned that the two trees in the middle of the garden of Eden represent two different ways of thinking and living, I modified the title to *Seeing the Forest despite the Tree*.

It was to be a big picture of the truth of God that we were kept from seeing because we were so focused on the Tree of Knowledge of Good and Evil that we could not see the ways of God, which lead to life. I learned that the "tree" that I saw in my near-death experience, which

I used to describe the place of All Knowledge, was symbolically the Tree of Life.

As an example of how God connects Christians together to help each other grow in knowledge and faith, a series of events helped me learn about the two different trees and led me to modify the title of the book God called me to write.

First I was invited by my neighbor and good friend Sandy Sather to talk about my near-death experience at a hot topics forum at Calvary Lutheran. When I described the place of All Knowledge that I went to as being like a tree and like a library, after my talk, someone in the audience asked me, "Rick, have you ever considered that the place of All Knowledge was the Tree of Life?" I replied, "No, I haven't, but that's a good idea!"

A couple of years later, a coworker came to me and said, "I think my brother had a near-death experience similar to the one you had." When we got together over lunch, his brother described how he had been addicted to drugs, and when he was dying he had an experience of going to a place where there was a Tree of All Knowledge, just as I experienced. But he said that he covered his eyes and did not want to look at it. When I asked why, he said that he knew that the truth would convict him and condemn him, and so he cried out to Jesus to save him. When I asked him what he thought about us having such different reactions to the Tree of Life, he said, "You had Jesus with you." His brother has since given up drugs and joined a very spiritual Bible-teaching church.

About a year after that, the brother introduced me to someone who had an experience where he saw that same Tree of Life. He described an experience in which Satan was in a car with him and was trying to kill him. It was an intervention of Jesus that saved him. When I met him he had the telltale signs of someone who has been rescued from death by the love of Jesus. He had a worn and ragged Bible full of highlighting and handwritten notes before him, and he was busy taking notes on paper.

And that is why God put a hunger for the Word of God on my heart that I cannot explain—because the knowledge of the truth that I experienced when I was near death and fighting for life is found in the Word of God. And so I began with a passion to re-create the knowledge I learned in that truth-and-love experience by studying the Bible, that I might share the truth that God shared with me with as many as will seek it. This truth will set them free from this world of sin and death.

I search for the truth in God's Word like a buried treasure of inestimable worth like I described my near death experience. And this is how Jesus describes the knowledge of the truth that leads to eternal life in heaven: "Again, the **kingdom of heaven is like treasure hidden in a field**, which a man found and hid; and **for joy over it** he goes and sells all that he has and buys that field. [45] Again, the **kingdom of heaven is like a merchant seeking beautiful pearls**, [46] who, when he had found one **pearl of great price**, went and sold all that he had and bought it" (**Matthew 13:44–46**).

Come with me as we search for the hidden truths in the Word of God that will help us understand the meaning and purpose of this temporary life on this temporary earth. That these truths are hidden is revealed by the fact that the word "mystery" is found twenty-one times in the Bible. The Scriptures are full of metaphors, signs, symbolism, and events on earth that help us picture realities in heaven, and Jesus speaks to us in parables that have deeper meanings. Let us consider how the hidden truth in the Bible will be revealed to those who seek after the truth:

> Therefore do not fear them. For there is **nothing covered** that will not **be revealed**, and **hidden** that will not be **known**. [27] Whatever I tell you in the dark, speak in the light; and what **you hear in the ear, preach on the housetops**. (**Matthew 10:26–27**)

> At that time Jesus answered and said, "I thank You, Father, Lord of heaven and earth, that You have **hidden these things from** *the* **wise and prudent** and have **revealed them to babes**." (**Matthew 11:25**)

"For there is **nothing hidden which will not be revealed**, nor has **anything been kept secret but that it should come to light**. [23] If anyone **has ears to hear, let him hear**." [24] Then He said to them, "Take heed **what you hear**. With the same measure you use, it will be measured to you; and **to you who hear, more will be given**. [25] For whoever has, to him more will be given; but whoever does not have, even what he has will be taken away from him." (**Mark 4:22–25**)

But **their minds were blinded**. For until this day **the same veil remains unlifted in the reading of the Old Testament**, because **the *veil* is taken away in Christ**. [15] But even to this day, when Moses is read, **a veil lies on their heart**. [16] Nevertheless **when one turns to the Lord, the veil is taken away**. [17] Now **the Lord is the Spirit**; and where the Spirit of the Lord *is,* there *is* liberty. (**2 Corinthians 3:14–17**)

We will learn who is hiding the truth, who is revealing the truth, and when and why they are hiding the truth beginning in the chapter "Blindness" and throughout the rest of book. Be prepared to be surprised and amazed at what we will learn and understand!

THE WISDOM OF MAN

AT THE TIME of my physical recovery and spiritual learning, I recognized that the more I knew, the more I knew how much I did not know and how much man did not know. I found the following quotations to be humorous examples of man's limited ability to imagine new concepts and ideas.

THE DARWIN AWARDS

"Computers in the future may weigh no more than 1.5 tons."

—*Popular Mechanics*, forecasting the relentless march of science, 1949

"I think there is a world market for maybe five computers."

—Thomas Watson, Chairman of IBM, 1943

"I have traveled the length and breadth of this country and talked with the best people, and I can assure you that data processing is a fad that won't last out the year."

—the editor in charge of business books for Prentice Hall, 1957

"But what ... is it good for?"

—engineer for the IBM Advanced Computing Systems project, 1968, commenting on the microchip

"There is no reason anyone would want a computer in their home."

> —Ken Olson, president, chairman, and founder of Digital Equipment Corp., 1977

"This 'telephone' has too many shortcomings to be seriously considered as a means of communication. The device is inherently of no value to us."

> —Western Union internal memo, 1876

"The wireless music box has no imaginable commercial value. Who would pay for a message sent to nobody in particular?"

> —David Sarnoff's associates in response to his urgings for investment in the radio in the 1920s

"The concept is interesting and well-formed, but in order to earn better than a 'C,' the idea must be feasible."

> —a Yale University management professor to Fred Smith's paper proposing reliable overnight delivery service (Smith went on to found Federal Express Corp.)

"I'm just glad it'll be Clark Gable who's falling on his face and not Gary Cooper."

> —Gary Cooper on his decision to not take the leading role in *Gone with the Wind.*

"A cookie store is a bad idea. Besides, the market research reports say America likes crispy cookies, not soft and chewy cookies like you make."

> —response to Debbi Field's idea of starting Mrs. Field's Cookies

"We don't like their sound, and guitar music is on the way out."

> —Decca Records Co. rejecting the Beatles, 1962

"Heavier-than-air flying machines are impossible."

> —Lord Kelvin, president, Royal Society, 1895

"If I had thought about it, I wouldn't have done the experiment. The literature was full of examples that said you can't do this."

—Spencer Silver on the work that led to the unique adhesives for 3M Post-it notes

"So we went to Atari and said, 'Hey, we've got this amazing thing, even built with some of your parts, and what do you think about funding us? Or we'll give it to you. We just want to do it. Pay our salary, we'll come work for you.' And they said, 'No.' So they went to Hewlett-Packard, and they said, 'Hey, we don't need you. You haven't got through college yet.'"

—Apple Computer Inc. founder Steve Jobs, on attempts to get Atari and HP interested in his and Steve Wozniak's personal computer

"Professor Goddard does not know the relation between action and reaction and the need to have something better than a vacuum against which to react. He seems to lack the basic knowledge ladled out daily in high schools."

—1921 *New York Times* editorial about Robert Goddard's revolutionary rocket work

"You want to have consistent and uniform muscle development across all of your muscles? It can't be done. It's just a fact of life. You have to just accept inconsistent muscle development as an unalterable condition of weight training."

—response to Arthur Jones, who solved the "unsolvable" problem by inventing Nautilus

"Drill for oil? You mean drill into the ground and try to find oil? You're crazy."

—drillers whom Edwin L. Drake tried to enlist to his project to drill for oil in 1859

"Stocks have reached what looks like a permanently high plateau."

—Irving Fisher, professor of economics, Yale University, 1929

"Airplanes are interesting toys but of no military value."

—Marechal Ferdinand Foch, professor of strategy, Ecole
Superiure de Guerre

"Everything that can be invented has been invented."

—Charles H. Duell, commissioner, US Officer of
Patents, 1899

"Louis Pasteur's theory of germs is ridiculous fiction."

—Pierre Pachet, professor of physiology at Toulouse, 1872

"The abdomen, the chest, and the brain will forever be shut from
the wise and humane surgeon."

—Sir John Eric Ericksen, British surgeon appointed surgeon-
extraordinary to Queen Victoria, 1873

"640K ought to be enough for anybody."

—Bill Gates, 1981

STRUCK WITH AWE

THE INSPIRING WORD OF GOD

As WE BEGIN our study of the Bible, God's powerful and transforming words of truth and love to fallen man, we will find ourselves in the company of some world-changing men and women:

> "The secret of my success? It is simple. It is found in the Bible."
>
> **—George Washington Carver**

> "It is impossible to enslave mentally or socially a Bible-reading people. The principles of the Bible are the groundwork of human freedom."
>
> **—Horace Greeley**

> "The existence of the Bible is a book for the people. It's the greatest benefit the human race has ever experienced. Every attempt to belittle it is a crime against humanity."
>
> **—Immanuel Kant**

> "I believe the Bible is the best gift God has ever given to man."
>
> **—Abraham Lincoln**

> "The Bible has been the Magna Carta of the poor and the oppressed. The human race is not in a position to dispense with it."
>
> **—Thomas Huxley**

"The Bible is no mere book, but it's a living creature with a power that conquers all who oppose it."

—Napoleon

"The Bible is ... as necessary to spiritual life as breath is to natural life. There is nothing more essential to our lives than the Word of God."

—Jack Hayford

"It is impossible to rightly govern the world without God and the Bible."

—George Washington

"Our constitution was made only for a moral and religious people ... so great is my veneration of the Bible that the earlier my children begin to read, the more confident will be my hope that they will prove useful citizens in their country and respectful members of society."

—John Adams

"A nation of well-informed men who have been taught to know the price of rights which God has given them cannot be enslaved."

—Benjamin Franklin

"That Book (the Bible) is the rock on which our Republic rests."

—Andrew Jackson

"The Bible is the cornerstone of liberty ... students' perusal of the sacred volume will make us better citizens, better fathers, and better husbands."

—Thomas Jefferson

"The Bible is worth all other books which have ever been printed."

—Patrick Henry

"If we will not be governed by God, then we will be ruled by tyrants."

—William Penn

"Bible reading is an education in itself."

—Lord Tennyson

"There are more sure marks of authenticity in the Bible than in any profane history ... I have a fundamental belief in the Bible as the Word of God, written by men who were inspired. I study the Bible daily."

—Sir Isaac Newton

"The New Testament is the very best book that ever was or ever will be known in the world."

—Charles Dickens

"The whole hope of human progress is suspended on the ever growing influence of the Bible."

—W. H. Seward

"The Bible was written in tears, and to tears it yields its best treasures."

—A. W. Tozer

"It is clear that there must be difficulties for us in a revelation such as the Bible. If someone were to hand me a book that was as simple to me as the multiplication table, and say, 'This is the Word of God. In it He has revealed His whole will and wisdom,' I would shake my head and say, 'I cannot believe it; that is too easy to be a perfect revelation of infinite wisdom.' There must be, in any complete revelation of God's mind and will and character and being, things hard for the beginner to understand; and the wisest and best of us are but beginners."

—R. A. Torrey

"My advice to Sunday Schools no matter what their denomination is: Hold fast to the Bible as the sheet anchor of your liberties; write its precepts in your heart, and practice them in your lives. To the influence of this Book we are indebted for the progress made in true civilization and to this we must look as our guide in the future. 'Righteousness exalteth a nation, but sin is a reproach to any people' (**Proverbs 14:34**)."

—Ulysses S. Grant

"At this time I both read and studied all kinds of literature: cosmography, histories, chronicles, and philosophy and other arts, to which our Lord opened my mind unmistakably to the fact that it was possible to navigate from here to the Indies, and He evoked in me the will for the execution of it; and with this fire I came to Your Highnesses. All those who heard of my plan disregarded it mockingly and with laughter. All the sciences of which I spoke were of no profit to me nor the authorities in them; only in Your Highnesses my faith, and my stay. Who would doubt that this light did not come from the Holy Spirit, anyway as far as I am concerned, which comforted with rays of marvelous clarity and with its Holy and Sacred Scriptures."

—Christopher Columbus

"All that we hear and read should be measured for accuracy by the standard of the Bible and the 'Holy Ghost filter.'"

—Betty Miller

BLINDNESS

So THERE I was, still struggling to survive, suffering from the effects of cancer, hydrocephalus, and radiation treatments. God had given me this incredible gift of going to a place that I call All Knowledge. And I, after having been shown knowledge and given understanding that was so far above what we know, had then lost most of the remembrance of that knowledge, except for the two specific words "truth" and "love," along with the feeling of connectedness or oneness and some general concepts, ideas, and feelings. On the inside I was filled with the unspeakable joy and excitement of having seen this hidden treasure of truth and knowledge; but on the outside I was suffering from a body that had been devastated by the effects of cancer. I realized through this near-death experience that although I was near death, I was also near life—eternal life!

I kept wondering why God would show me all this exciting and thrilling truth and knowledge and then not allow me to recall most of it. At first I kind of blamed myself. I reasoned that God had entrusted me with this precious knowledge, though I could not even remember what it was. But then I reasoned that there must be a reason. God could certainly enable me to remember the things I had forgotten if He wanted to. As I became more familiar with the ways of God from studying the Bible, I realized that He has a reason and a purpose for not revealing all the truth to us, at least not until we are ready to hear it. Jesus gave a similar message to His disciples: "I still have many things to say to you, but you **cannot bear** *them* **now**" (**John 16:12**).

Also, there is another player in this story, "that Serpent of old, called the Devil and Satan" (**Revelation 20:2**). It is Satan who deceived fallen man with a lie that has trapped us as slaves in bondage to him. He certainly has a purpose in keeping us from knowing the truth, because knowing the truth would destroy the deception of his lie and set us free from being his slave. As Jesus proclaimed, "And you shall **know the truth**, and the **truth shall make you free**" (**John 8:32**).

While God may not always reveal the whole truth to us, we should know that when He does not, it is for our own good. On the other hand, Satan always tries to keep the truth from us for his own good, not ours. Know also that unlike Satan, God cannot and will not lie, for He is a God of truth. "*He is* the Rock, His work *is* perfect; For all **His ways** *are* **justice**, A **God of truth** and without injustice; **Righteous and upright** *is* **He**" (**Deuteronomy 32:4**). And this is exactly what the apostle Paul says to Titus in a letter: "Paul, a bondservant of God and an apostle of Jesus Christ, according to the **faith of God's elect** and the **acknowledgment of the truth** which accords with **godliness**, [2] in hope of eternal life which God, **who cannot lie**, promised **before time began**" (**Titus 1:1–2**).

In comparison, Satan is the father of lies, as Jesus proclaims to the Pharisees, the religious leaders of the Jews: "You are of *your* **father the devil** and the desires of your father **you want to do**. He was a murderer from the beginning, and *does not* **stand in the truth**, because **there is no truth in him**. When he speaks a lie, he speaks from his own *resources,* for **he is a liar** and **the father of it**. [45] But because **I tell the truth**, you do not believe Me" (**John 8:44–45**).

We also have to understand that an omniscient God knows things that we are incapable of understanding, "For My thoughts *are* not your thoughts, Nor *are* your ways My ways," says the LORD. [9] "For *as* **the heavens are higher than the earth,** So are **My ways higher than your ways,** And **My thoughts than your thoughts**" (**Isaiah 55:8–9**). God also knows that it is not wise to try to share the truth with those who do not want to listen and are still violently rejecting Him and His truth: "Do not give what is holy to the dogs; nor **cast**

your pearls [of wisdom] **before swine,** lest they trample them under their feet, and turn and tear you in pieces" (**Matthew 7:6**).

Before we get started re-creating this truth-and-love experience and discovering the meaning and purpose for life on earth, we need to consider that there is truth being withheld from us for a number of reasons. We need to be prepared to seek the truth like hidden treasure, because it really is a treasure of inestimable worth. That idea is exactly what the Bible expresses: "Again, the **kingdom of heaven** is like **treasure hidden** in a field, which a man found and hid; and **for joy over it** he goes and **sells all that he has** and **buys that field**" (**Matthew 13:44**). "For what will it **profit a man** if he **gains the whole world**, and **loses his own soul?** [37] Or what will a man give in exchange for his soul?" (**Mark 8:36–37**).

On the way to work one day, I was thinking about how I was intending to first show how ignorant man can be at times and then describe the awesome intelligence of God and finally talk about blindness and how I have come to believe that all our human knowledge is a gift of God and that we are at His mercy to receive it. I got to thinking about the examples in the chapter "The Wisdom of Man" and the fact that some of the world's most brilliant and successful people have made some of the most ignorant comments and blunders, and I considered that perhaps they got the outside help of God at some times but not others.

So then I got to the place where I work, and I chose a quote of the day from about fifty candidates to print and display for my coworkers to enjoy. After printing the quote I suddenly realized that my selection really fit what I had been thinking about on the way to work. The quote "I" chose for the day was, *"When the solution is simple, God is answering" (Albert Einstein)*. Sounds like Albert had discovered the same thing as I was discovering, or rather I should say that God was teaching me the same thing He taught Albert. Thank You, Lord. Now let us consider some passages from the Bible as examples of how God and Satan use blindness.

The Veil—Blindness—Jesus, the Light of the World

> But even if our **gospel is veiled**, it is veiled to those who are perishing, [4] whose **minds** the **god of this age has blinded**, who **do not believe**, lest the **light of the gospel** of the glory of Christ, **who is the image of God**, should shine on them. [5] For we do not preach ourselves, but Christ Jesus the Lord, and ourselves your bondservants for Jesus' sake. [6] For it is the **God who commanded light** to **shine out of darkness**, who has shone in our hearts to give the **light of the knowledge** of the glory of God in the face of Jesus Christ. (**2 Corinthians 4:3–6**)

Satan is the "god" of this age who has blinded us to the truth with his lies for his evil purposes, and God did not lift the veil in the beginning to reveal the truth for His righteous purposes. God wants all to know and understand the truth, but if proud and arrogant people think they already know everything and refuse to listen or even consider a different way of thinking, the only thing God can do is work in their lives to show them they are wrong—sometimes painfully wrong. But I have been there, and the truth is worth the pain.

And Jesus is the Son of God who has come to **remove the veil** that we may know the truth that will set us free, "But their **minds were blinded**. For until this day the **same veil remains unlifted** in the **reading of the Old Testament**, because the *veil* **is taken away in Christ**. [15] But even to this day, when Moses is read, a **veil lies on their heart**. [16] Nevertheless **when one turns to the Lord**, the **veil is taken away**" (**2 Corinthians 3:14–16**).

The Mysteries of the Kingdom of God—Blindness—Predestination

> "He who has ears to hear, let him hear!" [10] And the disciples came and said to Him, "Why do You speak to them in parables?" [11] He answered and said to them, "Because **it has been given to you to know** the **mysteries of the kingdom of heaven**, but **to them it has not been given**. [12] For whoever has, to him more will be given, and he will have abundance; but whoever **does not have**, even what he has will be **taken away from**

him. [13] Therefore **I speak to them in parables**, because **seeing they do not see**, and **hearing they do not hear, nor do they understand**. [14] And in them the prophecy of Isaiah is fulfilled, which says: '**Hearing you will hear** and **shall not understand**, And **seeing you will see** and **not perceive**; [15] For the **hearts of this people have grown dull**. Their ears are hard of hearing, And their eyes **they** have closed, Lest they should see with their eyes and hear with their ears, Lest they should **understand with their hearts and turn**, So that **I should heal them**.' [16] "But **blessed are your eyes** for **they see**, and **your ears** for **they hear**; [17] for assuredly, I say to you that many prophets and righteous men desired to see what you see, and did not see it, and to hear what you hear, and did not hear it. [18] Therefore hear the parable of the sower: [19] When anyone hears the **word of the kingdom**, and does not understand it, then the **wicked one comes** and **snatches away what was sown in his heart**." (**Matthew 13:9–19**)

Jesus had just spoken the parable of the sower of seeds to the multitude, and as was His custom, afterward He explained it to His disciples in plain language. Mark records this for us: "But without a parable He did not speak to them. And when they were alone, He **explained all things to His disciples**" (**Mark 4:34**). And His disciples asked Him, "Why do You speak to them in parables?" and Jesus answered by saying, "Because **it has been given to you to know the mysteries** of the **kingdom of heaven**, but to them **it has not been given** … Therefore I speak to them in parables, because **seeing they do not see**, and **hearing they do not hear, nor do they understand**." (**Matthew 13:11b, 13**).

The question we have is, what does Jesus already know about the disciples that makes them worthy to know and understand, and how and when does Jesus know this about them? When was it given to the disciples to know the mysteries of the kingdom of heaven, and why? We will find an answer to this question and many others in the Bible as we seek to know and understand the truth.

Blindness

At that time Jesus answered and said, "I thank You, Father, Lord of heaven and earth, that **You have hidden these things** from the **wise and prudent** and have **revealed them to babes.** [26] Even so, Father, for so it seemed good in Your sight. [27] All things have been delivered to Me by My Father, and no one knows the Son except the Father. Nor does anyone know the Father except the Son, and **the one to whom the Son wills to reveal Him.** [28] Come to Me, all you who labor and are heavy laden, and I will give you rest. [29] **Take My yoke upon you** and **learn from Me,** for **I am gentle** and **lowly in heart,** and you will **find rest** for **your souls.** [30] For **My yoke is easy** and **My burden is light.**" **(Matthew 11:25–30)**

Blind Leaders of the Blind

When He had called the multitude to Himself, He said to them, "Hear and understand: [11] Not what goes into the mouth defiles a man; but what comes out of the mouth, this defiles a man." [12] Then His disciples came and said to Him, "Do You know that the Pharisees were offended when they heard this saying?" [13] But He answered and said, "**Every plant** which **My heavenly Father has not planted** will be **uprooted.** [14] Let them alone. They are **blind leaders** of the **blind.** And if the **blind leads the blind,** both will **fall into a ditch.**" **(Matthew 15:10–14)**

The Keys of the Kingdom of Heaven

"And I will give you the **keys of the kingdom of heaven,** and whatever you **bind** on earth will be **bound** in heaven, and whatever you loose on earth will be loosed in heaven." [20] Then He commanded His disciples that **they should tell no one** that **He was Jesus the Christ. (Matthew 16:19–20)**

Why does Jesus not want anyone to be told that He is the Christ?

Oh, Now I See—The Blind Will See, and the Seeing Will Be Made Blind

> And Jesus said, "For judgment I have come into this world, that **those who do not see may see**, and that **those who see may be made blind**." [40] Then some of the Pharisees who were with Him heard these words, and said to Him, "**Are we blind also?**" [41] Jesus said to them, "**If you were blind**, you would have no sin; but now you say, '**We see.**' Therefore your sin remains." (**John 9:39–41**)

Seeing the lies of Satan in this world as truth means being blinded to the real truth of God and being guilty of sin.

Temporary Blindness for a Purpose

> "Let these words sink down into your ears, for the Son of Man is about to be betrayed into the hands of men." [45] But **they did not understand** this saying, and **it was hidden from them so that they did not perceive it**; and they were afraid to ask Him about this saying. (**Luke 9:44–45**)

It appears that Jesus was trying very hard to have His disciples understand what was going to happen to Him as He went to the cross, but they did not understand, so it was hidden from them. Was the reason for their lack of understanding that their thinking was so focused on themselves and worldly things that they could not perceive the truth Jesus was trying to show them, which only made sense from the spiritual perspective? Since God does not cast spiritual pearls of wisdom among swine, had they wasted the chance to know greater truth and thereby been blinded from knowing it? Does the same thing happen to us?

The very next verses reveal what they were focused on: "Then a dispute arose among them as to which of them would be greatest. [47] And Jesus, **perceiving the thought of their heart**, took a **little child** and set him by Him, [48] and said to them, 'Whoever receives this little child in My name receives Me; and whoever receives Me receives Him who sent Me. For **he who is least among you all will be great**'" (**Luke 9:46–48**). It is in the nature, the heart, and the mind-set of little children, who know they cannot survive on their own, to be dependent on their father and mother and to be eager to listen to and learn what they do not know—that which makes us eligible to enter the kingdom of God. "Assuredly, I say to you, whoever does not receive the kingdom of God **as a little child** will by no means enter it" (**Mark 10:15**).

I like the way the New International Version of the Bible renders this passage: "I tell you the truth, anyone who will not receive the kingdom of God **like a little child** will never enter it" (**Mark 10:15 NIV**). That way people do not think that baptism when they are a child is necessary to enter the kingdom of heaven. Remember the criminal on the cross beside Jesus!

Hidden From Our Eyes

> Now as He drew near, He saw the city and wept over it, [42] saying, "If you had **known**, even you, especially in this **your day**, the things that make for your peace! **But now they are hidden from your eyes**. [43] For days will come upon you when your enemies will build an embankment around you, surround you and close you in on every side, [44] and level you, and your children within you, to the ground; and they will not leave in you one stone upon another, **because you did not know** the **time of your visitation**." (**Luke 19:41–44**)

The Jews missed the coming of their Messiah because they thought that He would bring them deliverance from the Roman domination and peace by power and military might. They did not expect a meek and mild Savior that would die on a cross to be their deliverer from Satan's domination, using gentleness, self-sacrifice, and love. They did not read their Old Testament Bibles to understand, and they killed the prophets that God gave them who spoke of what the Messiah would be like, because they were too focused on the ways and things of this world.

Paul Was Blinded

> And the men who journeyed with him stood speechless, hearing a voice but seeing no one. [8] Then Saul arose from the ground, and **when his eyes were opened he saw no one**. But they led him

by the hand and brought him into Damascus. ⁹ And he was **three days without sight**, and neither ate nor drank. (**Acts 9:7–9**)

Ironically, God made Paul blind to things of the world so he could "see" the reality of the spiritual world. I can relate to that experience.

Paul's Experience—His Blindness Removed

But rise and stand on your feet; for I have appeared to you for this purpose, to make you a minister and a witness both of the things **which you have seen** and of the things which **I will yet reveal to you.** (**Acts 26:16**)

There are certain things in Paul's experience that are similar to my experience and it makes me fall down on my knees and tremble.

Blindness—Hearts Grown Dull

So when they did not agree among themselves, they departed after Paul had said one word: "The **Holy Spirit spoke** rightly through Isaiah the prophet to our fathers, ²⁶ saying, 'Go to this people and say: "**Hearing you will hear**, and **shall not understand**; And **seeing you will see**, and **not perceive**; ²⁷ For **the hearts of this people** have **grown dull**. Their ears are **hard of hearing**, And their eyes **they** have closed, Lest they should **see with their eyes** and **hear with their ears**, Lest they should **understand with their hearts and turn**, So that I should heal them."' ²⁸ Therefore let it be known to you that the **salvation of God has been sent to the Gentiles**, and they will hear it!" ²⁹ And when he had said these words, the Jews departed and had a great dispute among themselves. (**Acts 28:25–29**)

This passage clearly shows us that their blindness is a free-will choice on their part in the phrase "Their eyes **they** have closed."

Blindness—Seeing in a Mirror Dimly

"When I was a child, I spoke as a child, I understood as a child, I thought as a child; but when I became a man, I put away childish things. [12] For **now we see in a mirror, dimly,** but then face-to-face. Now **I know in part**, but then I shall know just as I also am known. [13] And now abide **faith, hope, love**, these three; but the **greatest of these is love.**" (1 Corinthians 13:12)

Ignorance of Understanding—Blindness of Heart

This I say, therefore, and testify in the Lord, that you should no longer walk as the rest of the Gentiles walk, in the **futility of their mind,** [18] having **their understanding darkened**, being alienated from the **life of God**, because of the **ignorance that is in them**, because of the **blindness of their heart;** [19] who, being **past feeling**, have **given themselves** over to lewdness, to work all uncleanness with greediness. (**Ephesians 4:17–19**)

He Who Is of God Hears

He who is of God **hears God's words**; therefore you **do not hear**, because **you are not of God**. (**John 8:47**)

God Opens Our Understanding to Remove Blindness

But their **eyes were restrained, so that they did not know Him**. [17] And He said to them, "What kind of conversation is this that you have with one another as you walk and are sad?" [18] Then the one whose name was Cleopas answered and said to Him, "Are You the only stranger in Jerusalem, and have You not known the things which happened there in these days?" [19] And He said to them, "What things?" So they said to Him, "The things concerning Jesus of Nazareth, who was a Prophet mighty in deed and word before God and all the people, [20] and how the chief priests and our rulers delivered Him to be condemned to death, and crucified Him. [21] But we were hoping that it was He who was going to redeem Israel. Indeed, besides all this, today is the third day since these things happened.

²² "Yes, and certain women of our company, who arrived at the tomb early, astonished us. ²³ When they did not find His body, they came saying that **they had also seen a vision of angels who said He was alive**. ²⁴ And certain of those who were with us went to the tomb and found it just as the women had said; but Him they did not see." ²⁵ Then He said to them, "O foolish ones, and **slow of heart to believe** in all that the prophets have spoken! ²⁶ Ought not the Christ to have suffered these things and to enter into His glory?" ²⁷ And **beginning at Moses** and **all the Prophets, He expounded to them** in all the **Scriptures** the **things concerning Himself**.

²⁸ Then they drew near to the village where they were going, and He indicated that He would have gone farther. ²⁹ But they constrained Him, saying, "Abide with us, for it is toward evening, and the day is far spent." And He went in to stay with them. ³⁰ Now it came to pass, as He sat at the table with them, that He took bread, blessed and broke it, and gave it to them. ³¹ Then **their eyes were opened** and they **knew Him**; and **He vanished from their sight**.

³² And they said to one another, "Did not our heart burn within us while He talked with us on the road, and **while He opened the Scriptures to us**?" … Then He said to them, "These are the words which I spoke to you while I was still with you, that all things must be fulfilled which were written in the Law of Moses and the Prophets and the Psalms concerning Me." ⁴⁵ And **He opened their understanding**, that they might **comprehend the Scriptures. (Luke 24:16–32, 44–45)**

God, in His Word has given us all we need to recognize Jesus as the Son of God and our Savior. But He can blind the eyes of those who do not believe, and He can open the understanding of those who seek Him diligently by prayer and the humble study of His word. "But without faith *it is* impossible to please *Him,* for he who comes to God **must believe that He is**, and *that* **He is a rewarder** of those who **diligently seek Him" (Hebrews 11:6).**

The Elect Are Given Eyes to See and Ears to Hear

> What then? Israel has not obtained what it seeks; but the **elect have obtained it**, and the **rest were blinded**. [8] Just as it is written: "God has given them a **spirit of stupor, Eyes** that they **should not see** And **ears** that they **should not hear**, To this very day." [9] And David says: "Let **their table** become a snare and **a trap**, A stumbling block and a recompense to them. [10] Let their **eyes be darkened**, so that they **do not see**, And bow down their back always." (**Romans 11:7–10**)

As we will learn, because Israel rejected Jesus as their long-prophesied Messiah, God has blinded the eyes of most of the Israelites for the time of the Gentiles that all who are not Jews may hear the truth of God and be saved. This is the time that we live in!

Their Understanding Was Opened

> "And He **opened their understanding**, that they might **comprehend the Scriptures**." (**Luke 24:45**)

God can open our understanding, allowing us to comprehend the Bible. This is what we need to pray for constantly as we seek to understand the truth in the Bible that will make us free.

Their Understanding Was Darkened

> This I say, therefore, and testify in the Lord, that you should no longer walk as the rest of the Gentiles walk, in the futility of their mind, [18] **having their understanding darkened**, being **alienated from the life of God**, because of the **ignorance that is in them**, because of the **blindness of their heart**; [19] who, being **past feeling**, have **given themselves over** to lewdness, to work all uncleanness with greediness. (**Ephesians 4:18**)

The Blind Shall See, and the Seeing Shall Be Made Blind

> And Jesus said, "For judgment I have come into this world, that **those who do not see may see**, and that **those who see may be made blind**." (**John 9:39**)

This does not contradict what Jesus said about not coming to judge, for we will be judged when Jesus comes a second time, but the first time He came, He came to save us. If we respond to what Jesus teaches, it will save us from a future judgment, as the apostle John describes: "And if anyone hears My words and does not believe, **I do not judge him**; for I **did not come to judge** the world but to **save the world**. **⁴⁸** He who **rejects Me**, and **does not receive My words**, has that which judges him–the **word that I have spoken will judge him in the last day**" (**John 12:47–48**). By our response to the truth that He came to teach us, by the way we live our lives, we will judged. Concerned about our future judgment, Jesus came into this world to witness of the truth.

I would be extremely negligent if I did not share this great truth that I learned from another Bible scholar, and it is biblical: "But **the natural man** does not receive the things of **the Spirit of God**, for they are foolishness to him; **nor can he know** *them,* because they are **spiritually discerned** ... However, when He, **the Spirit of truth**, has come, He will **guide you into all truth**" (**1 Corinthians 2:14; John 16:12–13a**).

This truth was made abundantly clear to me when I began my first year of Bible Study Fellowship. I was very successful at learning and understanding science and math on my own with hard work and self will." So when I was filled with the hunger to know and understand as much about the Word of God as I could, I began by getting Bible commentaries and different translations of the Bible and threw **myself** at the **work** of Bible study.

The result was disastrous. The harder I tried in my own strength, the less I understood. Then one week a veteran student of Bible Study Fellowship suggested that I get rid of all my commentaries and quit trying to learn and understand with my own abilities. Instead he told me that I should get on my knees and pray and ask for help from the Holy Spirit before each Bible study session. At first that sounded and felt a little strange, and indeed it was strange to me. But when I laid aside all my auxiliary sources and purchased a simple Bible with no commentaries, just the Word of God, and prayed on my knees for the help of the Holy Spirit, I was often filled with Holy Ghost bumps, and my understanding of the Holy Scripture exploded.

I have prayed many different prayers before studying the Bible in the last twenty years, depending on where I was, but in the last five years or so, as I finished this book, this is the prayer I prayed before studying the Bible:

> Heavenly Father, I pray that You would fill me with a mighty indwelling of Your Holy Spirit of truth and love, knowledge, understanding, and wisdom. I pray that You would open my eyes to see the spiritual truth, open my ears to hear the spiritual truth, and that I may discern the spiritual truth in the core of my being.
>
> Father, I pray that my spirit would be one with Your Holy Spirit; that I might receive Your guidance, Your direction and correction; that I might hear Your still, small voice leading me to the truth, leading me in the way I should walk and the path I should take.
>
> Heavenly Father, I pray that You would open my understanding to everything in Your Holy Word that points to the fall from heaven; the need and purpose for creating the universe, the heavens, and the earth; the meaning of life on planet earth; and Your plan to reconcile us back to You through the revelation of the truth and who You are in Your Holy Word, and then sending Your only begotten Son, Jesus Christ, my Savior and Lord, into this world to

witness of the truth that will make us free, and then suffer and die on the tree that we would have died on, out of His great love for us, out of Your great love for us.

Father I pray that You would grant me an open mind and a teachable heart that I might cast out the lies, the error, the wrong thinking, the bad habits, the greed and selfishness, the pride and arrogance and replace it with humility, humbleness, truth and love, knowledge, understanding, and wisdom, righteousness, and a hunger for Your Word, Your will, and Your ways.

In Jesus' name I pray. Amen.

We will learn and understand why we need the Holy Spirit of Jesus Christ to understand the truth of God as we continue on.

GOD IS IN CONTROL

THERE ARE THOSE who accept that there was a God that created the heavens and the earth and everything in it but believe that He has left the earth alone and has not interacted with it. But that is not what the Bible says: "The king's heart *is* **in the hand of the** LORD, *Like* the rivers of water; He turns it wherever He wishes" (**Proverbs 21:1**).

God Is in Control

This day **I will begin to put** the dread and fear of you upon the nations under the whole heaven, who shall hear the report of you, and shall tremble and be in anguish because of you. (**Deuteronomy 2:25**)

God Is in Control—We Are Precious to God

And I say to you, My friends, do not be afraid of those who kill the body, and after that have no more that they can do. ⁵ But I will show you whom you should fear: Fear Him who, after He has killed, **has power to cast into hell**; yes, I say to you, fear Him! ⁶ Are not five sparrows sold for two copper coins? And not one of them is forgotten before God. ⁷ But the very hairs of your head are all numbered. **Do not fear** therefore; you are of more value than many sparrows. (**Luke 12:6–7**)

God Is in Control—Everything We Have is From Him

John answered and said, "**A man can receive nothing unless it has been given to him from heaven.** ²⁸ You yourselves bear me witness, that I said, 'I am not the Christ,' but, 'I have been sent before Him.' [29] He who has the bride is the bridegroom; but the friend of the bridegroom, who stands and hears him, rejoices greatly because of the bridegroom's voice. Therefore this joy of mine is fulfilled. [30] He must increase, but I must decrease. [31] **He who comes from above is above all; he who is of the earth is earthly** and **speaks of the earth**. He who comes from heaven is **above all**.

[32] "And what He has seen and heard, that He testifies; and no one receives His testimony. [33] He who has **received His testimony** has certified that **God is true**. [34] For He whom God has sent speaks the words of God, for God does not give the Spirit by measure. [35] The Father loves the Son, and **has given all things into His hand**. [36] **He who believes** in the **Son has everlasting life**; and he who does not believe the Son shall not see life, but the wrath of God abides on him." (**John 3:27–36**)

Webster's Student Dictionary © 1959 says "receive" can mean "to assimilate through the mind or senses as with new ideas." No one can receive anything without it being given to him from heaven. He who receives Jesus' testimony as true must have received it from God, or was allowed to understand it by the Holy Spirit, who is of God. Anyone who has been indwelled by the Holy Spirit has already believed in God or certified that God is true. Is this not the same as saying that the truth of God is spiritually discerned?

And this is exactly what the apostle Paul teaches: "Now we have received, **not the spirit of the world**, but the **Spirit who is from God**, that we might know the things that have been freely given to us by God. [13] These things we also speak, not in words which **man's wisdom teaches** but which **the Holy Spirit teaches**, comparing **spiritual things** with **spiritual**. [14] But the **natural man** does not receive the things of the **Spirit of God**, for they are **foolishness to him**; nor can he know *them,* because **they are spiritually discerned**" (**1 Corinthians 2:12–14**).

God Is in Control—He Protects His Son

> Therefore they sought to take Him; but **no one laid a hand on Him**, because **His hour had not yet come**. (John 7:30)

How awesome is this? A number of times when the unbelieving Jews would try to take Jesus by force, He would just walk away. This is to let us know that the when they did take Jesus to crucify Him, they were able to do so only because He let them. Jesus makes this an important point in **Matthew 26:52–54**: "But Jesus said to him, "Put your sword in its place, **for all who take the sword will perish by the sword.** ⁵³ Or do you think that I cannot now pray to My Father, and He will provide Me with more than twelve legions of angels? ⁵⁴ How then could the Scriptures be fulfilled, that it must happen thus?" Jesus voluntarily suffered and died for us. Notice Jesus' phrase, "**for all who take the sword will perish by the sword.**" This is important because the kingdom of God is one of freewill choice, not one of force.

If God Made Us This Way, Why Are We Responsible?— If God Is in Control, Why Are We Responsible?

> What shall we say then? Is there unrighteousness with God? Certainly not! ¹⁵ For He says to Moses, "I will have mercy on whomever I will have mercy, and I will have compassion on whomever I will have compassion." ¹⁶ So then it is not of him who wills, nor of him who runs, but of God who shows mercy. ¹⁷ For the Scripture says to Pharaoh, "**For this very purpose I have raised you up**, that **I may show My power in you**, and that My name may be declared in all the earth." ¹⁸ Therefore He has mercy on whom He wills, and whom He wills He hardens. ¹⁹ You will say to me then, "Why does He still find fault? For who has resisted His will?"
>
> ²⁰ But indeed, O man, who are you to reply against God? Will the thing formed say to him who formed it, "Why have you made me like this?" ²¹ Does not the potter have power over the clay, from the same lump **to make one vessel for honor** and **another for dishonor**? ²² **What if God**, wanting to show His wrath and to make His power known, **endured with much longsuffering**

the **vessels of wrath prepared for destruction**, [23] and that He might make known the riches of His glory on the vessels of mercy, **which He had prepared beforehand** for glory, [24] **even us whom He called, not of the Jews only**, but also **of the Gentiles**? (**Romans 9:14–24**)

This passage may leave us confused about who God is. But the fact that God prepared **"vessels for destruction"** and **"vessels for mercy"** *beforehand* gives us a clue that there is more going on here than what we can see from our vantage point on earth as fallen man. By the end of this book, you will understand, as the disciples did, how this and many other formerly confusing things in the Bible will make sense in the light of the truth.

As we will learn, God made and created man to enter into fellowship and a loving relationship with Him. God is more powerful than man and can trump any bad decision that we make that would be harmful to others in the community of heaven, but we do have a free will to choose whether to be in that relationship or not. God will not keep us in heaven against our will. When He cannot convince dissenters of what is right, He turns them over to live in their sin like prodigal children, hoping they will have a change of heart when they find out that God and His ways are right and realize that they made a big mistake out of ignorance, arrogance, and pride.

God Is in Control—The Most High Rules in the Kingdom of Men

The king spoke, saying, "Is not this great Babylon, that I have built for a royal dwelling by my mighty power and for the honor of my majesty?" [31] While the word *was still* in the king's mouth, a voice fell from heaven: "King Nebuchadnezzar, to you it is spoken: the kingdom has departed from you! [32] And they shall drive you from men, and your dwelling *shall be* with the beasts of the field. They shall make you eat grass like oxen; and seven times shall pass over you, until you know that **the Most High rules in the kingdom of men**, and gives it to whomever He chooses."

³³ That very hour the word was fulfilled concerning Nebuchadnezzar; he was driven from men and ate grass like oxen; his body was wet with the dew of heaven till his hair had grown like eagles' *feathers* and his nails like birds' *claws*. ³⁴ And at the end of the time I, Nebuchadnezzar, lifted my eyes to heaven, and **my understanding returned to me**; and I blessed the Most High and praised and honored Him who lives forever: For His dominion *is* an everlasting dominion, And His kingdom *is* from generation to generation. ³⁵ All the inhabitants of the earth *are* reputed as nothing; **He does according to His will** in the **army of heaven** And *among* the **inhabitants of the earth**.

No one can restrain His hand Or say to Him, "What have You done?" ³⁶ At the same time my reason returned to me, and for the glory of my kingdom, my honor and splendor returned to me. My counselors and nobles resorted to me, I was restored to my kingdom, and excellent majesty was added to me. ³⁷ **Now I, Nebuchadnezzar, praise** and **extol** and **honor** the **King of heaven**, all of whose **works** *are* **truth**, and **His ways justice**. And those who **walk in pride** He is able to put down. (**Daniel 4:30–37**)

God has not left the world and those He created to be on their own, He is very much involved in the minutest details of our lives on earth.

"Therefore I say to you, **do not worry about your life**, what you will eat or what you will drink; nor about your body, what you will put on. Is not life more than food and the body more than clothing? ²⁶ Look at the birds of the air, for they neither sow nor reap nor gather into barns; yet your heavenly Father feeds them. Are you not of more value than they? ²⁷ Which of you by worrying can add one cubit to his stature?

²⁸ "So why do you worry about clothing? Consider the lilies of the field, how they grow: they neither toil nor spin; ²⁹ and yet I say to you that even Solomon in all his glory was not arrayed like one of these. ³⁰ Now if God so clothes the grass of the field, which today is, and tomorrow is thrown into the oven, *will He* not much more *clothe* you, **O you of little faith**? ³¹ Therefore do not worry, saying, 'What shall we eat?' or 'What shall we drink?' or 'What shall we wear?' ³² For after all these things the

Gentiles seek. For your heavenly Father knows that you need all these things. [33] But **seek first the kingdom of God** and **His righteousness**, and **all these things shall be added to you."** (**Matthew 6:25–33**)

Even though **Genesis 2:1–3** says that God rested from the work of creation, "Thus the heavens and the earth, and all the host of them, were finished. [2] And on the seventh day God ended His work which He had done, and He rested on the seventh day from all His work which He had done. [3] Then God blessed the seventh day and sanctified it, because in it He **rested from all His work which God had created and made**." Jesus informs us that though God rested from His work of the things He had already created, His Father and He are still working for the salvation of fallen man: "But Jesus answered them, '**My Father has been working until now**, and **I have been working'**" (**John 5:17**).

The Truth Branch

As YOU WILL recall, there were three things that I distinctly remembered from my experience of being before All Knowledge, which I described as being like a tree and like a library. All knowledge was arranged in branches of knowledge. The first two that I could remember were the topics of truth and love, and I am not sure if the third was a branch or not or if it was an overall feeling of oneness or connectedness. These branches of knowledge were connected, and living and nonliving things were connected in ways that we do not fully know or understand. Since I was taught by God about truth before love, and since oneness was kind of an all-encompassing feeling that embraced the whole experience, I will start with truth.

I did not remember any specific things about the topic of truth during my experience other than that I reveled in how good and necessary truth is and that at some point it left me with a bad feeling because of what I learned. I know that God has been leading me and guiding me as I have studied His Word to re-create what He once showed me, and my hope and prayer is that thoughts and ideas of my own, that are not of God, have been kept out.

There is, though, one important characteristic about truth that will help me and you know whether something is true or not. Truth never contradicts another truth. All truth is consistent. "Truth" can be defined as "that which conforms to reality; fact; the body of real things; events; facts; fidelity to an original or a standard; or just how things really are." I hold the Bible to be the inerrant and inspired Word of God and to be the Word of Truth. If anything I write conflicts with the Word of God, then it is I that has erred, not God. It is clear that the apostle John understood the difference between the contradiction of lies and the fidelity of truth: "I have not written to you because you do not know the truth, but because you know it, and that **no lie is of the truth**" (**1 John 2:22**).

Mathematicians use this property of noncontradiction of truth to prove new mathematical theories in some interesting and clever ways. Sometimes they will assume the opposite of what they are trying to prove to be true. They will perform a number of proven mathematical operations that are known to be true on the proposition, and when they reach a contradiction, that means their opposite assumption is wrong and the actual theory they were trying to prove is true. Ponder that for a while.

With truth, there are only two possibilities when it comes to a single proposition or statement; either it is true or it is false. This is reflected in many real-word scenarios, such as computer scientists using the two-value binary numbering system, which contains only the two numbers 1 (one) and 0 (zero); the two states of a switch being "on" and "off"; and the high and low voltage of circuits used to perform complex calculations that are sure to be true, accurate, and factual.

Computer programmers and logisticians use "truth tables" to show the truth value of compound statements by showing the truth value of each component statement that is arrived at by using operations that follow the rules of math and logic. A computer programmer uses a truth table to show the output of a computer logic circuit for each value of input. Computers are powerful tools, and they can perform billions of calculations in seconds that a man could not complete in a lifetime. On top of that, the computer would end up with the correct answer, whereas man often makes mistakes.

People often blame computers for mistakes and problems, but a bad circuit is never the problem; human error is almost always the source of the problem. They are the ones that design the bad logic in the computer programs, the circuits just do what the laws of physics make them do. Truth is the basis on which our computers run. Computers are what make our complex modern world possible. We will learn that truth is what makes a complicated human society possible as well.

In high school I was taught that there are two kinds of truth: objective truth, which applies to everyone (such as $2 + 2 = 4$), and subjective truth, which depends on personal feelings, preferences, and sensibilities (such as one person liking vanilla ice cream and another liking chocolate). All truth can be said to be absolute if one defines truth as referring to its reference. For example, it is true for all people everywhere that I think strawberry ice-cream shakes are the best. Adding the reference "I think" to the statement "strawberry shakes are the best" makes this subjective truth an absolute truth. I am not sure that this adds anything to our understanding of truth, though; there are still truths that need to refer to a personal preference to be absolutely true, and some that do not need to refer to an individual's preference to be absolutely true. For the purposes of this book, truth will refer to objective, absolute truth.

Absolute truths are independent of what anyone thinks or feels. Truth is just the way things are. A king cannot proclaim something to be true if is not, though he may try. A nation cannot hold an election and vote on what is true and what is not. Truths cannot be invented; they can only be discovered. Subjective truths are based on human preference, feelings, and emotions, and those may change with time, but objective truth is absolute truth, and it does not change, as the apostle Paul teaches, "for **we can do nothing against the truth**, but **for the truth**" (**2 Corinthians 13:8**). In this book the word "truth" will always refer to absolute truth unless otherwise indicated as we did with "subjective" truth.

The truth is even independent of God, in that not even God can redefine what is true and call it false; nor can He take something that is false and now define it to be true. Some have implied that what is true is determined by God's nature. While it is true that God's nature and the truth are synonymous, the reason that is so is the other way around; God's nature is determined by what is true. For example, even God cannot make two plus two equal five.

God certainly has a free will. Actually, because He is all powerful, He has the only truly sovereign free will and no one else can make Him do what He does not want to do. God is a god of truth because He chooses to be a God of truth, to only live according to what is true, and so God's nature is determined by what is true. God speaks of this through the prophet Isaiah: "'For **My thoughts** *are* not **your thoughts**, Nor *are* your ways My ways,' says the LORD. [9] 'For *as* the **heavens are higher** than the **earth**, So are **My ways higher** than **your ways**, And **My thoughts** than **your thoughts**'" (**Isaiah 55:8–9**). Because God knows all things, He knows which are true and which are not.

And since God has a free will and He chooses to always do what is true, what is right, and what is good, He is righteous and holy. To be holy simply means to be set apart to righteousness; to only do what is right and true by self-discipline and intent. And because absolute truths do not change, God does not change. "For **I** *am* **the** LORD, **I do not change**; Therefore you are not consumed, O sons of Jacob" (**Malachi 3:6**). It is God's loving and forgiving nature that keeps Him from immediately executing judgment for our evil and sinful ways.

Because God does not change, we can determine what is true by looking at God's nature, because God's thinking and ways are always based on what is true. And this truth about God is expressed in the Bible by Moses: "*He is* the Rock, **His work** *is* **perfect**; For **all His ways** *are* **justice**, A **God of truth** and **without injustice**; **Righteous and upright** *is* He" (**Deuteronomy 32:4**). And as David sings in a psalm, "Into Your hand **I commit my spirit**; You have redeemed me, **O** LORD **God of truth**" (**Psalm 31:5**). And Isaiah prophesies, "So that he who blesses himself in the earth Shall bless himself **in the God of truth**" (**Isaiah 65:16**). And Jesus, who is God, gives witness: "Jesus said to him, "**I am the way, the truth**, and **the life**. No one comes to the Father except through Me" (**John 14:6**).

We also have a will and can choose to live according to the truth or not. But because we are not all-powerful, as God is, we are not sovereign, as He is, and God can do with us whatever He wants to based on the way we choose to live. We will see that the truth is powerful but lies bring corruption, misery, sorrow, and death. "Behold, **you trust in lying words that cannot profit**. [9] Will you steal, murder, commit adultery, swear falsely, burn incense to Baal, and walk after **other gods** whom you do not know?" (**Jeremiah 7:8–9**). The Hebrew word for "gods" in the phrase "walk after **other gods** whom you do not know" is H430 *elohym*, which we will become familiar with because this is the Hebrew word translated as "God" throughout the first chapter of Genesis, where the creation story is told.

Truth may be hard to discover, but that does not mean it does not exist. I can remember back when I was younger and I was fishing in a boat with my dad, grandfather, and brothers. The fish weren't biting, and there was plenty of time for contemplation. I wondered how many fish there were in this lake that had the opportunity to bite on my hook but had declined. I mean, the lake could be totally drained and the number of fish could be counted. I reckoned that would never happen and I would never know the answer, but that did not mean there was not an answer. Truth is like that. Truth always exists, but it is not always easy for us to discover.

Truth is important in human relationships. We want our doctor to tell us the truth about our health. We would not want him to lie about things that could harm us or end our lives or lie about what could heal us and save our lives. We do not want a bank to lie about how much money we have in a savings account, especially if their lie is that we have less money than we know we have. We do not want people to lie in court when we are accused and are on trial for something that we did not do. We do not want to enter a business relationship with people who are habitual liars.

In my hunger to know and understand the truth of God that was shown me in my near-death truth-and-love experience, I sought out and participated in all kinds of Bible studies. The most thorough, enlightening, and amazing Bible study I have ever found is Bible Study Fellowship, BSF. It is a worldwide Bible study that studies a portion of the Bible every Monday night for eight months out of the year from mid-September to mid-May.

Every BSF study in every city works on the same lesson at the same time. If you travel, you can sit in on a lesson in another city and continue the study without missing a beat! At the time I was going through the program, there were seven different yearly studies, and I started with what turned out to be my favorite, the study of the book of John. Today they have added a study on the book of Isaiah, which I am hoping to attend, God willing.

After I completed the seven-year cycle, I was debating on whether I should continue with BSF or check out another Bible study. But because the next Bible study was about the book of John, my first and favorite study, I decided to continue on, and I was immediately glad I did. Though I had taken this study of John seven years prior, I found it amazing how much I had learned in the last seven years and how much better I was at understanding things that I had not picked up on the first time around. I have heard similar comments from other scholars who have studied the Bible for many years; one day they will suddenly "see" and understand a verse that pops out at them—one that they do not remember being in the Bible!

I think there is more going on with that than we know. I think it is an example of what we discussed in the chapters "Blindness" and "God Is in Control." God is in control, and He knows when we are ready and worthy to understand a certain truth. Jesus said to His disciples, "I still have many things to say to you, but **you cannot bear *them* now**" (**John 16:12**) and "**Do not give what is holy to the dogs; nor cast your pearls** [of wisdom] **before swine**, lest they trample them under their feet, and turn and tear you in pieces" (**Matthew 7:6**).

The book of John, the last of the four Gospels to be written, is different from the other three. Whereas the first three Synoptic (meaning "a common harmonious view") Gospels are mainly historical accounts of the life of Jesus that pretty much agree with each other, John's gospel records things that the other three leave out and leaves out things that the others record. Perhaps one reason for that is that after years of teaching what he himself had heard from Jesus and studying the writings of the other disciples, and with the inspiration of the Holy

Spirit, the apostle John started to see deeper meanings in the things Jesus said and did.

Similarly, after studying the Bible for seven years, God started showing me deeper meanings of verses in the Bible. And this is exactly what the Bible says: "I love those who love me, And **those who seek me diligently will find me** ... But **without faith** *it is* impossible to please *Him,* for he who comes to God **must believe that He is**, and *that* He is a rewarder of **those who diligently seek Him**" (**Proverbs 8:17; Hebrews 11:6**).

Many call the gospel of John "the Book of Signs," and the apostle John gives us reason to in **John 2:11,** after Jesus has turned the water into wine at a wedding in Cana. John writes, "This **beginning of signs Jesus did in Cana of Galilee**, and manifested His glory; and His disciples believed in Him." Read **John 2:1–10** and see if you can understand the sign that this miracle represents like John did. We will learn the meaning of the sign in "The "Oneness Branch"!

The biggest of the new revelations I experienced my second time around studying the book of John occurred when I came to the discussion that Jesus had with Pontius Pilate in **John 18:3**. "Pilate therefore said to Him, 'Are You a king then?' Jesus answered, 'You say rightly that I am a king. **For this cause I was born** and **for this cause I have come into the world**, that **I should bear witness to the truth**. Everyone who is **of the truth** hears My voice.'" I remember where I was in a BSF lecture when those words struck me like a bolt of lightning out of the blue. *That means that I am living a lie!* I thought.

I reasoned to myself that if Jesus' purpose for being born and coming into this world is to reveal the truth to the world, then all of us are living a lie! Combine that with another verse found in John, **John 8:31–32,** where Jesus said to the Jews who believed in Him, "If you abide in **My word**, you are My disciples indeed. And **you shall know the truth** and **the truth shall make you free**." All of a sudden I had a powerful and exciting new perception of what the world is really about. How can the truth set us free unless a lie is keeping us in bondage?

As I have said previously, I do not, or was not allowed to, recall what truth I was shown in my truth-and-love experience. I knew only that I was learning about truth reveling in the goodness of it. And so I will feebly and humbly attempt to re-create the way that God taught me. Like leaves on a tree branch or pieces of a great puzzle, I will select a sampling of verses that I found to be particularly enlightening out of the many verses in the Bible that speak of truth. I will let the verses of the Bible teach the truth found in the inspired Word of God.

The Bible says some pretty amazing things about the truth, such as what Paul writes to Titus in a letter: "Paul, a bondservant of God and an apostle of Jesus Christ, according to **the faith of God's elect** and the **acknowledgment of the truth** which **accords with godliness**, ² in **hope of eternal life which God**, who cannot lie, **promised before time began**, ³ but has in **due time manifested His word through preaching**, which was committed to me according to the commandment of God our Savior" (**Titus 1:1–3**).

It is made obvious by these words that the apostle Paul, who was writing these things to Titus, knows some truths that we do not know. Who are the elect who acknowledged the truth, which is about godliness, and who have hope of eternal life, which God "**promised before time began?**" How is it that there is a time before time began? Paul says that God has revealed this truth in "**due time**." "Due time" must refer to the ages of time it took before God sent Jesus into the earth to be a witness of the truth. In later branches we will learn what God had to do before He sent Jesus into the world. These are the ages of time separated by four-hundred-year periods of time when God was silent to delineate and delimit the different ages.

THE TEACHING EXPERIENCE OF PAUL

It is most intriguing and reassuring to sinners like me that Paul, formerly known was Saul, who was actually persecuting the early church after Jesus was resurrected and ascended into heaven, was personally taught by Jesus in a vision:

It is doubtless not profitable for me to boast. I will come to **visions** and **revelations** of the Lord: [2] I know a man in Christ who fourteen years ago – **whether in the body** I do not know, **or whether out of the body** I do not know, God knows–such a one **was caught up** to the **third heaven.**

[3] And I know such a man–whether **in the body** or **out of the body** I do not know, God knows – [4] how **he was caught up into Paradise** and **heard inexpressible words**, which **it is not lawful for a man to utter.** [5] Of such a one I will boast; yet of myself I will not boast, **except in my infirmities.** [6] For though I might desire to boast, **I will not be a fool**; for **I will speak the truth.** But I refrain, lest anyone should think of me above what he sees me *to be* or hears from me. [7] And **lest I should be exalted above measure** by the **abundance of the revelations, a thorn in the flesh was given to me,** a messenger of Satan **to buffet me,** lest I be exalted above measure. (**2 Corinthians 12:1–7**)

The Greek word for the phrase "caught up" is G726 ***harpazo,*** which means "**to seize, catch (away, up), pluck, pull, take by force**" and is the same Greek word that is used for the rapture of the saints when they are "caught up" in the clouds to be with Christ.

Paul provides more detail about his experience when he speaks to King Agrippa:

"At midday, O king, along the road I saw **a light from heaven, brighter than the sun,** shining around me and those who journeyed with me. [14] And when we all had fallen to the ground, I heard a voice speaking to me and saying in the Hebrew language, '**Saul, Saul, why are you persecuting Me?** *It is* hard for you to kick against the goads.' [15] So I said, 'Who are You, Lord?' And He said, '**I am Jesus**, whom you are persecuting.

[16] 'But rise and stand on your feet; for I have appeared to you for this purpose, **to make you a minister** and **a witness** both of the **things which you have seen** and of the **things which I will yet reveal to you.** [17] I will **deliver you from the** *Jewish* **people,** as well as *from* **the Gentiles,** to whom **I now send you,** [18] **to open their eyes,** *in order* to **turn** *them* **from darkness**

to light, and *from* the **power of Satan to God**, that they may **receive forgiveness of sins** and an **inheritance** among those who are **sanctified by faith in Me**.' [19] "Therefore, King Agrippa, **I was not disobedient** to the **heavenly vision**." **(Acts 26:13–19)**

By the end of this study of the Bible, we will understand the things that Paul understood and preached, and most every question that people ask about the Bible, in a way that makes sense and is easy to understand; and it will not require that you be trained as a theologian.

THE TWO COMPETING TRUTH CLAIMS FROM THE BEGINNING

We will start at the beginning of time on earth and examine what the Bible says about the truth. Right away within the first three chapters of Genesis, the first book of the Bible, there are two competing truth claims presented to the first two human beings, Adam and Eve. **Genesis 2:9** records for us, "And out of the ground the LORD God made every tree grow that is pleasant to the sight and good for food. The **tree of life** *was* also in the **midst** of the garden, and the **tree of the knowledge of good and evil**." The word "midst" is translated from the Hebrew word H8432 *tavek*, which means "From an unused root meaning **to sever**; **a bisection**, that is (by implication), the **center**:- among, **between**, **half**, middle, midst." So not only were the two trees in the middle of the garden, but there is also a sense that in some way they divided or separated the garden in two.

In **Genesis 2:17** God speaks to Adam: "Then the LORD God **took the man and put him** in the **garden of Eden** to tend and keep it. [16] And the LORD God commanded **the man**, saying, 'Of every tree of the garden you may freely eat; [17] but **of the tree of the knowledge of good and evil you shall not eat**, for **in the day that you eat of it you shall surely die.**'"

Then in **Genesis 3:1–5**, the Serpent speaks to Eve: "Now **the serpent** was **more cunning** than any **beast** of the field **which the LORD God**

had made. And he said **to the woman**, 'Has God indeed said, "You shall not eat of every tree of the garden?"' [2] And **the woman** said to the serpent, 'We may eat the fruit of the trees of the garden; [3] but of the fruit of the tree which *is* in the midst of the garden, God has said, "You shall not eat it, nor shall you touch it, **lest you die**."' [4] **Then the serpent said to the woman, 'You will not surely die**."' The word "**cunning**" is translated from the Hebrew word H6175 *arum*, which means "cunning (**usually in a bad sense**), crafty, prudent, subtle." Webster's Student Dictionary says that the "synonyms **cunning, crafty, artful**, and **wily** agree in implying an aptitude **for attaining an end** by **secret or devious means**. Cunning implies skill, especially in **getting around a person** or **difficulty**."

First we will notice that **Revelation 12:9** reveals that the **Serpent is Satan**: "So the great dragon was cast out, **that serpent of old**, called **the Devil and Satan**, who **deceives the whole world**; he was **cast to the eart**h, and **his angels were cast out with him**." So in the beginning, man was confronted with two opposing truth claims by God and Satan about the "**eating** of the **tree of the knowledge of good and evil**." God said we "**shall surely die**," and Satan said you "**will not surely die**."

Now, this "**tree of the knowledge of good and evil**" is not a literal tree that bears literal fruit, such as an apple, but symbolically it is a tree of knowledge, whose fruit is the consequences of living according to the knowledge of good and evil. Jesus speaks of knowing a tree by the fruit it bears, which is symbolic for the different deeds produced by a man with a good heart compared to those of a man with an evil heart.

> Either **make the tree good** and **its fruit good**, or else **make the tree bad** and **its fruit bad**; for **a tree is known by *its* fruit**. [34] Brood of vipers! How can you, **being evil**, speak **good things**? For out of the abundance of the heart the mouth speaks. [35] A good man out of the good treasure of his heart brings forth good things, and an evil man out of the evil treasure brings forth evil things. [36] But I say to you that for every idle word men may speak, they will give account of it in the Day of Judgment. [37] For

by your words you will be justified, and by your words you will be condemned. (**Matthew 12:33–37**)

Do these words of Jesus not remind us of the fruit of the Tree of Knowledge of Good and Evil?

What God is saying through this metaphor of a tree bearing fruit is that living according to the knowledge of good *and* evil will surely cause death or—in the symbolic language of the Bible—bear the fruit of death, while Satan is claiming that living according to the knowledge of good and evil will surely not lead to the consequence of death.

Because these are contradictory claims, by the law of noncontradiction we know they cannot both be true. So how does one know whose truth claim is really true? Well, this issue about what the truth is and how to know the truth or come to the knowledge of the truth is the central issue of the Bible, and because it is a matter of eternal life and eternal death, it should be the major concern of our lives. For the acknowledgment of the truth is everlasting life, as we find in this amazing verse that we looked at earlier: "… according to **the faith of God's elect** and the **acknowledgment of the truth** which accords with **godliness,** [2] in **hope of eternal life** which God, who cannot lie, **promised before time began**" (**Titus 1:1b–2**). Truth is the acknowledgment of reality, the way things really are.

So how did Adam and Eve react to a challenge of the truth of God, the Creator, by Satan, the one whom God created? We find the answer to that question in **Genesis 3:6**: "So when the woman saw that the tree *was* good for food, that it *was* pleasant to the eyes, and **a tree desirable to make *one* wise**, she took of its fruit and **ate**. She also gave to her husband with her, **and he ate**" (**Genesis 3:6**). And how did God respond to their choice? We get that answer from **Genesis 3:23–24**: "Therefore the LORD God sent him out of the garden of Eden to till the ground from which he was taken. [24] So He drove out the man; and He placed cherubim at the east of the **garden of Eden**, and a flaming sword which turned every way, to guard the way to the **tree of life**."

So God cast them out of **the garden of Eden** to let them experience the fruit, the consequences of choosing to believe the lie of Satan and follow him, to live in the knowledge of the ways of good and evil.

> Then to Adam He said, "Because you have heeded the voice of your wife, and **have eaten from the tree of** which **I commanded you**, saying, 'You shall not eat of it': Cursed *is* **the ground for your sake**; In **toil** you shall **eat** *of* it All the days of your life. [18] Both thorns and thistles it shall bring forth for you, And you shall eat the herb of the field. [19] **In the sweat of your face** you shall **eat bread Till you return to the ground,** For out of it you were taken; **For dust you** *are,* And **to dust you shall return."** (Genesis 3:17–19)

Consider for a moment that when God says, "In **toil** you shall **eat** *of* **it**" He may symbolically be speaking of the knowledge of Good and Evil, because God earlier in this passage accused Adam of having "**eaten from the tree of** which **I commanded you**, saying, '**You shall not eat of it?**'"

> And Adam called his wife's name Eve, because she was the **mother of all living**. [21] Also for Adam and his wife the LORD God **made tunics of skin**, and **clothed them**. [22] Then the LORD God said, "Behold, the **man has become like one of Us**, **to know good and evil**. And now, lest he put out his hand and take also of **the tree of life**, and eat, and **live forever** – [23] therefore the LORD God **sent him out of the garden of Eden to till the ground from which he was taken**. [24] So **He drove out the man**; and He placed cherubim at the **east of the garden of Eden**, and a flaming sword which turned every way, **to guard the way to the tree of life**. (Genesis 3:20–24)

And the apostle Paul speaks of the consequence of that same choice for all mankind in his letter to the Romans: "Therefore God also **gave them up** to uncleanness, in the **lusts of their hearts**, to dishonor their bodies among themselves, [25] who **exchanged the truth of God for the lie**, and worshiped and served the **creature rather than the Creator**, who is blessed forever. Amen. [26] For this reason **God gave them up** to vile passions" (**Romans 1:24–26a**). We will learn how we all made that same choice in the chapter "The Meaning and Purpose of Life on Earth."

Now we know that God and His kingdom are in heaven, so Adam and Eve and their descendants were separated from God in heaven to live on earth under the rule and reign of Satan, whom they had believed and followed. And Satan kept them from knowing the truth that God is a god of love and would forgive them if they repented and changed their heart and mind, by reminding them that God said they would surely die if they ate of the fruit of the Tree of Knowledge of Good and Evil. And God's word cannot be broken, as God declares in **Isaiah 55:11**: "**So shall My word be** that goes forth from My mouth; **It shall not return to Me void**, But **it shall accomplish what I please**, And **it shall prosper** *in the thing* **for which I sent it**."

Satan reminding them that they had eaten of the Tree of Knowledge of Good and Evil when God told them they should not, kept them trapped under the fear of death all their lifetime, as the author of Hebrews explains: "Inasmuch then as **the children have partaken of flesh and blood, He Himself likewise shared in the same**, that **through death He might destroy him** who had **the power of death**, that is, **the devil**, [15] and release **those who through fear of death were all their lifetime subject to bondage**" (**Hebrews 2:14–15**). In the chapter "The Third Age of the Church," we will learn how the truth can make us free from the lie of Satan as Jesus said in **John 8:32**: "And you shall **know the truth**, and the truth shall **make you free**." This refers to the promise of everlasting life even after God said "You shall surely die."

And so we all have fallen from the grace of God, thinking we can do better on our own, in control of our own lives, wanting to throw off the minimal restrictions that God gave us to restrain us and give us life. And many of us still think that way. "Why do the nations rage, And the people plot a **vain** thing? [2] The **kings of the earth** set themselves, And the **rulers take counsel together**, Against **the LORD** and **against His Anointed**, *saying*, [3] '**Let us break Their bonds in pieces** And **cast away Their cords from us**.' [4] He who sits in the heavens shall

92

laugh; **The LORD shall hold them in derision**. ⁵ Then He shall speak to them in His wrath, And **distress them in His deep displeasure**: ⁶ "Yet I have **set My King** On My holy hill of Zion" (**Psalm 2:1–6**). Thinking we were wise, we became fools. And that is exactly how Paul describes it: "Professing to be wise, **they became fools**" (**Romans 1:22**).

But Jesus reveals the truth, as He figuratively reveals the reality of life in that we are totally dependent on God,

> **I am the true vine**, and **My Father is the vinedresser**. ² Every branch in Me that does not bear fruit He takes away; and **every *branch* that bears fruit He prunes**, that it may **bear more fruit**. ³ You are already clean **because of the word which I have spoken to you**. ⁴ Abide in Me, and I in you. As **the branch cannot bear fruit of itself**, unless **it abides in the vine, neither can you**, unless you abide in Me.
>
> ⁵ I am the vine, **you *are* the branches**. He who abides in Me, and I in him, **bears much fruit**; for **without Me you can do nothing**. ⁶ If anyone does not abide in Me, he is cast out as a branch and **is withered**; and they gather them and **throw *them* into the fire**, and they are **burned**. ⁷ If you abide in Me, and My words abide in you, **you will ask what you desire**, and it **shall be done for you**. ⁸ By this My Father is glorified, that you bear much fruit; so you will be My disciples. (**John 15:1–8**)

A picture comes to mind of a child in his mother's womb before he is born who wants to cutoff the umbilical cord so that he may be be more free to move. This is exactly like Jesus saying He is the vine and we are the branches. How foolish is the desire to cut ourselves free from the one thing that can give us life. To be free from what gives us life is not freedom at all but rather is death.

But Jesus says out of His love for us, "**Come to Me**, all *you* who labor and are heavy laden, and **I will give you rest**. ²⁹ Take **My yoke upon you** and **learn from Me**, for I am **gentle** and **lowly in heart**, and **you will find rest for your souls**. ³⁰ For **My yoke *is* easy** and **My burden is light**" (**Matthew 11:28–30**). Jesus is crying out to us to know and understand the truth that there is a better way to live if only we are willing to listen and learn from Him. Jesus wants us to know there is a way of living that leads to peace, prosperity, unspeakable joy, and eternal life.

On the other hand, those who want to cast off His cords and live separated from God, free from even His minimal rules for civilized living, free to do anything they want, where survival and prosperity is for the fittest, will find out that it leads to all kinds of evil, corruption, misery, sorrow, and death. They will find out that freedom is not free. The proverbs teach us the truth that when we shed blood for gain, we end up shedding our own blood: "My son, do not walk in the way with them, Keep your foot from their path; [16] For their feet **run to evil**, And **they make haste to shed blood**. [17] Surely, in vain the net is spread In the sight of any bird; [18] But **they lie in wait for their *own* blood**, They lurk secretly for **their *own* lives**. [19] **So *are* the ways of everyone who is greedy for gain**; It **takes away the life of its owners**" (**Proverbs 1:15–19**). And Jesus teaches us this truth in **Matthew 26:52**: "But Jesus said to him, 'Put your sword in its place, for **all who take the sword will perish by the sword**.'"

The truth is that living according to the truth benefits all; the lie only benefits in the short term the one who is deceiving others, but in the long run it will end up killing him as well. This is like what I learned in my truth-and-love experience when I described the connectedness and oneness of people as being such that if I should cut off another's hand it would be like cutting off my own hand. When we fight with and kill others, we are killing the very thing that keeps us alive. We need each other. Why this is true will become clear as we consider the branches of love and oneness and life.

The truth is that this life on earth is our second chance to recognize that we all chose the wrong way to live. We chose to live by the ways of Satan, the ways that lead to death. There is one thing that even God cannot do and will not do. He can lead us to the truth, but He cannot make us drink of it. That we must do for ourselves, because love can only be of a free-will choice.

The truth is that only the Holy Spirit can lead us to the truth. "On the last day, that great *day* of the feast, Jesus stood and cried out, saying, '**If anyone thirsts**, let him **come to Me and drink**. [38] He who believes in Me, as the Scripture has said, **out of his heart** will flow rivers of **living water**.' [39] But this He spoke concerning **the Spirit**, whom **those believing in Him would receive**; for the **Holy Spirit** was not yet *given,* because Jesus was not yet glorified" (**John 7:37–39**). It is the "**Spirit of truth**" who leads us to know the truth. "I still have many things to say to you, but **you cannot bear** *them* **now**. [13] However, when He, **the Spirit of truth**, has come, **He will guide you into all truth**; for He will not speak on His own *authority,* but whatever He hears He will speak; and **He will tell you things to come**" (**John 16:12–13**).

So the truth claim of Satan is essentially that God was holding out on us by not telling us that we could do better free from God's rule and on our own; that we could be like God, in charge and in control of our own lives with no one to tell us what to do. The truth claim of God is that Satan was lying and his ways lead to our death. Who is right? This is the question that raged at the time of the fall from the grace of God and the question that rages still. So to prove to all in heaven and on earth that God's ways are the true ways of eternal life and that Satan's ways are a lie that lead to eternal death, God called the courts of heaven into session. And we will see in the chapter "The Meaning and Purpose of Life on Earth" and in the four ages how God as Judge carries out the trial of Satan and his fallen angels on earth and proves that His ways are the true way to eternal life as Jesus proclaims. "Jesus said to him, "I am **the way**, **the truth**, and **the life**. No one comes to the Father except through Me" (**John 14:6**).

THE TRUTH IS THAT THIS LIFE ON EARTH IS NOT ALL THERE IS

This world of the flesh is not all there is. There is another realm or reality, the spiritual realm of heaven, which is above everything in this universe. The Bible speaks of three heavens. The first heaven is the atmosphere, where the birds fly, the clouds float, and the rain falls. The second heaven is outer space, where the sun and the moon and the stars exist. The heaven above those two is the third heaven, where the kingdom of God is. Paul describes the third heaven in his experience: "Such a one was **caught up** to the **third heaven** ... how he was caught up **into Paradise** where he heard inexpressible words ..." (**2 Corinthians 12:2b, 4a**).

The Greek word for "Paradise" is G3857 *paradeisos*, which means "a **park**, that is, (special) **an Eden** (place of **future happiness**) – paradise." This harkens back to the garden of **Eden** in **Genesis 2:8**: "The Lᴏʀᴅ God **planted a garden eastward in Eden**, and there He put the man whom He had formed." The Hebrew word for "Eden" is H5731 *eden*, which means "The same as H5730 *Eden*, the region of **Adam's home**." The Hebrew word for the Strong's number H5730 is *eden ednah*, which means "**Pleasure; delicate delight**."

Webster's Student Dictionary defines "Eden" as follows: "LL, fr. Heb. *'eden* a delight, **a place of pleasure**, Eden. a) Bible. The **garden where Adam and Eve first dwelt; Paradise**." And "Paradise" is the word Jesus uses for the place where the criminal hanging on the cross beside Him, who came to belief in Jesus, would go after he died in the flesh: "And Jesus said to him, 'Assuredly, I say to you, today **you will be with Me in Paradise**'" (**Luke 23:43**). Here Jesus is using the same Greek word, G3857 *paradeisos*.

This should challenge our thinking about where the real garden of Eden is and that the garden of Eden that God planted on earth might be a picture of or copy of the one in heaven, just as the Tabernacle of God on earth is a copy of the true tabernacle in heaven. "Therefore *it was* necessary that **the copies of the things in the heavens** should be purified with these, but **the heavenly things themselves** with better sacrifices than these. ²⁴ For Christ **has not entered** the **holy places made with hands,** *which are* **copies of the true**, but **into heaven itself,** now to appear in the **presence of God** for us" (**Hebrews 9:23–24**). (See also **Hebrews 8:4–5**.)

Jesus speaks of the truth of these two realms in a conversation with Nicodemus in **John 3:1–13**:

> There was a man **of the Pharisees** named Nicodemus, a ruler of the Jews. [2] This man **came to Jesus by night** and said to Him, "Rabbi, we know that You are a teacher come **from God**; for **no one can do these signs that You do** unless **God is with him**." [3] Jesus answered and said to him, "Most assuredly, I say to you, unless one is **born again**, he **cannot see the kingdom of God**." [4] Nicodemus said to Him, "How can a man be born when he is old? Can he enter a second time into his mother's womb and be born?"
>
> [5] Jesus answered, "Most assuredly, I say to you, unless **one is born of water** and **the Spirit**, he cannot enter the kingdom of God. [6] **That which is born of the flesh is flesh**, and **that which is born of the Spirit is spirit**. [7] Do not marvel that I said to you, **'You must be born again.'** [8] The **wind blows** where it wishes, and **you hear the sound of it**, but **cannot tell where it comes from** and **where it goes. So is everyone who is born of the Spirit**."
>
> [9] Nicodemus answered and said to Him, "How can these things be?" [10] Jesus answered and said to him, "**Are you the teacher of Israel**, and **do not know these things**? [11] Most assuredly, I say to you, We speak what We know and **testify what We have seen**, and you **do not receive Our witness**. [12] **If I have told you earthly things** and **you do not believe, how will you believe if I tell you heavenly things**? [13] No one has ascended to heaven but He who came down from heaven, *that is,* **the Son of Man who is in heaven**."

So to return to our home in heaven, we must be born again of the Spirit. We will learn exactly what this means and when and how this happens in later chapters.

Just because we cannot see this realm where God rules as King with our eyes does not mean that this spiritual realm does not exist. But as Jesus says about the wind, even though we cannot see some things with our eyes, we can observe with our eyes the effects on things around us that we can see. It is the gathering of these observations that collectively develops our faith that something we cannot see actually exists. We cannot see electrons, but we believe they exist. We can know they exist because we can see how they can heat up a wire and create light. We can see how they can make a magnetic field that can drive a motor, we can see how they spark in lightning, and we can feel their effects when they give us a shock and when they make our hair stand on end with static electricity.

With the evidence of things we can see, we can use logic and reason to know the existence of something that we are not able to see with our eyes or any microscope because of the wave–particle duality of matter and the uncertainty principle of physics. If we can have faith that electrons exist, we can have much more faith that God exists, because He has provided so much evidence in all areas of science that has been discovered in the last one hundred years or so. This is exactly like what Jesus said about the Spirit to Nicodemus; it is like the wind, in that you cannot see it but you can hear and see the effects, just as when the wind rustles through the tall grass or the leaves on a tree. We can see the effects of invisible things on things we can see. The apostle Paul uses this reasoning to prove the existence of God, whom we cannot see:

> For the wrath of God is revealed from heaven against all ungodliness and unrighteousness of men, who **suppress the truth in unrighteousness**, [19] because **what may be known of God is manifest in them**, for **God has shown *it* to them**.
>
> [20] For since the creation of the world His invisible *attributes* are clearly seen, being understood by the things that are made, *even* His eternal power and Godhead, so that they are without excuse, [21] because, although they knew God, they did not glorify *Him* as God, nor were thankful, but became futile in their thoughts, and their foolish hearts were darkened. [22] Professing to be wise, they became fools. (**Romans 1:18–22**)

Paul speaks of "**what may be known of God**" being revealed by **what is in us**. Scientists today can see all the incredible complexity of human life in DNA and the amazing workings required in the smallest living cell in molecular biology. And we can see a grand

and magnificent universe, which Albert Einstein has proven with his general relativity theory to have begun when time, space, and matter exploded into existence from nothing. These and many other scientific discoveries of man indicate that they must be the result of an incredible intelligence and the design of a creator, and yet many scientists, but certainly not all, claim that there is no God. "**Professing to be wise, they became fools.**"

Notice also what Nicodemus says of Jesus in **John 3:2**: "**Rabbi, we know that You are a teacher come from God**; for **no one can do these signs that You do** unless **God is with him**." Because Jesus did miraculous things outside of the natural things that happen in this world, Nicodemus knew He was from another realm outside of this world, he knew He was from God.

And it still is true today that God gives supernatural events and abilities to Christians of deep faith, such as gifts of healing, speaking in tongues, miraculous answers to prayers, prophecy, and many events in our lives that are far beyond the chance of being a coincidence, so that we may know and those we share with can know that God is with us and for us. "And the LORD, He *is* the one **who goes before you. He will be with you, He will not leave you nor forsake you**; do not fear nor be dismayed" (**Deuteronomy 31:8**). And this is exactly what Jesus says of casting out demons: "Then the disciples came to Jesus privately and said, 'Why could we not cast it out?' [20] So Jesus said to them, '**Because of your unbelief**; for assuredly, I say to you, **if you have faith as a mustard seed**, you will say to this mountain, "Move from here to there," and it will move; and **nothing will be impossible for you**'" (**Matthew 17:20**).

THESE TWO REALMS HAVE DIFFERENT WAYS OF THINKING AND VIEWING REALITY

Let us read the teaching that the apostle Paul gave to the Corinthians concerning Satan, the god of this age, the spirit of this world, who has blinded our hearts and minds to know only the things of this world that are of his thinking and his ways.

> However, we speak wisdom among those who are mature, **yet not the wisdom of this age**, nor of the **rulers of this age**, who are coming to nothing. ⁷ But **we speak the wisdom of God in a mystery**, the **hidden** *wisdom* which God ordained **before the ages** for our glory, ⁸ which none of the rulers of this age knew; for **had they known**, they would not have **crucified the Lord of glory**. ⁹ But as it is written: "*Eye has not seen, nor ear heard, Nor have entered into the heart of man The things which God has prepared for those who love Him.*"
>
> But God has **revealed** *them* **to us** through **His Spirit**. For the Spirit searches all things, yes, **the deep things of God**. ¹¹ For what man **knows** the things of a man except **the spirit of the man which is in him**? Even so **no one knows the things of God** except the **Spirit of God**. ¹² Now we have received, **not the spirit of the world**, but the **Spirit who is from God**, that we might know the things that have been freely given to us by God. ¹³ These things we also speak, not in words which **man's wisdom teaches** but which **the Holy Spirit teaches**, comparing **spiritual things** with **spiritual**. ¹⁴ But the **natural man** does not receive the things of the **Spirit of God**, for they are **foolishness to him**; nor can he know *them*, because **they are spiritually discerned**. ¹⁵ But **he who is spiritual** judges all things, yet he himself is *rightly* judged by no one. ¹⁶ For "*who has known the mind of the* Lord *that he may instruct Him?*" But **we have the mind of Christ**. (**1 Corinthians 2:6–16**)

In the chapter "The Tree of Life" and and in greater depth in the chapter "The Beginning as Seen from Earth," we will learn that man is a spirit in a body of flesh. Those who are in a body of flesh without the Holy Spirit do not know the whole truth, and so they cannot judge rightly.

"But even **if our gospel is veiled**, it is **veiled to those who are perishing**, ⁴ whose minds **the god of this age has blinded**, who **do not believe**, lest the **light of the gospel** of the **glory of Christ**, who is the **image of God**, should shine on them" (**2 Corinthians 4:3–4**). The word "gospel" comes from two Greek words: G2097 *euaggelizo*, which means "to **announce good news**," and G2098 *euaggelion*, which means "a **good message**." The first is a verb, and the second a noun.

Jesus has come into the world to proclaim the good news that He is the Son of God and that God is a god of forgiveness and love and a god of the second chance. Even though we will surely die if we continue in Satan's ways of death, the good news is that if we turn from the ways of the world and believe and put our faith and trust in God and His ways with all our heart and mind, we can have eternal life.

The apostle Paul tells us that without God, we only know the things that Satan wants us to know. At some point we should ask ourselves whom we should expect to know and understand more truth—the creator of the creature or the creature? If Satan only knows part of the truth, could he be wrong? And if we know less than Satan, could we be wrong?

The truth is that we do only know part of the truth, as Paul explains:

> For **we know in part** and *we prophesy* **in part**. [10] But when that which is perfect has come, then that **which is in part** will be done away. [11] When I was a child, I spoke as a child, **I understood as a child, I thought as a child**; but when I became a man, I **put away childish things**. [12] For now **we see in a mirror, dimly**, but then **face-to-face**. Now **I know in part**, but **then I shall know** just as **I also am known**. [13] And now abide **faith, hope, love**, these three; but **the greatest of these *is* love**." (**1 Corinthians 13:9**)

"Prophesy" can refer to the foretelling of future events, but it also refers to speaking of the hidden truth of God by inspiration. We can see what Paul is talking about in this saying by Mark Twain: "When I was a boy of fourteen, my father was so ignorant I could hardly stand to have the old man around. But when I got to be twenty-one, I was astonished at how much the old man had learned in seven years." We all start out in life thinking we know better than our parents, but we find out later in life that we had a lot to learn. The understanding that we do not know, it all is something that God wants us to learn not only from our parents, but from Him, our Father in heaven, as well. God seeks to share the truth with us, but if we do not understand the truth, it does us no good.

> My son, if you receive my words, And **treasure my commands** within you, ² So that you incline your ear to **wisdom**, *And* **apply your heart to understanding**; ³ Yes, if you **cry out for discernment**, *And* **lift up your voice for understanding**, ⁴ If you seek her as silver, And **search for her as** *for* **hidden treasures**; ⁵ Then **you will understand** the **fear of the** L ORD, And find the **knowledge of God**. ⁶ For the L ORD **gives wisdom**; From His mouth *come* **knowledge** and **understanding**;
>
> ⁷ He stores up **sound wisdom** for the **upright**; *He is* a shield to those who walk uprightly; ⁸ He guards the paths of justice, And **preserves the way of His saints**. ⁹ Then you will **understand righteousness** and **justice**, Equity *and* every good path. ¹⁰ When **wisdom enters your heart**, And **knowledge is pleasant to your soul**, ¹¹ Discretion will preserve you; **Understanding** will **keep you**, ¹² To **deliver you from the way of evil**, From the man who speaks perverse things. (**Proverbs 2:1–12**)

Paul tells us that a limited knowledge of the truth puffs us up with pride but that love builds us up: "Now concerning things offered to idols: We know that we all have knowledge. **Knowledge puffs up**, but **love edifies** [builds up]. ² And **if anyone thinks** that he **knows anything, he knows nothing yet** as he **ought to know**. ³ But if anyone **loves God**, this one is **known by Him**" (**1 Corinthians 8:1–3**). The Hebrew word for the phrase **"puffs up"** is G5448 *phusioo* which figuratively means **"to make proud."**

Webster's Student Dictionary defines "pride" as "**a Unreasonable self-esteem; conceit. 2. Proud** or **haughty behavior** or treatment; **insolence; disdain**." And "disdain" is defined as "1 To **consider unworthy**, unsuitable, or the like. 2 To reject as not deserving of one's notice; **to scorn** to accept, do, recognize, etc. **–Syn**. See DEPSPISE. **–n. A feeling of contempt** for that which is **regarded as beneath one**; scorm."

Pride—the thought that we know more than we really do and are more than we really are—was the downfall of Satan, the Devil. **"This is a faithful saying: If a man desires the position of a bishop, he desires a good work. ² A bishop then must be blameless ...** not a novice, **lest being puffed up with pride he fall into the *same* condemnation as the devil"** (**1 Timothy 3:6**).

We say a little knowledge is dangerous, because it leads us to think and do things that, we would not have done if we had known more. Pride is the thought that we are better than others because we think we know more than others. If we think we know something, we know nothing like we ought; a little knowledge is dangerous. In "The Oneness Branch," we will discover how Lucifer's pride caused his fall from heaven.

And knowing only a little truth is exactly the situation we are in with God. "For **My thoughts *are* not your thoughts, Nor *are* your ways My ways**," says the LORD. ⁹ "For *as* the heavens are higher than the earth, So are **My ways higher** than **your ways**, And **My thoughts** than **your thoughts**" (**Isaiah 55:8–9**).

This reminds me of a saying by Marc Kirsch: "The more I know, the more I know how much I don't know." When we think we know more than others, it can make us feel superior and fill us with pride, and we can become arrogant, but when we understand how little we know compared to God, we are humbled, and our minds are opened, and our hearts are teachable, and we are ready to learn.

RESPECT FOR GOD IS THE BEGINNING OF WISDOM

How should we react to God, who has knowledge, understanding, and wisdom vastly superior to ours? The Bible says we should respect Him and His knowledge, understanding, and power so that we can learn from Him. "The **fear** of the LORD *is* the **beginning of wisdom**, And the **knowledge** of the **Holy One** *is* **understanding**" (**Proverbs 9:10**).

The word translated as "fear" is the Hebrew word H3374 *yirah*, which means **"fear, morally reverence:- dreadful, exceedingly, fearfulness."** But God loves us and does not want us to be afraid of Him but rather respect Him for who He is. The apostle John tells us that love casts out fear: "There **is no fear in love**; but **perfect love casts out fear**, because fear involves torment. But he who fears has not been **made** perfect in love" (**1 John 4:18**).

A passage in Proverbs says, **"Trust in the LORD** with **all your heart,** And **lean not on your own understanding;** ⁶ In all your ways **acknowledge Him,** And He shall direct your paths. ⁷ **Do not be wise in your own eyes;** Fear the LORD and **depart from evil** ... But **fools die for lack of wisdom"** (**Proverbs 3:5–7; 10:21b**).

The apostle Paul urges us to "Be of the same mind toward one another. **Do not set your mind on high things,** but **associate with the humble. Do not be wise in your own opinion.** ¹⁷ Repay no one evil for evil. Have regard for good things in the sight of all men. ¹⁸ If it is possible, **as much as depends on you, live peaceably with all men.** ¹⁹ Beloved, **do not avenge yourselves,** but *rather* give place to wrath; for it is written, '*Vengeance is Mine, I will repay,*' says the Lord" (**Romans 12:16–19**).

The apostle Peter states, "Likewise you younger people, **submit yourselves to** *your* **elders.** Yes, all of *you* be **submissive** to **one another,** and be clothed with **humility,** for '*God resists the proud, But gives grace to the humble.*' ⁶ Therefore **humble yourselves** under the mighty hand of God, that **He may exalt you in due time,** ⁷ casting all your care upon Him, for **He cares for you"** (**1 Peter 5:5–7**). "**Do not be wise in your own eyes;** Fear the LORD and depart from evil. ⁸ It will be health to your flesh, And strength to your bones" (**Proverbs 3:7–8**).

Consider the blessing of wisdom. "**Happy** *is* **the man** *who* **finds wisdom,** And the man *who* **gains understanding;** ¹⁴ For her proceeds *are* **better than the profits of silver,** And her gain than fine gold. ¹⁵ She *is* **more precious than rubies,** And all the things you may desire cannot compare with her. ¹⁶ **Length of days** *is* in her right hand, In her left hand **riches and honor**. [17] Her ways *are* ways of **pleasantness**, And all her paths *are* **peace**. [18] She *is* a **tree of life** to **those who take hold of her**, And happy *are all* who retain her" (**Proverbs 3:13–18**).

> How long, you simple ones, will you love simplicity? For scorners delight in their scorning, And **fools hate knowledge**. [23] **Turn at my rebuke; Surely I will pour out my spirit** on you; **I will make my words known to you**. [24] Because **I have called** and **you refused, I have stretched out my hand** and **no one regarded**, [25] Because **you disdained all my counsel**, And would have none of my rebuke, [26] I also will laugh at your calamity; I will mock when your terror comes, [27] When your terror comes like a storm, And **your destruction** comes like a whirlwind, When distress and anguish come upon you.
>
> [28] Then they will call on me, but I will not answer; They will seek me diligently, but they will not find me. [29] Because **they hated knowledge** And **did not choose the fear of the LORD**, [30] They would **have none of my counsel** *And* despised my every rebuke. [31] Therefore **they shall eat the fruit of their own way**, And be filled to the full with **their own fancies**. [32] For the **turning away** of the simple **will slay them**, And the **complacency of fools will destroy them**; [33] But whoever **listens to me** will dwell safely, And will be secure, **without fear of evil**. (**Proverbs 1:22–33**)

Here in this proverb inspired by God, Solomon figuratively uses fruit to describe the produce, or the consequences, of choosing the ways of the knowledge of good and evil. This harkens back to the eating of the fruit from the Tree of Knowledge of Good and Evil (**Genesis 2:17; 3:3**).

God's "punishment" for not obeying the truth is not so much something He does to us, but more something that He cannot convince us to not do to ourselves, because we refuse to listen. Anyone can deny the truth, but no one can change the truth, because it is the way things are; truth is reality. God's "punishment" is to separate those who think they are wise but are not from those who seek after truth and wisdom. Those who refuse the knowledge of the truth, understanding, and wisdom will destroy themselves by their own choice.

"Whatever I tell you in the dark, **speak in the light**; and what you hear in the ear, preach on the housetops. **28** And **do not fear those who kill the body** but **cannot kill the soul**. But rather **fear Him** who is able to destroy both **soul and body** in **hell**" (**Matthew 10:27–28**). God loves us and does not want any of His children to perish,

> For **God so loved the world** that He gave His only begotten Son, that **whoever believes in Him should not perish** but have **everlasting life**. **17** For God did not send His Son into the world **to condemn the world**, but that **the world through Him might be saved**.
>
> **18** He who **believes in Him is not condemned**; but he who **does not believe is condemned already**, because he has not believed in the name of the only begotten Son of God. **19** And **this is the condemnation**, that the **light has come into the world**, and **men loved darkness rather than light**, because their deeds were evil. **20** For everyone practicing evil **hates the light** and does not come to the light, **lest his deeds should be exposed**. **21** But **he who does the truth comes to the light**, that his deeds may be clearly seen, that they have been done in God. (**John 3:16–21**)

We will learn and understand when all of us on earth did not believe in Jesus, who of us "**loved darkness rather than light**," and who of us "**comes to the light**" when we come to the chapters "The Meaning and Purpose for Life on Planet Earth" and "The Beginning as Seen from Earth."

THE VALUE OF THE KNOWLEDGE OF THE TRUTH, UNDERSTANDING, WISDOM, AND VIRTUE

Webster's Student Dictionary defines the word "know" as "To **recognize as true**; to **perceive with understanding** and **conviction**." The word "knowledge" is defined as "The **act of understanding**; clear perception of **truth**; clear perception of **facts**." And "**wisdom**" is defined as "The capacity of **judging soundly** and dealing broadly

with facts; it often implies the **ripeness of experience**." And *Webster's Student Dictionary* defines "virtue" as "**Moral practice or action**."

Let us consider well a proverb that personifies knowledge of the truth with understanding, and wisdom as though it is a person speaking to us. This proverb sounds as though God is speaking because only God speaks of what is true, out of understanding, wisdom, and virtue:

> To you, O men, I call, And **my voice** *is* **to the sons of men**. ⁵ O you simple ones, **understand prudence**, And you fools, **be of an understanding heart**. ⁶ Listen, for I will speak of excellent things, And from the opening of my lips *will come* **right things**; ⁷ For **my mouth will speak truth**; Wickedness *is* an abomination to my lips. ⁸ All the words of my mouth *are* with righteousness; Nothing crooked or perverse *is* in them. ⁹ They *are* **all plain to him who understands**, And right to **those who find knowledge**.
>
> ¹⁰ Receive my **instruction**, and **not silver**, And **knowledge rather than choice gold**; ¹¹ For **wisdom** *is* **better than rubies**, And all the things one may desire cannot be compared with her. ¹² "**I, wisdom**, dwell with **prudence**, And find out **knowledge** *and* **discretion**. ¹³ The **fear of the LORD** *is* to **hate evil**; **Pride** and **arrogance** and **the evil way** And the perverse mouth I hate. ¹⁴ Counsel *is* mine, and sound wisdom; **I** *am* **understanding, I have strength** [H1369 *geburah* power, might]. ¹⁵ By me kings reign, And rulers decree justice. ¹⁶ By me princes rule, and nobles, All the judges of the earth. ¹⁷ **I love those who love me**, And **those who seek me diligently will find me**. ¹⁸ Riches and honor *are* with me, **Enduring riches and righteousness**. ¹
>
> ⁹ My **fruit** *is* better **than gold**, yes, than fine gold, And **my revenue** than **choice silver**. ²⁰ I traverse the **way of righteousness**, In the midst of the paths of **justice**, ²¹ That **I may cause those who love me to inherit wealth**, That I may fill their treasuries.
>
> ²² "The LORD **possessed me** at the **beginning of His way**, Before His works of old.

²³ I have been established from everlasting, From the beginning, **before there was ever an earth**. ²⁴ When *there were* no depths I was brought forth, When *there were* no fountains abounding with water. ²⁵ Before the mountains were settled, Before the hills, I was brought forth; ²⁶ While as yet He had not made the earth or the fields, Or the primeval dust of the world.

²⁷ When **He prepared the heavens, I *was* there**, When He drew a circle on the face of the deep, ²⁸ When **He established the clouds above**, When He strengthened the **fountains of the deep**, ²⁹ When He assigned to the sea its limit, So that the waters would not transgress His command, When He marked out the foundations of the earth, ³⁰ Then I was beside Him *as* a master craftsman; And **I was daily *His* delight**, Rejoicing always before Him, ³¹ **Rejoicing in His inhabited world**, And **my delight** *was* **with the sons of men**.

³² "Now therefore, **listen to me**, *my* **children**, For blessed *are those who* **keep my ways**. ³³ **Hear instruction** and be **wise**, And do not disdain *it*. ³⁴ Blessed is the man who **listens to me**, Watching daily at my gates, Waiting at the posts of my doors. ³⁵ For **whoever finds me finds life**, And obtains favor from the LORD; ³⁶ But **he who sins against me wrongs his own soul; All those who hate me love death**." **(Proverbs 8:4–36)**

If wisdom were a person, it would say the same things God says to us. If knowledge of the truth, understanding, and wisdom is the power by which God created us and the universe, it is no wonder that He says to us to seek Him diligently that we might find Him and be like Him. "My son, do not despise **the chastening of the LORD**, Nor detest His **correction**; ¹² For **whom the LORD loves He corrects**, Just as a father the son *in whom* he delights. ¹³ **Happy** *is* the **man *who* finds wisdom**, And the **man *who* gains understanding**" **(Proverbs 3:11–13)**.

My son, if you **receive my words**, And **treasure my commands** within you, ² So that you **incline your ear to wisdom**, *And* apply **your heart to understanding**; ³ Yes, if you **cry out for discernment**, *And* lift up your voice for **understanding**, ⁴ If you seek her as silver, And search for her as *for* **hidden treasures**;

[5] Then you will **understand the fear of the LORD**, And find the **knowledge of God**. [6] For the LORD **gives wisdom**; From His mouth *come* **knowledge and understanding**;

[7] He stores up **sound wisdom** for the upright; *He is* **a shield** to those who walk uprightly; [8] He guards the paths of justice, And **preserves the way of His saints**. [9] Then you will **understand righteousness** and justice, Equity *and* every good path. [10] When **wisdom enters your heart**, And **knowledge is pleasant to your soul**, [11] **Discretion** will **preserve you**; **Understanding will keep you**, [12] To **deliver you from the way of evil**, From the man who speaks perverse things. (**Proverbs 2: 1–12**)

When we know and understand the truth of God and with wisdom know what to do with that understanding and then in virtuous action actually do it, that truth will make us free. "Then Jesus said to those Jews who believed Him, "If you **abide in My word**, you are My disciples indeed. [32] And you shall **know the truth**, and the **truth shall make you free**" (**John 8:31–32**).

IN CLOSING, CONSIDER NOW THESE TRUTHS FROM THE BIBLE

Love Rejoices in Truth

Love … does not rejoice in iniquity, but **rejoices in the truth**. (**1 Corinthians 13:6**)

This verse shows there is an interrelationship between truth and love that I experienced in my truth-and-love experience. "We know that whoever is **born of God** does not sin; but he who has been **born of God** keeps himself, and the **wicked one** does not touch him. [19] We know that **we are of God**, and the **whole world lies** *under the sway of* the wicked one" (**1 John 5:18–19**).

"**Do not love the world** or the **things in the world**. If anyone **loves the world**, the **love of the Father is not in him**. [16] For all that *is* in the world—the lust of the flesh, the lust of the eyes, and the pride of life—is not of the Father but is of the world. [17] And the **world is passing away**, and the lust of it; but **he who does the will of God abides forever**" (**1 John 2:15–17**). Because "the **whole world lies** *under the sway of* **the wicked one**," when we love the world, we are choosing the wicked ways of Satan.

God Desires All to Come to the Knowledge of the Truth

> The Lord is not slack concerning His promise, as some count slackness, but is longsuffering toward us, **not willing that any should perish** but that all should **come to repentance** ... For this is good and acceptable in the sight of God our Savior, [4] **who desires all men to be saved** and to **come to the knowledge of the truth**. (**2 Peter 3:9; 1 Timothy 2:3–4**)

The Truth of the Gospel Is Simple

> But I fear, lest somehow, as the **serpent deceived Eve** by his craftiness, so your minds may be corrupted from **the simplicity that is in Christ**. (**2 Corinthians 11:3**)

We do not have to be theologians to understand the truth of the gospel. The truth of God that sets us free is so simple that a child of the age of understanding can know and understand it. It is the craftiness of Satan that makes us think it is so complicated.

> But the **righteousness of faith** speaks in this way, *"Do not say in your heart, 'Who will ascend into heaven?'"* (that is, to bring Christ down *from above*) [7] or, *"'Who will descend into the abyss?'"* (that is, to bring Christ up from the dead). [8] But what does it say? *"The word is near you, in your mouth and in your heart'* (that is, the word of faith which we preach): [9] that if you **confess with your mouth the Lord Jesus** and **believe in your heart that God has raised Him from the dead, you will be saved**. [10] For **with the heart** one believes unto righteousness, and **with the mouth** confession is made unto **salvation**." (**Romans 10:6–10**)

Understanding God's Truth

> As it is written in the Law of Moses, all this disaster has come
> upon us; yet we have not made our prayer before the Lord our
> God, that we might **turn from our iniquities** and **understand
> Your truth. (Daniel 9:13)**

Testing the Spirit of Truth and the Spirit of Error

> Beloved, do not believe every **spirit**, but **test** the **spirits**,
> whether they are of God; because many **false prophets** have
> gone out into the world. [2] By this you know the **Spirit of God**:
> Every **spirit** that **confesses that Jesus** *Christ* has **come in
> the flesh is of God**, [3] and **every spirit that does not confess**
> that **Jesus Christ has come in the flesh** is not of **God**. And
> **this is the spirit of the Antichrist**, which you have heard was
> coming, and is now already in the world. [4] You are of God, little
> children, and have overcome them, because **He who is in you
> is greater than he who is in the world**. [5] They are of the
> world. Therefore they speak as of the world, and the world hears
> them. [6] We are of God. He who knows God hears us; **he who
> is not of God does not hear us**. By this we know **the spirit
> of truth** and **the spirit of error**. (1 John 4:1–6)

Notice that this passage speaks of men, whether they believe in God or
not, as spirits. As we will see in the chapter "The Beginning as Seen
from Earth," man is an eternal spirit in a temporary body of flesh.

The Plain Truth

> Therefore, since through God's mercy we have this ministry,
> we do not lose heart. [2] Rather, we have renounced secret and
> shameful ways; **we do not use deception, nor do we distort
> the word of God**. On the contrary, **by setting forth the truth
> plainly** we commend ourselves to every man's conscience in the
> sight of God. (2 Corinthians 4:1–2)

Love of the Truth Saves

And then the **lawless one** will be revealed, whom the Lord will consume with the breath of His mouth and destroy with the brightness of His coming. [9] The coming of the **lawless one** is according to the **working of Satan**, with all power, signs, and **lying** wonders, [10] and with all **unrighteous deception** among those who perish, because **they did not** receive the **love of the truth**, that they **might be saved**. [11] And for this reason God will send them strong **delusion**, that they should **believe the lie**, [12] that they all may be condemned **who did not believe the truth** but **had pleasure in unrighteousness**. (**2 Thessalonians 2:8–12**)

We Are Saved by Belief in the Truth

But we are bound to give thanks to God always for you, brethren beloved by the Lord, because God **from the beginning chose you for salvation** through **sanctification by the Spirit** and **belief in the truth**, [14] to which He called you by **our gospel**, for the obtaining of the glory of our Lord Jesus Christ. (**2 Thessalonians 2:13–14**)

Knowledge of the Truth

For if we **sin willfully** after we have received the **knowledge of the truth**, there no longer remains a sacrifice for sins, [27] but a certain **fearful** expectation of judgment, and fiery indignation which will devour **the adversaries**. [28] Anyone who has rejected Moses' law dies **without mercy** on the testimony of two or three witnesses. [29] Of how much worse punishment, do you suppose, will he be thought worthy who has **trampled the Son of God underfoot**, counted the **blood of the covenant** by which **he was sanctified** a **common thing**, and insulted the **Spirit of grace**? (**Hebrews 10:26–29**)

Word of Truth

Do not be **deceived**, my beloved brethren. [17] Every good gift and every perfect gift is **from above**, and comes down from the

Father of lights, with whom **there is no variation or shadow of turning**. [18] **Of His own will He brought us forth** by the **word of truth**, that we might be a kind of firstfruits of His **creatures**. (James 1:16–18)

Sanctified by the Truth

But now I come to You, and these things I speak in the world, that they may have **My joy** fulfilled in themselves. [14] I have given them Your word; and the world has **hated them because they are not of the world**, just as I am not of the world. [15] I do not pray that You should take them out of the world, but that You should **keep them from the evil one**. [16] They **are not of the world**, just as I am not of the world. [17] **Sanctify them by Your truth. Your word is truth**. [18] As You sent Me into the world, I also have sent them into the world. [19] And for their sakes I sanctify Myself, that they also may be **sanctified by the truth**. (John 17:13–19)

The word "sanctify" is translated from the Greek word G37 *hagiazo*, which means "to **make holy**, that is, (ceremonially) **purify** or **consecrate**; (mentally) to venerate, hallow, **be holy**." And Webster defines "**sanctify**" as, "1) To **set apart as sacred**; **consecrate**; to **hallow**. 2) To **make pure and holy** by **freeing from all desires** that **turn one from God**, as man is **sanctified** by **suffering**."

The Father Seeks Those Who Worship in Spirit and Truth

Jesus said to her, "Woman, believe Me, the hour is coming when you will neither on this mountain, nor in Jerusalem, worship the Father. [22] You worship what you do not know; we know what we worship, for salvation is of the Jews. [23] But the hour is coming, and now is, when the true worshipers will **worship the Father** in **spirit** and **truth**; for the Father is seeking such to worship Him. [24] **God is Spirit**, and **those who worship Him** must **worship in spirit** and **truth**." (John 4:21–23)

113

Father of Truth vs. Father of Lies

"I know that you are **Abraham's descendants**, but you seek to kill Me, because My word has no place in you. [38] **I speak what I have seen with My Father**, and you do what **you have seen with your father**." [39]

They answered and said to Him, "Abraham is our father." Jesus said to them, "If you were Abraham's children, you would do the works of Abraham. [40] But now you seek to kill Me, **a Man who has told you the truth** which **I heard from God**. Abraham did not do this. [41] **You do the deeds of your father**."

Then they said to Him, "We were not born of fornication; we have one Father—God." [42] Jesus said to them, "If God were your Father, you would love Me, for I proceeded forth and came from God; nor have I come of Myself, but He sent Me. [43] **Why do you not understand My speech**? Because you are not able to listen to My word. [44] **You are of your father the devil**, and the **desires of your father you want to do. He was a murderer from the beginning**, and **does not stand in the truth**, because **there is no truth in him**.

"When he speaks **a lie**, he speaks from his own resources, for **he is a liar and the father of it**. [45] But **because I tell the truth, you do not believe Me**. [46] Which of you convicts Me of sin? And **if I tell the truth**, why do you not believe Me? [47] **He who is of God hears God's words**; therefore **you do not hear**, because **you are not of God**." (John 8:37–47)

We Are Helpless to Know the Truth without God

In that hour Jesus rejoiced in the Spirit and said, "I thank You, Father, Lord of heaven and earth, that **You have hidden these things** from the **wise and prudent** and **revealed them to babes**. Even so, Father, for so it seemed good in Your sight. [22] All things have been delivered to Me by My Father, and no one knows who the Son is except the Father, and who the Father is except the Son, and the one to whom the Son wills to reveal Him." [23] Then He turned to His disciples and said privately, "Blessed are the eyes which see the things you see; [24] for I tell you that **many prophets and kings have desired to see what you see**, and **have not seen it**, and **to hear what you hear**, and **have not heard it**." (Luke 10:21–24)

We, in our own abilities, are helpless to know the truth; it is a gift of God.

God Desires Truth in Our Inner Parts

Behold, You desire **truth** in the inward parts, And in the **hidden part** You will make me to **know wisdom**. (**Psalm 51:6**)

The truth convicts us of our sin; Jesus Himself explains about His coming to earth to witness of the truth: "If I had not come and spoken to them, **they would have no sin**, but now **they have no excuse for their sin**" (**John 15:22**). The truth is that this world is temporary; this world is passing away, as the apostle John says: "And the **world is passing away**, and **the lust of it**; but he who does the will of God **abides forever**" (**1 John 2:17**). The fact that the earth is passing away and that believers will have eternal life tells us that this world was never intended to be our home.

I think the point in my experience of learning about the truth of God that gave me a feeling that the truth was in some way holding something bad for me was when I learned about what God said in **Romans 1:22–26b**: "**Professing to be wise, they became fools**, and changed the glory of the incorruptible God into an image made like corruptible man – and birds and four footed animals and creeping things. Therefore God also **gave them up to uncleanness**, in the lusts of their hearts, to dishonor their bodies among themselves, **who exchanged the truth of God for the lie**, and **worshiped and served the creature rather than the Creator**, who is blessed forever. Amen. **For this reason God gave them up to vile passions**." It gave me that sinking feeling you might feel after you had been scammed out of everything you own, out of everything you will inherit, and out of your very life.

One change that my near-death experience created in me was my perception of truth. I realized that there was a lot of truth I did not

115

know, though I had thought I knew the basic truths of life. I had always thought that my job as a Christian was to not fall for the lie of Satan, as Adam and Eve had done, but now I understand that it is too late to try to keep from falling for the lie; it has already happened. That ship has already sailed. My job now as a Christian is to seek, discover, understand, and believe the truth of God.

"Sin" is defined by *Merriam-Webster's Collegiate Dictionary*, 10th ed., as a "**Transgression of the law of God**, a state of human nature in which **the self is estranged** from God." The word "estranged" is defined as "**Alienated, removed from customary environment or associations**, to **arouse mutual enmity** or **indifference** in where there had **formerly been love and affection**." And I think that is exactly right. When we believed the lies of Satan, that sin was incompatible with the Holy and Righteous God and His Kingdom, and we were alienated from God. He removed us from our customary environment or associations, and this sin aroused mutual enmity or indifference where there had formerly been love and affection in our relationship with God.

"Enmity" is the word God uses in describing the broken relationship between God and Satan and those who believed and followed him: "So the LORD God said to the serpent: 'Because you have done this, **You** *are* **cursed** more than all cattle, And more than every beast of the field; On your belly you shall go, And you shall eat dust All the days of your life. [15] And I will put **enmity Between you** and **the woman**, And **between your seed** and **her Seed**; He shall bruise your head, And you shall bruise His heel'" (**Genesis 3:14–15**). And Webster defines "**enmity**" as "Ill will; hatred; especially mutual hatred or ill will. Synonym: hostility." The Hebrew word for "seed" is H2233 *zara,* which means "seed; figuratively fruit, plant, **posterity**, carnally, **child**, fruitful, sowing-time."

DISCOVERING THE TRUTH THAT LEADS TO ETERNAL LIFE

If the truth of God leads to eternal life, then we should want to know what that truth is. Let us end this study of the truth with some passages that show us where to look that we might discover the truth that leads to eternal life in order to prepare ourselves for the branches, which we will study next. If you have a lot of unanswered questions, that is good thing. We will find the answers that have been lost by neglect and lost in translations over time.

But do know and believe that the first disciples of Jesus Christ understood what they were saying and were so excited by what they knew and understood that they were willing to give their lives to share that truth with others. We will go into the Ancient Hebrew and Greek when necessary to learn the truth found in the pages of the Bible. And we will find a truth that literally is to die for!

> We **know** that we **have passed from death to life**, because we **love the brethren**. He who **does not love his brother abides in death**. [15] Whoever hates his brother is a murderer, and you know that no murderer has eternal life abiding in him. [16] **By this we know love**, because **He laid down His life for us**. And **we also ought to lay down our lives for the brethren**. [17] But whoever has this world's goods, and sees his brother in need, and shuts up his heart from him, how does the love of God abide in him? [18] My little children, **let us not love in word or in tongue**, but **in deed and in truth**. [19] And **by this we know that we are of the truth**, and shall assure our hearts before Him. (**1 John 3:14–19**)

In this passage and the ones below, we see the connectedness that I experienced in my truth-and-love vision.

The Word of God is calling out to us. "If indeed you have **heard Him** and **taught by Him**, as the **truth is in Jesus**: that you put off, concerning your former conduct, the old man which grows corrupt according the deceitful lusts, and **be renewed in the spirit of your mind**, and that you **put on a new man which was created according**

117

to God, in true **righteousness** and holiness. Therefore, **putting away lying**, 'Let **each one of you speak truth** with his neighbor, for **we are members of one another**'" (Ephesians: 4:21–25).

Speaking the Truth in Love

> that we should **no longer be children**, tossed to and fro and carried about with every wind of doctrine, by the trickery of men, in the cunning craftiness of deceitful plotting, [15] but, **speaking the truth in love**, may grow up in all things into Him **who is the head–Christ–** [16] from whom **the whole body, joined** and **knit together** by what **every joint supplies**, according to the effective working by which every part does its share, **causes growth of the body** for the **edifying of itself in love. (Ephesians 4:14–16)**

In these three verses we can see truth, love, and oneness, all three branches—the very ones that I could distinctly remember from my near-death experience.

Now let us see what some important people have said about truth over the years.

> "Every truth passes through three stages before it is recognized. In the first, it is ridiculed. In the second, it is opposed. In the third, it is regarded as self-evident."

> **—Schopenhauer**

> "The man who fears no truths has nothing to fear from lies."

> **—Thomas Jefferson**

> "A lie can travel half way around the world while the truth is putting on its shoes."

> **—Mark Twain**

"Repetition does not transform a lie into the truth."

—Franklin D. Roosevelt

"The truth of the matter is that you always know the right thing to do. The hard part is doing it."

—General H. Norman Schwarzkopf

"When I despair, I remember that all through history the way of **truth** and **love** has always won. There have been tyrants and murderers and for a time they seem invincible but in the end they always fall – think of it, ALWAYS."

—Mahatma Gandhi

"The truth does not change according to our ability to stomach it."

—Flannery O'Connor

"The highest compact we can make with our fellow is – "Let there be truth between us two forever."

—Ralph Waldo Emerson

"Truth, like surgery, may hurt, but it cures."

—Han Suyin

"There is no greatness where there is not simplicity, goodness, and truth."

—Leo Tolstoy

"The truth, which is indestructible, has a way of accumulating against pride and arrogance, and then sweeping them from its path."

—Mark Helprin of the *Wall Street Journal*

"Morality is truth in full bloom."

—Victor Hugo

"Through kindness, through affection, through honesty, through truth and justice toward all others we ensure our own benefit."

—Dalai Lama

"Integrity is telling myself the truth. And honesty is telling the truth to others."

—Spencer Johnson

"We cannot forever hide the truth about ourselves from ourselves."

—John McCain

"Truth is eternal, knowledge is changeable. It is disastrous to confuse them."

—Madeline L'Engle

"Familiarity breeds contempt. How accurate that is. The reason we hold truth in such respect is because we have so little opportunity to get familiar with it."

—Mark Twain

"A mind opened by truth can never be closed by lies."

—Marc Kirsch

"A mind closed by lies can only be opened by truth."

—Larry Atneosen

"The nice thing about telling the truth is that one is so much more likely to sound convincing."

—Susan Howatch

"The prideful mind is able to defend any position regardless of the truth."

—Marc Kirsch

"If you are out to describe the truth, leave elegance to the tailor."

—Albert Einstein

"As scarce as truth is, the supply has always exceeded demand."

—Josh Billings

"When you decide that you know all there is to know about the truth, you have shifted your mind into park."

—Marc Kirsch

"The truth doesn't hurt unless it ought to."

—St. Francis of Assisi

"Unlike the lie, truth can stand up to scrutiny."

—Marc Kirsch

"Pretty much all the honest truth-telling there is in this word is done by children."

—Oliver Wendell Holmes

"Every natural fact is a symbol of some spiritual truth."

—Ralph Waldo Emerson

"No person can consistently behave in a way that's inconsistent with the way he perceives the truth."

—Marc Kirsch

"What you know to be true determines what you do."

—Franklin Graham

"Truth is the most valuable thing we have. Let us economize it."

—Mark Twain

"The pursuit of truth and beauty is a sphere of activity in which we are permitted to remain children all our lives."

—Albert Einstein

"Man is least himself when he talks in his own person. Give him a mask and he will tell you the truth."

—Oscar Wilde

"He who asks questions cannot avoid the answers."

—Cameroonian Proverb

"In the land of the blind, the one eyed man is king."

—Author Unknown

"Truth exists; only falsehood has to be invented."

—George Braque

"In all affairs it's a healthy thing now and then to hang a question mark on the things you have long taken for granted."

—Bertrand Russell

"Men stumble over the truth from time to time, but most pick themselves up and hurry off as if nothing happened."

—Sir Winston Churchill

"There are some people so addicted to exaggeration that they can't tell the truth without lying."

—Josh Billings

"Truth is a hard master, and costly to serve, but it simplifies all problems."

—Ellis Peters

"Truth is stranger than fiction, but it is because fiction is obliged to stick to possibilities; truth isn't."

—Mark Twain

"Find the grain of truth in criticism - chew it and swallow it."

—D. Sutten

"Another good thing about telling the truth is that you don't have to remember what you said."

—Author Unknown

"Fight for your opinions, but do not believe that they contain the whole truth, or the only truth."

—Charles A. Danna

"There are two kinds of truths; small truth and great truth. You can recognize small truth because its opposite is a falsehood. The opposite of a great truth is another great truth."

—Niels Bohr

"Inasmuch as he who knows nothing is nearer to truth than he whose mind is filled with falsehoods and errors."

—Thomas Jefferson

"I have steadily endeavored to keep my mind free so as to give up any hypothesis, however much beloved, as soon as facts are shown to be opposed to it."

—Charles Darwin

"Knowledge rests not upon truth alone, but upon error also."

—C. G. Jung

"The truth will set you free but first it will make you miserable."

—Jim Davis, via Garfield

"Art is the lie that makes us realize the truth."

—Pablo Picasso

"Never apologize for showing feeling. When you do so you apologize for truth."

—Benjamin Disraeli

"The pursuit of the truth shall set you free – even if you never catch up with it."

—Author Unknown

"To a true artist only the face is beautiful which, quite apart from its exterior, shines with the truth within the Mahatma soul."

—Gandhi

"Oh, what webs we weave, when first we practice to deceive."

—William Shakespeare

"And you shall know the truth, and the truth will set you free."

—Jesus

Well, I found at least one quote that I know to be true. I also found that many of the above people thought that speaking the truth was a hard thing to do. Why would we feel that way? Ponder that question for a while. I think that answer is related to the meaning of life.

The Love Branch

ONE OF ONLY three topics I distinctly remember learning about in my truth-and-love experience, is love. The two things I remember about love besides just reveling in how good and necessary love is and exclaiming with joy inexpressible, "Oh, now I see; oh, now I see!" is that it came after I had learned about truth and it somehow took away the ill-boding and bad feeling that I had after I finished learning about truth.

As we learned in "The Truth Branch," the topics of truth and love are intimately connected. We will see the same connectedness as we study what God has to say about love in the Holy Scriptures. The fact that truth and love are so interconnected in the Bible is one of the things that confirmed in my mind that my experience was real and genuine. When I first learned that truth and love were the two words that summarized my entire experience, it boggled my mind and left me totally confused. But as you journey with me as we try to re-create that experience as best we can with God's help, you will experience for yourself how the two words "truth" and "love" summarize All Knowledge.

Let us now take a crash course in what God has to say about love by reading and pondering over the following verses from the Bible. If we are willing now to accept that God's ways are higher than our ways and His thoughts higher than our thoughts (**Isaiah 55:8−9**) and that there is a truth yet to be learned and understood, that belief will set us free.

WHAT IS LOVE?

In our attempt to understand what love has to do with All Knowledge, we first have to recognize that there is more than one kind of love, even though there is only one word for it in the English Language.

All Love Is Not the Same

In the Greek, there are five basic words for different kinds of love, but there are only three Greek words that we will be focused on in our study of the Bible.

The Greek word G25 *agapao* means "to **love** in a **social** or **moral** sense."

The Greek word G5368 *phileo* means "**to be a friend** to or to be **fond of an individual or an object**; to have affection for as a matter of **sentiment or feeling**; while G25 is **wider**, embracing especially the **judgment** and **deliberate assent of the will** as a matter of **principle**, **duty**, and **propriety**: the former (G5368 *phileo*) being chiefly of the heart and the latter (G25 *agapao*) being of the **head**; specifically to kiss (as a mark of **tenderness**)." *Webster's Student Dictionary* defines "**assent**" as "1. To give or express **one's agreement** or **accord**; to **consent**; as, to **assent to a proposal**. 2. To **admit a thing as true**."

So G5368 *phileo* is a matter of emotion and the heart, and G25 *agapao* is also a matter of the heart but is wider and also includes "to **love** in a **social** or **moral** sense," which means it is about **loving more than one person**. And because it involves "**admitting a thing is true**," it **is a matter of the mind** and a judgment of the **truth about morality and society**. And because it requires the "**deliberate consent of the will**" it is **a matter of choice**. Webster defines "**society**" as "1. **Companionship**, usually friendly, with **one's fellows**. 2. The **social order**, or **community life**, considered as a **system within which individual lives are shaped**. 3. Any part or section of a community bound together by **common aims**, **interests**, and **standards of living**. 4. A **voluntary associations** of persons for **common ends**."

Wikipedia defines two more Ancient Greek words for love. There is *eros*, which is "**passionate love**, with **sensual desire** and **longing**." Other sources describe *eros* as sensual, sexual, impulsive love. The word *eros* is not found in the New Testament. And then there is *storge*, which is "**natural affection**, like that felt by **parents for offspring**. Rarely used in ancient works, and then almost exclusively as a descriptor of relationships within the family. It is also known to express **mere acceptance** or **putting up with situations**, as in 'loving' the tyrant."

In **Mark 12:29–31,** we see Jesus quoting **Deuteronomy 6:4–6** in regard to a question as to which of the commandments was the greatest:

> Then one of the scribes came, and having heard them reasoning together, perceiving that He had answered them well, asked Him, "Which is the first commandment of all?" [29] Jesus answered him, "The first of all the commandments *is:* '*Hear, O Israel, the* LORD *our God, the* LORD *is one.* [30] *And you shall* **love the** LORD **your God** *with* **all your heart,** *with* **all your soul,** *with* **all your mind,** *and with* **all your strength.**' This *is* the first commandment. [31] And the second, like *it, is* this: '*You shall* **love your neighbor as yourself.**' There is **no other commandment greater than these.**"

Let us notice a few important things in this passage:

The Old Testament version of these words of Jesus is in **Deuteronomy 6:4–6**: "Hear, O Israel: The LORD our God, **the** LORD *is* one! [5] You shall **love the** LORD **your God** with **all your heart**, with **all your soul**, and with **all your strength**. [6] And these words which I command you today shall be **in your heart**." This does not include the words "*with* **all your mind**"; Jesus purposely adds these words to the way that we should love in the New Testament. Also notice that the Old Testament word for "love" in the Deuteronomy passage is H157 *ahab aheb,* which means "A primitive root; **to have affection for (sexually or otherwise)**:- **love, like, friend.**"

This word for "love" in the Old Testament is the Hebrew counterpart to both the Greek words G5368 *phileo* and *eros* in that it refers to the heart and emotions and sensuality of the flesh between two people and does not include the wider ideas of truth, morality, and social order;

nor does it speak of the free-will consent of other people. The word that Jesus uses for "love" in this passage where He is teaching us how we should love is the Greek word G25 *agapao*, which includes both the heart and the mind. This addition of loving with all our mind and loving "in a **social** or **moral** sense" is not a mistake by God or Jesus but is an intentional change in the way we should relate to each other in going from the Old Testament to the New Testament.

It is important for us to know that God is teaching something different in the New Testament from that which He taught in the Old Testament, and we will see that more clearly when we get to the chapter "The Third Age of the Church." But if we only have the emotional love of feelings in G5368 *phileo* and the sexual love of *eros* without the knowledge, understanding, and wisdom that come from the mind and produce sound judgment, we will chase after everything our heart desires, whether good or bad. "If it feels good, do it" is the motto of the world.

But Jesus warns His disciples what unrestrained desires of the heart lead to: "Beware of the scribes, who **desire** to go around in long robes, **love** greetings in the marketplaces, the best seats in the synagogues, and the best places at feasts, **47** who **devour widows' houses**, and for a pretense **make long prayers**. These will receive **greater condemnation**" (**Luke 20:46**). The word for love here is G5368 *phileo*, the love of the heart only, which is the world's kind of love. As Jesus points out, "If you were **of the world**, the world would **love** its own. Yet because **you are not of the world**, but **I chose you out of the world**, therefore **the world hates you**" (**John 15:19**). The Greek word for "love" in the phrase "the world would **love** its own" is G5368 *phileo*, which is the kind of love of the world that Jesus is speaking of here.

AGAPE LOVE—THE GOD KIND OF LOVE

Then there is the Greek word for love, G26 *agape*, which means "From G25; **love**, that is, **affection** or **benevolence**; specifically **in the plural a love feast**." This definition adds the sense that it involves many loving each other. But in the Bible God adds "unconditional," "sacrificial," and "voluntary" to this definition of love, which is known as the "God kind of love."

God Demonstrates His Own Love as Unconditional

> For when we were still without strength, in due time Christ **died for the ungodly**. [7] For scarcely for a righteous man will one die; yet perhaps for a good man someone would even dare to die. [8] But God **demonstrates His own love toward us**, in that **while we were still sinners, Christ died for us**. [9] Much more then, having now been **justified by His blood**, we shall be **saved from wrath** through Him. [10] For if when **we were enemies** we were **reconciled to God** through the **death of His Son**, much more, having been **reconciled**, we shall be **saved by His life**. [11] And not only *that,* but we also **rejoice in God** through **our Lord Jesus Christ**, through whom we have now **received the reconciliation**. (**Romans 5:7–11**)

God Demonstrates His Own Love as Sacrificial

> **Greater love** has no one than this, **than to lay down one's life for his friends**. (**John 15:13**)

Jesus died for all of us who are on earth because we are all sinners. God's *agape* love cares as much or more for others than for self. Compare that to the love of this world, which focuses on love of self, considering what is best for oneself, and asking "What's in it for me?" Jesus is telling us in this verse that *agape* love is the greatest form of love.

God Demonstrates His Own Love as Voluntary and of Free Will

> But Jesus said to him, "Put your sword in its place, for **all who take the sword** will **perish by the sword**. [53] Or do you think that I cannot now pray to My Father, and He will provide Me with more than twelve legions of angels? [54] **How then could the Scriptures be fulfilled**, that it must happen thus?" (**Matthew 26:52–53**)

Therefore My Father loves Me, because **I lay down My life** that I may take it again. [18] **No one takes it from Me**, but **I lay it down of Myself**. I have power to **lay it down**, and I have power to **take it again**. This command I have received from My Father. (**John 10:17–18**)

It was Jesus' free-will, unconditional, and sacrificial death which made His love *agape* love. If He had been forced to die and had no choice, it would not have been the kind of love that would save us. This is why Jesus said that He could call down a legion of angels to save Him if that was what He desired, and this is why Jesus asked the disciples to get a sword before He was arrested and then told Peter to put it away when He was arrested—to show everyone that what He was doing was of His own free will.

Love that is forced is not love at all but slavery. As the saying goes, "If you have something you love, set it free. If it returns to you, it is yours to keep; if it does not, it never was." The apostle Paul teaches that God's kind of "love **suffers long** *and* is **kind**; love **does not envy**; love **does not parade itself**, is **not puffed up**; [5] does not behave rudely, **does not seek its own**, is not provoked, **thinks no evil**; [6] **does not rejoice in iniquity**, but **rejoices in the truth**; [7] bears all things, **believes all things**, hopes all things, endures all things. [8] **Love never fails**" (**1 Corinthians 13:4–8a**).

The Greek word for "love" in this entire passage is G26 *agape*. And "**Believing all things**" can only happen in a loving environment. In an agape loving relationship there is truth, honesty, and integrity, so we do not have to question anything but can "believe all things."

Thinking back to my near-death truth-and-love experience, perhaps the point in that experience of learning about the truth, which gave me an ill-boding feeling and the feeling that truth was in some way holding something bad for me, was like what God said in **Romans 1:22–26b**: "**Professing to be wise, they became fools**, and changed the glory of the incorruptible God into an **image made like corruptible man** – and birds and four footed animals and creeping things. Therefore God also gave them up to uncleanness, in the lusts of their hearts, to dishonor their bodies among themselves, **who exchanged the truth of God for the lie**, and worshiped and served the creature rather than the Creator,"

Then the verses from the above passage in **Romans 5:8–9**: "But God **demonstrates His own love** toward us, in that **while we were still sinners, Christ died for us.** ⁹ Much more then, having now been **justified by His blood**, we shall be **saved from wrath** through Him," describing the amazing love and forgiveness that God still has for those who rejected Him and His truth must be like what God taught me about love that took away the ill-boding feeling that the truth had in store for me!

LOVE IS FORGIVENESS

Love Covers All Sin

> **Hatred stirs up strife**, But **love covers all sins. (Proverbs 10:12)**

He Who Is Forgiven Much Loves More

> Then one of the Pharisees asked Him to eat with him. And He went to the Pharisee's house, and sat down to eat. ³⁷ And behold, a woman in the city who was a sinner, when she knew that Jesus sat at the table in the Pharisee's house, brought an alabaster flask of fragrant oil, ³⁸ and stood at His feet behind Him weeping; and she began **to wash His feet with her tears**, and wiped them with the hair of her head; and she kissed His feet and anointed them with the fragrant oil. ³⁹ Now when the Pharisee who had invited Him saw this, he spoke to himself, saying, "This man, if He were a prophet, would know who and what manner of woman this is who is touching Him, for she is a sinner."
>
> ⁴⁰ **And Jesus answered and said to him**, "Simon, I have something to say to you." So he said, "Teacher, say it." ⁴¹ "There was a certain creditor who had two debtors. One owed five hundred denarii, and the other fifty. ⁴² And when they had

nothing with which to repay, he freely forgave them both. Tell Me, therefore, **which of them will love him more**?" [43] Simon answered and said, "**I suppose the one whom he forgave more**."

And He said to him, "**You have rightly judged**." [44] Then He turned to the woman and said to Simon, "Do you see this woman? I entered your house; you gave Me no water for My feet, but she has washed My feet with her tears and wiped them with the hair of her head. [45] You gave Me no kiss, but this woman has not ceased to kiss My feet since the time I came in. [46] You did not anoint My head with oil, but this woman has anointed My feet with fragrant oil.

[47] Therefore I say to you, **her sins, which are many, are forgiven, for she loved much. But to whom little is forgiven, the same loves little**." [48] Then He said to her, "**Your sins are forgiven**." [49] And those who sat at the table with Him began to say to themselves, "Who is this who even forgives sins?" [50] Then He said to the woman, "**Your faith has saved you**. Go in peace." (**Luke 7:36–50**)

This passage about the Pharisee, Jesus, and the woman is all about how those who are forgiven are the ones who love, but it is also true that because she loves, her sins are forgiven. And we cannot be forgiven our sin if we do not acknowledge we have sin that needs to be forgiven; nor will we recognize the great love of Jesus, who was willing to die for our sins, "If we **say that we have no sin**, we **deceive** ourselves, and **the truth is not in us**. [9] If we confess our sins, He is faithful and just to forgive us *our* sins and to cleanse us from all unrighteousness. [10] **If we say that we have not sinned, we make Him a liar**, and His word is not in us" (**1 John 1:8–10**). Jesus had this to say about forgiveness right after He taught us the Lord's Prayer: "For **if you forgive men their trespasses**, your heavenly Father **will also forgive you**. [15] But **if you do not forgive men their trespasses, neither will your Father forgive your trespasses**" (**Matthew 6:14–15**).

The Pharisee thought he was righteous under the law and did not acknowledge that he had any sin, but he was quick to point out the sins of others and even made the judgment that Jesus could not be a prophet because He was associating with this woman. All those who are on this earth have **"exchanged the truth of God for the lie**, and worshiped and **served the creature** rather than the Creator, who is blessed forever. Amen" (**Romans 1:25**).

"As it is written: '**There is none righteous**, **no**, **not one**; [11] There is **none who understands**; There is none **who seeks after God**. [12] They have all turned aside; They have **together** become unprofitable; There is none who does good, **no**, **not one**'" (**Romans 3:10–12**). So the prostitute walked away with her sins forgiven and the religious leader left with his sins intact and in his mind made Jesus a liar.

Jesus could not have "purchased" us by dying on the cross. If that were so, He would have taken us all home as His property. Buying and selling slaves is a worldly idea. God is a god of love, and as we will learn later in this branch, the economy of heaven is based on agape love. Love is a free-will thing, and it cannot be forced. Jesus had to win our love by first loving us. **"We love Him** because **He first loved us"** (**1 John 4:19**).

Jesus offers a loving relationship to us by dying on the cross for us, but it takes two to have a loving relationship. We have to accept His offer of a loving relationship and love Him and all others in return. It has to be true love, because God can see into the hearts of men. And true love only comes by knowing and understanding the truth of who God is and that love for God above all and loving our neighbors as ourselves makes for peace, power, prosperity, joy inexpressible, and eternal life.

THE TWO DIFFERENT KINDS OF LOVE OF JESUS AND PETER

Notice the two different kinds of love in this exchange between Jesus and Peter:

> So when they had eaten breakfast, Jesus said to Simon Peter, "Simon, *son* of Jonah, **do you love Me more than these?**"

He said to Him, "Yes, Lord; You know that **I love You**." He said to him, "Feed My lambs." [16] He said to him again a second time, "Simon, *son* of Jonah, **do you love Me**?" He said to Him, "Yes, Lord; You know that **I love You**." He said to him, "Tend My sheep." [17] He said to him the third time, "Simon, *son* of Jonah, **do you love Me**?" Peter was grieved because He said to him the third time, "**Do you love Me**?" And he said to Him, "Lord, You know all things; You know that **I love You**." Jesus said to him, "Feed My sheep. [18] Most assuredly, I say to you, when you were younger, you girded yourself and walked where you wished; but when you are old, **you will stretch out your hands**, and **another will gird you** and **carry *you* where you do not wish**." [19] This He spoke, signifying by what death he would glorify God. And when He had spoken this, He said to him, "Follow Me." (**John 21:15–19**)

This passage takes place after Jesus was crucified and had risen, when Peter said, "I am going fishing," and the others said, "We are going with you also" (**John 21:3**). Fishing was Peter's profession when Jesus first met him and called him and his brother to be "fishers of men." (See **Matthew 4:19**.) When Jesus asked Peter if he loved Him "more than these," perhaps Jesus was referring to the fish Peter had just caught and was asking Peter if he still wanted to follow Him or go back to his old way of life, but it may refer to the other disciples because of what Peter had said earlier, or it may be referring to both.

When Jesus asked Peter if he loved Him three times, perhaps He was giving Peter a chance to recommit his life to Jesus after having denied Him three times, but I also think Jesus was trying to humble Peter's pride because of what Peter said in an earlier event just before Jesus died.

> Then Jesus said to them, "**All** of you will be **made to stumble** because of Me this night, **for it is written**: '*I will strike the Shepherd, And the sheep of the flock will be scattered.*' [32] But after I have been raised, I will go before you to Galilee."
>
> [33] Peter answered and said to Him, "Even **if all are made to stumble** because of You, **I will never be made to stumble**." [34] Jesus said to him, "Assuredly, I say to you that this night, **before the rooster crows, you will deny Me three times**."

> ³⁵ Peter said to Him, "**Even if I have to die with You, I will not deny You!**" And so said all the disciples. (**Matthew 26:31**)

And indeed Peter did deny Jesus three times, which is described in **Matthew 26:69–75**.

There is an interesting interchange between Jesus and Peter that we do not see because the two different Greek words for love are translated into the one English word "love," and this is what we are missing. In the first two questions to Peter, Jesus used the Greek word G25 *agapao* for "love"; indicating love in the sense of a social, moral, community, or "many committed to each other as one," while Peter answered using the Greek word G5368 *phileo,* which indicates the fondness of a friend.

In the first two questions Jesus is reminding Peter how he had boasted that he would die for Jesus even if the other disciples would not, but Peter did not understand everything he thought he did, and when it came right down to it, he could not die for Jesus. And so Peter could not say that he had the sacrificial love for Christ that he thought he had. In the last question to Peter, Jesus also uses the Greek word *phileo*, knowing that Peter had been humbled enough and that it was now time to start building him back up.

Then Jesus, knowing that Peter was weak in the flesh and knowing that Peter would have the courage to die for Him when he received strength and courage from the Holy Spirit, acknowledged to Peter that he would die for Him and gave him a description of his death that sounds much like crucifixion: "But when you are old, **you will stretch out your hands**, and **another will gird you** and **carry *you* where you do not wish**." After this, to let Peter know that Jesus had forgiven him and accepted him as one in Him, He repeated what He had said to Peter when they first met: "**Follow Me.**"

Later, just before Jesus was taken up to heaven, He said to His disciples, "Behold, I send the **Promise of My Father** upon you; but tarry in the city of Jerusalem until you are **endued with power from on high**" (**Luke 24:49**). And so Peter, when he was filled with the Holy Spirit and understood the truth of why Jesus had to die, was able to die for his Lord and Savior, and he demonstrated his unconditional, sacrificial *agape* love for Him. Peter also learned what the apostle Paul experienced—that alone he could do nothing but that he could "**do all things through Christ who strengthens [him]**" (**Philippians 4:13**).

The sacrificial agape love is what Jesus has required of all of His disciples. "This is My commandment, that **you love one another** as **I have loved you**. [13] **Greater love has no one than this**, than to **lay down one's life for his friends**. [14] You are My friends if you do whatever I command you" (**John 15:12–14**).

And Paul teaches us by saying,

> "I beseech you, therefore, brethren, by the mercies of God, that you **present your bodies a living sacrifice**, holy, acceptable to God, *which is* **your reasonable service**. [2] And do not be conformed **to this world**, but be **transformed** by the **renewing of your mind**, that you may **prove** what *is* that **good** and **acceptable** and **perfect will of God**. [3] For I say, through the grace given to me, to everyone who is among you, **not to think** *of himself* **more highly than he ought to think**, but to think **soberly**, as God has dealt to each one a **measure of faith**. [4] For as we have **many members** in **one body**, but all the members do not have the same function, [5] so **we**, *being* **many**, are **one body in Christ**, and **individually members of one another**." (**Romans 12:1–4**)

Jesus then says to his disciples, "If anyone desires to come after Me, let him **deny himself**, and **take up his cross**, and **follow Me**. [25] For whoever **desires to save his life will lose it**, but whoever **loses his life for My sake will find it**. [26] For what profit is it to a man **if he gains the whole world**, and **loses his own soul**? Or **what will a man give** in exchange for **his soul**?" (**Matthew 16:24–26**).

Dying to this life of living by the ways of the world, and committing your life to Christ may seem like a hard thing to do until we understand that this life is not all there is and that it is not the main event. All of us on earth are spirits living in a temporary body of flesh, and our bodies will die one day, without exception, but our spirits will live on forever. The importance of this life on earth is that it is our one and only chance to change our hearts and minds and turn from the evil ways of Satan, which will lead to a second spiritual death, and to believe the ways of God, which will lead to eternal spiritual life, as God said from the beginning: "**I call heaven and earth as witnesses today against you**, *that* **I have set before you life and death, blessing and cursing**; therefore **choose life**, that **both you and your descendants may live**; [20] that you may **love the LORD your God**, that you may obey His voice, and that you may **cling to Him**, for **He *is* your life and the length of your days**; and that you may dwell in the land which the LORD swore to your fathers, to Abraham, Isaac, and Jacob, to give them" (**Deuteronomy 30:19–20**).

There is a lot more in these passages about *agape* love than meets the eye (e.g., being one body in Christ, choosing between life and death), but we will understand a deeper meaning as we learn the truth in "The Oneness Branch" and "The Tree of Life" chapter. And when we learn and understand the truth that Jesus came into this world to share with us, we will say what Peter said when others who did not understand turned away: "Then Jesus said to the twelve, 'Do you also want to go away?' [68] But Simon Peter answered Him, '**Lord, to whom shall we go? You have the words of eternal life.** [69] Also we have **come to believe** and know that You are **the Christ**, the **Son of the living God**'" (**John 6:67–69**). Neither will we be able to turn away from the living God once we know the truth.

THEN THERE IS THE WORLD'S DEFINITION OF LOVE OBTAINED BY SCIENCE

I once knew a much schooled and learned counselor who defined love as "total selfishness," and I remember thinking that this was exactly opposite to what the Bible says. Then, after thinking about it for a while, I concluded that he was a social scientist and that when one looks around the world, selfishness is exactly what one sees. The way in which fallen man loves others is "total selfishness," but that does not mean it is the right way to love.

I also remember reading a sociology book in college that talked about the trade-off that happens when we choose a mate. A man might not be handsome, but he might be rich; a woman might not be rich or educated, but she might be beautiful. And all the qualities of personality, humor, fame, power, social position, etc., come into play as each tries to get the best "deal" for what he or she has to offer.

Webster's Student Dictionary defines "science" as "Accumulated systematized **knowledge**, especially as it relates to **the physical world** – called also **natural** science" and defines "naturalism" as "1. Action, inclination, or thought based on natural desires and instincts **alone**. 2. Any **doctrine** that **denies a supernatural explanation** of origin, development, or end of the universe and holds that **scientific laws accounts for everything in nature**."

So science, by definition, excludes the spiritual realm and only considers the things of this world. But since Satan is the ruler of this world, we can only learn of his lies. And if we do not understand that there is a trial going on in heaven and carried out on this temporary earth to see who will seek the truth of God and learn and understand the truth and turn from their ways and be saved for eternal life, then we will perish with Satan. "In this **the children of God** and **the children of the devil** are manifest: Whoever **does not practice righteousness is not of God**, nor *is* **he who does not love his brother**" (1 John 3:10).

That there is a reality outside of the grasp of this world's science is just what Jesus said to Nicodemus:

> "That which is **born of the flesh** is flesh, and that which is **born of the Spirit** is spirit. [7] Do not marvel that I said to you, 'You must be **born again**.' [8] The **wind** blows where it wishes, and you hear the sound of it, but cannot tell where it comes from and where it goes. **So is everyone who is born of the Spirit**" ... Jesus answered and said to him, "Are you the teacher of Israel, and **do not know these things**? ... If I have **told you earthly**

things and **you do not believe**, how will you believe if I **tell you heavenly things?**" (**John 3:6–8, 10, 12**)

Thousands of years ago the apostle Paul, in a letter to Timothy, warned about the limitations of science and bad science done with ulterior motives: "O Timothy, keep that which is committed to thy trust, **avoiding profane** *and* **vain babblings**, and oppositions of **science falsely so called**: [21] Which some professing have erred concerning the faith. Grace *be* with thee. Amen" (**1 Timothy 6:20–21 KJV**).

But the Word of God Teaches a Love That Is Different from That of the World

> And if you do good to those who do good to you, what credit is that to you? For even **sinners do the same**. [34] And if you lend to those from whom you hope to receive back, what credit is that to you? For even sinners lend to sinners to receive as much back. [35] But **love your enemies, do good**, and **lend, hoping for nothing in return**; and **your reward will be great**, and you will be **sons of the Most High**. For He is kind to the unthankful and evil. [36] Therefore **be merciful**, just as your Father also is merciful. (**Luke 6:33–36**)

Walk in Truth and Love

> I rejoiced greatly that I have found some of your children **walking in truth**, as we received commandment from the Father. [5] And now I plead with you, lady, **not as though I wrote a new commandment to you**, but that which we have had **from the beginning: that we love one another.** [6] **This is love**, that **we walk according to His commandments**. This is **the commandment**, that as you have heard **from the beginning**, you should walk in it. (**2 John 1:4–6**)

The commandment they heard from the beginning was, "Hear, O Israel: The LORD our God, **the LORD** *is* **one!** [5] **You shall love the LORD your God** with all your **heart**, with all your **soul**, and with all your **strength**. [6] And **these words which I command you today**

shall be in your heart" (**Deuteronomy 6:4–6**). And we learned that the reason they could not love was that they did not understand the ways of God, because they thought they were foolishness. "But the **natural man** does not receive the things of the Spirit of God, for **they are foolishness to him**; nor can he know *them,* because they are **spiritually discerned**" (**1 Corinthians 2:14**).

The word "soul" in the phrase "with all your **soul**" comes from the Hebrew H5315 *nephesh*, which includes all aspects of the human being, including the "**bodily** and **mental**" senses. The soul is made up of the spirit, which possess the intellect and emotions combined with the body of flesh. "And the LORD God **formed** man *of* **the dust of the ground,** and breathed into his nostrils the **breath of life**; and man became a living **soul**" (**Genesis 2:7 KJV**).

The Hebrew word for "breath" is H5397 *neshamah*, which, among other things, means "**wind, divine inspiration, intellect**, and **spirit**." So man, or *adam* in the Hebrew, was "**formed**" by God taking dust of the earth and making a body of flesh and combining it with our spirit, in which is our mind and intellect. Remember that "wind" is the word that Jesus used to help Nicodemus understand what those "**born of the Spirit**" were like in **John 3:8**.

Jesus is not teaching anything new. God has told us from the beginning that it is because God is one that we should love Him and one another. Here we are taught that love is necessary for oneness. These words are important, and they are a key to eternal life, which we will see and fully understand in future branches. It is important to remember that in Jesus' time, there was no New Testament. Jesus explained the meaning of what God said in the Old Testament, and those teachings became the New Testament.

Truth and Love Saves

"But none of these things move me; **nor do I count my life dear to myself**, so that I may finish my race with **joy**, and the **ministry** which I **received from the Lord Jesus**, to **testify** to the **gospel** of the **grace** of God. [25] And indeed, now I know that you all, among whom I have gone preaching **the kingdom of God**, will see my face no more" (**Acts 20:24–25**). And so the apostle Paul gave his life to share the truth that will save the life of millions through the generations. And as we learned, laying down one's life for the life of others is the greatest form of love. "Greater **love** has no one than this, than **to lay down one's life for his friends**" (**John 15:13**).

The word "gospel" is translated from the Greek word G2098 *euaggelion*, which means "good message." One of *Webster's Student Dictionary* definitions of "gospel," besides "good news," is "something accepted as **infallible truth** or as a **guiding principle**." The guiding principle for the economy of the kingdom of God is love; so the gospel, simply put, is the good news that Jesus came into this world to witness of—the truth that *agape* love of God and our brothers and sisters will make us free from the bondage of this world under Satan, the ruler of this world. And we will see how love makes for the most prosperous and powerful economy later in this branch.

LOVE IS ABOVE ALL AND GREATER THAN ALL

Love Is Above Speaking in Tongues and Understanding All Knowledge

Though I speak with the **tongues of men and of angels**, but have not love, I have become sounding brass or a clanging cymbal. [2] And though I have the gift of **prophecy**, and **understand all mysteries** and **all knowledge**, and though I have **all faith**, so that I could remove mountains, but **have not love, I am nothing**. [3] And though I bestow all my goods to feed the poor, and though I give my body to be burned, but **have not love**, it **profits me nothing**.

> [4] Love suffers long and is kind; love does not envy; love does not parade itself, is not puffed up; [5] does not behave rudely, does not seek its own, is not provoked, thinks no evil; [6] does not rejoice in iniquity, but rejoices in the truth; [7] bears all things, believes all things, hopes all things, endures all things"

"Love never fails. But whether *there are* prophecies, they will fail; whether *there are* tongues, they will cease; whether *there is* knowledge, it will vanish away. [9] For we know in part and we prophesy in part. [10] But when that which is perfect has come, then that which is in part will be done away. (**1 Corinthians 13:1–10**)

Love Is Greater Than Faith and Hope

When I was a child, I spoke as a child, **I understood as a child, I thought as a child**; but when I became a man, I put away childish things. [12] For now we see in a mirror, **dimly**, but then **face-to-face**. Now **I know in part**, but then I shall **know just as I also am known**. [13] And now abide **faith, hope, love**, these three; but **the greatest of these is love**. (**1 Corinthians 13:11–13**)

Love Is Greater Than Knowledge

Now concerning things offered to idols: We know that we all have knowledge. **Knowledge puffs up**, but **love edifies**. [2] And if anyone **thinks that he knows anything**, he knows nothing yet as he ought to know. [3] **But if anyone loves God, this one is known by Him**. (**1 Corinthians 8:1–3**)

Our knowledge should lead us to love; if it does not, it is useless. Love is the end and goal of our knowledge and faith!

Love Is in All

Let **all that you do** be done with **love**. (**1 Corinthians 16:14**)

In all these verses above, the word translated as "love" comes from the Greek word G26 *agape*, which is the unconditional, sacrificial love of the kingdom of God.

Loving the Lord Jesus Christ Saves Us from the Curse of Death

> If anyone does not love the Lord Jesus Christ, **let him be accursed**. (**1 Corinthians 16:22**)

Webster's Student Dictionary defines "accursed" as "Being under or as if under a curse." Being accursed is not something that the apostle Paul wishes on someone or for someone. Being accursed is something we have already done to ourselves, not something done to us. "For God did not send His Son into the world to condemn the world, but that the world through Him might be saved. [18] He who believes in Him is not condemned; **but he who does not believe is condemned already, because he has not believed in the name of the only begotten Son of God**" (**John 3:17–18**).

All of us on earth are already accursed because of our fall from the grace of God. Paul is doing everything he can to provide everyone the truth that will set them free from the curse, but if people arrogantly, angrily, and violently refuse to listen to him and learn the truth of God, they will remain accursed, believing the lies of Satan.

LOVE DETERMINES WHOM WE WILL BELONG TO—JESUS OR SATAN

Love and Righteousness

> In this the **children of God** and the **children of the devil** are manifest [made known]: Whoever **does not practice righteousness** is not of God, nor is he who **does not love his brother**. [11] For this is the message that you heard from the beginning, that we should **love one another**, [12] not as Cain who was **of the wicked one** and **murdered his brother**. And why did he murder him? Because **his works were evil** and **his brother's righteous**. (**1 John 3:10–12**)

The criterion for being a son or daughter of God is to love and to practice righteousness. That does not mean that we will never sin while we are still living in this world of sin, but it means that our hearts and minds desire not to sin but do what is right and that we are actively trying to make that happen. Practicing, in this context, means trying to get better at actually doing what our heart and mind want to do, for our flesh is weak. "Watch and pray, lest you enter into temptation. The **spirit indeed *is* willing**, but the **flesh *is* weak**" (**Matthew 26:41**).

"Beloved, let us love one another, for **love is of God**; and **everyone who loves** is **born of God** and **knows God**. [8] He who **does not love does not know God**, for **God is love**" (**1 John 4:7–8**). Notice that the criterion for being "born of God" is being a person who loves.

Everyone who loves is born of God and knows God. When we fell from the grace of God in heaven, we did so because we rejected God and His truth and His love and we were born of the flesh. When we love God and love our brothers and sisters as much as much as we love ourselves, we are born of God again. If we submit our lives to God and serve God, it has to be by our choice, out of knowing and understanding that His ways are the best way for us and everyone else to live. Love is, by definition, of a free-will choice, because you cannot force anyone to love you.

Love

> For the kingdom of God **is not a matter of talk** but of **power**. [21] What do you prefer? Shall I come to you **with a whip**, or **in love** and **with a gentle spirit**? (**1 Corinthians 4:20–21**)

The power of the kingdom of God exists through the spiritual power of love and gentleness, which promotes unity, peace, productivity, and prosperity; not by power of physical force of the whip or the gun, which promotes division, decay, and death. But the kingdom of God will use its power to protect those who desire to live in love and peace from those who do not. Paul wants the Corinthians and us to recognize the difference. This is the difference of how Jesus and Satan rule and reign.

What Manner of Love

Behold what manner of **love** the Father has **bestowed on us,** that we should be called children of God! (**1 John 3:1**)

God Is Love

And we have **known** and **believed** the **love** that God has for us. **God is love**, and he who abides in love **abides in God**, and **God in him**. (**1 John 4:16**)

Love Hates Evil

Let **love** be without hypocrisy. **Abhor what is evil. Cling to what is good.** [10] Be kindly affectionate to one another with **brotherly love**, in honor **giving preference to one another;** [11] not lagging in **diligence, fervent in spirit**, serving the Lord. (**Romans 12:9–11**)

The first word for "love" in this passage comes from the Greek word G26 *agape*, and the rest of the passage indicates to us that **brotherly love**, G5360 *phlidelphia,* along with "**honor giving preference to one another; not lagging in diligence, fervent in spirit, serving the Lord,**" is what *agape* love is.

LOVE MAKES US UNITED AS ONE

Love One Another

In this is love, **not that we loved God,** but that **He loved us** and sent His Son to be the **propitiation** for our sins. [11] Beloved, **if God so loved us**, we also ought **to love one another.** [12] No one has **seen God** at any time. **If we love one another, God abides in us**, and His **love has been perfected** in us. (**1 John 4:10–12**)

Oneness in Love in Him

> ... just as He **chose us in Him before the foundation of the world**, that we should be **holy** and **without blame** before Him **in love**, [5] having **predestined us** to **adoption as sons** by Jesus Christ to Himself, according to the good pleasure of His will, [6] to the praise of the glory of His grace, by which He has **made us accepted in the Beloved. (Ephesians 1:4–6)**

If we were chosen before the foundation of the world, does that not mean that there was some kind of judgment by God before He created the world? We will discover what "predestined us" and what "He chose us in Him **before the foundation of the world**" mean in future chapters.

We Are Made One in Love and in One Are Made Perfect

> I do not pray for these alone, but also for those who will believe in Me through their word; [21] that **they all may be one**, as You, Father, are in Me, and I in You; **that they also may be one in Us**, that the world may believe that You sent Me. [22] And the glory which You gave Me I have given them, that **they may be one** just as **We are one**: [23] I in them, and You in Me; that they may be **made perfect in one**, and that the world may know that You have sent Me, and **have loved them as You have loved Me.**
>
> [24] Father, I desire that they also whom You gave Me **may be with Me where I am**, that they may behold My glory which You have given Me; for **You loved Me before the foundation of the world.** [25] O righteous Father! **The world has not known You**, but I have known You; and these have known that You sent Me. [26] And I have declared to them Your name, and will declare it, that **the love with which You loved Me may be in them**, and **I in them. (John 17:20–26)**

It is curious to note as a mathematician that in set theory, if a set of objects **A** is in the set of objects **B** and the set of objects **B** is in the set of objects **A**, then the set **A** and set **B** are one and the same. Also, if a set of objects **A** is in the set of objects **B** and the set of objects **B** is in the set of objects **C**, then the set of objects **A** is in the set of objects **C**. Do the math!

The Truth Is That Love Makes Many One

"The Jews answered him, 'We have a law, and according to our law He ought to die, because He made Himself the Son of God'" (**John 19:7**). One of the problems the Jews had with Jesus is that they believed there was only one individual being called God, and Jesus claimed to be the Son of God. The Jews did not understand the Scripture "Hear, O Israel: The Lord our God, the Lord is **one!**" (**Deuteronomy 6:4–6**). The Hebrew word for "one" is H259 *echad*, which means "A numeral from H258; **properly united**, that is, one." The word *echad*, properly understood, means that God is many living in love that are united together as though they are one.

They did not know that Jesus is the Son of God and that believers in the Word of God are "gods" living under the rule and reign of the Son of God:

> "My Father, who has given *them* to Me, is **greater than all**; and no one is able to snatch *them* out of My Father's hand. [30] **I and My Father are one**." [31] Then the Jews took up stones again to stone Him. [32] Jesus answered them, "Many good works I have shown you from My Father. For which of those works do you stone Me?"
>
> [33] The Jews answered Him, saying, "For a good work we do not stone You, but for blasphemy, and because You, being a Man, make Yourself God." [34] Jesus answered them, "Is it not written in your law, *'I said, "You are gods"'*? [35] If **He called them gods, to whom the word of God came** (and **the Scripture cannot be broken**), [36] do you say of Him whom the Father sanctified and sent into the world, 'You are blaspheming,' because I said, 'I am the Son of God'?" (**John 10:29–38**)

This is an amazing statement by our Lord Jesus that those of us who understand and believe the Word of God are gods! We will go deeper into the meaning and understanding of this passage in "The Oneness Branch" and the chapter "The Beginning as Seen from Earth."

Love Saves Us from Eternal Death and Gives Us Eternal Life

The Saving Love of God

> For **God so loved the world** that He gave His only begotten Son, that whoever believes in Him should not perish but have **everlasting life**. [17] For God did not send His Son into the world to condemn the world, but that the world through Him **might be saved**. [18] **He who believes in Him is not condemned; but he who does not believe is condemned already**, because **he has not believed** in the name of the only begotten Son of God. (**John 3:16–18**)

Jesus did not come into this world—which is under the sway of the ruler of this world, Satan—to condemn us or even to judge, but to show us His love for us and to save us with an understanding of the truth. This world is already under condemnation of our own making by believing the lie of Satan as described above, "**but he who does not believe is condemned already**." And the apostle John confirms this reality in **1 John 5:18–20**: "We know that whoever is **born of God** does not sin; but he who has been **born of God** keeps himself, and **the wicked one does not touch him**. [19] We know that **we are of God**, and the **whole world lies *under the sway of* the wicked one**. [20] And we know that the Son of God has **come and has given us an understanding**, that we may **know Him who is true**; and **we are in Him who is true**, in His Son Jesus Christ. This is the **true God** and **eternal life**."

By Love We Pass from Death to Life

> Do not marvel, my brethren, if the world hates you. We know that we have **passed from death to life**, because **we love the brethren**. He who **does not love his brother** abides **in death**. [15] Whoever **hates his brother is a murderer**, and you know that no murderer has eternal life abiding in him. [16] **By this we**

149

know love, because **He laid down His life for us**. And we also ought to **lay down our lives for the brethren**. [17] But whoever has this world's goods, and sees his brother in need, and shuts up his heart from him, **how does the love of God abide in him?** [18] My little children, let us not **love** in word or in tongue, but **in deed and in truth**. [19] And by this we know that we are **of the truth**, and shall **assure our hearts before Him. (1 John 3:13–19)**

Here the apostle John reveals that the ways of God that lead to eternal life are love, and he also explains the reason the ways of Satan lead to death. Satan rules over those who desire what is best for themselves and, by his greater power, forces everyone to do what he desires. God, on the other hand, rules over those whose desire is to do what is best for all others. With Satan there is division and strife, while with God there is unity and peace. When we express our love by the things we do, we know that we are "**of the truth**."

Love One Another with a Pure Heart

Since you have purified **your souls** in **obeying the truth** through **the Spirit** in sincere **love** of the **brethren, love one another fervently** with a **pure heart**, [23] having been **born again**, not of corruptible **seed** but incorruptible, **through the word of God** which **lives and abides forever. (1 Peter 1:22)**

Understanding and obeying the truth that the Spirit reveals to us is what purifies our hearts and minds and enables us to "**love one another**," and **love enables us to understand** and "**obey the truth**." This is a not a vicious circle, but a righteous circle of truth and love that leads to eternal life. When we understand the truth of how *agape* love leads us to peace, prosperity, inexpressible joy, and life everlasting, we will want to do what is right and true.

Made Perfect in Love

Love has been **perfected** among us in this: that we may have boldness in the **day of judgment**; because as He is, so are we in this world. [18] There **is no fear in love**; but **perfect love casts**

out fear, because **fear involves torment**. But **he who fears has not been made perfect in love**. [19] **We love Him** because **He first loved us**. [20] If someone says, "**I love God**," and hates his brother, he is a liar; for **he who does not love his brother** whom he has seen, how can **he love God whom he has not seen**? [21] And this commandment we have from Him: that **he who loves God must love his brother also**. (**1 John 4:17–21**)

If we fear, we are not trusting in God. Love requires trust. That we love God and not others is not love. God is holding all the cards. God has everything, and we have nothing without Him. "I am the vine, you *are* the branches. He who abides in Me, and I in him, bears much fruit; for **without Me you can do nothing**" (**John 15:5**). True love is the desire to enter into a relationship with someone for reasons other than that we can profit from the relationship for our own selfish interests, but that we can be enriched by a relationship in which all benefit by the synergism in an "all for one and one for all" commitment. True love is the desire for a relationship in which we ask what we can do for others, not what others can do for us. In this John Kennedy had it right.

The Love of Christ Compels Us to Become a New Creation

For the **love of Christ compels us**, because we judge thus: that if One died for all, then all died; [15] and He died for all, that those who live should **live no longer for themselves**, but for **Him who died for them** and **rose again**. [16] Therefore, from now on, we regard no one according to the flesh. Even though we have known Christ according to the flesh, yet now we know Him thus no longer. [17] Therefore, **if anyone is in Christ, he is a new creation**; old things have passed away; behold, all things have become new. (**2 Corinthians 5:14–17**)

We were a new creation when we fell from the grace of God by believing the lies of Satan and were born of Satan and were born in the image of fallen Adam, "and Adam lived one hundred and thirty years, and begot *a son* **in his own likeness, after his image**, and named him Seth" (**Genesis 5:3**).

We are a new creation and are born again in the image of God when we believe the truth of God and are set free from the lies that bind us to Satan. "So God **created** man **in His** *own* image; in the **image of God** He created him; male and female He created them ... And the LORD God formed man *of* the dust of the ground, and breathed into his nostrils the **breath of life**; and **man became a living being**" (**Genesis 1:27; 2:7**). We will learn the different meanings of the Hebrew word *"Adam"* and how it is possible to be born of flesh in the image of fallen Adam and then created in the image of God when we get to the chapters "The Meaning and Purpose of Life on Earth" and "The Beginning as Seen from Earth."

The Love of the Truth Saves Us

Let no one deceive you by any means; for *that Day* will not come unless the falling away comes first, and the **man of sin** is revealed, the **son of perdition**, [4] who opposes and exalts himself above **all that is called God** or that is worshiped, so that he **sits as God in the temple of God**, showing **himself** that he is God. [5] Do you not remember that when I was still with you I told you these things? [6] And now you **know what is restraining**, that he may be revealed in his own time. [7] For the mystery of lawlessness is already at work; **only He who now restrains** *will do so* **until He is taken out of the way**. [8] And then the **lawless one will be revealed**, whom the Lord will consume with the breath of His mouth and destroy with the brightness of His coming.

[9] The coming of the *lawless one* is according to the working of Satan, with all power, signs, and lying wonders, [10] and with **all unrighteous deception among those who perish**, because they **did not receive** the **love of the truth**, that **they might be saved**. [11] And for this reason God will send them strong delusion, that they should **believe the lie**, [12] that they **all may be condemned who did not believe the truth** but had **pleasure in unrighteousness**. [13] But we are bound to give thanks to God always for you, brethren beloved by the Lord, because **God from the beginning chose you for salvation** through sanctification **by the Spirit** and **belief in the truth**,

¹⁴ to which **He called you** by **our gospel**, for the obtaining of the glory of our Lord Jesus Christ. (**2 Thessalonians 2:3–14**)

Notice that this passage says that the "**love of the truth**" saves us, not just the knowledge of the truth of God, as James says about about merely having the belief of God but not loving God: "You **believe** that there is one God. You do well. **Even the demons believe–and tremble!**" (**James 2:19**)

There is a lot of teaching in this passage from Paul's second letter to the Thessalonians, such as the reference to *"that Day"*; the second coming of Jesus to earth; the "**son of perdition**," who is the Antichrist, the counterfeit version of Christ belonging to Satan who pretends He is God; the rapture of the church when God takes those who belong to Him "**out of the way**" before the coming of the Antichrist; the great tribulation; and the reference to the elect of God, whom God **chose from the beginning**! And we will learn and understand all these mysteries in future chapters.

WE LIVE BY LOVE, NOT BY POWER, MIGHT, AND CONTROL

In that hour Jesus rejoiced in the Spirit and said, "I thank You, Father, Lord of heaven and earth, that You have **hidden these things from** *the* **wise** and prudent and **revealed them to babes**. Even so, Father, for so it seemed good in Your sight. ²² All things have been delivered to Me by My Father, and no one knows who the Son is except the Father, and who the Father is except the Son, and *the one* to whom the Son wills to reveal *Him*." ²³ Then He turned to *His* disciples and said privately, "Blessed *are* the eyes which **see the things you see**; ²⁴ for I tell you that **many prophets** and **kings** have **desired to see what you see**, and **have not seen** *it,* and to **hear what you hear**, and **have not heard** *it*."

²⁵ And behold, a certain lawyer stood up and **tested** Him, saying, "Teacher, what shall I do to inherit **eternal life**?" ²⁶ He said to him, "**What is written in the law**? **What is your reading**

of it?" [27] So he answered and said, "'**You shall love the Lord your God with all your heart**, with **all your soul**, with all your **strength**, and with **all your mind**,' and '**your neighbor as yourself**.'" [28] And He said to him, "**You have answered rightly; do this and you will live.**" [29] But he, wanting to **justify himself**, said to Jesus, "And **who is my neighbor?**" **(Luke 10:21–29)**.

First notice that this lawyer must have been listening to the teachings of Jesus, because the Old Testament verse, which was the only Scripture of that day, does not contain loving the Lord your God "**with all your mind**" but rather reads, "Hear, O Israel: The LORD our God, **the LORD is one!** [5] You shall **love the LORD your God** with **all your heart**, with **all your soul**, and with all **your strength**" (**Deuteronomy 6:4–5**).

For example, when Jesus was asked by a scribe what the first commandment was, Jesus added "**with all your mind**" to the Deuteronomy passage, as we see in **Mark 12:29–31**: "Jesus answered him, 'The first of all the commandments *is:* "*Hear, O Israel, the* LORD *our God, the* LORD *is one.* [30] *And you shall love the* LORD *your God with all your heart, with all your soul, with all your mind, and with all your strength.*" This *is* the **first commandment.** [31] And **the second**, like *it, is* this: "*You shall love your neighbor as yourself.*" There is no other commandment greater than these.'"

This lawyer had a correct understanding of the law, that loving God above all and loving your neighbor as you love yourself fulfills the requirements of the law. But wanting to be able to keep this commandment to show *himself* righteous, while knowing he could not keep this commandment if the definition of "neighbor" was too large, he asked Jesus to define "neighbor." Jesus answered with the parable of the good Samaritan, which says that we are to love *everyone* as ourselves. (See **Luke 10:30–37**.) Notice that Jesus adds "love your enemies" in **Luke 6:27**: "But I say to you who hear: **Love your enemies, do good** to those **who hate you**, [28] **bless those** who **curse you**, and **pray for those** who **spitefully use you**."

But also notice that the second greatest commandment in the Old Testament is, "You shall **not take vengeance, nor bear any grudge** against **the children of** *your people*, but you shall **love your neighbor as yourself**: I *am* the LORD" (**Leviticus 19:18**).

So the question we might ask is, did Jesus broaden the definition of "neighbor"? The Old Testament passage, because it speaks of "**the children of** *your people*," makes it sound as though that is who your neighbors are; whereas Jesus in the New Testament says to love even your enemies. "**You have heard** that it was said, '*You shall love your neighbor* and **hate your enemy**.' ⁴⁴ But **I say to you, love your enemies, bless those who curse you, do good to those who hate you**, and **pray for those who spitefully use you** and **persecute you**, ⁴⁵ that *you may be* **sons of your Father** in heaven" (**Matthew 5:44–45a**). And the gospel of Luke adds, "But **love your enemies**, do good, and lend, **hoping for nothing in return**; and your reward will be great, and you will be **sons of the Most High**. For **He is kind** to the **unthankful** and **evil**" (**Luke 6:34**).

Here Jesus is saying that they have heard it said, "*You shall love your neighbor* and **hate your enemy**." Where would His audience have heard that or learned that from? "You shall hate your enemy" is not found anywhere in the Bible except, of course, in this verse that Jesus is speaking. This saying is contrary to God's teaching and the ways of the kingdom of God. So where would that teaching have come from?

We have already learned that Jesus added "with all your mind" to **Deuteronomy 6:5,** which says, "You shall **love the LORD your God** with **all your heart**, with **all your soul**, and with all **your strength**." We will see many changes as we go from the Old Testament to the New Testament even though God says, "For **I** *am* **the LORD, I do not change**; Therefore you are not consumed, O sons of Jacob" (**Malachi 3:6**). In the chapters concerning the three ages, the three periods of time separated by four hundred years during which God is silent, we will learn why the Old Testament seems so harsh compared to the New Testament. But always remember, *God does not change.*

This teaching, "***You shall love your neighbor*** and **hate your enemy**," was part of the ways of Satan, who, being more powerful than we are, was trying to build a kingdom based on the ways of living by power, might, and force; the ways that are contrary to God's ways of love. As we will learn, from the beginning we all heard and believed Satan's lie that "**You will not surely die ... you will be like God**," meaning that we all could be in charge of our own lives like God, and it caused us to fall from the grace of God. It is important to know that the Word of God is teaching us about two opposite ways of living; one leads to eternal life and one leads to eternal death. And between these two ways of living we all must choose (**Deuteronomy 30:15–20; Genesis 15:5–7; Hebrews 11:12–16**).

The Law Was Never Meant to Keep Us from Doing Good

> Now it happened on another Sabbath, also, that He entered the synagogue and taught. And a man was there whose right hand was withered. [7] So the scribes and Pharisees watched Him closely, whether He would heal on the Sabbath, that they might find an accusation against Him. [8] But **He knew their thoughts**, and said to the man who had the withered hand, "Arise and stand here." And he arose and stood.
>
> [9] Then Jesus said to them, "I will ask you one thing: **Is it lawful on the Sabbath to do good** or to **do evil, to save life or to destroy**?" [10] And when He had looked around at them all, He said to the man, "Stretch out your hand." And he did so, and his hand was restored as whole as the other. [11] But **they were filled with rage**, and **discussed with one another what they might do to Jesus**. (**Luke 6:6–11**)

Jesus was trying to show them that the law was meant to keep them from doing wrong, not to prevent them from them from doing good. When God gave the law to Moses to write, these laws were not to be the end of all what is good, but an example with the goal of doing good in mind. "Then the LORD said to Moses, "Write these words, for **according to the tenor of these words** I have made a covenant with you and with Israel." (**Exodus 34:27**). Using the law to do what is good and right is doing something "in the spirit of the law." Heartlessly using the law to do what is senseless, bad, and wrong is doing something "in the letter of the law."

The apostle Paul expressed a similar idea as he was speaking to the Corinthians about needing a letter (epistle) of commendation, written in ink on paper, as the Jews did to show that they were *bona fide* teachers of the law of God

> Do we **begin again to commend ourselves**? Or do we need, as some *others,* epistles of commendation to you or *letters* **of commendation from you**? ² You are our epistle **written in our hearts**, known and read by all men; ³ clearly *you are* **an epistle of Christ**, ministered by us, written not **with ink** but by **the Spirit of the living God**, not on **tablets of stone** but on **tablets of flesh**, *that is,* **of the heart.**
>
> ⁴ And we have such trust through Christ toward God. ⁵ Not that we are sufficient of ourselves to think of anything as *being* from ourselves, but **our sufficiency** *is* **from God**, ⁶ who also made us sufficient as ministers of the **new covenant, not of the letter** but **of the Spirit**; for the **letter kills**, but the **Spirit gives life.** (**2 Corinthians 3:1–6**)

Paul's letter of commendation that he and those with him were teachers of the New Covenant was evidenced by the changed hearts and lives of the Corinthians whom they taught.

The Sabbath Was a Gift of Love to Free Us, Not a Law to Enslave Us

> Now it happened that He went through the grain fields on the Sabbath; and as they went His disciples began to pluck the heads of grain. ²⁴ And the Pharisees said to Him, "Look, **why do they do what is not lawful on the Sabbath?**" ²⁵ But He said to them, "Have you never read what David did when **he was in need and hungry,** he and those with him: ²⁶ how he went into the house of God in the days of Abiathar the high priest, and ate the showbread, **which is not lawful**

157

to eat, except for the priests, and also gave some to those who were with him?" [27] And He said to them, "The **Sabbath was made for man**, and **not man for the Sabbath**. [28] Therefore the **Son of Man** is also **Lord of the Sabbath**." (**Mark 2:23–28**)

The issue here is not taking grain out of someone else's field as though stealing, for God had given a law stating that farmers were not to harvest every little bit from the field, but to leave some for the poor: "When you reap the harvest of your land, **you shall not wholly reap the corners of your field**, nor shall you **gather the gleanings of your harvest.** [10] And you shall not **glean your vineyard**, nor shall **you gather** *every* **grape of your vineyard**; you shall **leave them for the poor and the stranger**: I *am* the LORD your God" (**Leviticus 19:9–10**).

The issue of the Pharisees was that they were working to get something to eat on the Sabbath. But God had made the Sabbath day a blessing for man to rest from his work and be refreshed, having time to fellowship with God and remember that God made them and the heavens and earth, and to remember how God had rescued them from bondage in Egypt. "Therefore the children of Israel shall keep the Sabbath, to observe the Sabbath throughout their generations *as* a perpetual covenant. [17] **It** *is* **a sign** between Me and the children of Israel forever; for *in* six da**ys the LORD made the heavens and the earth**, and on the **seventh day He rested** and was refreshed" (**Exodus 31:16–17**).

And God's Word tells us that we should

> observe the Sabbath day, to keep it holy, as the LORD your God commanded you. [13] Six days you shall labor and do all your work, [14] but the seventh day *is* the Sabbath of the LORD your God. *In it* you shall do no work … that your male servant and your female servant may rest as well as you. [15] And **remember that you** were a **slave in the land of Egypt**, and the LORD **your God brought you out from there** by a **mighty hand** and by an **outstretched arm**; therefore the LORD your God commanded you to keep the Sabbath day. (**Deuteronomy 5:12–15**)

The Sabbath was a gift of mercy from a loving God, and the remembering "that **you were a slave in the land of Egypt**, and the LORD your **God brought you out from there by a mighty hand** and by an outstretched arm" was a "**sign**" given to man as foreshadowing of things to come that they and we might know that God would rescue us "**by a mighty hand**" from the slavery in this world under Satan, the ruler of this world. Satan is the ruler of this world who will be judged (**John 12:31; 14:30; 16:11**). But the Pharisees made the Sabbath to be a burden for men, and they were trying to tell the Son of God what the Sabbath was for, but Jesus said to them, "For the Son of Man **is Lord even of the Sabbath**" (**Matthew 12:8**). We will learn and understand in future chapters how rescuing His children from slavery was the purpose for which God created the heavens and the earth.

Hate This Life on Earth, Love Others and Gain Eternal Life in Heaven

Then He lifted up His eyes toward His disciples, and said: "Blessed are you poor, For yours is the kingdom of God. [21] Blessed are you who hunger now, For you shall be filled. **Blessed are you who weep now**, For **you shall laugh**. [22] Blessed are you when **men hate you**, And when they **exclude you**, And **revile you**, and **cast out your name as evil**, For the Son of Man's sake. [23] **Rejoice in that day** and leap for joy! For indeed **your reward is great in heaven**, For in like manner their fathers did to the prophets.

[24] "But **woe to you who are rich**, For you have received **your consolation**. [25] Woe to you who are full, For you shall hunger. Woe to you who laugh now, For you shall mourn and weep. [26] Woe to you when all men speak well of you, For so did their fathers to the false prophets. [27] "But I say to you who hear: **Love your enemies, do good to those who hate you**, [28] **bless those who curse you**, and **pray for those who spitefully use you**." (Luke 6:20–26)

Love Fulfills the Law

Owe no one anything except to love one another, for **he who loves another has fulfilled the law ...** [10] **Love does no**

harm to a neighbor; therefore **love** *is* **the fulfillment of the law.** (**Romans 13:8, 10**)

When we love God, we are also loving others as ourselves because we are all One with God, and those who believe are all *in* God. This commandment or law is easy to fulfill because it is the desire of our heart, and thus love fulfills the law. This is important and worth pondering for a while. A critical teaching of God is for people who have a heart and mind that do not want to be told what to do; when the law comes along and tells them what they must do, it stirs up in their heart the desire to do just the opposite. This is the heart and mind we all had when we fell from the grace of God by believing the lies of Satan. People no longer living by the law is another change in going from the Old Testament to the New Testament, when Jesus comes to us with knowledge, understanding, love, and a free-will choice.

The Great Commandments of Love Fulfill the Law and the Prophets

> Jesus said to him, "'**You shall love the LORD your God** *with all your heart, with all your soul, and with all your mind.*' [38] This is *the* first and **great commandment**. [39] And *the* second *is* like it: '*You shall love your neighbor as yourself.*' [40] On these two commandments **hang all the Law and the Prophets.**" (**Matthew 22:37–40**)

From Law to Love

> Previously saying, "Sacrifice and offering, burnt offerings, and offerings for sin **You did not desire, nor had pleasure in them**" (**which are offered according to the law**), [9] then He said, "Behold, I have come to do Your will, O God." **He takes away the first** that **He may establish the second**. [10] By that will we have been **sanctified** through the **offering** of the **body of Jesus Christ once for all**. (**Hebrews 10:8–10**)

From the beginning, God did not desire the law and the sacrifices it required, but He gave the law to teach them and us that alone as individuals they could not keep the law and they could not live by the law. Love, on the other hand, fulfills the requirements of the law.

Love Our Neighbors as Ourselves—Love Fulfills the Law

For the commandments, "You shall not commit adultery," "You shall not murder," "You shall not steal," "You shall not bear false witness," "You shall not covet," and if there is any other commandment, **are all summed up in this saying**, namely, "**You shall love your neighbor as yourself**. [10] Love does no harm to a neighbor; therefore love *is* the fulfillment of the law" (**Romans 13:9–10**).

Love must be a free-will choice, but the law is an obligation that must be adhered to whether you want to or not. How is it possible that love fulfills the law? When you want to do with all your heart that which the law says you must do whether you want to or not, the obligation becomes a moot point. You will do it out of love and fulfill the obligation. Love fulfills the Law.

From Law to Love

> The **Law and the Prophets** were proclaimed until **John**. Since that time, the **good news** of the **kingdom of God** is being preached, and everyone is forcing his way into it. [17] **It is easier for heaven** and **earth to disappear** than for **the least stroke of a pen to drop out of the Law.** (Luke 16:16–17)

The principles in the moral law are absolute truths that never change. The good news of the kingdom of God does not replace the law, as though the law is in error. It is the realization that fallen man with the heart of a lawbreaker cannot keep the law to be righteous that has to be learned. It is not the law that needs to change; it is we who need to change. It is our hearts and minds that need to change.

Fallen man had chosen to live in the ways of the prince of this world, Satan:

> "And you *He made alive,* **who were dead in trespasses and sins,** [2] in which **you once walked** according to the course of

this world, **according to the prince** of the **power of the air**, the **spirit who now works** in the **sons of disobedience**, [3] among whom also **we all once conducted ourselves** in the **lusts of our flesh**, fulfilling the **desires of the flesh** and of the mind, and **were by nature children of wrath, just as the others**." (Ephesians 2:1–3)

If we want to be Jesus' disciples, we have to change by having minds that understand the truth and hearts that love. "A **new commandment** I give to you, that you **love one another; as I have loved you**, that you also **love one another.** [35] By this **all will know that you are My disciples**, if you have **love for one another**" (**John 13:34**). For the pure of heart, the law is not needed. For the lawbreaker, the law cannot work.

TRIALS AND SUFFERING ARE GOD'S TOUGH LOVE

Being born again in the image of God is a lifelong process on earth, as we will see in the chapter "The Meaning and Purpose of Life on Earth" chapter. And creating us in His image is the purpose of God for creating the heavens and the earth, "for we know that the whole **creation groans** and **labors** with **birth pangs** together until now. [23] Not only *that,* but we also who have the **firstfruits of the Spirit**, even **we ourselves groan within ourselves**, eagerly waiting **for the adoption**, the redemption of our body" (**Romans 8:22–23**).

Here the apostle Paul is comparing the suffering and tribulations of all God's creation on earth, which was created to help us learn the truth that we cannot live on our own without God and therefore causes us to come to God to be born again in the Spirit, to the birth pangs of our earthly mothers who went through pain and suffering for us to be born to this world in the flesh. Being born again in God's image and likeness is the purpose for our life on earth, as we shall see by examining the truth in the Bible. As we shall learn, the purpose of God for creating the universe, the heavens, and the earth was to reconcile us back to Him by allowing us to be born again in Christ Jesus.

GOD TESTS US, SATAN TEMPTS US

The Word of Truth by Sincere Love

> But in all things we commend ourselves as ministers of God: in much patience, in **tribulations**, in **needs**, in **distresses**, [5] in **stripes**, in **imprisonments**, in **tumults**, in **labors**, in **sleeplessness**, in fastings; [6] by purity, by **knowledge**, by **longsuffering**, by kindness, by the **Holy Spirit**, by **sincere love**, [7] by the **word of truth**, by the **power of God**, by the armor of **righteousness** on the right hand and on the left. (**2 Corinthians 6:4–7**)

God's Tough Love

> In this you greatly rejoice, though now for a little while, if need be, **you have been grieved by various trials**, [7] that the **genuineness of your faith**, being **much more precious than gold** that perishes, though it **is tested** by fire, **may be found to praise**, **honor**, and **glory** at the **revelation of Jesus Christ**, whom **having not seen you love**. Though now you do not see Him, yet believing, you rejoice with **joy inexpressible** and full of glory. (**1 Peter 1:6–8**)

Trials not only test our faith but actually raise us up in faith and love, which is precious to God. My cancer wake-up call has been the best thing that ever happened to me. I would not *want* to go through it again, but if I had to I most certainly would, because I would not have this most precious relationship with God without it. I know myself, and I know that to be true.

God Tests Us That We May Be Found Worthy of Salvation

> And you shall remember that the LORD your God led you all the way these forty years in the wilderness, **to humble you** *and* **test you**, to **know what** *was* **in your heart**, whether you would keep His commandments or not. [3] So **He humbled you**, allowed you to **hunger**, and **fed you with manna** which **you**

> **did not know nor did your fathers know**, that He might
> make you know that **man shall not live by bread alone**; but
> man lives **by every *word* that proceeds from the mouth of
> the Lord.** ⁴ Your **garments did not wear out** on you, nor did
> your **foot swell** these forty years. ⁵ You should know in your
> heart that as a man **chastens his son**, *so* the Lord **your God
> chastens you. (Deuteronomy 8:2–5)**

There are two kinds of life being discussed here. Bread symbolically
sustains the life of the flesh, and the Word of God sustains the life of
the spirit that dwells in our body of flesh. God fed them in the desert
with food from heaven that they did not know. Manna symbolizes the
words of God and the Word of God, Christ, which they did not know
would give and sustain their spiritual life: "Our fathers ate the manna
in the desert; as it is written, *'He gave them bread from heaven to eat.'* " ³²
Then Jesus said to them, "Most assuredly, I say to you, Moses did not
give you the bread from heaven, but **My Father gives you the true
bread from heaven.** ³³ For **the bread of God is He who comes
down from heaven and gives life to the world.**" ³⁴ Then they said
to Him, "Lord, give us this bread always." ³⁵ And Jesus said to them, "**I
am the bread of life**. He who comes to Me shall never hunger, and
he who believes in Me shall never thirst." **(John 6:31–35)**

The fact that their garments did not wear out and their feet did not
swell while they sojourned in the wilderness showed them that God
loved them and provided for them. This should have made them know
that God did not chasten them to punish them but to correct them and
raise them for their own good like a loving father on earth chastens his
son rather than letting him go down the path that would destroy him.

And as Moses continues to write,

> When your heart is lifted up, and you forget the Lord your God
> who brought you out of the **land of Egypt**, from **the house
> of bondage**; ¹⁵ who led you through that **great and terrible
> wilderness**, *in which were* fiery serpents and scorpions and thirsty
> land where there was no water; **who brought water for you
> out of the flinty rock**; ¹⁶ who **fed you** in the wilderness
> **with manna**, which your fathers did not know, that **He might**

humble you and that **He might test you, to do you good in the end--** [17] then you say in your heart, "**My power** and the might of **my hand** have gained me this wealth." [18] And you shall **remember the LORD your God**, for *it is* **He who gives you power to get wealth**, that He may establish His covenant which He swore to your fathers, as *it is* this day. (**Deuteronomy 8:14–18**)

Satan Tempts and Entices Us to Do Evil

Blessed *is* the man who **endures temptation**; for when he has been approved, he will receive the **crown of life** which the Lord has **promised to those who love Him**. [13] **Let no one say** when **he is tempted**, "I am tempted by God"; for **God cannot be tempted by evil**, nor does **He Himself tempt anyone**. [14] But each one is **tempted** when **he is drawn away by his own desires** and **enticed**. [15] Then, when **desire has conceived**, it **gives birth to sin**; and sin, when it is full-grown, **brings forth death**. [16] **Do not be deceived**, my beloved brethren. [17] **Every good gift** and **every perfect gift is from above**, and comes down from the **Father of lights**, with whom there is **no variation** or **shadow of turning**. (James 1:1–17)

God Chastens Whom He Loves

As many as I love, I rebuke and chasten. Therefore be zealous and repent. (**Revelation 3:19**)

AGAPE LOVE REQUIRES ACTION

But **be doers of the word**, and **not hearers only**, deceiving yourselves. [23] For if anyone is a hearer of the word and not a doer, he is like a man observing his natural face in a mirror; [24] for he observes himself, goes away, and immediately forgets what kind of man he was. [25] But **he who looks into** the **perfect law of liberty** and **continues in it**, and is not a *forgetful hearer* but a **doer of the work**, this one will be **blessed in what he does**.

165

²⁶ If anyone among you thinks he is religious, and does not **bridle his tongue** but deceives his own heart, this one's religion is useless. ²⁷ Pure and undefiled religion before God and the Father is this: **to visit orphans** and **widows in their trouble,** and to keep oneself unspotted from the world. **(James 1:22–27)**

Those whose religion, whose practice, is doing what is best for themselves while restrained by the law, do not go out and help the poor and sick, because that is not in their best interest and there is no law telling them they must help the poor. The pure, undefiled religion of God requires helping those who have less than we do and caring as much about others as we care about ourselves.

Actions Prove Love

I speak not by commandment, but I am **testing the sincerity of your love** by the diligence of others. ⁹ For you know the grace of our Lord Jesus Christ, that **though He was rich,** yet for **your sakes He became poor,** that you **through His poverty might become rich**. ¹⁰ And in this I give advice: It is to your advantage not only to be doing what you began and were desiring to do a year ago; ¹¹ but now you also must **complete the doing of it**; that as there was a readiness to **desire it**, so there also may be a completion out of what you have. ¹² For if there is first a **willing mind**, it is accepted **according to what one has,** and not according to what he does not have ... Therefore show to them, and before the churches **the proof of your love** and of our boasting on your behalf. **(2 Corinthians 8:8–12, 24)**

In the end we will always do what our mind believes to be true and our heart desires. The smallest good deed is better than the grandest intention.

THE GOLDEN RULE IS THE GOD KIND OF LOVE

The Golden Rule

> And just as you **want men to do to you**, you also **do to them likewise**. (**Luke 6:31**)

There is a sense that living under the law on earth is like someone trying to be righteous and yet living for himself or herself. This type of living means doing whatever you want as long as you do not hurt others. Stated as a law it would be, "Do not do to others what you would not want them to do to you." While this rule, if kept, may bring peace, it does not require the love found in the Golden Rule of the Bible.

The Golden Rule requires everyone to help others in a time of need, because that is what we would want if we were in a time of need. On the other end of the spectrum, anarchy would be all people doing whatever they wanted to whomever they wanted. These three ways of living might be called The Golden Rule, the Silver Rule, and the Iron Rule (or No Rule). And we will see these three distinct ways of living together in three distinct ages of time in the Bible: the age of anarchy, the age of the law, and the age of the millennium.

It is most important to note that only the Golden Rule provides the synergy, prosperity, peace, and unspeakable joy that lead to the God kind of life—eternal life. But the Golden Rule cannot be kept where there is not love, for in the long run we will do what our hearts desire, whether good or bad. For the pure of heart, the law is not needed; for those with the heart of the lawbreaker, the law is useless."

The Golden Rule Fulfills the Law and the Prophets—The Golden Rule Is Agape Love

> Therefore, **whatever you want men to do to you**, **do also to them**, for this is the Law and the Prophets. (**Matthew 7:12**)

167

Love Does No Harm

> **Love does no harm to a neighbor**; therefore **love is the fulfillment of the law**. (Romans 13:10)

The word translated as "love" in this verse is G26 **agape**, which is the unconditional, sacrificial love of others that is the God kind of love. The phrase "Love does no harm" is the passive part of **agape** love and the Golden Rule. The active part of **agape** love and the Golden Rule is doing what is good for another in need—and we are all in need of each other. The passive part, doing no harm, does not require action; it does not require us to do anything.

The passive part fulfills the law if perfectly followed, but the active part of the Golden Rule is the God kind of love, which is higher than the law and which allows a group of individuals to work together as one and creates a synergy that produces power, prosperity, inexpressible joy, and the God kind of Life for a nation, a business, a family, or any other kind of relationship. This is the kind of love Jesus pointed out in the parable of the good Samaritan. The Jews passed by the man in dire need, so they did not break the letter of the law. They did him no harm, but since they did not help him, they did not keep the spirit of the law. They did not love him with the sacrificial, unconditional agape love of God. (See **Luke 10:25–37.**)

THE TRUE INVISIBLE HAND DOCTRINE IS FROM GOD

In a letter to the Philippians, the apostle Paul speaks of a teaching of Jesus about agape love that it has taken a couple thousand years for man to discover:

> Therefore if *there is* any consolation in Christ, if any **comfort of love**, if any fellowship of the Spirit, if any affection and mercy, ² fulfill my joy by **being like-minded**, having **the same love**, *being* of **one accord**, of **one mind**. ³ *Let* nothing *be done* through **selfish ambition or conceit**, but in **lowliness of mind** let **each esteem others better than himself**. ⁴ Let

each of you look out **not only for his own interests**, but **also for the interests of others**. ⁵ Let this mind be in you which was also in Christ Jesus, ⁶ who, **being in the form of God**, did not **consider it robbery** to be **equal with God**, ⁷ but **made Himself of no reputation**, taking the **form of a bondservant**, *and* coming in the **likeness of men**.

⁸ And being found in appearance as a man, **He humbled Himself** and became **obedient to** *the point of* death, even the **death of the cross**. ⁹ Therefore God also has highly exalted Him and given Him the name which is above every name, ¹⁰ that **at the name of Jesus every knee should bow, of those in heaven**, and of **those on earth**, and of **those under the earth**, ¹¹ and *that* **every tongue** should confess that **Jesus Christ** *is* **Lord**, to the glory of God the Father. (**Philippians 2:1–11**)

As we have learned, in **Philippians 2:1**, the Greek word translated as "love" is G26 *agape*, which means "love, that is, affection or **benevolence**; specifically **a love feast**, a **feast of charity, dear, love**." *Webster's Student Dictionary* defines "benevolence" as "**Generous gift as to charity**." The Bible defines what God's version of *agape* love is; it goes beyond any human definition of "love" with these words from Jesus Himself, where the Greek word *"agape"* is also translated as "love": "This is My commandment, that you **love** one another as I have **loved** you. ¹³ Greater **love** has no one than this, than **to lay down one's life for his friends**" (**John 15:12–13**). Agape is the unconditional, sacrificial love that Jesus has for us in that He would lay down His life for us who have rejected Him.

The invisible hand doctrine of man came from the thoughts of Adam Smith, who has been called the father of economics, as expressed in his 1776 book *The Wealth of Nations*, by these famous words:

> Every individual necessarily labours to render the annual revenue of the society as great as he can. He generally, indeed, neither intends **to promote the public interest**, nor knows how much he is promoting it. By preferring the support of domestic to that of foreign industry, he intends only **his own security**; and by directing that industry in such a manner as its produce may be

of the greatest value, **he intends only his own gain**, and he is in this, as in many other cases, **led by an invisible hand to promote an end which was no part of his intention. Nor is it always the worse for the society that it was no part of it. By pursuing his own interest he frequently promotes that of the society more effectually than when he really intends to promote it**. I have never known much good done **by those who affected to trade for the public good**.

Smith is also quoted as saying, "It is not from **the benevolence** of the butcher, the brewer, or the baker, that we can expect our dinner, but from their regard to their **own interest**" and "By directing that industry in such a manner as its produce may be of the greatest value, **he intends only his own gain**, and he is in this, as in many other cases, led by an **invisible hand** to promote an end which was no part of his intention."

Simply stated, the invisible hand doctrine is the belief that when every individual works to do what is in his own best interest, it is in the best interest of society as a whole, even if this is not intended. In fairness to Adam Smith, who was profoundly religious, he recognized that the society had to have a strong moral order for this "invisible hand" to work.

Then, 218 years later, in 1994, American mathematical genius John Nash won a Nobel Prize for mathematically proving that the invisible hand doctrine of Adam Smith was wrong. John's claim is basically that **It is not** when all are doing what is in their own best interest that an 'invisible hand' guides the economy and does what is in the best interest of all. Amazingly, John Nash mathematically proved that doing what is in your own best interest **and the best interest of others** is the most powerful economy. He said his life's work showed him that love was the most important thing that he had learned.

John Nash mathematically proved what Jesus has been saying all along! We can see the "true" invisible hand doctrine of John Nash in the words of the **Philippians 2:1–11** passage above and in the words of the apostle Paul, who was taught by Jesus: "See that **no one** renders

evil for evil to anyone, but always **pursue what is good both for yourselves and for all**" **(1 Thessalonians 5:15)**. As we will learn, agape love is the only thing that can make for unity and oneness. It is when many individuals work together as if they were of one mind, one heart, and one body that synergism, prosperity, and peace can flourish. The economy of the kingdom of God is agape love. Do the math!

I first made this connection, with help from the Holy Spirit, while watching the award-winning movie *A Beautiful Mind*. And this is exactly what is taught by the apostle Peter, a fisherman by trade who was taught by Jesus. "Finally, all *of you* **be of one mind**, having **compassion for one another; love as brothers,** *be* **tenderhearted,** *be* courteous; **⁹ not returning evil for evil** or **reviling for reviling**, but **on the contrary blessing**, knowing that you were called to this, that you may **inherit a blessing**" **(1 Peter 3:8–9)**.

When things are "***done* through selfish ambition** or **conceit**," this is not God's way but is fallen man's version of the invisible hand doctrine, as the Bible warns of in **Philippians 2:3a: "Let nothing *be done* through selfish ambition or conceit**." And this invisible hand doctrine of Adam Smith is the basis of Western economies, or it was until recently. This is the free market and capitalism, and if it does not have strong moral structure, as Adam Smith said about his invisible hand doctrine, it will lead to corruption, decay, and the death of a society, just as the Bible warns. If all do not live in truth, integrity, honesty, and faith in the God kind of love, it will breed corruption and destruction, as the US found out in the fall of 2008.

The invisible hand doctrine of Adam Smith is not the best economy, as Jesus and John Nash pointed out, but the best economy can be fully enjoyed only when *all* love each other as themselves, which we cannot experience on earth until the millennium reign of Christ or later in the kingdom of heaven. But worse yet is an economy in which there is no faith in God and in which citizens must put their faith in a government that rules them by force, and in which even the motivation of selfishness is taken away and replaced with futility and hopelessness. As Adam

Smith pointed out, "I have never known much good done **by those who affected to trade for the public good**."

THE TRUE INVISIBLE HAND BELONGS TO GOD

There was another American who saw *the* true Invisible Hand that guides the affairs of a nation. That man was **George Washington**, and he described that Invisible Hand in his first inaugural address: "No people can be bound to acknowledge and adore **the Invisible Hand** which **conducts the affairs of men** more than those of the United States. Every step, by which **they have advanced to the character of an independent nation**, seems to have been distinguished by some token of **providential agency**."

Webster's Student Dictionary defines the word "providence" as "1. **Divine guidance or care**; also an instance of such guidance or care. 2. **Especially God as a guide** and **protector of men**."

On the other hand, we can certainly recognize who is attached to that other invisible hand, the one who claims that we can live better on our own, separate from God, looking after our own best interests and not worrying about others. This was the lie that Satan deceived us with when we fell from the grace of God and believed the creature instead of the Creator.

This is the truth that Jesus came into this earth to teach us:

> till we all come to the **unity of the faith** and of the **knowledge** of the Son of God, to a perfect man, to the measure of the stature of the fullness of Christ; [14] that we should **no longer be children, tossed to and fro** and **carried about with every wind of doctrine**, by the trickery of men, in the cunning craftiness of deceitful plotting, [15] but, **speaking the truth in love**, may **grow up in all things into Him who is the head–Christ–** [16] from whom the **whole body, joined and knit together** by what **every joint supplies**, according to the **effective working by which every part does its share**,

causes growth of the body for the **edifying** [building up] of *itself* **in love. (Ephesians 4:13–16)**

Love Trumps Our Individual Liberty

I know and am convinced by the Lord Jesus that there is nothing unclean of itself; but to him who considers anything to be unclean, to him it is unclean. [15] **Yet if your brother is grieved because of your food**, you are no longer **walking in love. Do not destroy with your food the one for whom Christ died.** [16] Therefore do not let your good be spoken of as evil; [17] for the kingdom of God is not eating and drinking, **but righteousness** and **peace** and **joy in the Holy Spirit. (Romans 14:14–16)**

Truth is interwoven with righteousness. If what is right in regard to the best way for individuals to live and interact with each other is defined as maximizing personal prosperity, peace, satisfaction, fulfillment, and joy **for all**, and there are many different ways **to try** to do that, then there must be a way that is the best. That one best way would be called righteousness. There is a truth about what is right and what is wrong. Righteousness requires truth. Yielding our liberty to do what is best for another is love. The truth is that love is righteousness.

The way many choose to live and relate to each other is an economy. *Webster's Student Dictionary* defines economy as "**Management of a community**, **business**, or **estate**, so as to **keep down expenses** while **maintaining value**, **productiveness** and **income**." As we see the world around us, there are many different ways to run an economy, but Jesus said that the best way is to love one another, and that makes love the economy of the kingdom of God. John Nash has mathematically proven that Jesus' ways are the right ways, and he has been awarded a Nobel Prize for that discovery.

There is also a time element here that I don't know exactly how to describe yet. It is about doing in the short term what is best in the long run; sacrificing in the present for what is better in the future. The Bible talks about this in verses such as the following: "You shall not boil a young goat in its mother's milk" (**Deuteronomy 14:21**). This saying is something like "Don't kill the goose that laid the golden egg." If you eat the young goat before its mother, the mother may become too old to have any more young, and the population of the herd will suffer.

Another saying that goes something like, "Do not eat the last of your grain, because you will need some to use for seeds to plant next year's crop." Today we might say, "Do not get into credit card debt, for it will decrease your prospects for the future; rather, save for the future that it may bigger and better." And the Bible says that we should, **"Owe no one anything** except to **love one another**, for he who **loves another** has **fulfilled the law**" (**Romans 13:8**).

The apostle Paul talks about this time element in the New Testament: **"If the dead don't rise, 'Let us eat and drink for tomorrow we die'"** (**1 Corinthians 15:32b**). If we think we are going to die in a few years and this life is all there is, then we will think differently than if we know we are going to live forever. Christians think differently because they know and are assured that they are going to live forever.

Also note that **"love your neighbor as yourself"** includes loving yourself as much as your neighbor. Agape love is a mutually beneficial thing. When we are doing what is in the best interest of all concerned, we are part of that "all concerned" and we are really doing what is best for us. When we are practicing sacrificial love, we are sacrificing something in the present for something much greater in the future. When Jesus sacrificed Himself for us by suffering and dying on the cross, He did it for the joy set before Him in the future. "Therefore we also, since we are surrounded by **so great a cloud of witnesses**, let us lay aside every weight, and the sin which so easily **ensnares *us*,** and let us run with endurance the race that is set before us, ² looking unto Jesus, the **author and finisher of *our* faith, who for the joy** that was **set before Him endured the cross**, despising the shame, and has sat down at the right hand of the throne of God" (**Hebrews 12:1–2**).

BECAUSE CHRIST LAID DOWN HIS LIFE FOR US, WE OUGHT TO DO THE SAME

God is not trying to keep us from having joy; He is trying to teach how to have a joy that is "to die for!" "For if you live **according to the flesh you will die**; but if **by the Spirit** you **put to death** the deeds of the body, **you will live** … I beseech you therefore, brethren, by the mercies of God, that you present your bodies **a living sacrifice**, holy, acceptable to God, *which is* your reasonable service. ² And do not be conformed to this world, but **be transformed** by the **renewing of your mind**, that you may **prove** what *is* that good and acceptable and perfect will of God" (**Romans 8:13, 12:1**).

Being in Jesus in Faith and Love Is to Die For

> I have been **crucified with Christ**; it is no longer I who live, but **Christ lives in me**; and the life which I now live in the flesh I live **by faith** in the Son of God, **who loved me** and **gave Himself for me**. (**Galatians 2:20**)

The apostle Paul proclaims, "For to me, **to live *is* Christ**, and **to die *is* gain**" (**Philippians 1:21**).

> Then Jesus said to His disciples, "If anyone desires to come after Me, **let him deny himself**, and take up his cross, and follow Me. ²⁵ For **whoever desires to save his life will lose it**, but **whoever loses his life for My sake will find it**. ²⁶ For **what profit is it to a man** if he **gains the whole world**, and loses **his own soul**? Or **what will a man give in exchange for his soul**?" (**Matthew 16:24–26**)

> By this we know love, because **He laid down His life for us**. And **we also ought to lay down *our* lives for the brethren**. (**1 John 3:16**)

If we still think that we can have more joy on our own, we do not know the truth of God. We only know the lies of Satan.

Now let us compare what God says about love to what the best of the world says:

"The beauty of a child is in its infinite capacity to love."

—Author Unknown

"Life is eternal and love is immortal, and death is only a horizon; and a horizon is nothing save the limit of our sight."

—Rossiter Worthington Raymond

"Love cures people, both the ones who give it, and the ones who receive it."

—Karl Menninger

"To be able to love a butterfly we must care for a few caterpillars."

—Author Unknown

"One word frees us of all the weight and pain in life. That word is love."

—Sophocles

"The greatest thing a father can do for his children is to love the children's mother."

—Rev. Theodore M. Hesburg

"We can do no great things - only small things with great love."

—Mother Teresa

"Choose a job you love and you will never have to work a day in your life."

—Confucius

"Love is a fruit of all times and within the reach of every hand."

—Mother Teresa

"We may give without loving but we cannot love without giving."

—Author Unknown

"Let a man avoid evil deeds as a man who loves life avoids poison."

—Buddha

"There are no guarantees. From the viewpoint of fear, none are strong enough. From the viewpoint of love, none are necessary."

—Emmanuel

"The love of liberty is the love of others; the love of power is the love of ourselves."

—William Hazlitt

"When someone you love becomes a memory, that memory becomes a treasure."

—Author Unknown

"I'd rather be a failure at something I love than a success at something I hate."

—George Burns

"For one human being to love another; that is perhaps the most difficult of all our tasks, the ultimate, the test and proof, the work for which all other work is but preparation."

—Rainer Maria Rilke

"To love what you do and feel that it matters - how could anything be more fun."

—Katherine Graham

"A coward is incapable of exhibiting love; it is the prerogative of the brave."

—Mahatma Gandhi

"You cannot control someone and love them at the same time."

—Marc Kirsch

"When I despair, I remember that all through history the way of **truth and love** has always won. There have been tyrants and murderers and for a time they seem invincible but in the end they always fall – think of it, ALWAYS."

—Mahatma Gandhi

"Love is the strongest force the world possesses, and yet it is the Greatness that is a road leading toward the unknown."

—Charles deGaule

"Faith is love taking the form of aspiration."

—William Ellery Channing

"Money can't buy love. The only way to get love is by freely giving it away."

—Marc Kirsch

"If you judge people, you have no time to love them."

—Mother Teresa

"Finally, all of you, have unity of spirit, sympathy, love of the brethren, a tender heart and a humble mind."

—Simon Peter

"Love is an act of endless forgiveness, a tender look which becomes a habit."

—Peter Ustinov

"It is easy to half the potato where there is love."

—Irish Proverb

"We come to love not by finding a perfect person but by learning to see an imperfect person perfectly."

—Sam Keen

"Real success is finding your lifework in the work that you love."

—David McCullough

"If you are lucky enough to find a way of life you love, you have to find the courage to live it."

—John Irving

"We love because it is the only true adventure."

—Nikki Giovanni

"No machine can replace the human spark; spirit, compassion, love and understanding."

—Louis V. Gertsner Jr.

"Gravitation is not responsible for people falling in love."

—Albert Einstein

"God made man because he loves stories."

—Elie Wiesel

The Oneness Branch

CONNECTEDNESS, OR ONENESS, is the last of the three branches, or areas of knowledge, that I *distinctly* remember from my truth-and-love experience. I remember this feeling that people are so connected to each other that if we would hurt someone else it would be like hurting ourselves. And in some way all knowledge was connected together and all creation was connected together with us in some way that we do not understand. The apostle Paul speaks of the connection of all creation with man in a letter to the Romans: "For the earnest expectation of **the creation eagerly waits** for the **revealing of the sons of God. 20** For **the creation was subjected to futility**, not willingly, but because of Him who subjected *it* **in hope;** 21 because **the creation itself** also will be **delivered** from the **bondage of corruption** into the glorious **liberty of the children of God. 22** For we know that **the whole creation groans** and labors with birth pangs together until now" (**Romans 8:19**).

In this branch and in the chapter "The Tree of Life" we will learn how connectedness and oneness is essential to our very lives. So let us take a look and learn what God says about oneness in the Bible.

THE CHURCH OF CHRIST IS ONE

Now I plead with you, brethren, by the name of our Lord Jesus Christ, that you all speak **the same thing**, and that there be **no divisions** among you, but that you **be perfectly joined together in the same mind** and **in the same judgment**.

[11] For it has been declared to me concerning you, my brethren, by those of Chloe's household, that there are **contentions among you**. [12] Now I say this, that each of you says, "I am of Paul," or "I am of Apollos," or "I am of Cephas," or "I am of Christ." [13] **Is Christ divided**? Was Paul crucified for you? Or were you baptized in the name of Paul? (**1 Corinthians 1:10–14**)

Jesus Himself warns us in **Matthew 12:25** about the dangers of division: "But Jesus knew their thoughts, and said to them: '**Every kingdom divided against itself is brought to desolation**, and every **city** or **house divided** against itself will not stand.'"

Many in One

For as **the body is one** and has **many members**, but **all the members** of that **one body**, being many, are **one body, so also is Christ**. (**1 Corinthians 12:12**)

The body of Christ has many members, and the Bible compares it to the human body and its parts, but the body of Christ can also be compared to the members of a governmental body, with a leader as its head and the members as its body. As an earthly example, consider the US House of Representatives, with the Speaker of the House as its leader, or head, and the Congressmen and Congresswomen as its body (and they are often referred to in those terms).

In fact, using similar terms, the angel Gabriel, speaking to Mary of her future son, Jesus, said that He would reign over a house and rule over a kingdom: "He will be great, and will be called the **Son of the Highest**; and the Lord God will give Him the **throne of His father David**. [33] And He will **reign over the house of Jacob** forever, and of His **kingdom there will be no end**" (**Luke 1:32–33**).

Now consider that believers will be subjects in a kingdom with Jesus Christ as the King, where there are many subjects living under His rule and reign that act together as one kingdom or one body. If this is what the Son of God is like, is this not what the God the Father is like? And a Son being like His Father is exactly what the author of Hebrews tells us: "God ... ² has in these last days spoken to us **by *His* Son**, whom He has appointed heir of all things, through whom also He made the worlds; ³ **who being the brightness of *His* glory** and **the express image of His person**" (Hebrews 1:1–3).

This should help with the understanding of the Trinity being three personalities and yet one God, because God is really like two rulers— God the Father and God the Son—in a hierarchy of authority over a kingdom of many. This would explain why God calls Himself "**Us**" in **Genesis 1:26**: "Then God said, 'Let **Us** make man in **Our** image, according to **Our** likeness; let **them** have dominion over the fish of the sea, over the birds of the air, and over the cattle, over all the earth and over every creeping thing that creeps on the earth.'"

And this would explain why the Hebrew word for "God" in the entire first chapter of Genesis, the story of creation, is H430 *elohym*, which means "**gods in the ordinary sense; but specifically used in the plural, especially with the article of the supreme God**; occasionally applied by way of deference to **magistrates**; and sometimes as a **superlative – angels**, exceeding, **God** (**gods**), great, mighty, **judges**." In the next branch, we will learn that those of us who believe and are saved will be judges in the kingdom of God.

One for All and All for One

> Yet for us there is **one God, the Father**, of whom are all things, and we for Him; and **one Lord Jesus Christ**, through whom are all things, and **through whom we live**. (**1 Corinthians 8:6**)

Jesus speaks of this oneness of many believers in God in **John chapter 17**:

THE ONENESS OF JOHN CHAPTER 17

> I pray for them. I do not pray for the world but for **those whom You have given Me**, for **they are Yours**. ¹⁰ And **all Mine are Yours**, and **Yours are Mine**, and I am glorified in them. ¹¹ Now I am no longer in the world, but these are in the world, and I come to You. Holy Father, keep through Your name those

whom You have given Me, that **they may be one as We are**.
(**John 17:9–11**)

This passage tells us we belonged to the Father before He gave us to Jesus. Is this when God the Father chose and anointed Jesus to be King over us instead of Jesus' bright and showy but prideful brother Lucifer? (See **Isaiah 14:3–27.**)

Oneness in God

> ... the **Spirit of truth**, whom the world cannot receive, **because it neither sees Him nor knows Him**; but you know Him, for **He dwells with you** and **will be in you**. [18] **I will not leave you orphans**; I will come to you. [19] A little while longer and the world will see Me no more, but you will see Me. **Because I live, you will live also**. [20] At that day you will know that **I am in My Father**, and **you in Me**, and **I in you**. (**John 14:17–20**)

Jesus has not left us as orphans, because He has left us with His Holy Spirit. It is the Holy Spirit that was dwelling *with* His disciples until Jesus died, and then He sent His Holy Spirit to dwell *in them* beginning at Pentecost. And the Holy Spirit will be in all of us who believe in Jesus the Christ and commit our lives to Him.

Made Perfect in One

> I do not pray **for these alone**, but **also for those who will believe in Me through their word**; [21] that they **all may be one, as You, Father, are in Me**, and **I in You; that they also may be one in Us**, that the world may believe that You sent Me. [22] And the glory which You gave Me I have given them, that **they may be one** just as **We are one**: [23] **I in them**, and **You in Me**; that they may be **made perfect in one**, and that the world may know that You have sent Me, and **have loved them as You have loved Me**. (**John 17:21–23**)

As Jesus is praying to the Father that those who belong to Him will be made perfect in one, He lets us know that God the Father has loved us the same as He has loved Jesus. To think that we who believe are going to be one with Jesus and the Father! How unimaginably and incredibly awesome is our future life in Jesus and God the Father!

Love Makes Oneness

> Father, I desire that they also **whom You gave Me may be with Me where I am,** that they may behold My glory which You have given Me; for You loved Me **before the foundation of the world.** [25] O righteous Father! The **world has not known You,** but I have known You; and these have known that You sent Me. [26] And I have declared to them Your name, and will declare it, that **the love with which You loved Me may be in them,** and **I in them. (John 17:24–26)**

Jesus is praying for believers to be in Him! Can you see us in Jes*us*?

TEST FOR SPIRITS OF GOD OR SPIRITS OF ANTICHRIST

The Apostle John Speaks of Us as Spirits in a Body

> Beloved, do not believe every **spirit,** but **test the spirits,** whether they are **of God**; because many **false prophets** have gone out into the world. [2] By this you know **the Spirit of God**: Every **spirit** that **confesses that Jesus Christ** has **come in the flesh is of God,** [3] and every **spirit** that **does not confess** that Jesus Christ has come in the flesh **is not of God.** And **this is the spirit of the Antichrist,** which you have heard was coming, and is now already in the world. [4] You are of God, little children, and have **overcome** them, because **He who is in you is** greater than **he who is in the world.**
>
> [5] They are of the world. Therefore they speak as **of the world,** and the world hears them. [6] We are **of God.** He who **knows God hears us**; he who **is not of God** does not **hear us.** By this we **know the spirit of truth** and **the spirit of error.** [7] Beloved, **let us love one another,** for **love is of God**; and everyone who **loves** is **born of God** and knows God.

[8] He who **does not love** does not **know God**, for **God is love**. [9] In this the love of God was manifested toward us, that God has sent His only begotten Son into the world, that we might live through Him. [10] **In this is love**, not that we loved God, but that **He loved us** and **sent His Son** to be the **propitiation for our sins**.

[11] Beloved, if God so loved us, we also ought to **love one another**. [12] No one has seen God at any **time**. If we **love one another**, God abides in us, and His love has been perfected in us. [13] By this we know that we **abide in Him**, and **He in us**, because **He has given us of His Spirit**. [14] And we have seen and testify that **the Father has sent the Son as Savior of the world**. [15] Whoever confesses that Jesus is the Son of God, **God abides in him**, and **he in God**. [16] And we have known and believed the love that God has **for us**. **God is love**, and he who **abides in love abides in God**, and **God in him**. [17] **Love** has been perfected among us in this: that we may have boldness in the **day of judgment**; because as He is, so are we in this world.

[18] There is **no fear in love**; but **perfect love casts out fear**, because fear involves torment. But **he who fears has not been made perfect in love**. [19] **We love Him because He first loved us**. [20] If someone says, "**I love God**," and **hates his brother**, he is a **liar**; for he who does not love his brother whom he has seen, how can he love God whom he has not seen? [21] And this commandment we have from Him: that **he who loves God must love his brother also**. (**1 John 4:1–21**)

Notice how intimately linked love is with oneness. Notice also that when the apostle John speaks of spirits, he is speaking of men and women who are spirits in a temporary body of flesh. And when God says no one can love Him and hate his brother, He is referring to the brothers who were united as one with God before the fall and can be again, and so hating his brother means hating God's fallen sons and daughters. Jesus speaks of the oneness with His children, our brothers and sisters:

"When did we see You a stranger and take *You* in, or naked and clothe *You?* [39] Or when did we see You sick, or in prison, and come to You?' [40] And the King will answer and say to them, 'Assuredly, I say to you, **inasmuch as you did *it* to one** of the **least of these My brethren, you did *it* to Me**" (**Matthew 25:38–40**). And Jesus reinforces the notion of unity in an exchange with Phillip, who does not understand the inseparable unity and nature of Jesus and His Father: "Philip said to Him, 'Lord, show us the Father, and it is sufficient for us.' [9] Jesus said to him, "Have I been with you so long, and yet you have not known Me, Philip? **He who has seen Me has seen the Father**; so how can you say, 'Show us the Father'?" (**John 14:8–9**).

One for All and All for One

> For the **love of Christ compels us**, because we judge thus: that if **One died for all, then all died**; [15] and **He died for all**, that those who live should **live no longer for themselves**, but for Him who died for them and rose again. [16] Therefore, from now on, we **regard no one according to the flesh**. Even though we have known Christ according to the flesh, yet now we know Him thus no longer. [17] Therefore, **if anyone is in Christ**, he is **a new creation**; old things have passed away; behold, **all things have become new**. (**2 Corinthians 5:14–19**)

Love is the economy, and living by the Spirit in oneness is the constitution of the kingdom that is God. We have known each other by the flesh that Jesus once lived in and that we currently live in as individuals, but when we believe in Jesus, we know Him and others as spirits in oneness. Jesus is our head, and we are His body; Christ is our king, and we are subjects and citizens in His kingdom.

THE DIVINE LIFE "ASSURANCE" PLAN OF GOD

One in Christ

> For if there is first **a willing mind**, it is accepted **according to what one has**, and **not according to what he does not have**. [13] For I do not mean that others should be eased and you burdened; [14] **but by an equality**, that now at this time **your abundance may supply their lack**, that **their abundance also may supply your lack – that there may be equality**. [15] As it is written, "He who gathered much had nothing left over, and he who gathered little had no lack." (**2 Corinthians 8:12–15**)

Oneness in Christ provides "that their hearts may be encouraged, being **knit together in love**, and attaining to **all riches** of the **full assurance of understanding**, to the **knowledge of the mystery of God**, both of the Father and of Christ, [3] in whom are **hidden all the treasures** of **wisdom** and **knowledge**" (**Colossians 2:2–3**).

Is this not what All Knowledge would be: "being **knit together in love**," the "full **understanding** and the **knowledge** of the **mystery of God**," and "**all the treasures** of **wisdom** and **knowledge**"? If anyone were to be shown this mystery of God in a way that they could know and understand, it would be so far above what they currently know that they would surely cry out in joy, "Oh, now I see! Oh, now I see!"

THE LORD GOD IS ONE

> Hear, O Israel: The LORD our God, **the LORD *is* one**! [5] You shall love the LORD your God with **all your heart**, with **all your soul**, and with **all your strength**. [6] And these words which I command you today shall be in your heart. (**Deuteronomy 6:4–6**)

This is the verse that many non-Christians interpret as saying God is one person or personality, but the Hebrew word translated as "one" here is H259 *echad*, which means "**properly united**."

The Hebrew word translated as "Israel" here is H3478 *yisrael*, which is defined as "From H8280 and H410; he will rule **as God**; Jisrael, a **symbolic name of Jacob**; also (typically) of his posterity:- Israel." The Hebrew word H8280 *sarah* means "**to prevail:-have power as a prince**" and H410 *el* means "strength; as adjective **mighty**; especially the Almighty but used also of any deity: God or **god**." The story of Jacob's name change to Israel is most intriguing,

> Then Jacob was left alone; and **a Man wrestled with him** until the breaking of day. ²⁵ Now when He saw that **He did not prevail against him**, He touched the socket of his hip; and the socket of Jacob's hip was out of joint as **He wrestled with him**. ²⁶ And He said, "Let Me go, for the day breaks." But he said, "I will not let You go unless You bless me!" ²⁷ So He said to him, "What *is* your name?" He said, "Jacob." ²⁸ And He said, "**Your name shall no longer be called Jacob**, but **Israel**; for **you have struggled with God and with men**, and **have prevailed**." (**Genesis 32:24–28**)

What God is saying to His people, Israel, is that God has chosen them for His special purpose and they will have to wrestle with God and men and cling to Him for His blessing and their very life. "I call heaven and earth as witnesses today **against you**, *that* I have **set before you life and death, blessing and cursing**; therefore **choose life**, that both you and your descendants **may live**; ²⁰ that you may love the LORD your God, that you may obey His voice, and that **you may cling to Him**, for **He *is* your life** and the **length of your days**; and that you may dwell in the **land which the LORD swore to your fathers**, to Abraham, Isaac, and Jacob, **to give them**" (**Deuteronomy 30:19–20**).

Jacob had a hunger, passion, and desire for the blessing of God, but he went about getting that blessing in his own strength, using the ways of the world, trickery, and deception to earn the blessing of God. All his life he was "wrestling with God and men" to get what he wanted. It was only when God physically caused him to be weak and helpless by putting his hip out of joint, leaving Jacob with no choice but to cling to God and submit to Him, that he finally received God's blessing and was given power from God to be a prince.

And so it is with us. If we have a heart and a mind that desire to seek God and His blessings but we try to earn them in our own strength, God will wrestle with us, causing us to experience ever-increasing suffering until we are broken and cling to God for our very life; God can then freely give us what we worked so hard to earn. And "Israel" is a **"symbolic name of Jacob"** and his descendants, because it is not all the physical descendants of Israel that receive God's blessing and power to be a prince, but the spiritual sons and daughters of Abraham and Jacob, the ones out of every nation who believe the promise of God:

"But it is not that the word of God has taken no effect. For **they *are* not all Israel who *are* of Israel,** [7] **nor *are they* all children** because they are **the seed of Abraham**; but, *'In Isaac your seed shall be called.'* [8] That is, **those who *are* the children of the flesh**, these *are* **not the children of God; but the children of the promise** are counted as the seed" (**Romans 9:6–8**). God has made a number of promises to fallen man, but we will see which promise of God this passage refers to in the chapter "First Age of Anarchy."

Those who believe in God and believe that His words and His ways are truth and life everlasting will become again the gods—or in the Hebrew, the *elohym*—the "children of the Most High" they originally were in the kingdom of God, as Jesus Himself confirms: "Jesus answered them, 'Is it not written in your law, *"I said, 'You are gods'"* ? [35] If **He called them gods**, to whom the **word of God came** (and the **Scripture cannot be broken**), [36] do you say of Him whom the Father sanctified and **sent into the world**, "You are blaspheming," because I said, "I am the Son of God"?'" (**John 10:34–36**).

That we were "gods" and children of God Most High is seen from the Old Testament passage that Jesus is quoting from, **Psalm 82:5–6**: "They **do not know, nor do they understand**; They **walk about in darkness**; All the **foundations of the earth are unstable**. [6] I said,

"**You** *are* **gods**, And all of you *are* **children of the Most High**." The word "gods" comes from the Hebrew word H430 *elohym,* which means "**gods in the ordinary sense**; but specifically used (in the plural thus, especially with the article) of the **supreme God**; occasionally applied by way of deference to **magistrates** as a superlative:- **angels**, exceeding God (**gods**), great, **judges, mighty**."

And the apostle Paul confirms that there are many gods: "For even if there are so-called **gods**, whether **in heaven or on earth (as there are many gods and many lords)**, [6] yet for us *there is* **one God, the Father**, of whom *are* all things, and we for Him; and **one Lord Jesus Christ**, through whom *are* all things, and **through whom we** *live*. [7] However, *there is* not in everyone **that knowledge**; for some, with consciousness of the idol, until now eat *it* as a thing offered to an idol; and their conscience, being weak, is defiled" (**1 Corinthians 8:5–7**).

We will learn and understand what these amazing verses mean in future chapters, and we will learn that there was another life before this life on earth!

BY ONE SPIRIT WE HAVE ACCESS TO THE FATHER

For **through Him** we both have **access by one Spirit** to the Father. [19] Now, therefore, you are no longer **strangers** and **foreigners**, but **fellow citizens** with the **saints** and **members** of the **household of God**, [20] having been built on the **foundation of the apostles** and **prophets, Jesus Christ** Himself being the **chief corner stone**, [21] in whom the whole building, being **joined together**, grows into a **holy temple** in the Lord, [22] in whom you also are **being built together** for a **dwelling place of God in the Spirit**. (Ephesians 2:18–22)

A careful reading of this verse tells us that we, as individual spirits, when we are no longer in bodies of flesh, will have access to the Father "by one Spirit." The phrase "You also are **being built together** for a dwelling place of God **in the Spirit**" tells us that we will be spirits united in one just as God is one. Since we will be holy as God is holy, we would be one Holy Spirit with Jesus as our leader, head, and King!

The gospel of Mark explains how this gathering together as one in Jesus will happen: "Then they will see the Son of Man coming in the clouds with great power and glory. **²⁷** And then He will send His angels, and **gather together His elect** from the four winds, from the farthest part of **earth** to the farthest part of **heaven**" (**Mark 13:26–27**). This is confirmed by Matthew: "And He will **send His angels** with a great sound of a trumpet, and they will **gather together His elect** from the **four winds**, from one end of **heaven** to the other" (**Matthew 24:31**).

Notice that there will be angels who will gather together angels from heaven that will be gathered together with "**elect**" angels from earth at the end of the ages. And the apostle Paul uses the phrase "**elect angels**" in a letter to Timothy: "I charge *you* before God and the Lord Jesus Christ and the **elect angels** that you observe these things without prejudice, doing nothing with partiality" (**1 Timothy 5:21**).

This was the plan of God from before the beginning on earth, "having made known to us the **mystery of His will**, according to His good pleasure which He purposed in Himself, ¹⁰ that in the **dispensation of the fullness of the times** He might **gather together in one all things in Christ**, both which are **in heaven** and which are **on earth – in Him**. ¹¹ In Him also we have obtained an inheritance, being **predestined** according to **the purpose of Him** who works all things according to the counsel of His will" (**Ephesians 1:9–11**). *Webster's Student Dictionary* defines "predestine" as "To destine, decree, etc. **beforehand**."

And God miraculously put His plan in the voice of one who was trying to defeat God's plan: "And one of them, Caiaphas, being high priest that year, said to them, 'You know nothing at all, ⁵⁰ nor do you consider that it is expedient for us that **one man should die for the people**, and not that the **whole nation should perish**.' ⁵¹ Now this he did not say on **his own** *authority;* but being high priest that year **he prophesied that Jesus would die for the nation**, ⁵² and not for that nation only, but also that **He would gather together in one the children of God who were scattered abroad**" (**John 11:49–52**).

THE ONENESS OF EPHESIANS CHAPTER 4

The apostle Paul in his letter to the Ephesians writes, "I, therefore, the prisoner of the Lord, beseech you to walk worthy of the calling with which **you were called**, ² with all lowliness and gentleness, with longsuffering, **bearing with one another in love**, ³ endeavoring to keep the **unity of the Spirit** in the bond of peace. ⁴ There is **one body** and **one Spirit**, just as you were called in **one hope** of your calling; ⁵ **one Lord, one faith, one baptism**; ⁶ **one God and Father of all**, who is **above all**, and **through all**, and **in you all**" (**Ephesians 4:1–6**).

Notice that just as there is one body on earth, the church, there is one Spirit in heaven, the Holy Spirit! As the church is the congregation of believers on earth that are holy (set apart to righteousness), so is the Holy Spirit the collection of spirits who are holy in heaven. "But to each one of us grace was given according to the measure of Christ's **gift**. ⁸ Therefore He says: 'When He ascended on high, **He led captivity captive**, And gave **gifts** to men.' ⁹ (Now this, 'He ascended' – **what does it mean** but that **He also first descended into the lower parts of the earth**? ¹⁰ **He who descended** is also the **One who ascended** far above all the heavens, that He might fill all things)" (**Ephesians 4:7–10**).

After Jesus sacrificed Himself for our sins, He first took those who died believing in the promises of God, who were captives by Satan in hell but now belonged to Jesus, and He brought them to be with Him in paradise. We will learn that the "lower parts of the earth" and "the deep" are just two of many names for hell, which is on earth. That Jesus first descended into hell before He ascended into heaven is part of most versions of the Apostles' Creed.

> And He Himself gave some to be a**postles**, some **prophets**, some **evangelists**, and some **pastors** and **teachers**, ¹² for the equipping of the saints for the work of ministry, for the edifying of the body of Christ, ¹³ **till we all come** to the **unity of the faith** and of the **knowledge of the Son of God**, to a **perfect**

man, to the measure of the stature of the fullness of Christ; [14] that we should no longer be **children**, tossed to and fro and carried about with every **wind of doctrine**, by the **trickery of men**, in the **cunning craftiness** of **deceitful plotting**,

[15] but, speaking the **truth in love**, may grow up in all things **into Him who is the head—Christ—** [16] from whom **the whole body, joined** and **knit together** by **what every joint supplies**, according to the **effective working** by which **every part does its share**, causes **growth of the body** for the edifying [building up] of itself **in love**. (**Ephesians 4:11–16**)

The "cunning craftiness of deceitful plotting" harkens back to the Serpent, who was cunning and deceitful: "Now the **serpent was more cunning** than any beast of the field which the Lord **God had made**" (**Genesis 3:1**), and we can see his influence on the world and the division it caused then and causes now. But in stark contrast, we can see the "**truth in love**" of Christ that builds us up united as one. Notice how verses **4:15–16** speak of how "**truth in love**" enables us to be "**knit together**" with Christ and that oneness and unity "**causes growth of the body**," which is the synergy of many working together as one that John Nash mathematically proved was the best and most prosperous way to live in "The Love Branch."

Paul continues in his letter to the Ephesians:

This I say, therefore, and testify in the Lord, that you should no longer walk as the rest of the Gentiles walk, in the **futility of their mind**, [18] having their **understanding darkened**, being **alienated from the life of God**, because of the **ignorance that is in them**, because of the **blindness of their heart;** [19] who, being **past feeling**, have **given themselves over** to **lewdness**, to work all **uncleanness** with **greediness**. [20] But you have not so learned Christ, [21] if indeed you have heard Him and have been taught by Him, as **the truth is in Jesus**: that you **put off**, concerning your former conduct, the **old man** which **grows corrupt** according to the **deceitful lusts**, [23] and **be renewed** in the **spirit of your mind**, [24] and that you put on the **new man** which was **created according to God**, in true **righteousness and holiness**. [25] Therefore, **putting away**

lying, "Let each one of you **speak truth** with his neighbor," for **we are members of one another. (Ephesians 4:17–25)**

Notice some important facts about our fallen nature. We have had our **"understanding darkened**," we are **ignorant** of the truth, and we have a **"blindness of the heart"** that is past feeling, but in God **"we are members of one another."**

And Paul admonishes us to not let anger get ahold of us:

> "Be angry, and do not sin": **do not let the sun go down on your wrath**, [27] **nor give place to the devil**. [28] Let him who stole steal no longer, but rather let him labor, working with his hands what is good, that he may have **something to give him who has need**. [29] Let no corrupt word proceed out of your mouth, but what is good for **necessary edification**, that it may impart grace to the hearers. [30] And do not grieve **the Holy Spirit of God**, by **whom you were sealed** for the **day of redemption**. [31] Let all bitterness, wrath, anger, clamor, and evil speaking be put away from you, with all malice. [32] And be **kind to one another**, tenderhearted, **forgiving one another**, just as **God in Christ forgave you. (Ephesians 4:26–32)**

When we put off the old "**man**," that means we have stopped living like the rest of the world. "Putting off the old man" means coming out of that belief system and lifestyle in which we once lived by following the lies of Satan. **Ephesians 2:1–7** describes the situation this way:

> And you *He made alive,* who **were dead** in trespasses and sins, [2] in which **you once walked according** to the **course of this world**, according to **the prince of the power of the air**, the **spirit who now works** in the **sons of disobedience**, [3] among whom also **we all once conducted ourselves** in the **lusts of our flesh**, fulfilling the **desires of the flesh** and of the mind, **and were by nature children of wrath, just as the others.**
>
> [4] **But God**, who is rich in mercy, because of **His great love with which He loved us**, [5] even **when we were dead** in trespasses, **made us alive together with Christ** (by grace you have been saved), [6] and raised *us* up together, and **made *us* sit together in the heavenly** *places* **in Christ Jesus**, [7] that in the

ages to come He might show the exceeding riches of His grace in His kindness toward us **in Christ Jesus**.

In this we see that it was the love of God that "**made us alive together with Christ**."

THE FIRST ADAM SATAN, THE SECOND ADAM CHRIST

The use of the word "man" in the New Testament can also refer to "mankind" in the same way as the Old Testament's use of the Hebrew word "*adam*," which, as we will see, can refer to either an individual man or Mankind. In **Genesis 5:2** in the NKJV, the Hebrew word "adam" is actually translated as "Mankind": "He created **them** male and female, and blessed **them** and **called them Mankind** in the **day they were created**." And now we will see how oneness is an important concept in the understanding of the Bible, the Spiritual reality, and the meaning of life on earth, but for now, consider that the words "*Adam*" in the Hebrew and "Man" in the English, with capital first letters, can refer to one individual man and his many followers, as in the next two passages.

> And so it is written, "*The first man Adam became a **living being*** ["living soul" in the KJV]." The **last Adam** *became* a **life–giving spirit**. [46] However, the spiritual is not first, but the natural, and afterward the spiritual. [47] The **first man** *was of the earth, made of dust*; the **second Man** *is* **the Lord from heaven**. [48] As *was* the *man* of dust, **so also** *are* those *who are made* of **dust**; and as *is* the **heavenly** *Man,* so also *are* those *who are* **heavenly**. [49] And as **we have borne the image of the** *man* **of dust**, we shall also bear **the image of the heavenly** *Man*. [50] Now this I say, brethren, that **flesh and blood cannot inherit the kingdom of God**; nor does corruption inherit incorruption. (**1 Corinthians 15:45–50**)

The apostle Paul adds some more detail to these two "men" who are leaders of mankind in his letter to the Romans:

Therefore, just as through **one man** sin entered the world, and **death through sin**, and thus **death spread to all men, because all sinned–** [13] (For until the law sin was in the world, but sin is not imputed when there is no law. [14] Nevertheless **death reigned from Adam to Moses,** even over those who had **not sinned according to the likeness** of the **transgression of Adam,** who is **a type** of **Him who was to come.** [15] But the **free gift** *is* not like the **offense**. For if by the **one man's offense many died,** much more the grace of God and the **gift** by the **grace** of the **one Man, Jesus Christ, abounded to many.**

[16] And the **gift** *is* not like *that which came* **through the one who sinned**. For the judgment *which came* from one *offense resulted* in **condemnation,** but the **free gift** *which came* from many offenses *resulted* **in justification.** [17] For if by the one man's offense **death reigned through the one,** much more those who receive abundance of grace and of the **gift of righteousness** will **reign in life through the One, Jesus Christ.**)

[18] Therefore, as through **one man's offense** *judgment* **came to all men,** resulting in **condemnation,** even so through **one Man's righteous act** *the free gift came* to all men, resulting in **justification of life.** [19] For as by **one man's disobedience** many were **made sinners,** so also by **one Man's obedience** many will be **made righteous.** [20] Moreover **the law entered** that the **offense might abound.** But where sin abounded, grace abounded much more, [21] so that as **sin reigned in death,** even so **grace might reign through righteousness to eternal life** through **Jesus Christ our Lord.** (**Romans 5:12–21**)

We will see how all of these things—which are hard to understand from the perspective of this realm on earth, where the fiefdom of Satan is—will make perfect sense and will be easy to understand when we consider them from the greater perspective of the heavenly realm, where the kingdom of God is, as we get into the chapters that follow these branches of knowledge.

For now, let us consider the meaning of the phrase "… even over those who had not sinned according to **the likeness** of the **transgression of Adam,** who is a **type** of Him who was to come." The word "type" is translated from the Greek word G5179 *tupos*, which has many meanings, including, "Figuratively, a **style** or **resemblance**, a **model**, or a **pattern**." *Webster's Student Dictionary* defines "type" as "A person, thing, or event, etc. that **foreshadows another person** or thing to come; a token; **sign**; **symbol**; as, to many **Old Testament characters and events** are *types* realized in the New Testament."

Let us look at the second part of that phrase first—"Adam, who is a **type** of Him who was to come." Jesus is the identity of "Him who was to come" in this passage, and as we will learn, Jesus was chosen and anointed to be King over us. Satan wanted to be king over us but was not chosen, and the only way he could be king was to deceive us by a lie that we could do better on our own, separated from the kingdom of God, and that is exactly what he did.

As we will learn, the English word "man" is translated from the Hebrew word "*adam*," which refers to beings that are **mean, of low degree**, of a **common sort**, and **hypocritical** that will put on flesh made of the **dust of the earth** and are called "man" (the species, mankind). And so Satan qualifies for the label of "man" or "Adam," and this explains how Adam was a "**type**" of Jesus who was to come. Both Satan and Jesus were leaders of their followers, those who believed in them. And Satan's lie and deception was the event that "as through **one man's offense *judgment* came to all men**, resulting in **condemnation**," and Jesus' suffering and dying for us on the cross out of His love for us is the event where "**one Man's righteous act** *the free gift came* to all men, resulting in **justification of life**."

When Jesus came to earth, He first witnessed of the truth that would make us free (**John 8:32**; **18:37**), and then He suffered and died on the tree we would have died on, out of His great love for us and out of the Father's great love for us. That selfless act of agape love gave those who believed in Him eternal life, united together as one man in the flesh with Jesus as the Head or Leader. This is the second "congregation of man," or Mankind, or *Adam* in the Hebrew. So the **second Adam** is Jesus and those on earth who believe His truth and follow Him and will be taken with Him from earth to heaven.

The first **Adam** is made up of the first man and woman, named Adam and Eve, and all their descendants, who were all deceived by the lie of the Serpent who led them all into a lifestyle that would cause their death. The death spoken of here is not the death of the flesh that all men and women on earth have experienced or will experience: "And as it is **appointed for men to die once**, but after this **the judgment**" (**Hebrews 9:27**). Rather, this is the "second death" spoken of in the book of Revelation: "Blessed and holy *is* he who has part in the **first resurrection**. Over such **the second death** has no power, but they shall be **priests** of God and of Christ, and shall reign with Him a thousand years … But the cowardly, **unbelieving**, abominable, murderers, sexually immoral, sorcerers, idolaters, and all liars shall have their part in the **lake which burns with fire and brimstone**, which is **the second death**" (**Revelation 20:6, 21:8**).

Now recall that the Serpent is the one who deceived the whole world, and understand that the title "Serpent" is one of the symbolic names for Satan, the Devil who came from heaven: "So the **great dragon** was cast out, that **serpent of old, called the Devil and Satan**, who **deceives the whole world**; he was **cast to the earth**, and **his angels were cast out with him**" (**Revelation 12:9**).

So then "Adam" in the phrase "**Adam**, who is a **type** of Him to come" is referring to Satan, who deceived the whole world with a lie. We will see in the chapter called "The Beginning as Seen from Earth" that the Hebrew word "*Adam*" basically refers to the lowly state of fallen angels or fallen spirits in bodies of flesh. And since Satan is the angel called Lucifer before the fall from grace, this qualifies Satan to be called *Adam*, because he was an angel that fell from heaven with one-third of heaven's angels: "**His tail drew a third of the stars of heaven** and **threw them to the earth**. And the **dragon** stood before the woman who was ready to give birth, to devour her Child as soon as it was born" (**Revelation 12:4**). So the **first Adam** is Satan and those who believed his lies and followed him and were all cast out of heaven and down to earth.

Notice that "first Adam" does **not** refer to the first man named Adam any more than "second Adam," a name that refers to Christ, refers to the first man named Adam. In fact, there are two different definitions in the Hebrew to separate the different uses of the word Adam. In the Hebrew, H120 *Adam* refers to an individual man or all mankind, and H121 *Adam* refers to the name of the first man, whose name is Adam. Both the first *Adam*, Satan, and the second *Adam*, Jesus, are the leaders of those who believe and follow them. The first man, named Adam, was deceived by Satan just as we all were. To clarify this point, the Bible speaks of Eve as the person who sinned first, not the first man, named Adam.

Now let us look at the first part of that phrase: "Death reigned from Adam to Moses, even over those who **had not sinned according to the likeness of the transgression of Adam**." Lucifer, now called Satan, is the angel that *deceived* us with a lie in heaven and is symbolically called the Serpent on earth. *Webster's Student Dictionary* defines "deceive" as "**To catch**, to mislead; **delude**; **cheat**; **trick**."

The first Adam, Satan, knew what he was doing when he purposely and intentionally deceived us, who were ignorant of the truth and believed his lies and followed him into his trap. And Jesus Himself warns us not to be one who causes another to not believe and to sin: "But whoever **causes one of these little ones who believe in Me to stumble**, it would be better for him if a millstone were hung around his neck, and he were thrown into the sea" (**Mark 9:42**).

That is why it says that we are fallen angels or spirits (*adam*) in bodies of flesh, "who had not sinned according to the likeness of the transgression of Adam," who deceived and led us, "the whole world," astray. The Bible reveals that we did not know what we were doing; we were ignorant: "For **they being ignorant of God's righteousness**, and seeking **to establish their own righteousness**, have not **submitted to the righteousness of God**" (**Romans 10:3**).

The author of Hebrews, speaking of Jesus, tells us that "**He can have compassion** on those who are **ignorant** and **going astray**, since he himself is also subject to **weakness**" (**Hebrews 5:2**). And this ignorance of man is confirmed by Jesus with these words: "If I had not come and spoken to them, **they would have no sin**, but now they **have no excuse** for their sin" (**John 15:22**). In fact, this ignorance of the truth is why Jesus came into the world. "**For this cause I was born**, and **for this cause I have come into the world**, that I should **bear witness to the truth**. Everyone who is of the truth hears My voice" (**John 18:37b**).

While the first Adam, Lucifer (now called Satan), deceived and trapped us and led us into sin and death: "How **you are fallen from heaven, O Lucifer**, son of the morning! *How* you are **cut down to the ground**, You who **weakened the nations!** [13] For **you have said in your heart**: **'I will ascend into heaven, I will exalt my throne above the stars of God**; I will also sit on the mount of the congregation On the farthest sides of the north; [14] **I will ascend above the heights of the clouds, I will be like the Most High'"** (**Isaiah 14:13–14**), the second Adam, Jesus, was without sin, and He voluntarily and intentionally made Himself lower than the high and anointed "**Angel of the LORD**" that He was. He came to earth and put on flesh like we did so He could be like us in order to save us from our sin: "Let this mind be in you which was also in **Christ Jesus**, [6] who, **being in the form of God**, did not consider it robbery to be **equal with God**, [7] but **made Himself of no reputation**, taking the **form of a bondservant**, *and* coming in the **likeness of men**. [8] And being found in appearance as a man, **He humbled Himself** and became **obedient to *the point of* death**, even the **death of the cross**" (**Philippians 2:5–8**).

GOOD AND EVIL CANNOT BE UNITED TOGETHER AS ONE

The Loss of Oneness with God

> And the Lord God said, "**It is not good that man should be alone**; I will make him a helper comparable to him." ... [24] Therefore a man shall leave his father and mother and be joined to his wife, and **they shall become one flesh**. [25] And

200

they were both naked, the man and his wife, and were not ashamed. (**Genesis 2:18, 24–25**)

In the six-day creation story of man and the world, found in the first chapter of Genesis, God continues to declare that what He has created is good, and **Genesis 2:18** is the first place He says that something in His creation is not good. The first man to put on flesh, named Adam, who is the earthly father of all mankind, was alone. Being alone is not the nature of God. In heaven, the kingdom of God consists of God the Father, God the Son, and God the Holy Spirit—that is, a great many angels or spirits who all live together as One in love.

We know that Adam was not in an intimate, loving relationship with anyone, and that includes God, because if he had been in a loving relationship with God, he would not have been alone. The first thing God did for the first man, named Adam, was give him a wife so that they, joined together as one, could have children to make a family on earth. This family was to replace the family Adam lost in heaven, for we know Adam was a son of God before the fall, as this is pointed out by Jesus' earthly lineage in the book of Luke: "Now **Jesus** Himself began *His ministry at* about thirty years of age, being (as was supposed) *the* **son of Joseph**, *the son* **of Heli** … *the son* **of Enos**, *the son* **of Seth**, *the son* **of Adam**, *the son* **of God**" (**Luke 3:23, 38**).

And as Adam had been a son of God before the fall, so were we all, for the Psalmist, speaking the words of God, says, "They **do not know, nor do they understand**; They walk about in darkness; All the foundations of the earth are unstable. [6] I said, "**You** *are* **gods**, And **all of you** *are* **children of the Most High**. [7] But you shall die like men, And fall like one of the **princes**" (**Psalm 82:5–7**).

And the inspired words of Moses reveal that we dwelled with God before God formed the earth: "A Prayer of Moses the **man of God**. LORD, **You have been our dwelling place** in all **generations**. [2] **Before the mountains were brought forth**, Or **ever You had formed the earth** and **the world**, Even from everlasting to everlasting, You *are* God. [3] You **turn man to destruction**, And say, "**Return, O children of men**" (**Psalm 90:1–3**).

The Hebrew word for "men" in **Psalm 90:3** is H120 *adam*, which refers to those who believed the lies of the Serpent, who is Satan, who is himself qualified to be called "*adam*." So the verse "Return, O children of men" means something like "Return, O children of Adam" or "Return, O fallen children of Satan who formerly dwelled as My children!" And this is what the apostle Paul says in a letter to the Romans, speaking about the meaning of the prophecy of Hosea: "As He says also in Hosea: '*I will call them My people, who were not My people, And her beloved, who was not beloved.* [26] *And it shall come to pass in the place where it was said to them, You are not My people,' There they shall be called sons of the living God*" (**Romans 9:25–26**). Symbolically, the people of Israel were the children of God, until harlotry with other gods caused God to disown them. But God will again call those who return to Him sons and daughters of God. And this foreshadows us, fallen mankind, to whom God said, "You are not my people," in heaven when we were cast to the earth with Satan; and those of us who believe in God will one day in heaven be called sons of the living God.

Recall what I explained in "The Love Branch" regarding how all of us believed the lie of Satan and were trapped by him, but those who learn the truth of God can be set free to return to God. "In this **the children of God** and **the children of the devil** are manifest: Whoever **does not practice righteousness** is **not of God**, nor *is* **he who does not love his brother**" (**1 John 3:10**). We will understand all of this and much more in the chapters that follow.

We know from the New Testament that when we are in God, we are never alone ("*Let your* conduct *be* without covetousness; *be* **content** with such things as you have. For He Himself has said, '*I will* **never leave you** *nor forsake you*'" [**Hebrews 13:5**]), and that Jesus said, "And I give them **eternal life**, and **they shall never perish**; neither shall anyone **snatch them out of My hand**. [29] My Father, who has given *them* to Me, **is greater than all**; and no one is able **to snatch** *them* **out of My Father's hand**. [30] I and *My* **Father are one**" (**John 10:28–29**).

While God will never leave us, we are not held by force against our will but are always free to leave Him. In fact, that is what we did when we all believed the lies of the Serpent, who is Satan. God will never force us to stay with Him, for God is a God of love, and love must be a free-will choice. To do otherwise would be like the slavery of Satan. But if people choose not to live in a loving relationship with God, to go off on their own, they must be cast out of His kingdom like a life-robbing cancer, for love is righteousness, and righteousness cannot exist with unrighteousness, as the apostle Paul declared to the Corinthians:

> Do not be **unequally yoked together with unbelievers**. For what fellowship has righteousness with lawlessness? And what **communion** has **light with darkness**? [15] And what accord has **Christ** with **Belial**? Or **what part has a believer** with an **unbeliever**? [16] And what agreement has the **temple of God** with **idols**? For **you are the temple** of the **living God**. As God has said: "*I will **dwell in them** And **walk among them**. I will be their God, And **they shall be My people**.*" [17] Therefore "***Come out from among them** And **be separate**, says the Lord. Do not touch what is unclean, And **I will receive you**.*" (**2 Corinthians 6:14–17**)

The word "Belial" refers to Satan, just as the word "Christ" refers to Jesus. The word "Belial" comes from the Greek word G955 *Belial*, which means "Of Hebrew origin H1100 *beliya'al*, worthlessness; Belial, as an epithet of **Satan**." *Webster's Student Dictionary* defines "Belial" as "A **devil**; **specifically, Satan**."

So if God declares that Adam is alone, then he is not in a loving relationship with God, and that means it is Adam that must have chosen to be separated from God, even though the first man, named Adam, had only just put on flesh in **Genesis 2:7** when "**man became a living soul**" (KJV). This issue, of having sinned and being alone and separated from God before we were born on earth by putting on flesh, is the issue of **Romans 9:10–13**: "And not only *this,* but when Rebecca also had conceived by one man, *even* by our father Isaac [11] (for *the children* **not yet being born, nor having done any good or evil**, that the purpose of God **according to election** might stand, **not of works** but **of Him who calls**), [12] it was said to her, '*The older shall serve the younger.*' [13] As it is written, '***Jacob I have loved,** but **Esau I have hated**.*'" This may be a bit confusing right now, but hang in there; this is a most important statement by God and is necessary to a proper understanding of the Bible. It is just a little hard for us to see the big picture all at once, especially while we have been and are being fed the lies of this world at the same time. Be patient and read what the apostle Paul has said best: "For whatever things were written before **were written for our learning**, that we through the **patience** and **comfort of the Scriptures** might have **hope**" (**Romans 15:4**).

WE ARE ALL PRODIGAL SONS AND DAUGHTERS OF GOD

Speaking of choosing separation from God and the oneness that He is, let us consider the story of the prodigal son as told by Jesus.

> Then He said: "A certain man had **two sons**. [12] And the younger of them said to *his* father, 'Father, give me the portion of goods that falls *to me.*' So he divided to **them** *his* livelihood. [13] And not many days after, the younger son gathered all together, journeyed to a **far country**, and there wasted his possessions with prodigal living. [14] But when he had spent all, there arose a severe famine in that land, and he began to be in want.
>
> [15] Then he went and **joined himself** to a citizen of that country, and he sent him into his fields to feed swine. [16] And he would gladly have filled his stomach with the pods that the swine ate, and **no one gave him** *anything*. [17] But **when he came to himself**, he said, 'How many of my father's hired servants have bread enough and to spare, and **I perish with hunger**! [18] I will arise and go to my father, and will say to him, "Father, I have sinned against heaven and before you, [19] and I am no longer worthy to be called your son. Make me like one of your hired servants."'
>
> [20] "And he arose and **came to his father**. But when he was still a great way off, his father saw him and had compassion, and ran and fell on his neck and kissed him. [21] And the son said to him, '**Father, I have sinned against heaven and in your sight**, and **am no longer worthy to be called your son**.' [22] But the father said to his servants, 'Bring out the best robe and put *it* on

204

him, and put a ring on his hand and sandals on *his* feet. ²³ And bring the fatted calf here and kill *it,* and let us eat and be merry; ²⁴ for this **my son was dead** and **is alive again**; he was **lost** and is **found**.' And they began to be merry." (**Luke 15:11–24**)

The Prodigal Son left his father, who had a loving family and could supply everyone with all they wanted and more. Many children are ignorant of what it takes to create the "oneness" that provides for their prosperity; their fallen nature longs for the freedom of being able to do what they want, but they do not understand that freedom is not free. They do not understand the synergy of many working together as one and that "**it is not good that man should be alone**" (**Genesis 2:18b**).

After the son left home and spent his father's money in prodigal living and a famine arose in the land, he began to understand the truth and reality of being alone. There was no one who gave him anything, as his father had done. In **verse 15**, when he "joined himself to a citizen of that country" and he was sent to feed swine, he was so hungry he wished he could eat the slop he was feeding them. To the Jews, swine were unclean animals that they would not eat, yet he had sunk so low as to wish to eat what they were eating.

It was at that point that he came to the end of himself and learned that being joined with someone who does not love you or care for you is a form of living that leads to death, and that is exactly what he said: "**I perish with hunger!**" When the Prodigal Son learned the truth of what makes for oneness, a truth that his father already knew, he had a profound change of heart and was humbled and now was in a position to enter into a true loving relationship with his father, and that is all the father was concerned about. The father was only concerned about the son he had lost, who was as good as dead to him; he cared nothing about the money he had squandered. The father valued a loving relationship with his son above all and celebrated, "for this my son **was dead** and is **alive again**; he **was lost** and **is found**."

This ought to strike a chord of resemblance and remembrance in our heart, because this is a picture of our relationship with our Father in heaven when we left home thinking we could do better on our own, for this is what Jesus said before He told this story: "I say to you that likewise there will be **more joy in heaven over one sinner who repents** than over ninety-nine just persons who need no repentance" (**Luke 15:7**). This is also what our Father in heaven warned us prodigal sons and daughters about before we left home to be on our own: "but **of the tree of the knowledge of good and evil you shall not eat**, for in the day that you eat of it **you shall surely die**" (**Genesis 2:17**).

The other son who had stayed at home with his father became angry and did not celebrate but focused on the money his brother had wasted:

> Now his **older son** was in the field. And as he came and drew near to the house, he heard music and dancing. [26] So he called one of the **servants** and asked what these things meant. [27] And he said to him, "Your brother has come, and because he has received him safe and sound, your father has killed the fatted calf."
>
> [28] But **he was angry** and would not go in. Therefore his father came out and pleaded with him. [29] So he answered and said to *his* father, "Lo, these many years **I have been serving you; I never transgressed your commandment at any time**; and yet you never gave me a young goat, that I might make merry with my friends. [30] But as soon as this son of yours came, **who has devoured your livelihood with harlots**, you killed the fatted calf for him." [31] And he said to him, "Son, you are always with me, and all that I have is yours. [32] It was right that we should make merry and be glad, for **your brother was dead** and is **alive again**, and was **lost** and is **found**." (**Luke 15:25–32**)

The older son was angry. He had been living with his father as though he were a servant, trying to earn what he would receive from his father, and he was more concerned about lost money than the welfare of his brother. I think the moral of this story is that in heaven, love and forgiveness are the economy that makes for prosperity, peace, and joy. Money is the reward for your individual work; it is the expectation of return for what you have done, and it is self-centered and a way that causes division and the loss of oneness. The Prodigal Son's father was wealthy and would always provide. In a community of Oneness, love trumps individual wealth. The Prodigal Son was forgiven much, and as we have learned, those who are forgiven much love more. "Therefore I say to you, her sins, *which are* many, are forgiven, for she loved much. But **to whom little is forgiven,** *the same* **loves little**" (**Luke 7:47**). The Prodigal Son came into a loving relationship with his father. He would thereafter do what his father asked out of love and a feeling of family unity.

The older son was not forgiven anything; nor does he think he needs forgiveness, though he is angry and does not love his brother, which is tearing his family apart. "He who says he is in the light, and **hates his brother, is in darkness until now**" (**1 John 2:9**), and "**whoever hates his brother is a murderer,** and you know that **no murderer has eternal life abiding in him.** [16] By this we know **love,** because **He laid down His life for us.** And we also ought to **lay down *our* lives for the brethren.** [17] But whoever has **this world's goods,** and **sees his brother in need,** and **shuts up his heart from him,** how does the **love of God** abide in him?" (**1 John 3:15**). Jesus warns us about the love of wealth elsewhere: "No one can **serve two masters;** for either he will hate the one and love the other, or else he will be loyal to the one and despise the other. **You cannot serve God and mammon**" (**Matthew 6:24**). Living for God and living for money are completely different ways of living.

MARRIAGE IS A FORESHADOWING OF ONENESS IN CHRIST

In the Beginning, God Made Us One

You cover the altar of the LORD with tears, With weeping and crying; So He does not regard the offering anymore, Nor receive *it* with goodwill from your hands. [14] Yet you say, "For what reason?" Because the Lord has been witness Between you and the wife of your youth, With whom you have dealt treacherously; Yet **she is your companion** And **your wife by covenant.** [15] But **did He not make them one,** Having a **remnant of the**

> **Spirit**? And **why one**? **He seeks godly offspring**. Therefore take heed to **your spirit**, And let none deal treacherously with the wife of his youth. **(Malachi 2:15)**

The word "remnant" is translated from the Hebrew word H7605 *shear*, which means "A remainder, other, **remnant, residue**, rest." Webster defines "remnant" as "2. a) A **small fragment**. b) An unsold end of a length of cloth, or the like. 3. A **surviving trace**" and defines "residue" as "1. That which remains when **a part** is **taken, separated, designated**."

God made us male and female to be one, and because of this, we are a "remnant," a surviving fragment or example of the Spirit that is Holy— the Holy Spirit. Why? That He may have godly children forming a godly family that is part of His family and no longer part of Satan's disconnected horde. God's Holy Spirit is the collection or union of holy spirits in heaven; and spirits in bodies of flesh who are united as a holy family on earth, the holy church of Christ, are an example or remnant on earth of His Holy Spirit in heaven.

This Oneness of the family is the great mystery of God, called in the Latin "*Unio Mystica*," which Satan does not understand and is trying to destroy.

> See then that you walk circumspectly, **not as fools but as wise**, ¹⁶ **redeeming the time**, because **the days are evil**. ¹⁷ Therefore **do not be unwise**, but **understand** what the will of the Lord *is* … **submitting to one another** in the fear of God. ²² Wives, submit to your own husbands, **as to the Lord**. ²³ For the husband is head of the wife, **as also Christ is head of the church**; and He is the Savior of **the body**. ²⁴ Therefore, just as **the church is subject to Christ**, so let the wives be to their own husbands in everything.
>
> ²⁵ Husbands, **love your wives**, just as **Christ also loved the church** and gave Himself for her, ²⁶ **that He might sanctify** and **cleanse her** with the **washing of water by the word**, ²⁷ that He might present her to Himself a glorious church, not having spot or wrinkle or any such thing, but that she should be **holy** and **without blemish**. ²⁸ So husbands ought to **love their**

own wives as their own bodies; he who loves his wife
loves himself. [29] For no one ever **hated his own flesh**, but
nourishes and cherishes it, **just as the Lord does the church**.

[30] For **we are members of His body**, of His flesh and of His
bones. [31] **"For this reason a man shall leave his father and
mother** and be **joined to his wife**, and **the two shall become
one flesh."** [32] This is **a great mystery**, but I speak concerning
Christ and the church. [33] Nevertheless let each one of you in
particular so **love his own wife as himself**, and let the wife
see that she **respects** her husband. (**Ephesians 5:15–17, 21–33**)

So the marriage of a man and a woman is a remnant of Christ and His
church.

In all this we have to remember that this world where we are temporarily
living in bodies of flesh is not our home but that heaven is our home.
We who have fallen are on trial to see how we respond to the truth
and discover what is in our hearts and minds that we may change our
hearts and minds and return home. We need to remember that being
male and female is only a temporary role that we have been given on
this earth to teach us about what it takes to live as one in preparation
for being in the Oneness of Christ where we all will joyfully, lovingly,
and willfully submit to the rule of God the Father, Jesus our Lord and
Savior, and submit to each other out of love for each other.

In heaven there will be no male and female:

Jesus answered and said to them, "You are mistaken, **not
knowing the Scriptures** nor **the power of God**. [30] For **in the
resurrection** they **neither marry** nor are given in marriage,
but **are like angels of God** in heaven." (**Matthew 22:29–30**)

There is neither Jew nor Greek, there is neither slave nor free,
there is **neither male nor female**; for **you are all one in
Christ Jesus**. (**Galatians 3:28**)

After the trial is over and those of us who belong to Christ are separated
from those who belong to Satan, each group will go the way they
chose in this life on earth. Those who belong to Jesus will enter into a

marriage-like covenant with Christ—who is the Lamb of God, as the apostle John relates to us in a revelation from God: "Then he said to me, 'Write: **"Blessed *are* those who are called to the marriage supper of the Lamb**!"'" And he said to me, 'These are the true sayings of God'" (**Revelation 19:9**). Those who belong to Satan will be thrown into a lake of fire: "Then Death and Hades were cast into the lake of fire. This is the **second death**. [15] And anyone not found written in the **Book of Life** was cast into the lake of fire" (**Revelation 20:14–15**).

SYNERGY—THE SOURCE OF POWER AND PRODUCTIVITY

We have already learned that American mathematician John Nash has mathematically proven that the most productive economy is one in which people do what is in their best interest *and* what is in the best interest of others, and that this is exactly what Jesus was teaching us about the effect of *agape* love and being united in one, some two thousand years ago. Synergy is the name given to that effect. *Merriam-Webster's Collegiate Dictionary* defines "Synergy" as coming from the Greek word "*synergos*," which means "*working* **together**. SYNERGISM: *broadly*: combined action or operation" and "synergism" is defined as "The interaction of discrete agencies (as industrial firms) agents or conditions such that the total effect is greater than the sum of the individual effects." To rephrase that using "people" instead of "discrete agencies" and "produce" for "effect" and "work" for "interaction," "synergism" would then mean "two or more people *working* together will produce more than the sum of the same number of individuals working separately." Notice that the definition of "synergy" speaks of work (interaction) and the effect or amount of production from that work. If one or more individuals do not work in an interactive way, they add nothing to the effect of synergy.

This concept of synergy was spoken of by Jesus in a verse quoted in our discussion of marriage: "You are mistaken, **not knowing the Scriptures** nor **the power of God**" (**Matthew 22:29**) and in thefollowing passage: "**Abide in Me**, and I in you. As the branch **cannot bear fruit of itself**, unless it abides in the vine, neither can you, unless you abide in Me. [5] I am the vine, **you *are* the branches**. He who **abides in Me**, and I in him, **bears much fruit**; for **without Me you can do nothing**" (**John 15:4–5**). When we believe and trust in Jesus and become united in One with the kingdom of God, we will tap into the power of God to accomplish the purposes that benefits all in the kingdom. "So Jesus said to them, ' … for assuredly, I say to you, **if you have faith as a mustard seed**, you will say to this mountain, "Move from here to there," and it will move; and **nothing will be impossible for you**'" (**Matthew 17:20**).

The thing with synergism is that the greater the number of individuals working together, the greater the synergistic effect. Also, when a large group of individuals working together synergistically breaks up into a number of smaller groups of individuals working together with each other, each having a synergistic effect within the individual groups, there is an even more powerful synergy among the synergistic groups working together than if there were no subgroups at all.

These ideas are easier to understand in an example. If we consider a group of ten million individuals all working alone for themselves, how long would it take an individual to build, for example, a car from scratch, if he were to do it all by himself? Obviously he would die before he even got close to completing one car. Consider just what it would take to build an alternator, which provides the electricity to run a car. Think of all the science and engineering you would have to know before you even began. Why, you would have to first mine the aluminum and other metals to create the body of the alternator and mine the copper for the windings for the motor. Then think about what it would take to do the precision machining and tooling that it would take to make the ball bearings that the motor would spin on. The work list goes on and on just to build one small part of a modern automobile. The problem is even worse if you consider that our hypothetical worker had to build his own house to live in and produce his own food to eat as he built his car, and then he would have nowhere to drive it until he built roads first. But the power of synergy is amazing:

Now consider this group of ten million people working together to build cars for all the individuals in the group. In the case of one large group working together as if they were one, all would mine the metals together, and then all would work together to build all the metal parts, and so on for all the different parts needed. But even before they started, they all would have to work together to grow food and build houses, and producing food is a chore that never ends. While this strategy is better than each working alone, it is obvious that there would be more productivity if the ten million would break up into many smaller synergistic groups of hundreds and thousands and tens of thousands to produce all the things necessary for modern life. A hierarchy of small synergistic groups working together for the same purpose creates more synergy than one large group working together. This concept is hard to put into words but easy to understand.

This power of synergy, individuals working together in a hierarchy of subgroups as though they were One is an important idea in the Word of God. This idea of the synergy of individuals in a group and the synergy of groups working together as one is shown in the Bible in the story of Moses. Moses was being worn out by being the judge of all the disputes between millions of Israelites all by himself, and it kept him from his other duties as their leader as well.

So God sent Moses' father-in-law to show Moses a better way. Instead of Moses trying to judge millions of Israelites by himself, he told Moses to select God-fearing men of truth and place them as rulers of thousands, rulers of hundreds, rulers of fifties, and rulers of tens to be judges. Then they would judge the matters that were small, and matters that were too great for them would go to Moses (**Genesis 18:13–27**). This hierarchy of judicial authority took the burden off of Moses and allowed him to do his work of leadership.

SOVEREIGNTY, POWER, AND FREE-WILL CHOICE

There is another aspect of trying to create "Oneness" that we need to consider. *Merriam-Webster's Collegiate Dictionary* defines "sovereignty" as "**Supreme power**, especially over a body politic; **freedom from external control**: Autonomy; **controlling influence**."

So we see by this definition that to be sovereign, one needs to have the most power to keep others from imposing their will upon one regardless of what their will desires. When two individuals are considered, the most powerful is sovereign. As more individuals enter the mix, the situation changes. Individuals who are not the most powerful can band together to overpower the most powerful individual. In order for an individual to be sovereign, that individual would have to be more powerful than all other individuals put together. In order for a group of individuals to be sovereign, they would have to be more powerful together than all the other individuals should they come together in one group.

For the most powerful group to be sovereign—to be in control, free from external control—they would also have to remain united in a common will. If this group were divided on an issue that affected the unity of the group, and if that caused them to divide into two or more independent groups, then they would all lose some of the power of synergy, and all but one of those groups would no longer be sovereign. And this is exactly what Jesus was talking about to the Pharisees: "But Jesus knew their thoughts, and said to them: 'Every kingdom **divided against itself** is **brought to desolation**, and every **city** or **house divided against itself will not stand**'" (**Matthew 12:25**).

I always find it interesting when I hear some small country being described as "the sovereign nation of Trinidad (or Luxembourg, or some other small country)." They are only sovereign because other nations let them be sovereign and do not challenge their claim of sovereignty. To be truly sovereign, an entity must be more powerful than all the rest combined.

Uniting into groups to gain power and sovereignty is part of the history of the world. In the early days on this earth, individuals planted crops and raised herds of animals for food, built houses to live in, and made flour mills, wine presses, plows, pottery and the things people needed to make a better life for themselves. But if a group who wanted what they had was more powerful than they were, that stronger group would just take what they had worked for, and maybe kill them to keep them from retaliating or keep them as slaves.

To keep this from happening, people banded together and built walls around their dwellings and made weapons to fight off those who would steal what they had worked for. To keep order in their group and keep them united and working together as One, they set a leader or a king over them so that the group would be of the same will—the king's will. People quickly recognized the synergy—the power, productivity, and prosperity—of many working together as One, but they learned it after they learned that some people believe that they can do better for themselves by taking advantage of the work of others.

Small nations or kingdoms made agreements and alliances for protection when they could not combine to make a larger kingdom for one reason or another. Some smaller nations negotiated agreements to pay a percentage of their produce to a more powerful nation for protection. That way they did not have to spend resources producing weapons of battle and have a large standing group of soldiers. **Genesis 14:1–24** is a biblical example of this during the days of Abraham and Lot.

In the community, there is a time and a place where some of the more glamorous talents are not important, but some other gift or talent that is less honorable is needed. I remember a time when the garbage haulers went on strike in New York City and it brought the city to its knees! Prosperity requires a variety of gifts and talents. The truth is that we all need each other and what we contribute to the community to make all successful and prosperous. The Apostle Paul expresses these ideas of synergy of the hierarchy of individuals working together in groups, the synergy of groups, and the role of power and sovereignty in the Church, which is the Body of Christ on earth, in **1 Corinthians Chapter 12**:

THE SYNERGY OF ONENESS IN THE BIBLE

In the New Testament the Bible speaks of what great things can be accomplished when individuals work together in a hierarchy of subgroups, "But the **manifestation of the Spirit** is given **to each one** for **the profit of all**: [8] for to one is given the **word of wisdom** through the **Spirit**, to another the **word of knowledge** through the **same Spirit,** [9] to another **faith** by the **same Spirit**, to another gifts of **healings** by the **same Spirit,** [10] to another the **working of miracles,** to another **prophecy,** to another **discerning of spirits,** to another different kinds of **tongues,** to another the **interpretation of tongues.** [11] But one and **the same Spirit** works all these things, distributing to each one individually as He wills" (**1 Corinthians 12:7–11**).

Here we get the sense that the "**Spirit**" who gives the "**spirits**" the gifts of knowledge, wisdom, discernment, healings, working of miracles, etc., is the Holy Spirit in heaven and the spirits are in the souls of man on earth.

And Paul describes the Body of Christ by using the human body as a picture, "For as **the body is one** and **has many members, but all the members of that one body, being many, are one body, so also** *is* **Christ.** [13] For **by one Spirit** we were all **baptized into one body**—whether Jews or Greeks, whether slaves or free—and have all been made to **drink into one Spirit.** [14] For in fact **the body is not one member but many.** [15] If the foot should say, "Because I am not a hand, I am not of the body," is it therefore not of the body? [16] And if the ear should say, "Because I am not an eye, I am not of the body," is it therefore not of the body? [17] If the whole body *were* an eye, where *would be* the hearing? If the whole *were* hearing, where *would be* the smelling? [18] But now **God has set the members, each one of them, in the body just as He pleased**" (**1 Corinthians 12:12–18**).

Here Paul is talking metaphorically about the Church thinking that just because they have been given different Spiritual gifts and talents and given different tasks to accomplish they should not think that they are not part of the whole Church, the Body of Christ, and be divided

215

because they have been given different roles to play and different gifts to use.

"And if they *were* all one member, where *would* the body *be?* [20] But now indeed *there are* **many members, yet one body**. [21] And the eye cannot say to the hand, "I have no need of you"; nor again the head to the feet, "I have no need of you." [22] No, much rather, **those members of the body which seem to be weaker are necessary**. [23] And those *members* of the body which we think to be less honorable, on these we bestow greater honor; and our unpresentable *parts* have greater modesty, [24] but our presentable *parts* have no need.

But God composed the body, having given greater honor to that *part* which lacks it, [25] that there should be **no schism in the body**, but *that* the members should have **the same care for one another**. [26] And **if one member suffers, all the members suffer with** *it;* or **if one member is honored, all the members rejoice with** *it.* [27] Now **you are the body of Christ**, and **members individually**" (**1 Corinthians 12:19–27**).

This helps us understand how God is three yet One. The Father is the head and leader, the Son is second in command, and the Holy Spirit is the Body of holy spirits in a hierarchy of authority in the Kingdom called God!

"And **God has appointed these in the church: first apostles, second prophets, third teachers**, after that **miracles**, then gifts of **healings**, helps, **administrations**, varieties of **tongues**. [29] *Are* all apostles? *Are* all prophets? *Are* all teachers? *Are* all workers of miracles? [30] Do all have gifts of healings? Do all speak with tongues? Do all interpret? [31] "But earnestly desire the best gifts. **And yet I show you a more excellent way**" (**1 Corinthians 12: 28–31**).

The very next words by Paul make up **1 Corinthians Chapter 13**, what many students of the Bible call the "Love Chapter." Love is what makes the unity of individuals into one possible and the rich benefits of the synergy of Oneness along with peace, joy, kindness, harmony, and fellowship. **Love is the more excellent way! Love is the way of God that leads us to eternal life!**

THERE IS POWER AND SAFETY IN NUMBERS

I had always been a little confused about the meaning of the parable in **Luke 11:14–26**:

> And He was casting out a demon, **and it was mute**. So it was, when the demon had gone out, **that the mute spoke**; and the multitudes marveled. [15] But some of them said, "He casts out demons by Beelzebub, the ruler of the demons." [16] Others, testing *Him,* sought from Him a sign from heaven. [17] But He, **knowing their thoughts**, said to them: "**Every kingdom divided against itself is brought to desolation**, and **a house *divided* against a house falls.**
>
> [18] **If Satan also is divided against himself, how will his kingdom stand**? Because you say I cast out demons by Beelzebub. [19] And if I cast out demons by Beelzebub, by whom do your sons cast *them* out? Therefore they will be your judges. [20] But if I cast out demons with the finger of God, **surely the kingdom of God has come upon you**.
>
> [21] When a strong man, fully armed, guards his own palace, his goods are in peace. [22] But **when a stronger than he comes upon him** and **overcomes him**, he takes from him all his armor in which he trusted, and divides his spoils. [23] **He who is not with Me is against Me**, and he who does not gather with Me scatters. [24] When an unclean spirit goes out of a man, he goes through dry places, seeking rest; and finding none, he says, 'I **will return to my house from which I came.'** [25] And when he comes, he finds *it* swept and put in order. [26] **Then he goes and takes with *him* seven other spirits more wicked than himself**, and **they enter and dwell there**; and **the last *state* of that man is worse than the first.**

Then I had an inspiration one morning about something I had been thinking about for quite some time. I thought about the idea of sovereignty and what it takes to be totally independent of anyone else. Then I got the idea that sovereignty is what this parable is about. The evil spirit in **Luke 11:14–26** that goes out and looks for rest (a better dwelling place) and finds none decides to return and finds the house he came from swept and put in order (living in righteousness), meaning he can no longer overcome his former host with his evil power alone, so he goes and finds seven spirits more evil than he, and they dwell there.

This parable is about not being able to live a righteous life alone and on your own when there are others around you who are more powerful than you and do not care about you. This is why God warned that it was not good that man should be alone in **Genesis 2:18**: "And the LORD God said, '*It is* **not good that man should be alone**; I will make him a helper comparable to him.' We are spirits who were given a temporary body of flesh to live in just like Jesus was given, '**Inasmuch then as the children have partaken of flesh and blood**, He Himself likewise shared in the same, that through death He might destroy **him who had the power of death, that is, the devil'**" (**Hebrews 2:14**).

The Devil has the power of death over us! Living in a way where there is survival of the fittest is the way of Satan, and it is the way of death because it destroys the life of the loving community where all work together as One that supports each individual for eternal life.

> And the LORD God commanded the man, saying, "Of every tree of the garden you may freely eat; [17] **but of the tree of the knowledge of good and evil you shall not eat**, for in the day that you eat of it you shall **surely die**." (**Genesis 2:17**)

> **For the wages of sin *is* death**, but the **gift of God *is* eternal life in Christ Jesus our Lord**. (**Romans 6:23**)

We are given dominion over our body of flesh that we live in, but other spirits may dwell in our bodies with us. Evil spirits want to overpower us and take control of us, but Jesus will not permit them to unless we choose to let them in by the way we live our life. The kingdom of God is all-powerful, but it is a kingdom of love and free-will choice.

Whereas Satan and his demons desire is to overpower us and indwell our bodies of flesh by force, God waits to be invited into our bodies to live with our spirit, to be one with our spirit. "Behold, **I stand at the door and knock. If anyone hears My voice** and **opens the door, I will come in to him** and **dine with him**, and **he with Me.** 21 **To him who overcomes I will grant to sit with Me on My throne**, as I also overcame and sat down with My Father on His throne" (**Revelation 3:20–21**).

There are many stories of Jesus casting out evil spirits from those who are possessed by them. In one case there was a legion of evil spirits cast out of the body of one man: "For He had commanded the unclean spirit to come out of the man. For it had often seized him, and he was kept under guard, bound with chains and shackles; and he broke the bonds and **was driven by the demon into the wilderness.** 30 Jesus asked him, saying, 'What is your name?' And he said, '**Legion,' because many demons had entered him**" (**Luke 8:30**).

When we have had the demons swept out of our life, we are not powerful enough to stand alone to keep them out; we need to invite Jesus into our life, for no one can overpower Him, and He loves us and cares for us besides. He alone can give us true freedom and eternal life. And this is exactly what the Psalmist sings of: "LORD, who *is* like You, Delivering the poor from **him who is too strong for him**, Yes, the poor and the needy from him who plunders him?" (**Psalm 35:10**).

Pride vs. Humility

Pride is focusing on oneself, and humility is focusing on the needs of others. "All things are lawful for me, but not all things are helpful; all things are lawful for me, but not all things **edify.** 24 **Let no one seek his own**, but **each one** the **other's** *well*-**being**" (**1 Corinthians 10:23–24**). The Bible says that the selfishness of the proud is the reason God resists the proud:

> Likewise you younger people, **submit yourselves to *your* elders.** Yes, **all of *you* be submissive to one another**, and be **clothed with humility**, for "*God resists the proud, But gives*

grace to the humble." [6] Therefore **humble yourselves** under the mighty hand of God, that He may exalt you in due time, [7] casting all your care upon Him, for **He cares for you**. (**1 Peter 5:5–7**)

Do you not know that **friendship with the world is enmity with God**? **Whoever therefore wants to be a friend** of the **world makes himself an enemy of God**. [5] Or do you think that the Scripture says in vain, **"The Spirit who dwells in us** yearns jealously"? [6] But He gives more grace. Therefore He says: *"God resists the proud, But gives grace to the humble."* [7] Therefore **submit to God. Resist the devil** and **he will flee from you**. [8] **Draw near to God** and **He will draw near to you**. Cleanse *your* hands, *you* sinners; and **purify *your*** hearts, *you* double-minded. (**James 4:4–8**)

In the end, we are not powerful enough to live on our own; that is just a lie of Satan to trap us as slaves under his rule. We will either voluntarily, joyfully, lovingly submit to God, who loves us and cares for us, or be forced by Satan to remain submitted to him under his rule as slaves to him, who does not care for us but cares only what we can do for him. And that is exactly what Paul teaches in a letter to Timothy: "And a servant of the Lord must not quarrel but be **gentle to all**, able to teach, **patient**, [25] in **humility** correcting those who are in opposition, if God perhaps will **grant them repentance**, so that **they may know the truth**, [26] and *that* **they may come to their senses** *and escape* **the snare of the devil**, having been **taken captive by him to** *do* **his will**" (**2 Timothy 2:24–26**).

This notion is also addressed in the book of Romans:

Do you not know that to whom you present yourselves **slaves to obey**, you are that one's slaves whom you obey, **whether of sin** *leading* **to death**, or of **obedience** *leading* **to righteousness**? [17] But God be thanked that *though* **you were slaves of sin**, yet you **obeyed from the heart** that form of doctrine to which you were delivered. [18] And having been **set free from sin**, you became **slaves of righteousness**. [19] I speak in **human** *terms* because of the weakness of your flesh. For just as you presented your members *as* **slaves of uncleanness**, and of **lawlessness** *leading* to **more lawlessness**, so now present your members *as* slaves *of* **righteousness** for holiness. [20] For when you were **slaves of sin**, you were **free in regard to righteousness**. [21] What **fruit did you have** then in the things of which you are now ashamed? For **the end of those things** *is* **death**. [22] But now having been set free from sin, and having become **slaves of God**, you have your **fruit to holiness**, and **the end, everlasting life**. [23] For **the wages of sin** *is* **death**, but the **gift of God** *is* **eternal life** in **Christ Jesus our Lord**. **(Romans 6:16–23)**

Jesus describes this becoming "**slaves of God**" as obeying the minimal things that are necessary for our life, freedom, and happiness:

Come to Me, all *you* who labor and are heavy laden, and **I will give you rest**. [29] **Take My yoke upon you** and **learn from Me**, for **I am gentle** and **lowly in heart**, and **you will find rest for your souls**. [30] **For My yoke** *is* **easy** and **My burden is light**. **(Matthew 11:28–30)**

Finally, all *of you be* of one mind, having compassion for one another; love as brothers, *be* tenderhearted, *be* courteous; [9] not returning evil for evil or reviling for reviling, but on the contrary blessing, knowing that you were called to this, that you may inherit a blessing. [10] For '*He who would love life And see good days, Let him refrain his tongue from evil, And his lips from speaking deceit*. [11] *Let him* **turn away from evil and do good***; Let him* **seek peace and pursue it**. [12] *For* **the eyes of the** LORD **are on the righteous**, *And His ears are open to their prayers; But* **the face of the** LORD **is against those who do evil***.*' [13] And who *is* he who will harm you if you become followers of what is good? **(1 Peter 3:8–13)**

In the end, we are not sovereign on our own; we are only free in Christ Jesus.

Now let us compare what God has said about unity and oneness with what the wisdom of man has discovered by living in this world that is separated from God. Over the years that I was collecting quotations, I did not find as many concerning oneness, or maybe I wasn't as good at recognizing it then. Or possibly all of fallen man, who rejected the truth of God thinking they could do better on their own, suffers from a self-inflicted blindness to the power of "Oneness. Anyway, take a look at what I have found:

> "Laughing at ourselves as well as with each other gives a surprising sense of togetherness."
>
> **—Hazel C. Lee**

> "We must live together as brothers or perish together as fools."
>
> **—Martin Luther King Jr.**

> "If we don't hang together, we will surely hang together."
>
> **—Benjamin Franklin**

> "A house divided against its self cannot stand."
>
> **—Abraham Lincoln**

That concludes the three topics, or branches, that I *distinctly* remember from my experience, as well as my feeble attempt to duplicate, at least in part, the way that God had taught me. With that background in God's Word, we are now ready to begin looking at how these three branches are part of the Tree of Life, which sustains the lives of the individuals.

The Tree of Life

THE WHOLE BIBLE is concerned with learning and living by the ways that God says will lead to eternal life and rejecting and turning from the ways of Satan, which will lead to eternal death. In a rebellion against his creator, Satan disputed what God says are the ways that lead to life and the ways that lead to death, and he claims his ways of good and evil will not lead to death but are really a better way to live: "Then the serpent said to the woman, '**You will not surely die**. ⁵ For God knows that in the day you eat of it your eyes will be opened, and **you will be like God**, knowing good and evil'" (**Genesis 3:4–5**).

Our temporary life on this temporary earth is all about God giving us an opportunity to experience both ways and choose again for ourselves what we believe to be true.

> See, **I have set before you today life and good, death and evil**, ¹⁶ in that I command you today **to love the LORD your God, to walk in His ways,** and to keep **His commandments,** His statutes, and His judgments, **that you may live** and multiply; and the LORD your God will bless you **in the land which you go to possess.**
>
> ¹⁷ But **if your heart turns away** so that **you do not hear,** and are **drawn away,** and worship **other gods** and **serve them,** ¹⁸ I announce to you today that **you shall surely perish**; you shall not prolong *your* days in the land which you cross over the Jordan to go in and possess. ¹⁹ **I call heaven and earth as witnesses today against you,** *that* **I have set before you life and death, blessing and cursing**; therefore **choose life, that both you**

and your descendants may live; [20] that you may **love the LORD your God, that you may obey His voice**, and that you may **cling to Him**, for **He *is* your life** and the length of your days; and that you may **dwell in the land which the LORD swore to your fathers**, to Abraham, Isaac, and Jacob, to give them. (**Deuteronomy 30:9–20**).

We will learn in the chapter "The First Age of Anarchy" that the land promised by God on earth is a foreshadowing of a land in heaven that God promised. "These all **died in faith, not having received the promises**, but **having seen them afar off** were assured of them, embraced *them* and confessed that **they were strangers** and **pilgrims on the earth** ... But now they desire a better, that is, **a heavenly country**. Therefore God is not ashamed to be called their God, for He has **prepared a city for them**" (**Hebrews 11:13–16**).

We learned earlier that if we love God and understand His ways, we will be able to keep His laws because our hearts and minds will desire to keep them: "Owe no one anything except **to love one another**, for **he who loves another has fulfilled the law**. [9] For the commandments, *'You shall not commit adultery,' 'You shall not murder,' 'You shall not steal,' 'You shall not bear false witness,' 'You shall not covet,'* and if *there is* any other commandment, **are *all* summed up in this saying**, namely, *'You shall love your neighbor as yourself'*" (**Romans 13:8–9**).

Since the ways that lead to life eternal are what the whole Bible is about, let us consider what the Bible says about the different kinds of life.

THE DIFFERENT WORDS FOR LIFE

You have probably already noticed that in all kinds of Bible literature the words "soul" and "spirit" are used rather interchangeably. Perhaps the reason for that is that when people use the word "soul" they are focusing on the spirit that resides in either a body of corruptible flesh on earth or an incorruptible body in heaven, as the apostle Paul describes: "For **this corruptible** must put on **incorruption**, and **this mortal** *must* put on **immortality**" (**1 Corinthians 15:53**).

To be outside of the incorruptible body in heaven is described as being "naked," as God and Adam acknowledge in **Genesis 3:9–11**: "Then the Lᴏʀᴅ God called to Adam and said to him, "Where *are* you?" ¹⁰ So he said, 'I heard Your voice in the garden, and **I was afraid because I was naked**; and I hid myself.' ¹¹ And He said, '**Who told you that you** *were* **naked**? Have you eaten from the tree of which I commanded you that you should not eat?'" Jesus confirms our nakedness in **Revelation 3:17–18a**: "Because you say, '**I am rich**, have become **wealthy**, and have **need of nothing**'–and do not know that you are **wretched, miserable, poor, blind**, and **naked**– ¹⁸ I counsel you to buy from Me gold refined in the fire, that you may be rich; and **white garments**, that you may be **clothed**, *that* the **shame of your nakedness may not be revealed**."

For the purposes of this book, "soul" refers to a spirit together with the body that the spirit is in, and "spirit" refers only to the angelic spirit, whether in a body or not.

THE WORDS FOR LIFE IN THE GREEK

The Greek word for the life of a soul, a spirit in a body of animal flesh, is the Greek word G5590 *psuche*, which means "From G5594; **breath**, that is, (by implication) **spirit**, abstractly or concretely (**the animal sentient principle only**; thus distinguished on the one hand from G4151, which is the rational and immortal **soul** [spirit]; and on the other from G2222, which is **mere vitality, even of plants**; these terms thus correspond respectively to the Hebrew H5315, H7307, and H2416."

The Greek word for the life of a spirit, angel, demon, or God is G4151 *pneuma*, which means "From G4154; a current of air, that is, breath (blast) or a breeze; by analogy or figuratively **a spirit**, that is, (**human**) **the rational soul**, (by implication) **vital principle**, mental disposition, etc., or (**superhuman**) an **angel, daemon**, or (divine) **God, Christ's spirit**, the **Holy Spirit**;- ghost, life, spirit, mind." Notice that when this concordance refers to a spirit in a soul, it puts "human" in parentheses.

The Greek word for the kind of life without intellect, emotions, or feelings, like that of plants, is G2222 *zoe* (pronounced dzo-ay'), which means "From G2198; **life** (literally or figuratively) **life**(time)." This is also apparent in the definition of G5590 above, where G2222 is described as the "mere **vitality**, even of **plants**."

THE WORDS FOR LIFE IN THE HEBREW

The Hebrew word in the Old Testament that refers to fallen spirits in bodies of flesh like those of animals is H5315 *nephesh*, which means "From 5314; properly breathing **creature**, that is, **animal** or (abstractly) **vitality**; used very widely as in a literal, accommodated or figurative sense (bodily or mental):- any, **appetite**, **beast**, breath, **creature**, **greedy**, heart, **life**, **lust**, **man**, **me**, **mind**, **mortality**, one, **own person**, **pleasure**, themselves, **soul**."

The Hebrew word for the life of a spirit is H5397 *neshamah*, which means "a puff, that is, wind, **vital** breath, **divine inspiration**, intellect, inspiration, soul, **spirit**." This is the Hebrew word used when God formed a body of flesh out of the dust of the earth and "**breathed**" the fallen spirit, or the first man, or H120 *adam*, into the first soul, named H121 *Adam*. And a similar word, H7307 *ruach*, which means "From H7306; **wind**; by resemblance **breath**, that is, a sensible (or even violent) **exhalation**; figuratively **life**, anger, by resemblance **spirit**, but only of **a rational being** (including its expression and functions)," is metaphorically used to represent the spirit in a living being or soul because wind is invisible but influences things that can be seen, as Jesus describes to Nicodemus: "The **wind blows** where it wishes, and **you hear the sound of it**, **but cannot tell where it comes from** and where it goes. **So is everyone who is born of the Spirit**" **(John 3:8)**.

The Hebrew word for mere life without intellect, emotions, or feelings is H2416 *chay* (pronounced khah'ee), which means "**Alive**; **fresh** (**plant**, water, year); **life** (or **living thing**); **quick**."

Thus a human being has two lives that can die: the life of body of flesh and the life of the spirit. Matthew teaches this: "And **do not fear** those who kill the body but **cannot kill the soul**. But rather **fear Him** who is able to destroy both **soul and body** in **hell**" (**Matthew 10:27–28**). This is important to know, as we will learn in the chapter "The Meaning and Purpose of Life on Earth."

THE LIFE OF ANIMALS WITH OR WITHOUT A SPIRIT

All the verses below that speak of a "soul" or "life" or "living creature" in this world are speaking of the life of animals or speaking of the life of animal-like bodies of flesh indwelled by fallen spirits and are translated from the Hebrew H5315 *nephesh* or the Greek word G5590 *psuche*.

> Therefore I say to you, do not worry about your **life**, what you will eat or what you will drink; nor about your body, what you will put on. Is not **life** more than food and the body more than clothing? (**Matthew 6:25**)

> And whoever desires to be first among you, let him be your slave— [28] just as the Son of Man did not come to be served, but to serve, and to give His **life** a ransom for many. (**Matthew 20:27–28**)

> Greater love has no one than this, than to lay down one's **life** for his friends. (**John 15:13**)

> For consider Him who endured such hostility from sinners against Himself, lest you become weary and discouraged in your **souls**. (**Hebrews 12:3**)

> Brethren, if anyone among you wanders from the truth, and someone turns him back, [20] let him know that he who turns a sinner from the error of his way will save a **soul** from death and cover a multitude of sins. (**James 5:19–20**)

> And the LORD God formed man *of* the dust of the ground, and breathed into his nostrils the breath of **life**; and man became a living **soul**. (**Genesis 2:7 KJV**)

> Out of the ground the LORD God formed every beast of the field and every bird of the air, and brought *them* to Adam to see what he would call them. And whatever Adam called each **living creature**, that *was* its name. ²⁰ So Adam gave names to all cattle, to the birds of the air, and to every beast of the field. But for Adam there was not found a helper comparable to him. (**Genesis 2:19–20**)

> But flesh with the **life** thereof, *which is* the blood thereof, shall ye not eat. ⁵ And surely your blood of your **lives** will I require; at the hand of every beast will I require it, and at the hand of man; at the hand of every man's brother will I require the **life** of man. (**Genesis 9:4–5 KJV**)

That man is a spiritual being in a body of flesh is clearly seen in verses like the following: "And Mary said: 'My **soul** magnifies the Lord, ⁴⁷ And **my spirit** has rejoiced in **God my Savior**'" (**Luke 1:46–47**). Here the worldly mother of our Lord Jesus recognizes she is a spirit in a body of flesh; sounds like she has been reading her Old Testament Scriptures and has been enlightened by the Holy Spirit.

THE LIFE OF SPIRITS WITHIN OR WITHOUT BODIES OF FLESH

All of the following verses speak of a "spirit"; they are speaking of the lives of spiritual beings within or without bodies of flesh and those who are righteous or not. Where the words "spirit" and "ghost" are used in all these New Testament passages, those words have been translated from the Greek word G4151 **pneuma**. And in all the Old Testament passages where the word "Spirit" is used, that word has been translated from the Hebrew word H7307 **ruach**.

> I indeed baptize you with water unto repentance, but He who is coming after me is mightier than I, whose sandals I am not worthy to carry. He will baptize you with the **Holy Spirit** and fire. (**Matthew 3:11**)

Blessed *are* the **poor in spirit**, For theirs is the kingdom of heaven. (**Matthew 5:3**)

But Jesus rebuked him, saying, "Be quiet, and come out of him!" [26] And when the **unclean spirit** had convulsed him and cried out with a loud voice, he came out of him. (**Mark 1:25–26**)

But immediately, when Jesus perceived **in His spirit** that they reasoned thus within themselves, He said to them, "Why do you reason about these things in your hearts?" (**Mark 2:8**). As we have learned, Jesus on earth is also a spirit in a body of flesh, "Inasmuch then as the **children have partaken of flesh and blood, He Himself likewise shared in the same**, that through death He might destroy him who had the power of death, that is, the devil, [15] and release those who through fear of death were all their lifetime subject to bondage." (**Hebrews 2:14–15**)

And behold, there was a man in Jerusalem whose name was Simeon, and this man was just and devout, waiting for the Consolation of Israel, and the **Holy Spirit** was upon him. (**Luke 2:25**)

*The **Spirit of the L**ORD ***is upon Me**, Because He has anointed Me To preach the gospel to the poor; He has sent Me to heal the brokenhearted, To proclaim liberty to the captives And recovery of sight to the blind, To set at liberty those who are oppressed;* [19] *To proclaim the acceptable year of the L*ORD. (**Luke 4:18–19**)

Jesus answered, "Most assuredly, I say to you, unless one is born of water and the **Spirit**, he cannot enter the kingdom of God. [6] That which is born of the flesh is flesh, and that which is born of the **Spirit** is **spirit**." (**John 3:5–6**)

For He whom God has sent speaks the words of God, for God does not give the **Spirit** by measure. (**John 3:34**)

But the hour is coming, and now is, when the true worshipers will worship the Father in **spirit** and truth; for the Father is seeking such to worship Him. [24] **God** *is* **Spirit**, and those who worship Him must worship in **spirit** and truth. (**John 4:23–24**)

Therefore, when Jesus saw her weeping, and the Jews who came with her weeping, He groaned in the **spirit** and was troubled. (**John 11:33**)

However, when He, the **Spirit** of truth, has come, He will guide you into all truth; for He will not speak on His own *authority,* but whatever He hears He will speak; and He will tell you things to come. (**John 16:13**)

The earth was without form, and void; and darkness *was* on the face of the deep. And the **Spirit** of God was hovering over the face of the waters. (**Genesis 1:2**)

And the LORD said, "My **Spirit** shall not strive with man forever, for he *is* indeed flesh; yet his days shall be one hundred and twenty years." (**Genesis 6:3**)

Now it came to pass in the morning that his **spirit** was troubled, and he sent and called for all the magicians of Egypt and all its wise men. And Pharaoh told them his dreams, but *there was* no one who could interpret them for Pharaoh. (**Genesis 41:8**)

And Pharaoh said to his servants, "Can we find *such a one* as this, a man in whom *is* the **Spirit of God**?" [39] Then Pharaoh said to Joseph, "Inasmuch as God has shown you all this, *there is* no one as discerning and wise as you." (**Genesis 41:38–39**)

Then the LORD spoke to Moses, saying: [2] "See, I have called by name Bezalel the son of Uri, the son of Hur, of the tribe of Judah. [3]And I have filled him with the **Spirit** of God, in wisdom, in understanding, in knowledge, and in all *manner of* workmanship." (**Exodus 31:3**)

Notice that even in the Old Testament, God filled some people with the Holy Spirit of God.

God of the Spirits of All Flesh

> Then they fell on their faces, and said, "O God, the God of the **spirits** of all flesh, shall one man sin, and You be angry with all the congregation?" (**Numbers 16:22**)

> Then a **spirit** passed before my face; The hair on my body stood up. [16] It stood still, But I could not discern its appearance. A form *was* before my eyes; *There was* silence; Then I heard a voice *saying:* [17] "Can a mortal be more righteous than God? Can a man be more pure than his Maker?" (**Job 4:15–17**)

Notice that in the Old Testament, just being in the presence of a holy spirit caused the hair on Job's body to stand up. In the New Testament church age, when the Holy Spirit can indwell our bodies, believers experience a tingling from head to toe that some call Holy Ghost bumps.

Spirits in a Body

> I, Daniel, was grieved in my **spirit** within *my* body, and the visions of my head troubled me. (**Daniel 7:15**)

The Spirit of Man

> The burden of the word of the LORD against Israel. Thus says the LORD, who **stretches out the heavens**, lays the foundation of the earth, and forms the **spirit** of man within him. (**Zechariah 12:1**)

THE LIFE THAT IS NOT THE LIFE OF LIVING BEINGS AND YET IS

There is another word that does not speak of the individual life of animals, spiritual beings, or human beings but rather speaks of the things that are necessary for the life of animals, spiritual beings, and human beings. Let us consider the English word "vital."

Webster defines the word "vital" as "1. Of, **relating to**, or **characteristic of**, **life**. 2. **Necessary** for the **continuance of life** or **vigor**; as, wounded in **a vital part**. 3. Animated; **full of life** and **vigor**. 4. **Fatal**; **mortal**; as, a **vital wound**. 5. Fundamental; basic; hence, **indispensable**; **requisite**; as, his aid is **vital to our cause**; loosely, highly important. 6. Having to do with data concerning **births, deaths**, etc.; as **vital statistics**. – noun a. **vital organs** as a heart or brain. b. Essential parts of a thing. **Vitality**, adverb."

An example of this vitality that is necessary for life in the Bible is when God created plant life: "Then God said, 'Let **the earth bring forth grass**, the **herb** *that* **yields seed**, *and* the **fruit tree** *that* **yields fruit according to its kind**, whose **seed** *is* **in itself**, on the earth'; and it was so. [12] And **the earth brought forth grass**, the herb *that* yields seed according to its kind, and **the tree** *that* **yields fruit**, whose **seed** *is* **in itself** according to its kind. And God saw that *it was* good" (**Genesis 1:11–12**).

Here God creates and arranges all the complicated DNA of the first plants so they can take the energy of the sun, the nutrients of the soil, and the water from rain and through photosynthesis have the ability to grow and produce seeds to replicate many more versions of themselves. As long as God keeps providing the sun and the rain and the honeybee, the earth will produce more plants in due season. And God promises what is vital for the life of the plants and man: "You shall keep My Sabbaths and reverence My sanctuary: I *am* the LORD. [3] '**If you walk in My statutes** and **keep My commandments**, and perform them, [4] then **I will give you rain in its season, the land shall yield its produce**, and the **trees of the field shall yield their fruit**. [5] Your threshing shall last till the time of vintage, and the vintage shall last till the time of sowing; you shall **eat your bread to the full**, and **dwell in your land safely** (**Leviticus 26:2–5**).

After God created the living creatures that dwell in the sea and the birds of the air, then in **Genesis 1:24–25** God created the beasts of the field, putting together the complicated DNA in the same way so that they can produce many replicas of themselves as long as God provides plants of the earth for the animals to eat.

Then God said, "**Let the earth bring forth the living creature according to its kind**: cattle and creeping thing and beast of the earth, *each* **according to its kind**"; and it was so. [25] And God made the beast of the earth according to its kind, cattle according to its kind, and everything that creeps on the earth according to its kind. And God saw that *it was* good.

> And God did provide them the food they needed to live, "Also, **to every beast of the earth**, to **every bird of the air**, and **to everything that creeps on the earth,** in which *there is* life, *I have given* every **green herb for food**"; and it was so. (**Genesis 1:30**)

The Hebrew word for "life" in this verse and all the verses of God's creation that use the words "life" or "living" are translated from the Hebrew word H2416 *chay* (pronounced khah'ee), which means "From H2421; **alive**; hence raw (flesh); fresh (**plant**, water, year), strong; also as a noun, especially in the feminine singular or the masculine plural) **life** (living thing) whether literally or figuratively ;- age, alive, **appetite**, (wild) beast, **company, congregation, living (creature, thing), maintenance, multitude, troop**."

Notice that God had already provided for the sustaining of the life of the flesh of fallen man, *Adam*, for they were to eat of the plant life God had created, just as the animals did. "Then to Adam He said, 'Because you have heeded the voice of your wife, and have **eaten from the tree of which I commanded** you, saying, "**You shall not eat of it**": Cursed *is* the ground for your sake; **In toil you shall eat** *of* it All the days of your life. [18] Both thorns and thistles it shall bring forth for you, And **you shall eat the herb of the field**'" (**Genesis 3:17–18**). Also notice in this definition of life that there is a sense of **maintenance** and that, to multiply and continue as a species, these living beings are **dependent on each other** to reproduce **and on God** to supply **the vital things they need to live**.

And when God put a body of flesh on the first fallen angelic spirit, named Adam, He also provided that which was vital for the **life of his spirit**, the **Tree of Life**: "And the LORD God **formed man** *of*

the dust of the ground, and breathed into his nostrils the **breath of life**; and man became a **living soul.** **8** And the **LORD God** planted a garden eastward in Eden; and there he put **the man whom he had formed.** **9** And out of the ground **made the LORD God to grow** every tree that is pleasant to the sight, and **good for food**; the **tree of life** also in the midst of the garden, and the **tree of knowledge of good and evil**" (**Genesis 2:7–9** KJV). We will learn more about God's "**forming**" of man in the chapter "The Beginning as Seen from Earth."

But most importantly, notice that in **Genesis 3:17**, after Adam had eaten from the Tree of Knowledge of Good and Evil, God made Adam metaphorically experience the "fruit," or consequences, of living by the knowledge of good and evil all the days of his life on earth: "Then to Adam He said, 'Because you have heeded the voice of your wife, and have **eaten from the tree of which I commanded** you, saying, "**You shall not eat of it**": Cursed *is* the ground for your sake; **In toil you shall eat** *of* **it All the days of your life**.'" In future chapters we will learn why and how this curse applies to everyone living on planet earth.

Although God made many trees that were "good for food" to sustain the life of the flesh, it is the **knowledge of the Tree of Life** that God provided that is vital to the survival of the **life of the spirit** that is in the body of flesh. In this "tree" is the knowledge and understanding of what is vital for the life of our spirits. That is the subject of this book, and the truth of this knowledge can only found in the Word of God. This knowledge and understanding of the truth that leads to life is what Jesus, called the Word of God, has come into this world to witness of. (See **John 18:37**.)

God wants us to know and understand that we are totally dependent on Him, our Creator, and each other for our life. And God wants us to know that He is the source of all life, as Jesus, the Son of God, explains: "I am the vine, you *are* the branches. **He who abides in Me**, and **I in him, bears much fruit**; for **without Me you can do nothing**" (**John 15:5**). All spiritual beings were created by God, our Father; even

Jesus, our Savior and King, and Lucifer/Satan, our adversary and the enemy of our souls. There is only one form of life that does not require maintenance to live, and that is the eternal source of all life, God the Father or Jehovah by name. It is only God the Most High, LORD God, that has always existed. The Hebrew word for "LORD" in the phrase "LORD God" found in **Genesis 2:8** is H3068 *yehovah* (pronounced yeh-ho-vaw'), which means "From H1961; (the) **self Existent** or **eternal**; **Jehovah**, Jewish national name of God;- Jehovah, the Lord."

The Hebrew word for "life" in the phrase "tree of life" in **Genesis 2:9** is H2416 *chay*, which refers to that which is vital for man's spiritual life. This Tree of Life on earth is symbolic for the Tree of Life in heaven as an angel showed the apostle John: "And he showed me a pure river of **water of life**, clear as crystal, proceeding from the throne of God and of the Lamb. ² In the middle of its street, and on either side of the river, *was* **the tree of life**, which bore twelve fruits, **each *tree* yielding its fruit** every month. The **leaves of the tree** *were* for the **healing** of the **nations**" (**Revelation 22:1–2**). The Greek word for the word "life" in the phrase "tree of life" is G2222 *zoe*.

ZOE—THE GOD KIND OF LIFE

In the New Testament we find the following passages that speak of eternal spiritual life in Christ and that which is vital to support the individual spirit lives. In every verse where the word "life" is found, it is translated from the Hebrew word *zoe*:

Life—Death

> For when you were slaves of sin, you were free in regard to righteousness. ²¹ What fruit did you have then in the things of which you are now ashamed? For the end of those things is death. ²² But now having been set free from sin, and having become slaves of God, you have your fruit to holiness, and the end, everlasting life. ²³ For the wages of sin is death, but the gift of God is eternal **life** in Christ Jesus our Lord. (**Romans 6:20–23**)

Being set free from sin by the truth and becoming the joyful slaves of God rather than slaves held in bondage by Satan to do his will are vital to everlasting life.

Being Carnally Minded Is Death—Being Spiritually Minded Is Life

For those who live according to the flesh set their minds on the things of the flesh, but those who live according to the Spirit, the things of the Spirit. [6] For to be carnally minded is death, but to be spiritually minded is **life** and peace. (**Romans 8:5–6**)

Walking according to the Spirit, living according to the Spirit and being spiritually minded are vital to life and peace in Christ Jesus.

The Law Kills, but Love Gives Life

I was alive once without the law, but when the commandment came, sin revived and I died. [10] And the commandment, which was to bring **life**, I found to bring death. [11] For sin, taking occasion by the commandment, deceived me, and by it killed me. [12] Therefore the law is holy, and the commandment holy and just and good. (**Romans 7:9–12**)

The **words that I speak** to you are spirit, and they are **life**. [64] But there are some of you who do not believe. (**John 6:63**)

Believing in the words of Jesus is vital to life.

Jesus Is the Resurrection and the Life

Jesus said to her, "I am the resurrection and the **life**. He who believes in Me, though he may die, he shall live. [26] And whoever lives and believes in Me shall never die. Do you believe this?" [27] She said to Him, "Yes, Lord, I believe that You are the Christ, the Son of God, who is to come into the world." (**John 11:25–27**)

Believing in Jesus is vital to not dying the second death of the spirit, which is spoken of by Jesus in **Revelation 2:11**: "He who has an ear, let him hear what the Spirit says to the churches. **He who overcomes shall not be hurt by the second death.**"

Eternal Life

> You search the Scriptures, for in them you think you have eternal **life**; and these are they which testify of Me. [40] But you are not willing to come to Me that you may have **life**. (**John 5:39–40**)

Coming to Jesus to understand the Scriptures is vital to eternal life.

Jesus Is the Way, the Truth, and the Life

> "In My Father's house are many mansions; if it were not so, I would have told you. I go to prepare a place for you. [3] And if I go and prepare a place for you, I will come again and receive you to Myself; that where I am, there you may be also. [4] And where I go you know, and the way you know." [5] Thomas said to Him, "Lord, we do not know where You are going, and how can we know the way?" [6] Jesus said to him, "I am the way, the truth, and the **life**. No one comes to the Father except through Me." (**John 14:2–6**)

Many Bible scholars call *Zoe* life the "God kind of life" because it refers to life eternal, which only God can give. So what if someone should ask, **"How can the life that is defined as mere vitality—even of life without intellect, emotions, or feelings, such as that of plants—be called the God kind of life?"**

The answer is that *Zoe* refers not to the life of individuals but rather the life of oneness, the community, the nation, the family, the health of the relationships. As we learned in "The Oneness Branch," the way many individuals choose to live and relate to each other is an economy. Jesus said that the best way to live together is to love one another, and that makes love the economy of the kingdom of God. And John Nash has mathematically proven that Jesus' ways of love are the best ways to relate to each other. It is the economy that provides for that which is vital for the life of the individuals that live in the community. The life of a nation is not the life of any individual. It does not have an intellect or emotions, but it is what provides the peace, prosperity, unspeakable joy, and eternal life for the citizens of that nation or kingdom.

RESTORING LIFE TO THAT WHICH IS DEAD OR DYING

In the first chapter of **Genesis**, as we will learn in the chapter "The Beginning as Seen from Earth," there are fallen spiritual beings who are not living in **Zoe**, the eternal life that only God can give, but are living in darkness, wickedness, and death. There are fallen spiritual beings already on earth that are currently in the image and likeness of Satan, those who believed his lies and fell from the grace of God. It is the purpose and plan of God in creating the universe, the heavens, and the earth to give these fallen spiritual beings a second chance at life eternal by having them experience what it would be like to live in the evil ways of Satan and compare it to the good ways of God and then choose again which way they want to live.

We learn from **Genesis 5:3** that we on earth were created in the image of Satan and not God: "And Adam lived one hundred and thirty years, and **begot *a son* in his own likeness, after his image**, and named him Seth." These events occur at a time when the first man, Adam, had already fallen by believing the lies of Satan. This brings new meaning to the earlier description of the creation of man in Genesis chapter one: "Then God said, "Let **Us make man** in **Our image**, according to **Our likeness; let them have dominion** over the fish of the sea, over the birds of the air, and over the cattle, over all the earth and **over every creeping thing that creeps on the earth**" (**Genesis 1:26**).

Obviously Adam and his son Seth were not in the image of God yet, God's creation of man in His image must happen at some time later in their life on earth. While both Adam and Eve had sinned, God does not hold children responsible for their parents' sin: "Fathers shall not be put to death for *their* children, **nor shall the children be put to death for *their* fathers**; a person shall be put to death **for his own sin**" (**Deuteronomy 24:16**). And if they are all born with Original

Sin, the same must be true of all of us. We must be made in the image of God during our temporary lifetime on this temporary earth if we are going to be made in His image at all.

And this fact that we are all guilty of sin from our birth is what Paul explains in **Romans 3:9–12**: "What then? Are we better *than they?* Not at all. For we have previously charged both Jews and Greeks that **they are all under sin**. [10] As it is written: '***There is none righteous, no, not one;*** [11] *There is* **none who understands**; *There is* **none who seeks after God**. [12] *They have* **all turned aside**; *They have together become* **unprofitable**; *There is* **none who does good, no, not one**.'" We will learn much more about why we are guilty of Original Sin from birth in the chapter "The Meaning and Purpose of Life on Earth," but for now consider what the Psalmist says: "Behold, I was **brought forth in iniquity**, And **in sin my mother conceived me**" (**Psalm 51:5**).

But by the loving mercy of God, He is giving those who will, those who want to, a second chance to humble themselves, listen, learn, and understand the truth of God that will make them free from death and give them eternal life. As we will learn, God's making us back into His image and likeness is a process that will last a lifetime on earth as we experience good and evil for ourselves and then choose again. This process begins by us fallen spiritual beings putting on a body of flesh like that of an animal, literally in **Genesis 2:7** and symbolically, looking back in retrospect, in **Genesis 3:21**. And so when we become living souls, we have the life of our bodies to sustain and the life of our spirits, and God is going to make us who believe, who were as good as dead, alive again:

> And you *He made alive,* who were **dead in trespasses and sins,** [2] in which **you once walked according** to the **course of this world, according** to the **prince** of the **power of the air,** the **spirit who now works** in the **sons of disobedience,** [3] among whom also **we all once conducted ourselves** in the **lusts of our flesh,** fulfilling the desires of the flesh and of the mind, and **were by nature children of wrath, just as the others.**

⁴ But God, who is rich in mercy, because of **His great love with which He loved us**, ⁵ even when we were **dead in trespasses, made us alive together with Christ** (by grace you have been saved), ⁶ and **raised** *us* **up together**, and made *us* **sit together in the heavenly** *places* **in Christ Jesus**, ⁷ that in **the ages to come** He might show the exceeding riches of His **grace** in *His* **kindness** toward us **in Christ Jesus**. ⁸ For by grace you have been **saved through faith**, and that **not of yourselves**; *it is* **the gift of God**, ⁹ **not of works**, lest anyone should boast. (**Ephesians 2:1–18**)

The Greek word for the phrase "**made us alive together with**" in **Ephesians 2:4** is G4806 *suzoopoieo* (pronounced sood-zo-op-oy-eh'-o), which means "From G4862 and G2227; to **reanimate conjointly with** (figuratively: -**quicken together with**." The word "conjoin" is defined by *Webster's Student Dictionary* as "To **join together** as in action or **purpose**; **unite**." And "conjoint" is defined as "1. **United**; conjoined. 2. Relating to, made up of, or carried on by **two or more in combination**; joint. – conjointly being the adverb." And the word "quicken" means "To **impart life, to revive, as from death**; to arouse; stimulate."

And this is exactly what the Word of God has been teaching us—that Satan, with a lie that we could do better on our own, separated us from God and each other. And that sin, or transgression of God's truth, caused us to be "**dead in trespasses and sins**." But God, "because of **His great love with which He loved us ... made us alive together with Christ**." And this is exactly what we learned in the truth, love, and Oneness branches. The truth is that loving God and loving others as ourselves fulfills the law of God, unites us again in Christ, and gives us eternal life.

In the Old Testament we see this process of God to restore us into His image in this Deuteronomy verse: "So **He humbled you, allowed you to hunger**, and fed you with manna which you did not know nor did your fathers know, that He might **make you know** that **man shall not live by bread alone**; but **man lives by every** *word* **that proceeds from the mouth of the** Lord" (**Deuteronomy 8:3**).

The words "live" and "lives" are both translated from the Hebrew word H2421 *chayah* (pronounced khaw-yaw'), which means "A prime root (compare H2331, H24240; to live, whether literally or figuratively **causatively to revive**;-**keep** (leave, **make**) **alive**, certainly, **give** (**promise**) **life**, (**let suffer**) **to live**, nourish up, **preserve alive**, recover, **repair**, **restore** (**to life**), revive, (**God**) **save** (**alive**, life, lives), surely, **be whole**." It is when God allows us to experience the suffering caused by evil that we are awakened form the lie that we can do better on our own, separated from God, and desire to seek the truth and long to go back home to live with our Father in heaven.

In this verse, the Hebrew version of God's restoration of life for those who are as good as dead includes ideas of a process to **revive**, **make alive**, and **restore to life**, as well as the words "**let suffer**," which is exactly right. Because we evidently did not believe the words of God or even listen to His words that He could reason with us, we have to experience the suffering that evil causes in order change our hearts and minds and believe from our own experience that God was right all along. I personally bear witness to this humbling from suffering in my own life that allowed me to come before God with a broken spirit and a contrite heart, along with an open mind and a teachable heart, hungry to let the Spirit of God teach me the truth that will make me free, instead of arrogantly trying to understand the truth with my own abilities and resources.

> But we speak **the wisdom of God in a mystery**, the **hidden wisdom which God ordained before the ages for our glory**, [8] which **none of the rulers of this age knew**; for had they known, they would not have crucified the Lord of glory. [9] But as it is written: "*Eye has not seen, nor ear heard, Nor have entered into the heart of man The things which God has prepared for those who love Him.*" [10] But God has **revealed** *them* **to us through His Spirit**. For **the Spirit** searches all things, yes, the **deep things of God**. [11] For what man knows the things of a man except the **spirit of the man which is in him**? Even so **no one knows the things of God except the Spirit of God.**

[12] Now we have received, **not** the **spirit of the world**, but **the Spirit who is from God**, that **we might know the things** that have been **freely given to us by God**. [13] These things we also speak, not in words which man's wisdom teaches but which **the Holy Spirit teaches**, comparing spiritual things with spiritual. [14] But **the natural man does not receive the things of the Spirit of God**, for they are **foolishness** to him; **nor can he know** *them*, because **they are spiritually discerned**. (**1 Corinthians 2:7–14**)

God Gives Life to the Dead

Therefore it is of **faith** that it might be according to **grace**, so that **the promise** might be sure **to all the seed**, not only to those who are of the law, but also to **those who are of the faith of Abraham**, who is the **father of us all** [17] (as it is written, "I have made you a father of many nations") in the presence of Him whom he believed—God, **who gives life to the dead** and **calls those things which do not exist as though they did.** (**Romans 4:16–17**)

The Greek word for life in the phrase "gives life to the dead" is G2227 *zooppoieo* (pronounced dzo-op-oy-eh'-o), which means "**Re-vitalize, make alive, give life, quicken,**" which we notice is part of the definition of G4806 *suzoopoieo* without the conjoining part, the joining together. And we see this Spirit gift of Life—G2227 *zooppoieo*—in **John 6:63**: "It is the Spirit who **gives life**; the flesh profits nothing." God *gives* life to the dead and makes something from nothing. We cannot earn a gift.

And this is the choice we all must make in this second chance of life on earth, having experienced good and evil for ourselves: do we believe our Creator, the all-wise source of all life and the lover of our souls who would gladly and freely die to save us, or the creature, the one whom God created and who would gladly and freely kill our life in the flesh to keep us in bondage as his personal slaves?

See, I have set before you today **life and good, death and evil**, [16] in that I command you today **to love the LORD your God**, to **walk in His ways**, and to keep His **commandments**, His **statutes**, and His **judgments**, that you may live and multiply; and the LORD your God will **bless you in the land which you go to possess**. ¹⁷ But **if your heart turns away so that you do not hear**, and are drawn away, and worship **other gods and serve them**, ¹⁸ I announce to you today that **you shall surely perish**; you shall not prolong *your* days in the land which you cross over the Jordan to go in and possess.

¹⁹ **I call heaven and earth as witnesses today against you**, *that* **I have set before you life and death, blessing and cursing; therefore choose life**, that both you and your descendants may **live**; ²⁰ that you may **love the LORD your God**, that you may **obey His voice**, and that you may **cling to Him**, for **He** *is* **your life** and the length of your days; and that you may **dwell in the land which the LORD swore to your fathers**, to Abraham, Isaac, and Jacob, to give them. (**Deuteronomy 30:15–20**)

Just as the fruit of the Tree of Knowledge of Good and Evil was not the same thing as the fruit we eat, such as apples, but the product of the knowledge of evil and good that led to death, so is the Tree of Life the knowledge, understanding, and wisdom concerning the ways of righteousness that lead to eternal life. Let us now consider what the Bible says about the Tree of Life,

THE TREE OF LIFE

Tree of Life

He who trusts in his riches will fall, But the **righteous** will flourish like **foliage**. ²⁹ He who troubles his own house will inherit the wind, And the fool *will be* servant to the wise of heart. ³⁰ The **fruit of the righteous** *is a* **tree of life**, And he who wins souls *is* wise. (**Proverbs 11:28–30**)

Tree of Life

A soft answer turns away wrath, But a harsh word stirs up anger. [2] The tongue of the wise uses knowledge rightly, But the mouth of fools pours forth foolishness. [3] The eyes of the LORD *are* in every place, Keeping watch on the evil and the good. [4] A **wholesome tongue** *is* a **tree of life**, But **perverseness** in it **breaks the spirit. (Proverbs 15:4)**

Tree of Life

And he showed me a pure river of water of life, clear as crystal, proceeding from the throne of God and of the Lamb. [2] In the middle of its street, and on either side of the river, *was* **the tree of life**, which bore twelve fruits, each *tree* yielding its fruit every month. The **leaves of the tree** *were* **for the healing of the nations. (Revelation 22:1–2)**

Tree of Life—Overcomers

He who has an ear, let him hear what the Spirit says to the churches. To him who overcomes, **I will give the right to eat from** the **tree of life**, which is in the **paradise** of God. **(Revelation 2:7)**

Tree of Life

"And behold, I am coming quickly, and **My reward** *is* **with Me**, to give to every one **according to his work**. [13] I am the Alpha and the Omega, *the* Beginning and *the* End, the First and the Last." [14] Blessed *are* those who do His commandments, that they may have the right to the **tree of life**, and may enter through the gates into the city. [15] But outside *are* dogs and sorcerers and sexually immoral and murderers and idolaters, and whoever **loves and practices a lie**. [16] "I, Jesus, have sent **My angel** to testify to you these things **in the churches**. I am the Root and the Offspring of David, the **Bright and Morning Star.**" **(Revelation 22:12–16)**

Now, with this basic understanding of God's Word learned from these three branches of the Tree of Life, we will put together the pieces of this great puzzle that we may know the meaning and purpose of God for this temporary life on this temporary earth. And when we understand so that we can believe and grow deeper in faith, we will "rejoice with joy inexpressible," as the apostle Peter said in **1 Peter 1:7–9**: "In this you **greatly rejoice**, though now for a little while, if need be, you have been **grieved by various trials,** [7] that the **genuineness of your faith,** *being* **much more precious than gold** that perishes, though it is **tested** by fire, may be found to praise, honor, and glory at the **revelation of Jesus Christ,** [8] whom having not seen you love. Though now you **do not see** ***Him,* yet believing,** you **rejoice with joy inexpressible** and full of glory, [9] receiving the **end of your faith**–the **salvation of** *your* **souls."**

> Of **this salvation** the **prophets have inquired** and **searched carefully,** who prophesied of the grace *that would come* to you, [11] searching what, or what manner of time, the **Spirit of Christ who was in them** was indicating when He testified beforehand the sufferings of Christ and the glories that would follow. [12] **To them it was revealed that, not to themselves, but to us** they were ministering the things which now have been reported to you through those who have **preached the gospel** to you **by the Holy Spirit** sent from heaven–**things which angels desire to look into.** **(1 Peter 1:10, 12)**

We will learn answers to things we never knew that we never knew.

Can you think of anything more important than knowing what the meaning and purpose of this life on earth is? I think the excitement comes from the gravity of the issues we will be wrestling with. This is the issue that people have been seeking the answer to since the beginning of time. The answer will tell us how we should be living our lives. Three things that I wanted to know after facing death by a cancerous brain tumor and then by hydrocephalus were (1) where am I going? (2) where did I come from? and (3) why am I here? We will discover the answer to these questions and many more as we walk together through this story that is revealed to us in God's Holy Word. This is His story and our history! Read and ponder the following, and if you are ready and willing, fall on your knees and pray for the Holy Spirit of truth to lead you into all truth, as Jesus taught: "However, when He, the **Spirit of truth**, has come, **He will guide you into all truth**; for He will not speak on His own *authority,* but whatever He hears He will speak; and **He will tell you things to come**" (**John 16:13**).

The Meaning and Purpose of Life on Planet Earth

The purpose for Life on planet earth actually has its beginning in heaven, and the Bible tells us that we were all sons of God called "gods" of the Most High God, as the Psalmist declares: "Deliver the poor and needy; **Free** *them* from the **hand of the wicked**. **⁵ They do not know, nor do they understand**; They **walk about in darkness**; All the foundations of the earth are unstable. **⁶ I said,** "**You** *are* **gods, And all of you** *are* **children of the Most High**" (**Psalm 82:4–8**). And Jesus confirms that we are gods and the lost children of the Most High God: "Jesus answered them, 'Is it not written in your law, *"I said, 'You are gods'"*? **³⁵ If He called them gods, to whom the word of God came** (and **the Scripture cannot be broken**), **³⁶** do you say of Him whom the Father sanctified and sent into the world, "You are blaspheming," because I said, "**I am the Son of God**"?'" (**John 10:34–36**). It is here in heaven where God first created us in His image. On earth God had to transform our fallen nature back into His image and likeness.

And Luke, describing the lineage of Jesus, tells us that the first man, named Adam, was a son of God the Father before the fall: "Jesus ... *the* son of Joseph ... *the son* of Enos, *the son* of Seth, *the son* of **Adam**, *the son* **of God**" (**Luke 3:23–24, 38**). So right away God the Father is telling us that we all were His "gods," and Jesus is telling us that those "**to whom the word of God comes**" can again be "gods" of the Most High God!

The Hebrew word for "gods" in the Psalm passage is H430 *elohym*, which means "**gods** in the ordinary sense; but **specifically used in the plural, especially** with the **article of the supreme God**; occasionally applied by way of deference to **magistrates**; and sometimes as a **superlative** – **angels**, exceeding, God (gods), **great, mighty, judges**." And of interest is the fact that in the entire first chapter of Genesis, where the Bible describes how God created the heavens and the earth and everything in it, the word "God" is translated from the Hebrew word H430 *elohym*. So the Hebrew word "*elohym*" can refer to the Supreme God as well as to gods or angels belonging to the Supreme God. This makes sense, because we learned in "The Oneness Branch" that God is many united together as one.

Among all the "gods" or "superlative angels" in heaven, there were two that stood above all the rest—Jesus and Lucifer. The brightest, most beautiful and powerful angel was called Lucifer. The prophet Ezekiel says of Lucifer, "You *were* the **seal of perfection, Full of wisdom** and **perfect in beauty**. [13] You were in **Eden**, the **garden of God** … [15] **You** *were* **perfect in your ways** from the day **you were created, Till iniquity was found in you** … [17] Your **heart was lifted up** because of **your beauty**; You **corrupted your wisdom** for the sake of **your splendor; I cast you** to the **ground**" (**Ezekiel 28:12b–13, 15, 17**).

Lucifer was probably the most popular angel in heaven because of his great beauty, wisdom, and power. Notice that Lucifer was in the garden of Eden in heaven before he was cast down to the earth. The word "ground" in the phrase "**I cast you** to the **ground**" is translated from the Hebrew word H776 *erets*, which means "**The earth**, wilderness, **world**."

And Jesus was the angel that was "gentle and lowly in heart" (**Matthew 11:29**), and the Psalmist said of Jesus, "You **love righteousness** and **hate wickedness**" (**Psalm 45:7a**). And when it came time for God the Father, God Most High, called "*Jehovah*" in the Hebrew, to choose one of His angels to be the king, the second in command, whose throne would be at the right hand of the Father, He chose Jesus over Lucifer, as described in **Hebrews 1:1–14**:

> God, who at various times and in various ways spoke in time past to the fathers by the prophets, ² has in these last days spoken to us by *His* Son, whom He has **appointed heir of all things**, through whom also He made the worlds; ³ who being the **brightness of *His* glory** and the **express image of His person**, and upholding all things by the word of His power, when He had by Himself **purged our sins**, sat down at the right hand of the Majesty on high, ⁴ having become **so much better than the angels**, as He has **by inheritance** obtained **a more excellent name than they**. ⁵ For to which of the angels did He ever say: *"You are My Son, Today I have begotten You"*? And again: *"I will be to Him a Father, And He shall be to Me a Son"*?
>
> ⁶ But when He again **brings the firstborn into the world**, He says: "Let all the angels of God worship Him." ⁷ And of the angels He says: "Who **makes His angels spirits** And His ministers a flame of fire." ⁸ But to the Son He says: "**Your throne, O God, is forever and ever**; A scepter of righteousness is the **scepter of Your Kingdom**. ⁹ **You have loved righteousness and hated lawlessness**; Therefore God, Your God, has **anointed You With the oil of gladness** more than Your companions."
>
> ¹⁰ And: "You, LORD, **in the beginning laid the foundation of the earth**, And the heavens are the work of Your hands. ¹¹ **They will perish**, but You remain; And they will all grow old like a garment; ¹² Like a cloak You will fold them up, And they will be changed. But **You are the same**, And Your years will not fail." ¹³ But to **which of the angels** has He ever said: "**Sit at My right hand**, Till **I make Your enemies Your footstool**"? ¹⁴ Are they not all **ministering spirits sent forth to minister for those who will inherit salvation**?

To be chosen to be king does not mean you are king yet but that you are consecrated or anointed to be king at some future time. King David is an example of God having Samuel anoint David to be king while Saul was still king. The word for a person anointed to be king is "Messiah," or in the Hebrew, H4899 *mashyach*, which means "From

H4886; **anointed**; usually a **consecrated** person (as a king, priest, or saint); especially the Messiah;- **anointed, Messiah**." In the Greek, the word for being anointed is G5547 *Christos*, which means "From G5548; **anointed**, that is, the **Messiah**, and epithet of Jesus:-Christ," from which we get the word "Christ."

THE REBELLION IN HEAVEN

So how do you think Lucifer took that decision of God the Father? Do you think that maybe Lucifer thought God would choose him to be king and that he would rule and reign with God Most High? Well, we do not have to imagine, because the prophet Isaiah records for us the mind of Lucifer, in that he did want to be king and rule over a kingdom and that his not being chosen to be king set off a rebellion in heaven: "**How you are fallen from heaven, O Lucifer, son of the morning**! *How* you are **cut down to the ground, You who weakened the nations!** [13] For you have said **in your heart: 'I will ascend into heaven, I will exalt my throne above the stars of God**; I will also sit on the mount of the congregation On the farthest sides of the north; [14] I will ascend above the heights of the clouds, **I will be like the Most High'**" (**Isaiah 14:12–14**). While Jesus was chosen to be a son at the right hand of God, Satan wanted to be above Jesus and like the Most High God.

The word "Lucifer" comes from the Hebrew word H1966 *heylel*, which is defined as "from H1984 (in the sense of **brightness**); the **morning star:-lucifer**." It is also derived from the Hebrew word H1984 *halal*, which means "To be clear, to **shine**; hence to **make a show**; to **boast**; and thus to be (**clamorously**) **foolish**; to **rave**; causatively to celebrate; also to **stultify**; glory, give [light], **be mad, rage**." *Webster's Student Dictionary* defines **stultify** as "1. To cause **to appear foolish** or **stupid**. 2. To cause to be considered **untrustworthy**; as, the witness, by **false testimony** has *stultified* himself; also, **to disgrace**."

Of interest is the definition of "Lucifer" in *Webster's Student Dictionary*: "1. The planet Venus, when it appears as the **morning star**. 2. *Bible*.

Satan, the rebel archangel who, like the morning star in old myths, **fell from heaven.**" Recall that in the Bible, **stars are symbolic for angels**. The words "cut down" from the phrase "*How* you are **cut down to the ground**" come from the Hebrew word H1438 *gada*, which means "To fell a tree; generally to destroy anything: **cut down.**" As we just learned, the word "ground" comes from the Hebrew word H776 **erets**, which means "**the earth.**" So Lucifer was fallen from heaven to earth, where he was called Satan.

We learn in **1 Timothy 3:1–2, 5–6** that pride is what caused Lucifer to fall from the glory he had with God to being God's arch enemy, now called by the names Satan and the Devil: "This *is* a faithful saying: If a man desires the position of a bishop, he desires a good work. ² A bishop then must be blameless, the husband of one wife, temperate, sober-minded, of good behavior, hospitable, able to teach ... (for if a man does not know how to rule his own house, how will he take care of the church of God?); ⁶ not a novice, **lest being puffed up with pride he fall into the *same* condemnation as the devil.**" And the Bible teaches us that "*God **resists the proud,** But **gives grace to the humble**"* (**James 4:6b**).

Other names that Lucifer, former archangel and son of God, is known by are The Serpent, the Dragon, the Devil, the accuser of the brethren, the ruler of this age, the prince of the power of the air, the spirit who now works in the sons of disobedience, the destroyer, the Evil One, the Wicked One, and Belial.

On the other hand, we know that Jesus was described as an "Angel of the Lord" and the great "I AM" in the Old Testament before He put on flesh and became a human being like we did. Jesus describes Himself **in Matthew 11:27–30** as being gentle and lowly in heart: "All things have been delivered to Me by My Father, and no one knows the Son except the Father. Nor does anyone know the Father except the Son, and *the one* to whom the Son wills to reveal *Him*. ²⁸ Come to Me, all *you* who labor and are heavy laden, and I will give you **rest**. ²⁹ **Take My yoke upon you** and **learn from Me**, for **I am gentle** and **lowly in heart,** and **you will find rest for your souls**. [30] For **My yoke *is* easy** and **My burden is light**."

Jesus is also known by these other names: Prince of Peace, Savior, the Redeemer, Word of God, Son of God, Son of Man, the great I AM, the Bread of Life, the Light of the World, the Lion of Judah, the Lamb of God, the Chosen One, the Messiah, the Christ, King of Kings, Lord of Lords, the Angel of the Lord, God's High Priest, the Seed, and the Way.

In order for Lucifer to become a king, he would have to have some citizens in his kingdom to rule and reign over, and because he cannot create angelic beings like God Most High can, the only place to get them from is the kingdom of God, of which he once was a citizen. Satan was probably the most powerful angel in heaven, but God is all-powerful, which means that Satan's power would not allow him to take citizens out of heaven. And this is exactly what Jesus says in **John 10:27–30**: "My sheep hear My voice, and I know them, and they follow Me. [28] And I give them eternal life, and they shall never perish; **neither shall anyone snatch them out of My hand**. [29] My Father, who has given *them* to Me, **is greater than all**; and **no one is able to snatch *them* out of My Father's hand**. [30] I and *My* Father **are one**."

Since taking citizens from heaven by force was not an option, Lucifer schemed to deceive some of the angels in heaven with a lie that he could provide them a better life than God could. He would tell them they could "be like God," on their own and in control of their own life, with no one to tell them what to do. Lucifer knew that they had never heard a lie before and that they would be easy targets for the scam, especially the ones who were impressed with his great glory and beauty. The angels could not see into his heart to detect his lie like God can. Lucifer knew that once the deceived angels believed him and his lie and rejected the truth of God, God would have to cast them out of heaven, and then they would be under his control since he was more powerful than they. They would have fallen into his trap, unable to go back home.

That God is able to see into the minds of those He created and to know what they are thinking and to see into their hearts to know their desires is evident from verses like the following:

252

For behold, He who forms mountains, And creates the wind, Who **declares to man what his thought** *is,* And makes the morning darkness, Who treads the high places of the earth– The LORD **God of hosts** *is* **His name.** *(Amos 4:13)*

O LORD, You have searched me and **known** *me.* [2] You know my sitting down and my rising up; You **understand my thought afar off.** [3] You **comprehend my path** and my lying down, And are **acquainted with all my ways.** [4] For *there is* not a word on my tongue, *But* behold, O LORD, **You know it altogether.** **(Psalm 139: 1–4)**

This ability is what enables God the Father to be completely fair and just in His judgments. Nothing that we think, say, or do is hidden from the LORD God. We will see that this ability of the God the Father to see into the hearts and minds to know who is lying and who is telling the truth is critical in order for the leader of a kingdom or a nation to keep order, unity, and peace. And the ability to see into hearts and minds is the ability the Father gave Jesus, His Son, when He anointed Him to be King: "But Jesus **knew their thoughts**, and said to them: 'Every kingdom **divided against itself** is brought to desolation, and every city or house **divided against itself will not stand.** [26] If Satan casts out Satan, **he is divided against himself. How then will his kingdom stand?**'" **(Matthew 12:25–26)**.

The angels in heaven had never experienced evil in heaven; nor had they ever heard a lie before. So God could not hold them accountable for what they did not know and understand. We will see that ignorance of the truth is an excuse for bad behavior in the eyes of God. And because God could see into the hearts and minds of those angels who were deceived by Lucifer, He knew who, like prodigal sons, would turn from the lies of Satan and believe the truth of God once they had experienced good and evil for themselves. And God also knew who had hardened their hearts and minds against the truth of God and were beyond hope of ever changing. Those who do not have open minds and teachable hearts cannot be helped by the truth of God because they will not even listen to it. Their minds are already made up; their hearts immovable as though set in stone.

The author of Hebrews speaks of the angels in heaven who were not deceived by Lucifer's lies as being sent by God to minister to the elect angels who were deceived but could be saved: "And of the angels He says: "*Who* **makes His angels spirits** *And His ministers a flame of fire* ... Are they not all **ministering spirits** sent forth to minister for those **who will inherit salvation?**" (**Hebrews 1:7, 14**). And the apostle Paul speaks of "those **who will inherit salvation**," the elect angels, in a letter to Timothy: "I charge *you* before God and the Lord Jesus Christ and the **elect angels** that you observe these things without prejudice, doing nothing with partiality" (**1 Timothy 5:21**).

THE ELECT OF GOD

The Bible refers in many places to the "elect of God"—those that God knew still had open minds and teachable hearts. These He selected to be forgiven and reconciled to Him before He created the world, for those whom He foreknew will come to know and understand the truth and will choose life. Let us consider how the Bible speaks of "**elect angels**," the elect sons and daughters in the following verses:

> **Colossians 3:12–15**: "Therefore, as *the* **elect of God**, holy and beloved, put on tender mercies, kindness, **humility**, meekness, longsuffering; [13] bearing with one another, and **forgiving one another**, if anyone has a complaint against another; **even as Christ forgave you, so you also** *must do*. [14] But above all these things **put on love**, which is **the bond of perfection**. [15] And let the **peace of God rule in your hearts**, to which also you **were called in one body**; and be thankful."

And the apostle Paul speaks of how God knew beforehand who would belong to Him after they experienced good and evil for themselves in the world that He would create:

> Now **He who searches the hearts knows what the mind of the Spirit** *is,* because **He makes intercession for the saints** according to *the will of* God. [28] And we know that **all things work together for good** to those **who love God**, to those **who are the called** according to *His* **purpose**. [29] For **whom**

254

He foreknew, He also **predestined** *to be* **conformed to the image of His Son**, that He might be the **firstborn among many brethren**. [30] Moreover whom **He predestined**, these **He also called**; whom He called, these **He also justified**; and whom He justified, these **He also glorified**. [31] What then shall we say to these things? **If God** *is* **for us, who** *can be* **against us** [32] He who did not spare His own Son, but delivered Him up for us all, how shall He not with Him also freely give us all things? [33] Who shall bring a charge against **God's elect**? *It is* God who justifies? (**Romans 8:29–33**)

Notice that the fallen angels were no longer in the image of God but that those God foreknew would be "**conformed to the image of His Son**." And the author of Hebrews tells us that Jesus is the express image of the Father:

God, who at various times and in various ways spoke in time past to the fathers by the prophets, [2] has in these last days spoken to us by *His* Son, whom He has appointed heir of all things, through whom also He made the worlds; [3] who being the **brightness of** *His* **glory** and the **express image of His person**, and upholding all things by the word of His power, when He had by Himself purged our sins, sat down at the right hand of the Majesty on high. (**Hebrews 1:1–3**)

And unless those days were shortened, no flesh would be saved; but for **the elect's sake** those days will be shortened. (**Matthew 24:22**)

For false christs and false prophets will rise and show great signs and wonders to deceive, if possible, **even the elect**. (**Matthew 24:24**)

And then He will send His angels, and **gather together His elect** from the four winds, from the farthest part of earth to the farthest part of heaven. (**Mark 13:27**)

And shall God not avenge **His own elect** who cry out day and night to Him, though He bears long with them? (**Luke 18:7**)

> What then? Israel has not obtained what it seeks; but the **elect** have obtained it, and the rest were blinded. (**Romans 11:7**)

> Therefore I endure all things for the sake of **the elect**, that they also may obtain the salvation which is in Christ Jesus with eternal glory. (**2 Timothy 2:10**)

The apostle Paul reveals an amazing truth concerning the "elect" before the world was created: "Paul, a bondservant of God and an **apostle of Jesus Christ**, according to the **faith of God's elect** and the **acknowledgment of the truth** which accords with **godliness**, ² in **hope of eternal life** which God, **who cannot lie, promised before time began**" (**Titus 1:1–3**).

God promised the elect the hope of eternal life before time began! This passage confirms that we who are fallen angelic spirits on earth lived in God's kingdom in heaven before we were cast down to earth with Satan because we believed his lies. There are many other verses that confirm our preexistence in heaven and our predestination to be freed from death by the trap of Lucifer and saved for eternal life by Jesus.

PREEXISTENCE AND PREDESTINATION

There are a lot of verses in the Bible that refer to things that happened "before the foundation of the world" with words and phrases like "**predestined**," "**before the beginning of time**," and "**foreknowledge**" (where the prefix "fore" seems to refer to "**before the creation of the world**"). With that in mind, consider the following verses:

> Your eyes saw my substance, being **yet unformed**. And in Your book they all were written, The days fashioned for me, **When as yet there were none of them**. (**Psalm 139:16**).

> LORD, **You have been our dwelling place in all generations.** ² **Before the mountains were brought forth**, Or **ever You had formed the earth and the world**, Even from everlasting to everlasting, You *are* God. ³You turn man to destruction, And say, "**Return, O children of men**." (**Psalm 90:1–3**)

The latter verse above is a prayer of Moses, the man of God. Moses is saying that we lived with God before the earth was formed and that God wants us to return to Him.

> Therefore do not be ashamed of the testimony of our Lord, nor of me His prisoner, but share with me in the **sufferings for the gospel** according to the power of God, ^{9} **who has saved us** and **called us with a holy calling**, not according to our works, but **according to His own purpose and grace** which was given to **us in Christ Jesus before time began. (2 Timothy 1:8–9)**

> These all died in faith, not having received the promises, but having seen them afar off were assured of them, embraced *them* and confessed that **they were strangers and pilgrims on the earth. (Hebrews 11:13)**

> "It is **the Spirit** who gives life; **the flesh profits nothing**. The **words that I speak** to you **are spirit**, and **they are life**. ^{64} But there are some of you who do not believe." For **Jesus knew from the beginning** who they were **who did not believe**, and who would betray Him. ^{65} And He said, "Therefore I have said to you that no one can come to Me unless it has been **granted to him by My Father." (John 6:63–65)**

> Blessed be the God and Father of our Lord Jesus Christ, who has blessed us with every spiritual blessing in the heavenly places in Christ, ^{4} just as **He chose us in Him before** the **foundation of the world**, that we should be holy and without blame before Him **in love**, ^{5} having **predestined us to adoption as sons** by **Jesus Christ to Himself**, according to the good pleasure of His will, ^{6} to the praise of the glory of His grace, by which He has made us accepted in the Beloved. **(Ephesians 1:3–6)**

So the Bible says we were chosen by God to be in Christ before the foundation of the world. Does that not mean that there was some kind of judgment by God before the creation of the world? And because this passage says that God has "**predestined** us to **adoption** as sons," that has to mean that before the beginning, before the foundation of the world, there was a time when we were sons of God and a later time when we were not sons of God.

> Then the word of the LORD came to me, saying: [5] "**Before I formed you in the womb I knew you; Before you were born I sanctified you**; I ordained you a prophet to the nations." (**Jeremiah 1:4–5**)

> For we are His workmanship, created in Christ Jesus for good works, **which God prepared beforehand** that we **should walk in them. (Ephesians 2:10)**

> … knowing that you were not redeemed with corruptible things, like silver or gold, from your aimless conduct received **by tradition** from your fathers, [19] but with the precious blood of Christ, as of a lamb without blemish and without spot. [20] **He indeed was foreordained before** the **foundation of the world**, but was **manifest in these last times for you. (1 Peter 1:18–20)**

> Nevertheless the solid foundation of God stands, having this seal: "**The Lord knows those who are His**," and, "Let everyone who names the name of Christ **depart from iniquity**." (**2 Timothy 2:19**)

> Now when the Gentiles heard this, they were glad and glorified the word of the Lord. And **as many as had been appointed to eternal life** believed. (**Acts 13:48**)

How amazing are these words from **2 Timothy 1:9**: "God, who has saved us and **called us** with **a holy calling**, not according to our works, but according to **His own purpose** and **grace** which was **given to us** in Christ Jesus **before time began**." And likewise these words from **Romans 8:28–30**: "And we know that all things work together for good to those who love God, to those **who are the called according to His purpose**. [29] For **whom He foreknew, He also predestined** to be **conformed to the image of His Son**, that He might be the firstborn among many brethren. [30] **Moreover whom He**

predestined, these **He also called; whom He called**, these **He also justified; and whom He justified**, these **He also glorified**."

Notice that this passage in Romans says God predestined us who love God to be "**conformed to the image of His Son**," who is the "**express image**" of God, as the author of Hebrews says: "God, who at various times and in various ways spoke in time past to the fathers by the prophets, ² has in these **last days** spoken to us by *His* **Son**, whom He has appointed heir of all things, through whom also He made the worlds; ³ **who being the brightness of *His* glory** and the **express image of His person** ..." (**Hebrews 1:1–3**).

So if God's purpose before time began was to predestine those He foreknew to be called and to be conformed to His image, does that not mean that we were not in the image of God before time began and that creating the earth might even be part of that purpose to **conform us to God's image**?

And now we have an understanding of that curious and confusing passage in **Romans 9:11–14**: "And not only *this,* but when Rebecca also had conceived by one man, *even* by our father Isaac ¹¹ (for *the children* **not yet being born, nor having done any good or evil**, that the **purpose of God according to election might stand**, not of works but of **Him who calls**), ¹² it was said to her, '*The older shall serve the younger.*' ¹³ As it is written, '*Jacob I have loved,* but *Esau I have hated.*' ¹⁴ What shall we say then? *Is there* **unrighteousness with God**? **Certainly not!**" God is not arbitrary or unrighteous, because He knew the natures of Jacob and Esau in heaven before they were born of flesh on the earth. Paul clearly understood what he was writing, and now we do too.

After considering these verses—and there are more like them—can anyone not conclude that there is more to life on earth than what happened after the creation of the world? This not only sounds like a plan for salvation: it sounds like a determination about the fallen angels or spiritual beings had already been made by God before time, and if it was before time, it was before the creation of the world. (According to Einstein's theory of general relativity, space, matter, and time were created from nothing and exploded into existence at the creation of the universe.)

Then, ironically, those whom Satan deceived to commit sin, he accused of sinning so that he could keep them under his rule and reign on earth, as the book of Revelation reveals: "Then I heard a loud voice saying in heaven, 'Now salvation, and strength, and the kingdom of our God, and the power of His Christ have come, for **the accuser of our brethren**, who **accused them before our God day and night**, has been cast down'" (**Revelation 12:10**). The apostle Paul speaks of our adversary ready to accuse those he deceived in **1 Timothy 5:14**: "Therefore I desire that *the* younger *widows* marry, bear children, manage the house, **give no opportunity** to the **adversary to speak reproachfully.** [15] For some have already **turned aside after Satan.**" The Greek word for "Satan" is G4567 *Satanas*, which means "**the accuser**, that is, the **devil:- Satan.**"

In a vision of Zechariah in the Old Testament, God reveals to us what is really happening behind the scenes in the spiritual reality where Satan stands to oppose us: "Then he showed me Joshua the high priest standing before the **Angel of the Lord**, and **Satan standing at his right hand to oppose him**" (**Zechariah 3:1**). Here Jesus is standing with Joshua, the high priest, to defend him before God the Father, and Satan is there to accuse him. The Hebrew word for Satan is H7854 *satan*, which aptly means "An **opponent**, especially **Satan, the arch enemy of good, adversary.**" Satan is God's adversary and the adversary of anyone who wants to follow God and live under God's reign and rule in heaven.

THE PLAN OF GOD

In order to deal with this rebellion by Satan, God called the courts of heaven into session to prove to all the angels in heaven, both those who were deceived and those who still believed in God but must have been in some level of doubt after one-third of their companions believed Lucifer, that the ways of Lucifer—being separated from God and on their own—would lead to their corruption, misery, sorrow, and death. And God had to prove that the ways of God are the only ways that lead to peace, prosperity, unspeakable joy, and eternal life. And because angels cannot see into hearts and minds, God also had to prove that His judgment was fair and just in choosing the elect—those He foreknew would turn from the ways of Satan and believe God after they experienced the evil ways of Satan.

To accomplish this, the God of forgiveness and the God of the second chance, for those who were ignorant of the truth, would give His elect and some of those who were evil beyond all hope a temporary life in a temporary world, separated from God, to experience good and evil for themselves. And by the way they lived their lives when they thought no one was watching, God would show to all that His judgment of who would belong to Him and who would belong to Satan was fair, just, and righteous. To prove that Satan's claim of a better way to live was a lie and would only lead to death and that God's ways are the only ways that lead to life, God would let the fallen angels live to experience both ways to prove that He was true and right.

In order for the trial to be fair, these fallen angels could not be allowed to recall the former glorious life with God, who had protected them and provided all their needs, as they would choose God out of greed and selfish motives. And so God had to put them in bodies made of the same dust that the earth is made of so that they could only perceive the things of that temporary, virtual world and would be blind to the heavenly, spiritual reality. And we will see how this plan of God is carried out in the Bible story. In fact, **Revelation 12:4, 9** reveals to us that this is exactly what happened: **"His tail drew a third** of the **stars of heaven and threw them to the earth** ... So the **great dragon** was cast out, that **serpent of old,** called the **Devil** and **Satan, who deceives the whole world; he was cast to the earth,** and **his angels** were **cast out with him**."

That God put a body of flesh on both the elect that belonged to God and the evil that belonged to Satan is exactly what Paul teaches us God did in **Romans 9:21–26**:

> Does not the potter have power over the clay, from the same lump to **make one vessel for honor** and **another for dishonor**? ²² *What* if God, wanting to show *His* wrath and to **make His power known**, endured with much longsuffering the **vessels of wrath prepared for destruction**, ²³ and that He might make known the riches of His glory on the **vessels of mercy**, which He had **prepared beforehand for glory**, ²⁴ *even* **us whom He called**, not of the Jews only, but also of the Gentiles? ²⁵ As He says also in Hosea:
>
> *"I will call them My people, who were not My people, And her beloved, who was not beloved."*
>
> ²⁶ *"And it shall come to pass in the place where it was said to them, 'You are not My people,' There they shall be called **sons of the living God**."*

That place where God said of us **"*You are not My people*"** was in heaven, and heaven is the place where God will call us **"*sons of the living God*."** And a return to our home in heaven for believers is exactly what the author of the book of Hebrews teaches will occur: "These all died in faith, **not having received the promises**, but **having seen them afar off** were assured of them, embraced *them* and confessed that **they were strangers** and **pilgrims on the earth** … ¹⁶ But now they desire a better, that is, a **heavenly** *country*. Therefore God is not ashamed to be called their God, for **He has prepared a city for them**" (**Hebrews 11:13, 16**). And as we learned, the promise that the patriarchs of faith received from God was as follows: "Then He brought him outside and said, '**Look now toward heaven**, and count the stars if you are able to number them.' And He said to him, '**So shall your descendants be**.' ⁶ And he **believed in the LORD**, and He **accounted it to him for righteousness**" (**Genesis 15:5–6**).

In all of this we can clearly see and understand the source of the doctrine of Original Sin, the doctrine that says that all of us on earth are guilty of sin from birth.

THE ORIGINAL SIN DOCTRINE

Psalm 51:5 tells us that we all were conceived in sin: "Behold, I was **brought forth in iniquity**, And **in sin my mother conceived me**." If we are guilty of sin at our birth on earth, and knowing that a righteous and holy God does not create anything evil and sinful but does create beings with a free-will choice because love must be of a free-will choice, then our sin must have come from a choice we made in heaven. And this helps us understand the source of our preexistence and predestination spoken of in the Bible.

The Original Sin doctrine is attributed to Bishop Irenaeus in the second century and is based on the teachings of the apostle Paul in **Romans 5:12–21** and **1 Corinthians 15:22**:

> Therefore, just as through one **man** sin entered the world, and **death through sin**, and thus **death spread to all men, because all sinned**– [13] (For until the law sin was in the world, but sin is not imputed when there is no law. [14] Nevertheless **death reigned from Adam to Moses**, even over those who had **not sinned according to the likeness** of the **transgression of Adam**, who is **a type** of **Him who was to come**. [15] But the **free gift** *is* not like the **offense**. For if by the **one man's offense many died**, much more the grace of God and the **gift** by **the grace of the one Man, Jesus Christ, abounded to many**.
>
> [16] And the **gift** *is* not like *that which came* **through the one who sinned**. For the judgment *which came* from one *offense resulted* in **condemnation**, but the **free gift** *which came* from many offenses *resulted* **in justification**. [17] For if by the one man's offense **death reigned through the one**, much more those who receive abundance of grace and of the **gift of righteousness** will **reign in life through the One, Jesus Christ**.)

[18] Therefore, as through **one man's offense** *judgment* **came to all men**, resulting in **condemnation**, even so through one **Man's righteous act** *the free gift came* to all men, resulting in **justification of life.** [19] For as by **one man's disobedience** many were **made sinners**, so also by **one Man's obedience** many will be **made righteous.** [20] Moreover **the law entered** that the **offense might abound**. But where sin abounded, grace abounded much more, [21] so that as **sin reigned in death**, even so **grace might reign through righteousness to eternal life** through **Jesus Christ our Lord**. (**Romans 5:12**)

"For as **in Adam** all die, even so **in Christ** all shall be made alive." (**1 Corinthians 15:22**)

As we learned in "The Oneness Branch," in the section "The First Adam Satan, the Second Adam" Christ," to be "in Adam" or "in Christ" refers to many being united together under a leader in a common belief, as though they all are One. We need to be careful, though, so that we do not blame the first man, named Adam, for our sinful nature but put the blame on Lucifer, called Satan, who deceived all of us in heaven. This is recounted for us on earth in the tale of Satan deceiving Adam and Eve in the form of the Serpent. In any case, it was the first woman, named Eve, who was deceived first, not the first man, named Adam. As we will learn, there are two definitions of the Hebrew word *adam*. The Hebrew word H121 *Adam* is defined as "Adam, **the name of the first man**." Then there is the other Hebrew word, H120 *adam*, which means "**Ruddy**, that is a human being (**an individual** or **the species, mankind**, etc.) **hypocrite, common sort, of low degree**."

As we learned in "The Oneness Branch," because "Adam" refers to fallen angels who have been made lower in status when they were cast down to earth and put on flesh, Satan qualifies for the label of "man" or "Adam," and this explains how Adam was a "**type**" of Jesus who was to come. Both Satan and Jesus are leaders, rulers, or kings of their followers, those who believed in them. And Satan's lie and deception was the event that "as through **one man's offense** *judgment* **came to all men**, resulting in **condemnation**," and Jesus' suffering and dying for us on the cross out of His love for us is the "one **Man's righteous act** *the free gift came* to all men, resulting in **justification of life**."

The phrase "even over those who had **not sinned according to the likeness** of the **transgression of Adam**" is referring to the fact that those who deceive others to sin bear a greater guilt than those who are deceived. And this is exactly what Jesus teaches: "But **whoever causes one of these little ones who believe in Me to stumble**, it would be better for him if a millstone were hung around his neck, and he were thrown into the sea" (**Mark 9:42**). The first man, named Adam, did not deceive others to sin but was among those of us who were deceived by Satan, as Eve explains to God in **Genesis 3:13**: "And the LORD God said to the woman, 'What *is* this you have done?' The woman said, 'The **serpent deceived me**, and I ate.'"

Jesus confirms that all of us on earth are already deserving of condemnation: "For God did not send His Son into the world to condemn the world, but **that the world through Him might be saved**. ¹⁸ He who believes in Him is not condemned; but **he who does not believe is condemned already**, because **he has not believed in the name of the only begotten Son of God**" (**John 3:17–18**). Everyone on earth has been cast out of heaven and down to earth with Lucifer/Satan and is "**condemned already**" for his or her belief in his lies instead of the truth of the Son of God.

The Beginning as Seen from Earth

IN ORDER FOR God to cast Lucifer (called Satan after the fall) and one-third of heaven's angels down to the earth, God would have to create the universe, the heavens, and the earth first. The Bible, the Word of God, describes this creation: "In the beginning **God created the heavens and the earth**. ² The earth was without form, and void; and **darkness *was* on the face of the deep**. And the Spirit of God was hovering over the face of the waters. ³ Then God said, '**Let there be light**'; and there **was light**. ⁴ And **God saw the light**, that *it was* **good**; and God **divided the light from the darkness**" (**Genesis 1:1–4**).

In this verse, the Bible agrees with the understanding of the science of the last century. The work of Albert Einstein and others have shown that the laws of physics predict that the universe began with a "big bang" when time, space, and matter exploded into existence from nothing. Previously the world thought that the universe had always existed. But the second law of thermodynamics tells us that everything moves from order to disorder, from more useable energy to less; according to this, the sun that provides our energy and warmth would have burned out long ago, as would every other star in the universe.

In these first four verses of Genesis, there is evidence of intelligent beings, the fallen angels from heaven, who are already present on the earth. The English word "darkness" in the phrase "**darkness *was* on the face of the deep**" is translated from the Hebrew word H2822 *choshek,* which figuratively means "**misery, destruction, death,**

ignorance, sorrow, and **wickedness.**" Now let us consider the fact that the water, rocks, and dirt of the earth cannot be good or evil. They cannot experience misery and death; nor can they be ignorant, sorrowful, or wicked—only living beings can do that.

Darkness is often used in the Bible as a metaphor for evil and doing what is wrong, because those things are done in darkness so others cannot see what is being done. "And this is the condemnation, that the **light has come into the world,** and **men loved darkness rather than light,** because their deeds were evil. [20] For **everyone practicing evil hates the light** and **does not come to the light,** lest his deeds should be exposed. [21] But **he who does the truth comes to the light,** that his deeds may be clearly seen, that they have been done in God" (**John 3:19–21**).

In the very next verse, we read, "Then God said, '**Let there be light**'; and there was light" (**Genesis 1:3**). Now we know that this light could not be the kind of light that we normally think of, because the sun, moon, and stars were not created until the fourth day in **Genesis 1:14–17, 19**:

> Then God said, "Let there be lights in the firmament of the heavens to divide the day from the night; and **let them be for signs** and seasons, and for days and years; [15] and let them be for lights in the firmament of the heavens **to give light on the earth**"; and it was so. [16] Then **God made two great lights**: the greater light to rule the day, and the lesser light to rule the night. *He made* the stars also. [17] God set them in the firmament of the heavens **to give light on the earth** ... So the evening and the morning were the **fourth day.**

The word "light" in **Genesis 1:3** is translated from the Hebrew word H216 *or,* which means "**illumination** or luminary **in every sense** including **happiness, etc.,**" while the word "lights" in **Genesis 1:14** is from a different Hebrew word, H3974 *ma'or ma'or me'orah me'orah,* which means "light (as an element) specifically lights **like a chandelier.**" The word translated as "light" in **verse 1:3** refers to the *illumination* **of the mind** to what is true and good. "**And God saw** the light, that *it was* good; and God divided the light from the darkness" (Genesis 1:4).

It is easy to see that illumination of the mind is what was meant when we remember that Jesus, who was there in the beginning, is the **Light of the World**, as we see in **John 8:12**: "Then Jesus spoke to them again, saying, 'I am **the light of the world**. He who follows Me shall not **walk in darkness**, but have the **light of life**.'" That Jesus came into this world to bring us the truth is evidenced by what Jesus said to Pontius Pilate: "Pilate therefore said to Him, 'Are You a king then?' Jesus answered, 'You say *rightly* that I am a king. **For this cause I was born**, and for this cause I have come into the world, **that I should bear witness to the truth**. Everyone who is of the truth hears My voice'" (**John 18:37**). And we shall see that Jesus, the "**light of the world**," was there on the earth in the beginning of the world with God.

All of this is described in the **first chapter of John**, where the beginning of the world is also discussed: "**In the beginning** was the Word, and **the Word was with God**, and **the Word was God**. He was **in the beginning** with God. All things were made through Him, and without Him nothing was made that was made. **In Him was life**, and **the life was the light** of men. [5] And **the light shines in the darkness**, and **the darkness did not comprehend it**" (**John 1:1–5**). To comprehend is something that is done with the mind, which confirms that the "light" in **Genesis 1:3** was for the illumination of the mind and that in the "darkness" were beings capable of understanding—just not capable of understanding the truth that leads to life.

Also consider what the apostle Paul says in **2 Corinthians 4:3–4**: "But even if our gospel is veiled, it is veiled to those who are perishing, [4] whose minds **the god of this age has blinded, who do not believe**, lest **the light of the gospel** of the glory of Christ, who is **the image of God**, should shine on them." And consider what the author of Hebrews says: "But **recall the former days** in which, **after you were illuminated**, you **endured a great struggle with sufferings**" (**Hebrews 10:32**).

Now notice that in the first day, in **Genesis 1:4**, "God **divided the light from the darkness**." In view of the previous discussion, consider the following facts: Because the sun, moon, and stars were not made yet, and because Jesus, the Light of the World, was there with God, the "light" in **Genesis 1:3** must be the revelation of truth coming from Jesus and His Holy Spirit, and we have learned that the Holy Spirit is the giver of truth and will lead us into all truth. "However, when He, the **Spirit of truth**, has come, He will **guide you into all truth**; for He will not speak on His own *authority,* but whatever He hears He will speak; and **He will tell you things to come**" (**John 16:13**).

Because life was in Jesus and "**the life was the light of men**," and because Jesus came into the world to witness of the truth, the light must be the "illumination" of the truth that leads to life. And because the apostle John said, "the **darkness did not comprehend it**," this confirms that the "darkness" refers to living beings capable of understanding and reasoning.

The pre-incarnate Jesus was there, bearing the light of life, or the truth that leads to life, and the darkness did not understand it, but that does not mean that there were not some who wanted to understand the light that leads to life and did come to the light to understand and believe the truth. And those who do are no longer considered to be in darkness, but in the light. It was only the darkness that did not understand the light of life and did not want to try to understand it because their deeds were evil and they did not want them to be exposed. These are the ones that Satan, the god of this age, has blinded to the truth, as we shall shortly learn from Scripture.

And the purpose of God to bring the light of truth to those who sit in darkness is exactly what Jesus said to Saul, later known as the apostle Paul, after Jesus had died and had risen and had ascended into heaven: "I will deliver you from the *Jewish* people, as well as *from* the Gentiles, to whom I now send you, [18] to **open their eyes**, *in order* to **turn *them* from darkness to light**, and *from* the **power of Satan to God**, that they may **receive forgiveness of sins** and an inheritance among **those who are sanctified by faith in Me**" (**Acts 26:18**).

269

And Jesus, while in flesh on earth, says as much in **John 12:36**: "While you **have the light, believe in the light**, that you may **become sons of light**." And consider the separation of darkness and light in **1 Peter 2:9**: "But you *are* a **chosen** generation, a royal priesthood, a holy nation, **His own special people**, that you may proclaim the praises of Him who **called you out of darkness into His marvelous light**." And again in **Romans 13:12**: "The night is far spent, the day is at hand. Therefore **let us cast off the works of darkness**, and **let us put on the armor of light**."

Remember that the Hebrew word for darkness, H2822 *choshek*, figuratively means "**Misery, destruction, death, ignorance, sorrow**, and **wickedness**." Misery, ignorance, and sorrow can apply only to living beings, and this definition allows for two kinds of living beings: those who are **wicked** and those who are **ignorant** and **sorrowful**. Both were **living in darkness** and the **ways of death** until God brought the **light of truth**, which some believed, and became sons of light, and some did not believe, and remained in darkness.

So now we have biblical support for the thinking that in the first day, God dividing the "darkness" from the "light" refers to His separating the evil from the good—the elect from those who were not chosen—which had already occurred in heaven. And the Bible story is full of that purpose of God to separate light from darkness that we see in the first day of creation in the fourth verse of Genesis:

> And have no **fellowship** with the **unfruitful works of darkness**, but rather **expose** *them*. [12] For it is shameful even to speak of those things which are done by them in secret. [13] But all things that are **exposed are made manifest by the light**, for **whatever makes manifest is light**. [14] Therefore He says: "Awake, **you who sleep, Arise from the dead**, And Christ will **give you light**." (**Ephesians 5:11–14** [spoken by Paul])

> Through the tender mercy of our God, With which the Dayspring from on high has visited us; [79] To **give light to those who sit in darkness** and the **shadow of death**, To guide our feet into **the way of peace**. (**Luke 1:78–79**)

I have come *as* **a light** into the world, that whoever **believes in Me** should not **abide in darkness**. **(John 12:46)**

And so now we have an answer for anyone who would ask, **"Why does God say 'Let there be light' in the first day of creation though He does not create the sun and the moon until the fourth day?"**

Let's take a moment to ponder what the Bible is telling us about this first day of creation. There were living, spiritual beings already on earth **before** man was "created" in the sixth day (**Genesis 1:27**). And all of these passages from the Bible are consistent with there being two kinds of fallen angels or spiritual beings on earth who were cast out of heaven with Lucifer, now called Satan: the elect of God, who are in the light seeking the truth that leads to life; and those who still believe the lies of Satan and are in the darkness and living in the ways of death. And this fall from heaven was confirmed by Jesus when He was on the earth in **Luke 10:18**: "And He said to them, "**I saw Satan fall like lightning from heaven**."

GOD CREATES A PLACE FOR MAN TO LIVE DURING THE TRIAL

As we have seen in the first day of Genesis, there was nothing but water, called "the deep" on the face of the earth, and by this we learn that spiritual beings can exist in water but man will need dry land to stand on. The Hebrew word for "the deep" is H8415 *tehom,* which means "An **abyss** (as a **surging mass of water**), especially the deep (the **main sea** or the **subterranean water supply**)."

In days two through six, God creates the atmosphere; the land; the sun, moon, and stars; the fish of the sea and the birds of the air; and all kinds of land animals. "Then God said, '**Let Us make man in Our image, according to Our likeness**; let them have dominion over the fish of the sea, over the birds of the air, and over the cattle, over all the earth and over every creeping thing that creeps on the earth.' [27] So God **created man in His *own* image**; in the **image of God He created him; male and female He created them**" (**Genesis 1:26–27**).

Notice that the fallen angels, or spirits, are called "man" or in the Hebrew H120 *adam* which means: "**ruddy**, that is a human being (**an individual** or **the species, mankind,** etc.) **hypocrite, common sort,** of **low degree.**" Also notice that "man" refers to the fallen nature of angels made lower by their fall from the grace of God, as confirmed in **Hebrews 2:6–7**: "But one testified in a certain place, saying: "*What is man that You are mindful of him, Or the son of man that You take care of him?* **7** *You have made him a little lower than the angels*" (**Hebrews 2:6–7**).

Being cast down to the earth made the fallen angels physically lower than the angels in heaven, and it made them lower in status as well. Now consider that since man—or *adam*, in the Hebrew—was a group of fallen angels that already existed on earth before God created dry land, then making "man" in God's image and likeness means that we were not in the image of God in the beginning of life on earth. This is consistent with fallen angels and all of our thinking and discussion so far.

But what if someone were to ask, "**Was man not in the image of God from the beginning?**"

That is a good question. Let us take a closer look at the sixth day of creation. In each of the previous five days, after God finished what He had created that day, God looked back and saw what He had created and "**saw that it was good**" five times. Then, in the sixth day, the Bible says, "And God **made** the beast of the earth according to its kind, **cattle** according to its kind, and everything that creeps on the earth according to its kind. And God **saw that** *it was* **good**" (**Genesis 1:25**). So God already **saw** that what God had created was good, because it was already done. He was finished with the process of creating the beasts and the cattle and every creeping thing, and He could actually see that it was good.

Later, but still in the sixth day,

> God said, "Let Us **make man** in Our own image, according to
> Our likeness; let them have dominion over the fish of the sea, the

birds of the air, and over the cattle, over all the earth and over all the wild animals of the earth, and over every creeping thing that creeps on the earth." So God **created man** in His *own* image; in the image of God He **created** him; **male and female** He created **them**. [28] Then **God blessed them**, and **God said to them**, "**Be fruitful and multiply; fill the earth and subdue it; have dominion over the fish of the sea**, over the birds of the air, and over every living thing that moves on the earth." (**Genesis 1:27–28**)

But the Bible conspicuously *does not say* of the **creation** of man that God saw that it was good. This can only mean that God could not see that what He was creating was good yet, as man still had the fallen and evil nature of Satan at that point because God was not finished creating man in His image yet. In fact, the Bible records for us, "And the LORD God said of the first man, '*It is* **not good** that **man should be alone**; I will make him a helper comparable to him'" (**Genesis 2:18**).

FALLEN MAN IS NOT IN THE IMAGE OF GOD AT BIRTH

There are a number of verses in the Bible that tell us that we are not born in the image of God and that the purpose of this temporary life on this temporary earth is to create us or transform us to the image of God:

> Behold, I was **brought forth in iniquity**, And in **sin my mother conceived me**. (**Psalm 51:5**)

> For whom He foreknew, **He also predestined *to be* conformed** to the **image of His Son**, that He might be the firstborn among many brethren. (**Romans 8:29**)

> But we all, with unveiled face, beholding as in a mirror the glory of the Lord, **are being transformed into the same image** from glory to glory, **just as by the Spirit of the Lord**. (**2 Corinthians 3:18**)

> Do not lie to one another, since you have put off the old man with his deeds, [10] and have put on the new *man* who is renewed

in knowledge according to the image of Him who created him. (**Colossians 3:9–10**)

But even **if our gospel is veiled**, it is veiled to those who are perishing, [4]**whose minds the god of this age has blinded**, who do not believe, lest the **light of the gospel** of the glory of Christ, **who is the image of God**, should shine on them. (**2 Corinthians 4:4**)

As it is written: *"There is none righteous, no, not one;* [11] *There is none who understands; There is none who seeks after God.* [12] *They have all turned aside; They have together become unprofitable; There is none who does good, no, not one."* (**Romans 3:10-12**)

The doctrine of Original Sin tells us that we are guilty of sin from our birth. And Jesus Himself tells us in the verses right after the most famous verse in the Bible, **John 3:16**, that all of us on earth are already condemned of sin, "For God did not send His Son into the world to condemn the world, but that the world through Him **might be saved.** [18] **He who believes in Him is not condemned**; but **he who does not believe** is **condemned already**, because he has not believed in the name of the only begotten Son of God" (**John 3:17–18**).

If we on earth are already guilty of the sin of not believing in Jesus, the Son of God, at birth, then the only other place that could have happened is in heaven. And this supports everything that we previously discussed in the chapter "The Meaning and Purpose of Life on Earth." This life on earth is our second chance to believe in the Son of God after we learn the truth of God. If we do not believe in Jesus during this life on earth, we will remain condemned.

We also have evidence that man was not yet in God's likeness in the beginning from **Genesis 5:3**, which speaks of the **birth** of the third son of Adam, Seth, who was born in fallen Adam's image and not God's image: "And **Adam** lived one hundred and thirty years, and **begot** *a son* **in his own likeness, after his image**, and named him Seth."

This shows us that we were not born on earth in God's image but in the image and likeness of fallen Adam, and we will learn that creating man in God's image is a process that lasts a lifetime on earth. A passage in the New Testament speaks of this very thing: "And as we **have borne the image of the *man* of dust**, we shall also bear the **image of the heavenly *Man***" (**1 Corinthians 15:49**). As we have learned, the "**image of the man of dust**" refers to "Satan," and the "**image of the heavenly *Man***" refers to Jesus Christ.

We will also see that the word "create" is translated from the Hebrew word H1254 *bara*, which tells us that making man into the image of God is a formative process. But first we will consider the seventh day of creation.

THE SEVENTH DAY OF CREATION

The Bible says that on the seventh day of creation, God rested from the work of creating an environment for man to live in, and in **Genesis 2:1–4** we see that the work of creating a temporary place in which to hold the trial of fallen mankind is already completed: "Thus the heavens and the earth, and all the host of them, **were finished**. ² And on the seventh day God ended His work which He **had done**, and He rested on the seventh day from **all His work which He had done**. ³ Then God blessed the seventh day and sanctified it, because in it He rested from all His work which God had **created and made**. ⁴ This *is* the history of the **heavens** and the **earth** when they **were created**, in the **day** that the LORD God **made the earth and the heavens**."

The Hebrew word translated as "day" in the phrase "in the **day** that the LORD God made the earth and the heavens" is H3117 *yom* (pronounced yome), which can mean "a day (as the **warm hours**), whether literally (from **sunrise to sunset**, or **one sunset to the next**), or figuratively (**a space of time defined by an associated term**), (often used adverbially): **age, season**, (full) **year**, etc." This is the same Hebrew word used for "day" in each of the days of creation. So in **Genesis 2:3** the Bible describes the whole six days of creation with the same word for "day" as it uses for each of the six days of the creation story.

But how should we answer anyone who would ask, "**Are the seven days of creation not twenty-four-hour days?**"

The answer is that we do not know for sure. But it seems unlikely they are twenty-four-hour days, because the sun, which was given for us to determine the length of a day, was not even created until day four of creation, but the word "day" was used in the first three "days," when a twenty-four-hour day could not have been defined by the sun: "Then God said, "**Let there be lights** in the firmament of the heavens to **divide the day from the night**; and let them be for signs and seasons, and **for days** and years" (**Genesis 1:14, 19**). Also consider that God is eternal and exists outside of time, as the apostle Peter reminds us: "But, beloved, do not forget this one thing, that **with the Lord one day *is* as a thousand years**, and **a thousand years as one day**" (**2 Peter 3:8**).

It is the position of this book that science, properly done, totally agrees with the Bible because truth never contradicts another truth. The fossil record shows a long history of the earth. And we see evidence of dinosaurs in the bones we find; they could not have lived and died in a twenty-four-hour day. And oil, coal, and other fossil fuels are part of what God created to provide us with the energy we need to live, and they are the result of the decay of plant and animal life that existed long ago, and their formation required long periods of time. Science, in many different fields, actually substantiates the biblical record and provides us with many proofs that there must be a creator. Biblical agreement with science is not the focus of this book, because many excellent books on this subject have already been written. We will focus on the meaning and purpose of God for life on planet earth.

But do be aware that some two thousand years ago, the apostle Paul was teaching the Romans and us that God's creation necessarily requires a highly intelligent creator: "For the wrath of God is revealed from heaven against all ungodliness and unrighteousness of men, who **suppress the truth in unrighteousness,** [19] because **what may be known of God is manifest in them,** for God has shown *it* to them. [20] For **since the creation of the world His invisible *attributes* are clearly seen, being understood by the things that are made,** *even* His **eternal**

power and **Godhead**, so that they are **without excuse**" (**Romans 1:19–20**).

But what if someone should ask, **"But doesn't the Bible say that there is evening and morning for each day? Doesn't that indicate a twenty-four-hour day?"** That is a good question. Let us look deeper into what the Bible actually says.

In the first day, in **Genesis 1:5,** the Word of God defines the relationship of day and night to light and darkness for us: "God called the **light Day**, and **the darkness He called Night**. So the **evening** and the **morning** were the first day." The Hebrew word for "darkness," we already learned, is H2822 *"choshek,"* which figuratively means "**Misery, destruction, death, ignorance, sorrow,** and **wickedness**." And we learned that "darkness" refers to the presence of the evil and wickedness of Satan and his fallen angels on earth. We also learned that the Hebrew word for "light" is H216 *or*, which means "**illumination** or luminary **in every sense** including **happiness, etc.**" And we learned that the "light" was the presence of the all-knowing, all-wise, omnipotent God, who had come to earth with the light—the knowledge and understanding of the truth that was the life of man.

Now we see that the Hebrew word for "evening" is H6153 *ereb*, which means "dusk :- + day even(-ing, tide), **night**" (note the meaning "night") and that the Hebrew word for "morning" is H1242 *boqer*, which means "properly dawn (as the break of **day**); generally morning, (+) **day**, early morning, morrow" (note the meaning "**day**"). So the night is a period of time when there is the absence of God, where there is ignorance, evil, and wickedness; and the day is a period of time when there is the presence of God on earth, where He uses His infinite knowledge, understanding, and wisdom to create the good things that fallen man will need.

Notice that when God creates plants, fish, birds, animals, and man, He creates them so that they can reproduce many copies of themselves by the "seeds" they produce. And so, all kinds of life can be generated by itself on earth as long as God in heaven provides "the sun and rain" that is needed to sustain life. The Bible refers to this part of the creation process with the words "Let **the earth bring forth** ..." This allows us to consider that when God comes to earth to create some new kind of life, that period of time is called day or morning, and when God returns to heaven to let the earth, by itself, complete the generation of what God started, that period of time is called night or evening.

This helps us understand the curious statement of Jesus in the "age" when He has come to earth to witness of the truth of God, which is the eternal life of man and which will create fallen man in His image: "I must **work** the works of Him who sent Me **while it is day**; *the* **night is coming when no one can work.** [5] As long as **I am in the world, I am the light of the world**" **(John 9:4)**. Later, after Jesus has been resurrected and is in heaven but will return again, Paul describes the time when Jesus is gone from the earth as night and the time of His return as day: "And *do* this, knowing the time, that now *it is* high time to awake out of sleep; for now our salvation *is* nearer than when we *first* believed. [12] **The night is far spent, the day is at hand**. Therefore let us **cast off the works of darkness,** and let us **put on the armor of light**" **(Romans 13:11–12)**.

This leads us to consider the length of the seventh day. Notice that the Bible does not speak of an end to the seventh day as it does of the rest of the six days of creation. Also consider that though God rested in the seventh day from the work of creating a habitation for man to live in, God did not rest from the work of creating man in His image. After all, the purpose of God in making a temporary home for fallen man was to have a place where He could create man in His image by having them experience good and evil for themselves.

In fact, Jesus informs the Jews who were trying to kill Him for healing a man on the Sabbath as though doing a good work for others was prohibited on the Sabbath: "But Jesus answered them, 'My Father **has been working until now**, and I **have been working**'" **(John 5:17)**. Here Jesus is making the point that He and God the Father are working on their Seventh and Sabbath day of rest to heal and restore us. In fact, the whole family of God has been working 24/7 to create us in His image and reconcile us to God the Father. "But to which of **the**

angels has He ever said: *'Sit at My right hand, Till I make Your enemies Your footstool'?* [14] Are they not **all ministering spirits sent forth to minister for those who will inherit salvation?**" (**Hebrews 1:13– 14**). Here we can see the "all for one and one for all" nature of God.

How can we not consider that we today are still in the seventh day, where Jesus, His Father, and His angels are all working together to create the elect in the image of God? After their environment was put in order, Adam and Eve put on bodies of flesh at the beginning of the seventh day in **Genesis 2:7–25** as the first step of God creating those He elected in His image.

And the family of Adam and Eve, of which all of us on earth are members, put on flesh in the seventh day as part of a lifelong process of creating us in the image of God. And this is exactly what the Bible says in **Genesis 5:1–2**: "This is the book of the genealogy of Adam. In **the day** that **God created man, He made him in the likeness of God**. [2] He created them male and female, and blessed them and **called them Mankind in the day they were created**." We are all living in the seventh day, and those who believe will be created or transformed in the image and likeness of God by the end of our lives on earth and by the end of the seventh day.

We get a glimpse of the end of the seventh day in God's revelation to the apostle John:

> And I heard a loud voice from heaven saying, "Behold, **the tabernacle of God** *is* **with men**, and **He will dwell with them**, and **they shall be His people**. God Himself will be with them *and be* their God. [4] And God will **wipe away every tear** from their eyes; there shall be **no more death, nor sorrow, nor crying**. There shall be **no more pain**, for the **former things have passed away**." [5] Then He who sat on the throne said, "Behold, **I make all things new**."
>
> And He said to me, "Write, for these words are true and faithful." [6] And He said to me, "**It is done**! I am the Alpha and the Omega, the Beginning and the End. I will give of the fountain of the **water of life** freely to him who thirsts. [7] **He who overcomes**

shall inherit all things, and I will be his God and **he shall be My son**. [8] But the cowardly, unbelieving, abominable, murderers, sexually immoral, sorcerers, idolaters, and all liars shall have their part in the lake which burns with fire and brimstone, **which is the second death**." (**Revelation 21:3–8**)

CREATING FALLEN MAN IN THE IMAGE OF GOD

Somewhere in my second yearlong study of the book of Genesis in Bible Study Fellowship, I learned that there were two distinct Hebrew words, "*asah*" and "*bara*," for the English words "make" and "create," respectively. That is, "make" or "made" is the translation of "*asah*," and "create" is used for "*bara*." The way I remember it being told to me is that one word meant that God made something from nothing and the other meant God fashioned something new out of things that already existed. The Hebrew word H6213 *asah* is defined as "Make, do, **accomplish**, and **become**," and the word H1254 *bara* is defined as "**Select, choose, cut down**, and **feed (as a formative process)**."

Anyway, I went through my Bible and looked up the Hebrew words and wrote "*asah*" and "*bara*" over their English counterparts throughout the first chapter of Genesis, which describes the six days of God's creation, but I did not see a pattern of making something from nothing versus fashioning something new out of things that already existed. Now we can see that the **selecting** and **choosing** of those that already existed is the part of the *bara* process that happened when God chose His elect angels in heaven, and the "**cut down**" part of that *bara* process happened when Satan and all of us who believed his lies were cast down to earth by God. The "**feeding**" part of the word "*bara*" is what God does when He supplies the "sun and the rain and the apple seed" to provide food for life of man's flesh and when He reveals the truth in the Word of God to provide the nourishment for the life of our spirit.

God, speaking through Moses, describes the feeding of the body and the spirit in this *bara* process of creating us in the image of God like this: "And you shall remember that the LORD your God led you all the way these forty years in the wilderness, **to humble you *and* test you**,

to know what *was* **in your heart**, whether you would **keep His commandments or not.** ³ "So **He humbled you, allowed you to hunger,** and **fed you with manna** which you did not know nor did your fathers know, that He might make you know **that man shall not live by bread alone**; but **man lives by every** *word* **that proceeds from the mouth of the** L<small>ORD</small>" **(Deuteronomy 8:2–3).**

Jesus compares this *bara* **process** of creating fallen man in the image of God to pruning:

> **I am the true vine**, and **My Father** is the **vinedresser.** ² Every branch in Me that does not bear fruit He takes away; and *every* *branch* **that bears fruit He prunes**, that it may **bear more fruit.** ³ You are already clean because of the word which I have spoken to you. ⁴ Abide in Me, and I in you. As the **branch cannot bear fruit of itself**, unless **it abides in the vine**, neither can you, unless you abide in Me.
>
> ⁵ **I am the vine, you** *are* **the branches.** He who **abides in Me, and I in him**, bears much fruit; for **without Me you can do nothing.** ⁶ If anyone does not abide in Me, he is **cast out as a branch** and **is withered**; and they gather them and throw *them* into the fire, and they are burned. ⁷ If **you abide in Me**, and **My words abide in you**, you will ask what you desire, and it shall be done for you. ⁸ By this My Father is glorified, **that you bear much fruit**; so **you will be My disciples. (John 15:1–8)**

But the writer of Hebrews explains that God does this pruning out of His love for us: "'*For whom the* L<small>ORD</small> *loves He chastens, And scourges every son whom He receives.*' ⁷ If you **endure chastening, God deals with you as with sons**; for what son is there whom a father does not chasten? ⁸ But **if you are without chastening,** of which all have become partakers, then **you are illegitimate** and **not sons.** ⁹ Furthermore, we have had human fathers who corrected *us,* and we paid *them* respect. Shall we not much more readily be **in subjection** to the **Father of spirits and live?**" **(Hebrews 12:6–9).**

The apostle Paul describes this *bara* **process** of creating fallen man in the image of God as "transforming" us: "But we all, with unveiled face, beholding as in a mirror the glory of the Lord, are **being transformed into the same image** from glory to glory, just as by the Spirit of the Lord" (**2 Corinthians 3:18**).

Indeed, Paul uses the same word, "**creation,**" in describing the final outcome of the formative process of God in making us in His image: "Therefore, **if anyone *is* in Christ**, *he is* a **new creation**; **old things have passed away**; behold, **all things have become new**" (**2 Corinthians 5:17**). Notice that Paul uses the word "**creation**" to refer to changing or making a man—a fallen spirit whose nature is made lower by sin, who is temporarily in a body of flesh, who already exists—into a new, reconciled, and saved soul who now has a higher and holy nature like God.

And Paul also describes this process of being created in the likeness of God as a renewing of the mind, a process of feeding us the spiritual truth in the Word of God to change what we think and believe to be true: "But you have not so learned Christ, [21] if indeed you have **heard Him** and have been **taught by Him**, as **the truth is in Jesus:** [22] that you put off, concerning your former conduct, the **old man** which grows corrupt according to the **deceitful lusts,** [23] and be **renewed in the spirit of your mind,** [24] and that you put on the **new man** which was **created** according to God, in **true righteousness and holiness**" (**Ephesians 4:20–24**).

Head Pastor Steve Dornbusch at Calvary, the church I belong to, spoke of the process God used to prepare Elijah for God's service as a process of "cutting down," just as the Hebrew word *bara* includes the meaning "cut down" regarding the process of God creating fallen man in His image. Pastor Steve likens it to boot camp that a new recruit has to go through before he is fit for service as a soldier in the military. Steve related to us that the drill sergeant's job is to cut the new recruits down to size and train them with harsh experiences until every bit of arrogance and self-importance is taken out of them, which pretty much gets them ready to face any kind of challenge that life throws at them.

I think that is a perfect illustration of what God is doing for all of us on earth who have fallen. We who are recruited are being trained in God's boot camp as a soldier in His holy army so we are prepared for anything life in this world throws at us. But in God's army, our weapons of war are the Word of God—declaring the truth of God out of love for God's enemies, who we all once were. "For if **when we were enemies** we were reconciled to God through the death of His Son, much more, having been reconciled, we shall be saved by His life" (**Romans 5:10**). (See also **Ephesians 6:13–17.**)

GOD PUTS HIS FALLEN SPIRITS IN BODIES OF FLESH

THE FIRST MAN PUTS ON FLESH

So after God chose which of the fallen angelic spirits would be male and which would be female in **Genesis 1:27**, in **Genesis 2:7–8** we see the work of God in the next step of the *bara* process of creating man , or *adam* in the Hebrew, in the image of God: "And the LORD God **formed** man *of* the dust of the ground, and breathed into his nostrils the **breath of life; and man became a living being.** ⁸ The LORD God **planted a garden** eastward in **Eden**, and there He put the man whom He had formed." The King James Version of the Bible translates the last part of **Genesis2:7** as "… and man became a **living soul.**"

Notice that these words describe the way God is changing the first man, a fallen angelic spirit, into something new for a purpose: "and man **became** a living being [soul]." The Hebrew word for "**formed**" is H3335 *yatsar* (pronounced yaw-tsar'), which means "Probably identical with H3334 (through the **squeezing into a shape**); (compare H3331); to **mould into a form**; especially **as a potter**; figuratively **to determine** (that is, form a resolution):- **earthen**, fashion, form, **frame**, make, **potter, purpose.**"

The Hebrew word for "breath" is H5397 *neshamah*, which means, among other things, "**Divine inspiration**, intellect, or **spirit.**" And the Hebrew word for both "being" and "soul" is H5315 *nephesh*, which can mean many things that relate to fallen man's nature, such as "breathing creature, **body**, breath, and **ghost, will, heart, mind**, and **soul; appetite, greedy, lust, mortality, pleasure, self, one, own, themselves**." And so the first man, named Adam, became a living being or a soul, which is a fallen spirit that is squeezed into a body molded by God the potter from the clay of the earth.

And if anyone should ask, **"Where in the Bible does it say that we are angelic spirits in a temporary body of flesh?"** That we are spirits in bodies made of clay or the dust of the earth is seen in many verses, such as the following:

SPIRITS IN BODIES OF FLESH

> I, Daniel, was grieved **in my spirit within *my* body**, and the visions of my head troubled me. (**Daniel 7:15**)

Angels in Houses of Clay

> If He puts no trust in His servants, If **He charges His angels with error**, [19] How much more **those who dwell in houses of clay**, Whose **foundation is in the dust**, Who are crushed before a moth? (**Job 4:18–19**)

Spirit and Body

> For you were bought at a price; therefore glorify God **in your body** and **in your spirit**, which are God's. (**1 Corinthians 6:20**)

God of the Spirits of All Flesh

> Then they fell on their faces, and said, "O God, the **God of the spirits of all flesh**, shall one man sin, and You be angry with all the congregation?" (**Numbers 16:22**)

The Spirit of Man

> The burden of the word of the LORD against Israel. Thus says the LORD, who stretches out the heavens, lays the foundation

of the earth, and **forms the spirit of man within him**. (**Zechariah 12:1**)

Two Spirits in a Body

Then **Satan entered Judas**, surnamed Iscariot, who was numbered among the twelve. [4] So he went his way and conferred with the chief priests and captains, how he might betray Him to them. (**Luke 22:3–4**)

Spirit in a Body

Then He came to the disciples and found them asleep, and said to Peter, "What? Could you not watch with Me one hour? [41] Watch and pray, lest you enter into temptation. The **spirit indeed** *is* **willing**, but the **flesh** *is* **weak**." (**Matthew 26:40–41**)

Our Earthly Home

For we know that if **our earthly house,** *this* **tent**, is destroyed, we have a building from God, a house not made with hands, eternal in the heavens. [2] For in this we groan, **earnestly desiring to be clothed** with our **habitation which is from heaven**, [3] if indeed, having been **clothed**, we shall **not** be **found naked**. [4] For **we who are** in *this* **tent** groan, being burdened, not because we want to be **unclothed**, but **further clothed**, that **mortality** may be swallowed up by **life**. [5] Now **He who has prepared us for this very thing** *is* **God**, who also has given us **the Spirit as a guarantee**. [6] So *we are* always confident, knowing that **while we are at home in the body** we are **absent from the Lord.** [7] For we walk by faith, not by sight. [8] We are confident, yes, **well pleased rather** to be **absent from the body** and to be **present with the Lord.** (**2 Corinthians 5:1–8**)

Jesus Put on Flesh Like We Did

Inasmuch then as the **children have partaken of flesh and blood, He Himself likewise shared in the same**, that **through death He might destroy him who had the power of death**, that is, the **devil**, [15] and release those who through fear

285

of death were all their lifetime subject to bondage. (**Hebrews 2:14–15**)

THE FIRST WOMAN PUTS ON FLESH

Now let us also consider how the first woman is formed in **Genesis 2:21–23**: "And the LORD God caused a deep sleep to fall on **Adam**, and **he** slept; and He took one of **his ribs,** and closed up the **flesh** in its place. ²² Then **the rib** which the LORD God had taken **from man** He made into a **woman**, and He brought her to **the man**. ²³ And Adam said: 'This *is* now bone of my bones And flesh of my flesh; **She shall be called Woman**, Because she was taken out of **Man.**'"

So the body of flesh for the woman was formed out of a part of Adam's body, but where did the spirit come from to make her the living being or living soul that she would need to be to make the first woman be a suitable helpmate for the first man, Adam? God had purposely brought all the animals to Adam so that he would realize that he was different from the animals, because he had the intellect and emotions of an angelic spirit in his body of flesh, which they did not have.

The word "Adam" in the phrase "the LORD God caused a deep sleep to fall on **Adam**, and **he** slept; and He took one of **his ribs**" is translated from the Hebrew word H121*Adam,* which means "Adam, **the name of the first man.**" And we can tell it is referring to one person by the phrases "**he** slept" and "one of **his** ribs." The word "man" in the phrase "Then **the rib** which the LORD God had taken **from man**" is translated from a different Hebrew word, H120 *adam,* which in this case means "**mankind.**" And we can tell that is the correct meaning because the Bible does not say "from **the man**" but rather says "**from man.**"

The English word "rib" is translated from the Hebrew word H6763 *tsela tsalah,* which can mean "a rib (as curved) but **literally means 'of the body.'**" Also notice in this passage that **God takes a "rib" twice**—once from the body of flesh of the first man, named Adam, and once from the "body" of mankind; and the use of the words "from **man**" when God takes a "rib" and the different words "to **the man**" when God brings her to Adam. The term **"the man"** definitely refers to an individual, but the word **"man"** refers to more than one man or mankind. From what we have learned, where else could the spirit for the woman come out of but from all of fallen Mankind, (or "man," or *"Adam"* in the Hebrew), whom God "made lower than the angels they were," which began the process of creating mankind "in the image of God" that was spoken of in the sixth day of creation and in **Genesis 5:2**?

Now notice that the word **"Man"** with an uppercase first letter in the phrase "She shall be called **Woman**, Because she was taken out of **Man**" is not translated from the Hebrew word H120 *adam*, as in "a single man" or "all mankind." Nor is it translated from H121*Adam*, the name of the first man. Rather, it is translated from the Hebrew word H376 *ysh* (pronounced eesh), which means **"Champion, husband**, mighty, **steward, mankind."** And the word **"Woman"** is translated from the Hebrew word H802 *ishshah nashym*, which is defined as follows: "Irregular **plural, wife**, often unexpressed in English." In the English, we do not often consider "wife" to include more than one person, but God does.

We can see how God is taking the next step in the *bara* process of creating fallen man in His image and likeness when the first man and woman are to become one in **Genesis 2:24**: "Therefore **a man** shall leave his father and mother and be joined to his **wife**, and **they** shall become **one flesh**." And when we think of Oneness, we should think of Jesus as the Bridegroom and His church as the bride, as Paul explains to the Ephesians and to us: "For **we are members of His body**, of His flesh and of His bones. [31] *'For this reason a man shall leave his father and mother and be joined to his wife, and the two shall become one flesh.'* [32] This is a **great mystery**, but I speak concerning **Christ and the church**" (**Ephesians 5:31–32**).

Now consider the word **"Man,"** which is translated from the Hebrew word H376 *ysh* and has the meaning of "a leader and their followers," "a king and his subjects," "a nation's ruler and its citizens," or "a husband and his wife and children" where the followers, subjects, citizens, or family are called in the Hebrew H802 ***ishshah nashym***. This concept is most important. This multitude of fallen angels called "man," "***adam***," or "mankind" is made up of a leader and his followers. So here the Bible is referring to Satan as the head or leader, who is the fallen archangel who deceived one-third of heaven's angels to follow him.

And because "***adam***" or "man" is the word that describes the nature of fallen angels made lower than they were in heaven, Satan is qualified to be called Adam—or, in the English language, Man! That Satan put on flesh made from the dust of the earth is seen from **Genesis 3:1**: "Now the serpent [Satan] was more cunning than any **beast of the field** which the Lord God **had made**." Recall that those in the flesh cannot perceive spirits without flesh, and notice that Adam and Eve did perceive the Serpent.

We see the result of being one with Satan or One with Christ in Paul's letter to the Corinthians: "For since by **man** *came* death, by **Man** also *came* the resurrection of the dead. ²² For as **in Adam** all die, even so **in Christ** all shall be made alive. ²³ But each one in his own order: **Christ the firstfruits**, afterward **those *who are* Christ's at His coming**. ²⁴ Then *comes* **the end**, when He delivers the kingdom to God the Father, when He puts an end to all rule and all authority and power" (**1 Corinthians 15:22–24**). The phrases "**in Adam**" and "**in Christ**" demonstrate the oneness between two different leaders and their followers.

Later, in **1 Corinthians 15:45–49,** Paul continues:

> And so it is written, "*The first man Adam became a living being* [soul]." The **last Adam** *became* a **life-giving spirit**. ⁴⁶ However, the spiritual is not first, but the natural, and afterward the spiritual. ⁴⁷ The **first man *was* of the earth, *made* of dust**; the **second Man *is* the Lord from heaven**. ⁴⁸ As *was* **the *man* of dust**, so also *are* those *who are made* of dust; and as *is* the **heavenly *Man***, so also *are* those *who are* **heavenly**. ⁴⁹ And **as we have borne** the **image of the *man* of dust**, we shall also bear the **image of the heavenly *Man***.

From this passage we can clearly see that we were not in the image of God when we were born of flesh, but rather in the image of Satan or *Adam* as a leader of his followers; and we can see that the purpose of God for the elect is to create us in His image in a *bara* process that lasts a lifetime on earth.

So when the Bible says, "**She shall be called Woman**, Because she was taken out of **Man**," it is referring to separating Satan the leader from those who were deceived and followed him, that they may have a second chance to choose a loving and righteous leader whom they would follow when they understood the truth. And we can see this idea of a leader and followers in **Jeremiah 31:32**: "Behold, the days are coming, says the LORD, when I will make a **new covenant** with the **house of Israel** and with the house of Judah– **32** not according to **the covenant that I made** with their **fathers in the day** *that* **I took them** by the **hand to lead them out** of the **land of Egypt**, My covenant which they broke, **though I was a husband to them**, says the LORD. **33** But this *is* the covenant that I will make with the house of Israel **after those days**, says the LORD: I will put **My law in their minds**, and **write it on their hearts**; and I will be **their God**, and they shall be **My people**."

And because both the English and the Hebrew word for "man" can refer to one individual or to all mankind, this allows us to consider that when God "created Adam" He had the same plan and process in mind for all mankind. And we know that God was "creating" a multitude of fallen angels into souls or living beings because of the way **Genesis 5:1–2** describes the "creation" of man (or *adam* in the Hebrew): "This is the book of the **genealogy of Adam. In the day that God created man**, He **made him in the likeness of God**. **2 He created them male and female**, and blessed them and **called them Mankind** in the day **they** were created."

Now that God has "created" the first man and the first woman by Himself in the sixth day, the Bible describes how God created the generations of fallen man in the seventh day, in a collaborative process that includes God, a man, and a woman, that we are all familiar with—well, at least the human body of flesh part. In **Psalm 139:13–16**, David speaks of God **"covering us"** in our mother's womb and God planning our days before we put on flesh and before we were **born of flesh**: "For You formed my inward parts; **You covered me in my mother's womb.** [14] I will praise You, for I am fearfully *and* wonderfully made; Marvelous are Your works, And *that* my **soul** knows very well. [15] My frame was not hidden from You, When **I was made in secret,** *And* skillfully wrought **in the lowest parts of the earth.** [16] Your eyes saw **my substance,** being yet unformed. And **in Your book they all were written,** The **days fashioned for me,** When *as yet there were* none of them."

And so the preparations for the trial in heaven are being carried out on earth. As we discussed, if this is to be a fair and just trial, fallen man may not be allowed to remember his glorious life in heaven, because those with an evil and selfish heart would choose God out of greed and selfishness, as Satan wrongly accuses Job of doing:

> Then the LORD said to Satan, "Have you considered My servant Job, that *there is* **none like him on the earth,** a **blameless** and **upright man,** one who **fears God** and **shuns evil**?" [9] So Satan answered the LORD and said, "Does Job fear God for nothing? [10] Have You not made a hedge around him, around his household, and around all that he has on every side? You have blessed the work of his hands, and his possessions have increased in the land. [11] But now, **stretch out Your hand** and **touch all that he has,** and **he will surely curse You to Your face!**" **(Job 1:8–11)**

Jesus experienced this selfishness of people choosing Him after He miraculously fed the five thousand with five loaves of bread and two small fish, because He could supply them with bread: "Jesus answered them and said, 'Most assuredly, I say to you, **you seek Me, not because you saw the signs,** but because **you ate of the loaves and were filled**'" **(John 6:26).**

Keeping us from remembering our spiritual past is accomplished by putting us in a body of flesh so that we can only perceive the things of this world with our five senses unless influenced by spiritual beings, as we discover in **1 Corinthians 2:12–14**:

But God has **revealed** *them* **to us through His Spirit**. For the Spirit searches all things, yes, the deep things of God. [11] For what man knows the things of a man except the **spirit of the man which is in him**? Even so **no one knows** the **things of God** except the **Spirit of God**. [12] Now we have received, **not the spirit of the world**, but the **Spirit who is from God**, that we might **know the things that have been freely given to us by God**. [13] These things we also speak, not in words which **man's wisdom teaches** but which the **Holy Spirit teaches**, comparing spiritual things with spiritual. [14] But the **natural man does not receive the things of the Spirit of God**, for they are **foolishness to him**; nor can he know *them*, because they are **spiritually discerned**.

We see this blindness to the Spiritual reality in our own lives and the lives of those around us. But rather ironically, even the demons that belong to Satan know who Jesus is, because they are spiritual beings without flesh:

Now in the synagogue there was a man who had a **spirit of an unclean demon**. And he cried out with a loud voice, [34] saying, "Let *us* alone! **What have we to do with You, Jesus of Nazareth?** Did You come to destroy us? **I know who You are—the Holy One of God!**" (**Luke 4:33–34**).

When He had come to the other side, to the country of the Gergesenes, there met Him two **demon-possessed** *men,* coming out of the tombs, exceedingly fierce, so that no one could pass that way. [29] And suddenly they cried out, saying, "**What have we to do with You, Jesus, You Son of God**? Have You come here to **torment us before the time**?" (**Matthew 8:28–29**)

This is also evidence that not all of the fallen angels put on flesh.

As you recall, there were the fallen angels who had taken on the image of the first *Adam*. These angels realized they had been deceived and had made the wrong choice in following Satan and his lies, and like prodigal sons and daughters, they wanted to go home. These God chose and covered with flesh, and in a formative process that would last a lifetime on earth, He would transform them into His image: "And the LORD

God **formed man** *of* **the dust of the ground**, and breathed into his nostrils the breath of life; and **man became a living being** ... Also for Adam and his wife the Lord God made **tunics of skin**, and clothed them" (**Genesis 2:7, 3:21**).

And there were some fallen angels that chose to remain with Satan that still had the self-centered hearts and minds of Satan and still believed that that they could do better on their own, without God, as we saw in the beginning on earth when God separated the light from the darkness. These are the fallen angels that belong to Satan, and they are called demons. These demons will be allowed to tempt those in the flesh to sin and follow in the ways of Satan.

And there were some fallen angels who were not chosen by God and yet remain on the surface of the earth, born into bodies of flesh, to provide the evil so that the elect of God may experience good and evil for themselves and learn that God is right. Both of these good and bad angels who put on flesh are to be put on trial in the courts of heaven to be tested and tried to show all in heaven and on earth that God's separation of the light from the darkness, the good angels from the bad, was fair, just, and right. In any case, both of these groups of fallen angels in bodies of flesh are given a chance to repent and turn and follow Jesus instead of Satan: "The Lord is not slack concerning *His* promise, as some count slackness, but **is longsuffering toward us**, **not willing** that **any should perish** but that **all should come to repentance**" (**2 Peter 3:9**).

These two different kinds of "souls," or good and evil spirits, in bodies of flesh are the ones that Paul speaks of in **Romans 9:22–24**: "***What if God***, wanting to show *His* wrath and to make His power known, **endured with much longsuffering** the **vessels of wrath prepared for destruction**, [23] and that He might make known the riches of His glory on the **vessels of mercy**, which **He had prepared beforehand for glory**, [24] *even* **us whom He called**, not of the Jews only, but **also of the Gentiles**?" Here the apostle Paul is identifying himself and his followers, who believe the gospel that he is preaching, as the "**vessels of mercy**" that God had prepared beforehand.

God had both types of souls live a temporary life on earth, separated from God in heaven, to experience good and evil for themselves and see that God is right and that His ways are the only ways that lead to eternal life and all other ways lead to death, that they might choose life and choose God. **"I call heaven and earth as witnesses** today against you, *that* **I have set before you life and death, blessing and cursing**; therefore **choose life**, that both you and your descendants may **live**; [20] that you may **love** the LORD your God, that you may obey His voice, and that you may cling to Him, for **He** *is* **your life** and the **length of your days**; and that you may dwell **in the land which the LORD swore to your fathers, to Abraham**, Isaac, and Jacob, to give them" (**Deuteronomy 30:19–20**).

So the souls, the spirits who put on flesh, were not allowed to remember the peace, the unspeakable joy, and the glory they had had once enjoyed in heaven with God, but they did have to know that they were fallen because of their having believed the lies of Satan and having rejected the truth of God. And so the event of the deception by Lucifer in heaven had to be recounted on earth as the deception by the Serpent, who is Lucifer and Satan, who deceived Eve into choosing to live by the ways of evil by symbolically eating of the Tree of Knowledge of Good and Evil rather than the Tree of Life in the story we all know: "Then the **serpent said to the woman, 'You will not surely die**. [5] For God knows that in the day you eat of it your eyes will be opened, and **you will be like God**, knowing good and evil.' [6] So when the woman saw that the tree *was* good for food, that it *was* pleasant to the eyes, and a tree desirable to make *one* wise, **she took of its fruit and ate**. She also gave to her husband with her, **and he ate**" (**Genesis 3:4–6**).

We know that Adam and Eve did not eat of the Tree of Life, because had they done so, they would have had eternal life. "Then the LORD God said, 'Behold, the **man has become like one of Us**, to **know good and evil**. And now, lest he put out his hand and **take also** of the **tree of life**, and **eat**, and **live forever'**– [23] therefore the LORD God sent him **out of the garden of Eden** to till the ground from which he was taken. [24] So **He drove out the man**; and He placed cherubim

293

at the east of **the garden of Eden**, and a flaming sword which turned every way, to guard the way to **the tree of life**" (**Genesis 3:22–24**).

Recall that the prophet Ezekiel said Lucifer was in Eden, the garden of God that was in heaven, before he was cast out and down to the earth. "You *were* the seal of perfection, Full of wisdom and perfect in beauty. [13] You were in **Eden**, the garden of God ... [15] **You *were* perfect in your ways** from the day **you were created**, Till **iniquity was found in you** ... [17] **Your heart was lifted up** because of **your beauty**; You **corrupted your wisdom** for the sake of **your splendor**; **I cast you to the ground**" (**Ezekiel 28:12b–13, 15, 17**).

Now let us consider that the Eden on earth is a symbolic copy of the Eden, or paradise, in heaven. The Hebrew word for the Eden in heaven described in the Ezekiel passage is the same as the Hebrew word for the Eden on earth described in **Genesis 2:8**: "The LORD God **planted a garden eastward in Eden**, and there He put the man whom He **had formed**." The Hebrew word for "Eden" is H5731 *eden*, which means "The same as H5730 *Eden*, **the region of Adam's home**." The Hebrew word for Strong's number H5730 is *eden* or *ednah*, which means "**pleasure; delicate delight**."

We know that those who believe in God will have a home in the Eden in heaven again, just as Jesus promised the criminal who was crucified on the cross beside Him, who believed in Him: "And Jesus said to him, 'Assuredly, I say to you, today **you will be with Me in Paradise**'" (**Luke 23:43**). The Greek word for "Paradise" is G3857 *paradeisos*, which means "a park, that is, (specifically) **an Eden (place of future happiness) – paradise**!" And *Webster's Student Dictionary* defines "Eden" as follows: "[LL, fr. Heb. *'eden* a delight, **a place of pleasure**, Eden.] a) Bible. The garden **where Adam and Eve first dwelt; Paradise**."

In order to make the situation on Earth reflect the reality in heaven, God made copies on earth of things in heaven. Not only did God make a copy on earth of the garden of Eden in heaven, but the Tabernacle of God on earth is also a copy of the true tabernacle in heaven. "Therefore *it was* necessary that the **copies of the things in the heavens** should be purified with these, but **the heavenly things themselves** with better sacrifices than these. [24] For Christ **has not entered** the **holy places made with hands,** *which are* **copies of the true,** but **into heaven itself,** now to appear **in the presence of God** for us" (**Hebrews 9:23–24**). The author of Hebrews writes, "For if He were on earth, He would not be a priest, since there are priests who offer the gifts according to the law; [5] **who serve the copy and shadow of the heavenly things,** as Moses was divinely instructed when he was about to make the tabernacle. For He said, *'See that you make all things according to the pattern shown you on the mountain.'* [6] But now He has obtained a more excellent ministry, inasmuch as He is also **Mediator of a better covenant,** which was established on **better promises"** (**Hebrews 8:4–6**).

The apostle Paul reveals to the Galatians and to us that the city Jerusalem is a copy of the true Jerusalem in heaven above:

> For it is written that Abraham had two sons: the one by a **bondwoman,** the other by a **freewoman.** [23] But he *who was* of the bondwoman was born **according to the flesh,** and he of the freewoman **through promise,** [24] **which things are symbolic.** For **these are the two covenants:** the one from Mount Sinai which gives birth to bondage, which is Hagar– [25] for this Hagar is Mount Sinai in Arabia, and **corresponds to Jerusalem which now is,** and is **in bondage with her children–** [26] but the **Jerusalem above is free,** which is the **mother of us all.** (**Galatians 4:22–25**)

In future chapters we will learn and understand what all this symbolism and foreshadowing is about. But for now it is most important to notice that the choosing of the two sons of Abraham is *symbolic.* And we must understand that those of the bondwoman Hagar, the descendants of Ishmael, are not all excluded from the promises of God to be saved by faith in Jesus, just as not all those of the free woman Sarai, the descendants of Isaac, are included. The apostle Paul says that the choice of sons was symbolic of two covenants: the promise of God by faith, which leads to **freedom** in Christ, and the covenant of the Law, which leads to the **bondage** of Satan. We need to understand that believers shall come from every nation so that we are to share the truth with everyone: "But in **every nation** whoever fears Him and works righteousness is accepted by Him" (**Acts 10:35**).

In **Revelation 21:1–4**, we see the New Jerusalem:

> Now I saw **a new heaven** and **a new earth**, for the first heaven and the first earth had passed away. Also there was no more sea. [2] Then I, John, **saw the holy city, New Jerusalem, coming down out of heaven from God**, prepared as a **bride** adorned for **her husband**. [3] And I heard a loud voice from heaven saying, "Behold, the tabernacle of God *is* with men, and He will dwell with them, and they shall be His people. God Himself will be with them *and be* their God. [4] And God will **wipe away every tear from their eyes**; there shall be **no more death, nor sorrow, nor crying**. There shall be **no more pain**, for the former things have passed away."

IN THIS TRIAL, SPIRITS TRY TO INFLUENCE US

In this trial, God sends His Holy Spirit, His holy angels in heaven, to try to influence their fallen brethren to return to God by reminding them of the truth that God is a god of love and forgiveness for those who recognize that they have been lied to and that the ways of Satan's world are corruption, misery, sorrow, and death, that they may have a change of heart and mind. And we have already seen evidence of this ministering of angels in **Hebrews 1:13–14**: "But to which of the angels has He ever said: *'Sit at My right hand, Till I make Your enemies Your footstool'?* [14] **Are they not all ministering spirits** sent forth **to minister for those who will inherit salvation**?" On the other hand, Satan sends his fallen angels, called demons, to influence us to deny the truth of God and think only about what is best for ourselves and tempt us to do evil by deceitful lies, to keep us captives in his fallen kingdom.

And by the way we respond to these spiritual influences, we give them or deny them permission to enter this body of flesh with us—this tent, this temporary place that we live in. When we respond to the influence of the Holy Spirit and believe in Jesus, the Holy Spirit can indwell us and teach us the truth of God that will make us free from the bondage of Satan: "Then Jesus said to those Jews who believed Him, 'If you **abide in My word**, you are **My disciples indeed**. [32] And **you shall know the truth**, and **the truth shall make you free**'" (**John 8:31–32**). And it is the Spirit of God that leads us to the life-saving truth: "However, when He, the **Spirit of truth**, has come, He will **guide you into all truth**; for He will not speak on His own *authority*, but whatever He hears He will speak; and He will tell you things to come" (**John 16:13**).

When we are indwelled with the Spirit of God, which is Holy, it is evidence that we belong to Jesus, the Son of God, as can be seen in **2 Corinthians**:

> For in this we groan, earnestly desiring to be clothed with our habitation which is from heaven, [3] if indeed, having been clothed, we shall **not be found naked**. [4] For we who are in *this* tent groan, being burdened, not because we want to be unclothed, but further clothed, that mortality may be swallowed up by life. [5] Now **He who has prepared us for this very thing** *is* **God, who also has given us the Spirit as a guarantee**. [6] So *we are* always confident, knowing that while we are at home in the body we are absent from the Lord. [7] For we walk by faith, not by sight. [8] We are confident, yes, well pleased rather to be **absent from the body** and **to be present with the Lord**. (2 Corinthians 5:2–8)

"Naked" is how **Genesis 3:9–11** describes fallen man after we were deceived by Satan, who is the Serpent: "Then the LORD God called to Adam and said to him, 'Where *are* you?' [10] So he said, 'I heard Your voice in the garden, and **I was afraid** because **I was naked**; and I hid myself.' [11] And He said, '**Who told you that you** *were* **naked**? Have you **eaten from the tree** of which **I commanded you that you should not eat**?'"

When we respond to the influence of demons by doing what is neither right nor good, we give them permission to influence us in even greater ways until we have finally given them permission to indwell this body we live in. The people of Jesus' time recognized when people were indwelled with demons. Jesus, whose power was greater than Satan's, could cast these demons out. This was evidence that the kingdom of God had come to earth to take back those who belonged to God from Satan the god of this world. "But if I **cast out demons** with the finger of God, surely **the kingdom of God has come upon you**. [21] When a strong man, **fully armed**, **guards his own palace**, his goods are in peace. [22] But **when a stronger than he comes upon him** and **overcomes him**, he **takes from him** all his armor in which he trusted, and **divides his spoils**" (**Luke 11:20**).

The intellectually sophisticated people of the world today who do not believe in God refer to the indwelling of demons as "split personalities" or "multiple personalities." But is that not just the same thing that the Bible is talking about—multiple persons in the same body?

Notice the stark difference between the two different types of spiritual indwelling. Jesus' Holy Spirit waits for permission to come into our earthly habitation: "Behold, **I stand** at the **door and knock**. If anyone **hears My voice** and **opens the door, I will come in to him** and **dine with him**, and he with Me. [21] To **him who overcomes** I will grant to **sit with Me on My throne**, as I also overcame and sat down with My Father on His throne" (**Revelation 3:20**). On the other hand, God restrains Satan's demons from coming into our body to overpower us and only lets him in when we give him permission by many increasing decisions to walk in the ways of evil, as the apostle Peter warns us: "Be sober, be vigilant; because **your adversary the devil** walks about like **a roaring lion, seeking whom he may devour.** [9] **Resist him, steadfast in the faith,** knowing that the **same sufferings** are experienced **by your brotherhood in the world.** [10] But may the God of all grace, **who called us** to His eternal glory by Christ Jesus, **after you have suffered a while, perfect, establish, strengthen**, and **settle** *you*" (**1 Peter 5:8–10**).

We need to know that God is working in our life for our good, as Paul teaches:

> Now He who **searches the hearts knows** what the **mind of the Spirit** *is,* because He **makes intercession** for the **saints** according to *the will of* God. [28] And we know that **all things work together for good** to those **who love God**, to those **who are the called according to** *His* **purpose.** [29] For **whom He foreknew**, He also **predestined** *to be* **conformed** to the **image of His Son**, that He might be the firstborn among many brethren. [30] Moreover **whom He predestined**, these **He also called**; **whom He called**, these He also **justified**; and whom He justified, these He also **glorified.** [31] What then shall we say to these things? **If God** *is* **for us**, who *can be* **against us**? (**Romans 8:27–31**)

And because God is for us, James, the brother of Christ, tells us, "Let no one say when he is tempted, 'I am tempted by God'; for **God cannot be tempted by evil**, nor does **He Himself tempt anyone.** [14] But each one **is tempted** when he is drawn away by **his own desires** and enticed" (**James 1:13–14**). God can see into the heart and mind, but for those who cannot, God tests us in this trial on earth so that He can prove to others that His judgment of who were the elect and who were not was true and righteous. The following verses are examples of God allowing us to have trials and tribulation to test and prove us before all:

> But as we **have been approved by God** to be entrusted with the gospel, even so we speak, not as pleasing men, but **God who tests our hearts.** (**1 Thessalonians 2:4**)

> Oh, let the wickedness of the wicked come to an end, But **establish the just**; For **the righteous God tests the hearts and minds.** (**Psalm 7:9**)

> The refining pot *is* for silver and the furnace for gold, But **the LORD tests the hearts.** (**Proverbs 17:3**)

The Hebrew word translated as "test" in the phrase "God tests the hearts and minds" in **Psalm 17:3** is H974 ***baw-khan***, which means "A primitive root; **to** *test* (especially metals); general and figurative to *investigate* :- **examine**, **prove**, tempt, **try** (**trial**)." *Webster's Student Dictionary* defines "test" as "2. Means of a **trial**; specifically: a. Subjection to conditions that **show the real character of a person** or thing."

We need to understand that we are on trial for our eternal lives, having become addicted to the lies and the ways of Satan, which will lead to our death. Sometimes it is only when we are on the brink of death that the tough love of God can help us come to the end of ourselves and realize how desperately we need Him. And when we seek God diligently, we will find Him, and He will save us—if not from the death of the body, certainly from the second death of our spirit or soul.

We see the tough love of God in the Old Testament: "And you shall remember that the LORD **your God led you** all the way these forty years in the wilderness, **to humble you** *and* **test you**, to **know what** *was* **in your heart**, whether you would keep His commandments or not. [3] So **He humbled you, allowed you to hunger**, and **fed you with manna** which you did not know nor did your fathers know, that **He might make you know** that **man shall not live by bread alone**; but **man lives by every** *word* that **proceeds** from the **mouth of the LORD**" (**Deuteronomy 8:2–3**). But Jesus assures us of peace in the New Testament: "These things I have spoken to you, that **in Me you may have peace.** In the **world you will have tribulation**; but be of good cheer, **I have overcome the world**" (**John 16:33**).

But what if someone should ask, **"If God is a god of love and God is all-powerful, why do we suffer?"**

The short answer is that we are not home yet. We chose to leave our home with God in heaven when we believed the lies of Lucifer that we could do better on our own, separated from God and living with Satan in his ways, where we would have our eyes opened and be like God, knowing good and evil. But, in reality, the wicked ways of Satan are unsustainable and will lead to our death. Because we would not even listen to God to reason with Him, He had to let us experience the misery and sorrow of living in the evil ways of Lucifer, now called Satan, on earth to convince us that we were wrong and had made a mistake. In this way we might be willing to repent of our ways and listen to the truth of God and understand and turn from the ways of Satan and return to the loving ways of God.

It is when we are broken and have come to the end of ourselves that we are ready and willing to reason with God, which is what He wanted us to do from the beginning. "'Come now, and **let us reason together,**' Says the LORD, 'Though your sins are like scarlet, They shall be as white as snow; Though they are red like crimson, They shall be as wool. ¹⁹ **If you are willing and obedient**, You shall eat the good of the land; ²⁰ But **if you refuse and rebel**, You shall be **devoured by the sword**'; For the mouth of the LORD has spoken" (**Isaiah 1:18–20**). Being "devoured by the sword" is not something God does to us; it is something we do to each other.

"For whom the LORD loves He chastens, And scourges every son whom He receives." ⁷ If you **endure chastening**, God **deals with you as with sons**; for what son is there whom a father does not chasten?" (**Hebrews 12:6–7**). The great love of God the Father and God the Son for us is the reason Jesus suffered and died for us sinners. And because of their Oneness, the Father suffered with Jesus when He was on the cross, as we shall learn in the chapter "The Third Age of the Church."

"**No temptation** has overtaken you except such as is common to man; but **God is faithful**, who will **not allow you** to be **tempted beyond what you are able**, but with the temptation will also **make the way of escape**, that **you may be able to bear** *it*" (**1 Corinthians 10:13**). Peter teaches us that if God saved Noah and delivered the righteous Lot oppressed by the filthy conduct of the wicked, "*then* the Lord **knows how to deliver the godly out of temptations** and to reserve the **unjust under punishment for the day of judgment**" (**2 Peter 2:9**).

THE COURTS OF HEAVEN

There are many passages in the Bible that make us think a trial is occurring. Because Adam and Eve, symbolically representing all mankind, rejected the truth of God and believed the lies of Satan, they were cast out of the garden of Eden in heaven, separated from God to live on earth under the rule of Satan. But because God is a god of love, forgiveness, and the second chance, He gave those who were ignorant of the truth and deceived by lies a second chance to learn and understand the truth of why God's ways are the only path to eternal life. And if that understanding of the truth leads them to repent and change their hearts and minds and seek God's forgiveness, they can be reconciled to God. The Bible describes the parties involved in the trial; we will examine these parties in the following section.

SATAN IS THE DECEIVER AND ACCUSER

The Serpent challenged God's truth claim and accused God of lying when he tempted Eve in the garden:

> Now the serpent was more cunning than any beast of the field **which the LORD God had made**. And he said to the woman, **"Has God indeed said**, 'You shall not eat of every tree of the garden'?" ² And the woman said to the serpent, "We may eat the fruit of the trees of the garden; ³ but of the fruit of the tree which *is* in the midst of the garden, God has said, 'You shall not eat it, nor shall you touch it, lest you die.'"
>
> ⁴ Then **the serpent said to the woman, "You will not surely die**. ⁵ For God knows that in the day you eat of it your eyes will be opened, and **you will be like God**, knowing good and evil." **(Genesis 3:1–4)**

So the first thing that is on trial is the truth about the ways that lead to life and the ways that lead to death.

From **Genesis 3:13** we know that Eve recognized that she had been deceived by the Serpent's lies: "And the LORD God said to the woman,

'What *is* this you have done?' The woman said, '**The serpent deceived me**, and I ate'" (**Genesis 3:13**). Then, amazingly, the shameless Satan accuses those he deceived to commit sin of sinning, as the book of Revelation reveals: "Then I heard a loud voice saying in heaven, 'Now salvation, and strength, and the kingdom of our God, and the power of His Christ have come, for **the accuser of our brethren**, who **accused them before our God day and night**, has been cast down'" (**Revelation 12:10**). This deception followed by accusation is the trap that Satan used on us in heaven when we fell from the grace of God, and Jeremiah the prophet speaks of those who try to trap us to keep us from being saved: "For **among My people** are found **wicked** *men;* They lie in wait as **one who sets snares**; **They set a trap**; **They catch men**" (**Jeremiah 5:26**).

This is the same trap that is still used today. Those who are evil promise grand but illegal gain, and when we bite on that hook, they use the threat of the law to trap us. And that is why Jesus came in the flesh: "Inasmuch then as **the children have partaken of flesh and blood, He Himself likewise shared in the same**, that through death He might destroy him who had the power of death, that is, the devil, [15] and release those who through **fear of death** were all their lifetime subject to bondage" (**Hebrews 2:15b**).

The Bible describes how once we are trapped, we are oppressed by the Devil, and "how God anointed Jesus of Nazareth with the **Holy Spirit** and **with power**, who went about **doing good** and **healing all who were oppressed by the devil**, for God was with Him" (**Acts 10:38**). *Webster's Student Dictionary* defines "**oppress**" as "1. to **weigh down spiritually**; to **burden** 2. to **crush or trample down by abuse of power or authority**; to **treat cruelly or with undue severity**." Oppression is the way Satan rules over his subjects.

JESUS AND THE HOLY SPIRIT OF GOD ARE OUR COUNSELORS AND DEFENDERS

While the lie of Satan trapped us and oppresses us, the truth of Jesus cries out to us: "Come to Me, **all *you* who labor and are heavy laden**, and I will **give you rest**. [29] Take My yoke upon you and **learn from Me**, for I am **gentle** and **lowly in heart**, and **you will find rest for your souls**. [30] For **My yoke** *is* easy and **My burden is light**" (**Matthew 11:29–30**).

Jesus speaks of the Holy Spirit as our spiritual lawyer in **John 14:15–17**: "**If you love Me, keep My commandments**. [16] And I will pray the Father, and He will give you **another Helper**, that He may **abide with you forever**– [17] the **Spirit of truth**, whom **the world cannot receive**, because it neither sees Him nor knows Him; but you know Him, for **He dwells with you** and **will be in you**."

Instead of the word "Helper" used in the NKJV, the *Amplified Bible* renders that word as "Comforter, **Counselor, Intercessor**, and **Advocate**, Strengthener, and Standby." The Greek word translated as "Helper" is G3875 *parakletos*, which means "**Intercessor**, consoler, comforter, or **advocate**," and Webster defines "advocate" as "1) **A person who pleads the cause of another as before a court; counselor**." Jesus identifies this "Helper" (or *parakletos* in the Greek), as the "**Spirit of truth**" and the one who will help us know **all truth,** and "when He, **the Spirit of truth**, has come, **He will guide you** into **all truth**" (**John 16:13**). "All truth" includes the truth that will set us free from the rule and reign of Satan, who oppresses us: "And you shall **know the truth**, and the **truth shall make you free**" (**John 8:32**).

WE ARE THE DEFENDANTS

The apostle Paul warns us and encourages us to live according to the truth of God:

> But in accordance with your **hardness** and your **impenitent heart** you are treasuring up for yourself **wrath** in the **day of wrath** and revelation of the **righteous judgment of God**, ⁶ who *"will render to each one according to his deeds"*: ⁷ **eternal life** to those who by **patient continuance in doing good** seek for glory, honor, and **immortality**; ⁸ but to those who are **self-seeking** and do not **obey the truth**, but **obey unrighteousness**–indignation and wrath, ⁹ **tribulation** and **anguish**, on every **soul of man who does evil**, of the Jew first and also of the Greek; ¹⁰ but **glory, honor,** and **peace** to everyone who **works what is good**, to the Jew first and also to the Greek.
>
> ¹¹ For **there is no partiality with God**. ¹² For as many as have sinned without law will also perish without law, and as many as have **sinned in the law will be judged by the law** ¹³ (for not the hearers of the law *are* just in the sight of God, but the **doers of the law will be justified**; ¹⁴ for when Gentiles, who do not have the law, **by nature do the things in the law**, these, although not having the law, are a law to themselves, ¹⁵ **who show the work** of the **law written in their hearts**, their **conscience also bearing witness**, and between themselves *their* **thoughts accusing or else excusing** *them*) ¹⁶ in **the day when God will judge the secrets of men** by Jesus Christ, **according to my gospel. (Romans 2:5–16)**

Also, Jesus stated, "But I say to you that for **every idle word men may speak**, they will **give account** of it in the **day of judgment**. ³⁷ For by your words you will be **justified**, and by your words you will be **condemned**" (**Matthew 12:36–37**). So by the thoughts of our minds and the desires of our hearts, which produce our words and deeds, God will show Satan and all the angels in heaven and on earth who is righteous and who is not and that His selection of the elect was fair and just.

The Witnesses of the Trial

Witnesses of the proceedings of this trial are in heaven and all around us: "Therefore we also, since we are **surrounded by so great a cloud of witnesses**, let us **lay aside every weight**, and the **sin which so easily ensnares** *us,* and let us run with endurance the race that is **set before us**" (**Hebrews 12:1**). The witnesses include all the angels in heaven and fallen angels on earth, whether they are in bodies of flesh or are the demons of Satan.

Unlike a trial on earth, there is no jury, because man and angels cannot see into the hearts of men to know whether they are guilty or not. A fair and just judgment can come from God alone: "Therefore **you are inexcusable, O man**, whoever you are **who judge**, for in whatever you **judge another** you **condemn yourself**; for you who judge practice the same things. [2] But **we know** that the **judgment of God** is **according to truth** against **those who practice such things**" (**Romans 2:1–2**).

God Is the Judge

The author of the book of Hebrew states,

> And let us consider one another in order **to stir up love** and **good works**, [25] not **forsaking** the **assembling of ourselves together**, as *is* the manner of some, but **exhorting** *one another,* and so much the more as you see **the Day** approaching. [26] For if we **sin willfully** after **we have received** the **knowledge of the truth**, there **no longer remains a sacrifice for sins**, [27] but a certain fearful **expectation of judgment**, and fiery indignation which will devour the **adversaries**.
>
> [8] Anyone who has rejected Moses' law dies without mercy on the testimony of two or three witnesses. [29] Of how much worse punishment, do you suppose, will he be thought worthy who has **trampled the Son of God underfoot**, counted the **blood of the covenant** by which **he was sanctified a common thing**, and insulted the **Spirit of grace**? [30] For we know Him who said,

"Vengeance is Mine, I will repay," says the Lord. And again, *"The* LORD *will judge His people."* (**Hebrews 10:24–30**)

The apostle John, who foresaw the end in a vision, reveals the following: "When He opened the fifth seal, I saw under the altar the souls of those who had been slain for the **word of God** and for the **testimony which they held**. ¹⁰ And they cried with a loud voice, saying, 'How long, O Lord, **holy and true**, until **You judge** and **avenge our blood** on those **who dwell on the earth?**'" (**Revelation 6:9–10**).

The White Throne Judgment

Then I saw a **great white throne** and Him who sat on it, from whose face the earth and the heaven fled away. And there was found no place for them. ¹² And I saw the dead, small and great, standing before God, and books were opened. And another book was opened, which is *the Book* of Life. And **the dead were judged according to their works,** by the **things which were written** in the **books**. (**Revelation 20:11–12**)

The apostle Paul states, "For we must **all** appear before the **judgment seat of Christ**, that each one may receive the things *done* **in the body**, according to what he has done, **whether good or bad**" (**2 Corinthians 5:10**).

AND GOD THE JUDGE SETS THE CONDITIONS OF THE TRIAL

These are the pretrial instructions that the Judge gave as the trial began in earnest:

For the LORD will again rejoice over you for good as He rejoiced over your fathers, ¹⁰ **if you obey the voice of the LORD your God, to keep His commandments and His statutes** which are written in this Book of the Law, *and* if you **turn to the LORD your God with all your heart** and **with all your soul**.

For **this commandment which I command you today** *is* **not** *too* **mysterious for you, nor** *is* **it far off**. ¹² It *is* **not in** heaven, that you should say, "Who will ascend into heaven for us and bring it to us, that we may hear it and do it?" [13] **Nor *is* it beyond the sea**, that you should say, "Who will go over the sea for us and bring it to us, that we may hear it and do it?" [14] But **the word *is* very near you, in your mouth** and **in your heart**, that you may **do it**.

[15] See, I have set before you today **life** and **good**, **death** and **evil**, [16] in that I command you today to **love the LORD your God**, to **walk in His ways**, and to **keep His commandments**, His statutes, and His judgments, that you **may live** and **multiply**; and the LORD your God will **bless you** in the **land which you go to possess**.

[17] But if your **heart turns away** so that **you do not hear**, and are drawn away, and worship **other gods** and serve them, [18] I announce to you today that **you shall surely perish**; you **shall not prolong *your* days** in the land which you cross over the Jordan to go in and possess.

[19] **I call heaven and earth** as **witnesses today against you**, *that* I have **set before you life and death, blessing and cursing**; therefore **choose life**, that both you and your descendants **may live**; [20] that you **may love the LORD your God**, that you may **obey His voice**, and that you may **cling to Him**, for He *is* **your life** and the **length of your days**; and that you may dwell in the land **which the LORD swore to your fathers,** to **Abraham**, Isaac, and Jacob, to give them. (**Deuteronomy 30:10–20**)

Especially notice that this admonition contains the way to keep God's commandments: "that you **may love the LORD your God**, that you may **obey His voice**." When we love God, we will automatically desire to do what He says, because He has our best interest at heart. True love involves trusting the object of our love.

In this trial, Satan probably thinks he has an airtight case against fallen man. After all, God said man would surely die if he partook of the fruit of good and evil. Man did partake, and Satan knows that God's word must be done, for God cannot lie, and His word must be done, as God Himself says: "So shall **My word be that goes forth from My mouth**; **It shall not return to Me void**, But it shall **accomplish what I please**, And it shall **prosper** *in the thing* **for which I sent it**" (**Isaiah 55:11**).

What Satan did not count on was the great wisdom of God and the fact that He is the God of the second chance and the God of forgiveness for those who will acknowledge their error, repent, and seek to understand the truth that will change what they think in their mind and believe with all their heart. When God gave the commandment that we would surely die if we partook of the fruit of good and evil, we were on earth in bodies of flesh. But God had previously given us the hope of eternal life while we were in heaven; He promised this to those whom He foreknew would believe in Him and His truth and ways while on earth. And that is exactly what Paul, having been taught by Jesus, recounts to Titus: "Paul, a bondservant of God and an apostle of Jesus Christ, according to the **faith of God's elect** and the **acknowledgment** of the **truth** which accords with **godliness**, ² in **hope of eternal life** which **God, who cannot lie, promised before time began**" (**Titus 1:1–2**). And if it was before time began, it was before we were "formed" in a body of flesh on earth.

THE TRIAL ON EARTH BEGINS

And so the trial being carried out on earth is ready to begin, and those in flesh on earth do not realize anyone is watching what they do and say, so that their true nature can be exposed. But when the elect begin to call on God and the Holy Spirit of God begins teaching them the truth concerning the reality of heaven above, they will come to understand that there are many angels in heaven witnessing, by the way we live our lives, how God was right about the ways of Satan—that they lead to death—and that the only way that leads to life eternal is to follow the ways of God. The author of Hebrews, who was taught by Jesus and His Holy Spirit, confirms this: "Therefore we also, **since we are surrounded by so great a cloud of witnesses,** let us **lay aside every weight,** and the sin which so easily ensnares *us,* and let us **run** with **endurance the race** that is **set before us,** ² looking unto Jesus, the **author** and **finisher** of *our* **faith,** who for the **joy that was set before Him endured the cross,** despising the shame, and has sat down at the right hand of the throne of God" (**Hebrews 12:1–2**).

God can see our deeds and hear our words, but He also knows our thoughts and the desires of our heart, and these He will record in a book for our judgment: "Then I saw a **great white throne** and Him who sat on it, from whose face the earth and the heaven fled away. And there was found no place for them. ¹² And I saw the dead, small and great, **standing before God,** and **books were opened.** And another book was opened, which is *the Book* of Life. And the dead were judged **according to their works,** by the **things which were written in the books**" (**Revelation 20:11–12**).

This trial will show that God's judgment about who the elect are— those that will belong God—is fair and just by how those in the flesh live their lives; by what they say and what they do. Jesus describes how we who are in bodies of flesh will be judged by the words we speak: "For **out of the abundance of the heart** the **mouth speaks.** ³⁵ A good man **out of the good treasure of his heart** brings forth **good things,** and an evil man **out of the evil treasure** brings forth **evil things.** ³⁶ But I say to you that for every idle word men may speak, they **will give account of it** in the **day of judgment.** ³⁷ For **by your words you will be justified,** and **by your words you will be condemned**" (**Matthew 12:334b–37**).

In the Old Testament, God begins the trial by showing us all that the ways of Satan bring corruption, misery, sorrow, and finally death. In the first age, God lets fallen man be free to do anything they want to. God gives them up to be in charge of their own lives, just as Satan promised they could. In the second age, separated from the first by four hundred years during which God is silent, God demonstrates another way that man can live under Satan's rule—by laws that we must obey. In this God shows us all that fallen man, with the heart and mind of the rebellious lawbreaker, cannot live by laws.

In the New Testament, God shows us His ways that lead to eternal life. In the third age, which is separated from the age of the law by four hundred years during which God is silent, Jesus comes to the earth He created as a witness for the trial and shows us the truth concerning the ways of God: that in loving God above all and loving each other as much as we love ourselves provides the unity that makes us One and the *zoe* life of the community, which provides the power and prosperity that gives eternal life to individuals. And we learn that good cannot live with evil. In the fourth age, the age of the millennial reign of Christ, which is separated from the church age by the rapture and the tribulation, God shows that when evil is kept separate from good, the ways of God lead to peace, prosperity, unspeakable joy, and eternal life. And once the elect have experienced both good and evil, they cannot be deceived again.

The First Age of Anarchy

IN THE FIRST age, right after the fall, God left everyone to be on their own, free to do whatever they desired and chose to do. And what they chose to do was live like Satan said they could when he deceived them with a lie. God does this when people refuse to believe Him, or even listen to Him that He may reason with them. The ways of God are logical and reasonable, and they make sense. But if we will not listen to reason, He cannot save us from ourselves and from Satan's trap. And so He is left with no other choice but to turn them over to live in their sin. And this is exactly what Paul teaches the Romans and us: "Therefore **God also gave them up to uncleanness**, in the lusts of their hearts, to dishonor their bodies among themselves, **25 who exchanged the truth of God for the lie**, and **worshiped** and **served the creature rather than the Creator**, who is blessed forever. Amen" (**Romans 1:24–25**).

God's kingdom is not one of captivity and slavery but one of glory, honor, and privilege for those who are worthy to belong. By turning nonbelievers over to practice their sin, God gives them an opportunity to learn the truth from experience and return as humble prodigal children. The result of this "dispensation of time," or age, was that it ended up in total chaos and anarchy. This age covered roughly the period of time from Adam until the time Abraham's descendants, named after Israel, went down to Egypt. The Bible refers to this time as the "Days of Noah," during which the world was so wicked that God destroyed it with a flood and started over with the righteous Noah and his family.

Right away in **Genesis 4:8**, Cain, the first man born to Adam and Eve, kills Abel, the second man born to them: "Now Cain talked with Abel his brother; and it came to pass, when they were in the field, that **Cain rose up against Abel his brother and killed him.**" In **Genesis 4:23**, Lamech, a descendant of Cain, brags of his power to kill in revenge: "Then Lamech said to his wives: 'Adah and Zillah, hear my voice; Wives of Lamech, listen to my speech! For **I have killed a man for wounding me, Even a young man for hurting me.** ²⁴ **If Cain shall be avenged sevenfold**, Then **Lamech seventy-sevenfold.**'"

> The only bright spot in this age was a descendant of Adam's third son, Seth, named Enoch. "And **Enoch walked with God**; and **he *was* not, for God took him**" (**Genesis 5:24**). This is a foreshadowing of the rapture of the saints that occurs before the tribulation, when those who belong to Christ will be caught up to be with Jesus in the air: "For **the Lord Himself** will **descend from heaven with a shout**, with the **voice of an archangel**, and with the **trumpet of God**. And the **dead in Christ will rise first**. ¹⁷ Then **we who are alive *and* remain shall be caught up together with them in the clouds to meet the Lord in the air**. And thus **we shall always be with the Lord**. ¹⁸ Therefore comfort one another with these words" (**1 Thessalonians 4:16–18**).

The word "took" in the phrase "**God took him**" is translated from the Hebrew word H3947 *laqach*, which means "**To take**, accept, bring, **carry away, fetch**, get, **seize, send for, take (away, up)**." The words "**caught up**" in the **1 Thessalonians** verse are translated from the Greek G726 *harpazo*, which has much the same meaning: "To **seize, catch (away, up), pluck, pull, take (by force)**." We will learn more about the rapture of the saints in the chapter "The Rapture."

In **Genesis 6:5–8**, God the Father Himself describes the situation like this: "Then the Lord saw that the wickedness of man *was* great in the earth, and *that* **every intent** of the **thoughts of his heart *was* only evil continually**. ⁶ And the Lord **was sorry that He had made man on the earth**, and He was **grieved in His heart**. ⁷ So the Lord said, 'I will destroy man whom I have created **from the face of the**

earth, both man and beast, creeping thing and birds of the air, for I am sorry that I have made them.' [8] But **Noah found grace in the eyes of the LORD**."

But in every age, God has a remnant that belong to Him, and Peter describes how God saved the righteous descendants of Noah who did not get to hear the saving truth of Christ's gospel: "For Christ also suffered once for sins, the just for the unjust, that He might bring us to God, **being put to death in the flesh** but made alive by the Spirit, [19] by whom also **He went and preached** to the **spirits in prison**, [20] **who formerly were disobedient**, when once the **Divine longsuffering waited** in the **days of Noah**, while *the* ark was being prepared, in which a few, that is, **eight souls**, were **saved through water**" (**1 Peter 3:18**).

But in a short time some of the descendants of Noah resisted the will of God to fill the earth, and rather built a city and tried to reach heaven using their own strength and abilities: "And they said, 'Come, **let us build ourselves a city**, and **a tower whose top** *is* **in the heavens**; **let us make a name for ourselves**, lest we be scattered abroad over the face of the whole earth'" (**Genesis 11:4**). So God started over with Abraham and spoke directly to him.

THE PROMISES OF GOD TO ABRAHAM

Then He brought him [Abraham] outside and said, "**Look now toward heaven**, and **count the stars** if you are able to number them." And He said to him, "**So shall your descendants be**." [6] And **he believed in the LORD**, and **He accounted it to him for righteousness**. [7] Then He said to him, "I *am* the LORD, who brought you out of Ur of the Chaldeans, to give you this land to inherit it." [8] And he said, "Lord GOD, **how shall I know that I will inherit it**?" [9] So He said to him, "Bring Me a three-year-old heifer, a three-year-old female goat, a three-year-old ram, a turtledove, and a young pigeon." (**Genesis 15:5–9**)

As we have learned, the Bible uses stars in heaven as a metaphor for angels in heaven. But, on the same day, God made another promise to

Abraham (who was still called Abram at that time): "**On the same day** the Lord made a covenant with Abram, saying: '**To your descendants** I have given this **land**, from the river of Egypt to the great river, the River Euphrates'" (**Genesis 15:18**).

We can see that this first promise of God, that Abraham and his descendants will be like angels in heaven, is very dear to Abraham's heart, because he asks God to guarantee His promise by entering into a unilateral contract of that day. By walking through these split animals, a person was saying in effect, "Let this happen to me if I break my part of the contract." We see that God alone completed the contract in **Genesis 15:17**: "And it came to pass, when the sun went down and it was dark, that behold, there appeared **a smoking oven** and **a burning torch** that **passed between those pieces**."

We can also see that Abraham and his descendants Isaac and Jacob were not as excited about the promise of land on earth that God made later that same day, because Abraham's life was focused on the Promised Land in heaven: "By faith he dwelt in the **land of promise** as *in* **a foreign country**, dwelling in tents with Isaac and Jacob, the **heirs with him of the same promise**; [10] for he **waited for the city which has foundations, whose builder and maker** *is* **God**" (**Hebrews 11:9–10**).

The author of Hebrews continues:

> These all died in faith, **not having received the promises,** but **having seen them afar off were assured of them,** embraced *them* and **confessed that they were strangers** and **pilgrims on the earth.** [14] For those who say such things declare plainly that **they seek a homeland.** [15] And truly if they had called to mind **that** *country* from which **they had come out,** they would have had opportunity to return. [16] But now **they desire a better,** that is, **a heavenly** *country.* Therefore God is not ashamed to be called their God, for **He has prepared a city for them.** (**Hebrews 11:13–16**)

We have already seen that the city God prepared for them is the new Jerusalem in heaven. (See **Revelation 21:2**.)

But what if someone should ask, **"So why don't the Israelites possess the land on earth that God promised to Abraham and his descendants?"**

The Hebrew word rendered as "descendants" in the phrase **"So shall your descendants be"** in the New King James Version of the Bible is actually "seed," as is noted in an explanatory footnote to **Genesis 13:15**: "Literally **seed**, and so throughout the Book [of Genesis]." The King James Version correctly renders this verse as "And he brought him forth abroad, and said, Look now **toward heaven**, and tell the stars, if thou be able to number them: and he said unto him, So shall thy **seed** be" (**Genesis 15:5** KJV).

THE SEED OF ABRAHAM

While **2 Peter 2:4** accurately describes our current desperate situation on earth under the rule and reign of Satan: "For if God **did not spare the angels who sinned**, but **cast *them* down to hell** [The deep on earth] and delivered *them* **into chains of darkness**, to be **reserved for judgment**," Hebrews 2:16 gives hope to the spirits in bodies of flesh, those who believe and are in Christ Jesus: "For indeed **He does not give aid to angels**, but **He does give aid** to the **seed of Abraham**." Abraham was a fallen angel/spirit that put on flesh, and his seed, or descendants, are also angels who have put on flesh, but how could we who are not descendants of Abraham in the flesh be of the ones that God gives aid to, and how can we be saved by the promises God gave to Abraham?

In the New Testament, the apostle Paul reveals to the Galatians and to us that when God made the promises to Abraham and his seed, He was referring to Abraham and his one Seed, Jesus:

> Now to **Abraham** and **his Seed** were the promises made. **He does not say**, "And to **seeds**," as of many, **but as of one**, "*And to your Seed*," **who is Christ**. [17] And this I say, *that* **the law**, which was **four hundred and thirty years later, cannot annul the covenant** that was **confirmed before by God in Christ**, that

it should make **the promise** of no effect. [18] For if the inheritance *is* **of the law**, *it is* no longer **of promise**; but **God gave** *it* **to Abraham by promise** ... For you are all **sons of God through faith in Christ Jesus**. [27] For as many of you as were **baptized into Christ** have **put on Christ**. [28] There is neither Jew nor Greek, there is neither slave nor free, there is neither male nor female; for **you are all one in Christ Jesus**. [29]And **if you** *are* **Christ's**, then **you are Abraham's seed**, and **heirs according to the promise**." (**Galatians 3:16–18, 26–29**)

When this passage speaks of "**the covenant** that was **confirmed before by God in Christ**," it refers to the time when God alone went between the animals split in half as a burning torch to confirm with a contract the promise God had made with Abraham, that his descendants who are in Christ—the Seed—would be like the stars (angels) in heaven.

Paul speaks of this very idea in a letter to the Romans: "But it is not that the word of God has taken no effect. For **they** *are* **not all Israel who** *are* **of Israel**, [7] **nor** *are they* **all children** because they are the **seed of Abraham**; but, '*In Isaac your seed shall be called.*' [8] That is, **those who** *are* **the children of the flesh**, these *are* **not the children of God**; but the **children of the promise are counted as the seed**" (**Romans 9:6–8**).

Let us take another look at the promise of God to Abraham, Isaac, and Jacob/Israel: "Then He brought him outside and said, 'Look now **toward heaven**, and count the stars if you are able to number them.' And He said to him, '**So shall your descendants ["Seed" in the KJV] be**.'" [6] And he **believed in the LORD**, and **He accounted it to him for righteousness**" (**Genesis 15:5**). The promise of God was made to Abraham and his one Seed, Christ, because all those who "**believe in Jesus**" and are "**in Christ**" are considered by God to be righteous.

In this promise for those in faith, God repeats to Abraham in the first age the promise He had already made to the elect in heaven before God created the world, which Paul teaches in the third age: "Paul a bondservant of God and an apostle of Jesus Christ, **according to the faith of God's elect** and the **acknowledgment of the truth** which **accords with godliness,** [2] in **hope of eternal life** which God, **who cannot lie, promised before time began,** [3] but has in **due time** manifested His word **through preaching,** which was committed to me according to the **commandment of God our Savior"** (**Titus 1:1**).

The reason the Israelites do not now possess the land that God promised Abraham is that the promise was not made for the physical descendants of Abraham, but for the spiritual descendants—those who believe in God and are in the One Seed of Abraham, Jesus Christ. And those who believe in the promise of God and are in Jesus will possess that land on earth as Christ rules over them as their King in the millennial reign of Jesus, and they will possess the Promised Land in heaven as angels in the kingdom of Christ Jesus forever.

The Second Age of the Law

WE WILL NEVER understand the Bible if we do not first recognize that these first two ages are **not** the ways of God. Remember that mankind fell because man was full of pride and arrogance and believed the lies of Lucifer. Because of our selfish, greedy, prideful, and arrogant nature, we would not even listen to the truth claims of God. And so, because He still loved us and knew that we could not live with this kind of heart and mind-set, He had no choice but to turn us over to live in the ways of Satan, whose lies we believed, that we may as prodigal sons and daughters find out for ourselves by experiencing for ourselves that living in the ways of Satan leads only to corruption, misery, sorrow, and death. Having recognized that, we as prodigal sons and daughters of God would want to come home. "**Professing to be wise, they became fools** ... [24] Therefore **God also gave them up to uncleanness**, in the **lusts of their hearts**, to dishonor their bodies among themselves, [25] **who exchanged the truth of God for the lie**, and **worshiped** and **served the creature** rather than **the Creator**, who is blessed forever. Amen" (**Romans 1:22, 24–25**).

In the second age of the law, God teaches His children on earth and in heaven that fallen man, who has the nature of a lawbreaker like Satan, cannot live by the law, even good law. When God gave Moses the Ten Commandments written on tablets of stone, there was a sense that God never meant that they were the end-all of how to live righteously: "Then the LORD said to Moses, 'Write these words, for **according to the tenor of these words** I have made **a covenant** with you and with Israel.' [28] So he was there with the LORD forty days and forty nights; he neither ate bread nor drank water. And **He wrote on the tablets** the words of **the covenant**, the Ten Commandments" (**Exodus 34:27–28**).

The author of Hebrews writes, "For **the law, having a shadow of the good things to come,** *and* **not the very image of the things,** can never with these same sacrifices, which they offer continually year by year, make those who approach perfect" (**Hebrews 10:1**). We cannot legislate morality, for it is the condition of the heart and mind. We will see in the chapter "The Third Age of the Church" that believers in God need to choose to "die" to the ways of Satan in this world, in what the Bible describes as a living sacrifice, so they can live in the ways of Christ: "I beseech you therefore, brethren, by the mercies of God, that **you present your bodies a living sacrifice,** holy, acceptable to God, *which is* your reasonable service. ² And do not be conformed to this world, but **be transformed** by the **renewing of your mind,** that you may **prove** what *is* that good and acceptable and perfect will of God" (**Romans 12:1**).

THE LETTER OF THE LAW VS. THE SPIRIT OF THE LAW

The goal of the law is to make us righteous and keep us from doing harm to each other, but sometimes circumstances conflict with that goal. For example, if the law says that "you shall not lie," we can agree that is a good law. But if you lived in Nazi Germany and you were trying to do good by hiding Jews in your home to save them from those who were trying to unjustly murder them, and a Nazi knocked on your door and asked you if you were hiding any Jews, what would you say? If you obeyed the law that says, "Thou shall not lie," you would end up doing great harm to innocents. If you made an exception to that law, then you would have to explain all the possible situations in which the law does not have to be followed and all the situations in which it must be followed. And because that is impossible to do, someone with the heart of the lawbreaker will try to use that law to take advantage of others in a way that is perfectly "legal."

Living strictly by what the law says, as if it is carved in stone with no exceptions no matter what, is referred to as "legalism" or "living by the letter of the law." Living by the intent of the law to do what is good is called "living by the spirit of the law." Living by the letter is strictly defined; it is written with many words in black and white that are hard to know and understand. Living by the spirit is very easy for the heart to understand. We can see this type of thinking in God the Father as we look again at **Genesis 34:27**: "Then the LORD said to Moses, 'Write these words, for **according to the tenor of these words** I have made a covenant with you and with Israel.'" *Webster's Student Dictionary* defines the word "tenor" as "1. **General tendency** or direction; course; procedure; trend. 2. **General drift of thought**; purport; **intent**; as, the *tenor* of the speech."

We can see how the Pharisees of Jesus' day used the law, as though it were carved in stone, not to do what was good for all but to benefit only them:

> At that time Jesus went through the grain fields on the Sabbath. And His disciples were hungry, and began to pluck heads of grain and to eat. ² And when the Pharisees saw it, they said to Him, "Look, Your disciples are doing **what is not lawful** to do **on the Sabbath!**" ³ But He said to them, "Have you not read what David did when he was hungry, he and those who were with him: ⁴ **how he entered the house of God** and **ate the showbread** which was **not lawful for him to eat**, nor for **those who were with him**, but **only for the priests**?
>
> ⁵ "Or have you not **read in the law** that on the Sabbath the priests **in the temple** profane the Sabbath, and are blameless? ⁶ Yet I say to you that in this place **there is One greater than the temple**. ⁷ But if you had known what this means, '**I desire mercy** and **not sacrifice**,' you would not have **condemned the guiltless**. ⁸ For the **Son of Man is Lord even of the Sabbath**" (**Matthew 12:1–8**).

In those days, those who harvested the fields were not supposed to scour the fields to get every little bit; they were to leave a little grain behind so that the poor could "glean" enough of the leftovers to keep from starving. So the taking of the grain by Jesus and His disciples was not the issue. The issue was doing work on the Sabbath. The Sabbath was intended to be a blessing for man—a day on which man did not have to work "in the sweat of his brow" but had time to ponder the truth of God, which would save him. If man did this, God would provide him with blessings to make up for the day he did not work.

The Sabbath was not a curse to prevent people from doing what is good and right for others, but the religious leaders used the law of the Sabbath to condemn Jesus out of jealousy because His teaching of love was contrary to their use of the law and was causing many to follow Him. Just because the Ten Commandments were carved in stone did not mean that the law was supposed to be applied that way. As Bible scholar Jonathan Preuse teaches, "The Pharisees always asked, 'Is it legal?' But they never asked, 'Is it right?'"

The truth is that man cannot write enough laws to tell him what is right and wrong, but when we have love in our hearts for one another, we automatically know what is right, for "**love does no harm** to a neighbor; therefore **love** *is* **the fulfillment of the law**" (**Romans 13:10**).

LAWS GIVEN IN TERROR DO NOT RESULT IN RIGHTEOUS

In the Old Testament, when God gave the people the law from Mount Sinai, He gave it to them in the way that Satan would give them laws—in fear and trembling. Remember that in the Old Testament, God is letting them experience what it would be like to live in the ways of Satan so that they may have a second chance to repent and choose the ways of God, which we will experience in the New Testament. Recall that when God gave the Ten Commandments in the Old Testament, He gave them to the people from Mount Sinai, which was burning with fire; there was lightning and thunder, and the people were trembling in terror, dread, and the fear of death. And so the people spoke to Moses, as he later reminds them with the words recorded for us in Deuteronomy:

So it was, when you **heard the voice** from the **midst of the darkness**, while the **mountain was burning with fire**, that you came near to me, **all the heads of your tribes** and your elders. [24] And you said: "Surely **the Lord our God has shown us His glory and His greatness**, and we have heard His voice from the **midst of the fire**. We have seen this day that **God speaks with man**; yet he *still* lives.

[25] "Now therefore, **why should we die?** For this **great fire** will **consume us**; if we **hear the voice of the Lord our God anymore**, then **we shall die**. [26] For who *is there* of all flesh who has heard the voice of the living God **speaking from the midst of the fire**, as we *have,* and lived? [27] You go near and hear all that the Lord our God may say, and tell us all that the Lord **our God says to you**, and **we will hear and do *it*.**" (Deuteronomy 5:23–27)

The people lived in fear of death from God, but they would listen to and obey Moses, who was like them and dwelled among them. And we see evidence of that today and throughout history; people who are ruled by terror and fear of death will risk their lives to be free of tyranny and live in freedom under a leader who cares for them and is like them and lives among them, or they will die trying.

God also knew that keeping the law was a matter of the heart; Moses refers to this when he recounts God's words to His people: "Then **the Lord heard** the **voice of your words** when **you spoke to me**, and the Lord said to me: 'I have heard **the voice of the words of this people** which they have spoken to you. **They are right *in* all that they have spoken.** [29] Oh, that they had such a heart in them** that they would **fear** Me and always keep all My commandments, **that it might be well with them** and with **their children forever!**'" (Deuteronomy 5:28–29).

Especially notice that God agrees with what the people said! They said that if God came to them with terror, dread, and fear of death to make them obey the law, they would **surely die**! Notice that God wishes that they had a different kind of heart in them, one that would change them from living in terror to living in respect and reverence so that they would be able to keep God's laws. And that was exactly what God was trying to teach them and us in the Old Testament—that if there were not *agape* love between a king and his people (that is, if the king did not care for those he ruled as if they were one with him and part of him, and did not live among them), there would be division in the kingdom. And as Jesus said, a kingdom that is divided cannot stand: "Every **kingdom divided against itself** is **brought to desolation**, and every city or house **divided against itself will not stand**" (**Matthew 12:25**). By giving the law in this way, God was showing them and us the way Satan would rule over us, and He was further showing that it would lead to division, corruption, desolation, misery, sorrow, and their death.

The word "fear" from the phrase "**Oh, that they had such a heart in them** that they would **fear** Me and always keep all My commandments" is translated from the Hebrew word H3372 *yare*, which means "To fear; **morally to revere**; causatively to **frighten**;-affright, be (make) **afraid**, **dread** (-full), (put in) **fear** (-full, -fully, -ing), (be had in) **reverence**, terrible (act, -ness, thing)."

The event that Moses recounts to the people in Deuteronomy occurred in **Exodus 20:18–20**: "Now all the people witnessed the **thunderings**, the **lightning flashes**, the **sound of the trumpet**, and the **mountain smoking**; and when the people saw *it*, **they trembled** and **stood afar off**. [19] Then they said to Moses, 'You speak with us, and we will hear; but **let not God speak with us, lest we die**.' [20] And Moses said to the people, 'Do not **fear**; for God has come to **test you**, and that **His fear** may be before you, so that you may not sin.'"

The Hebrew word for the first instance of "fear," in the phrase "Do not **fear**," is H3372 *yare*, which is defined above. The second instance of "fear," in the phrase "that His **fear** may be before you," is H3374 *yirah*, which means "**fear, morally reverence, dreadful, exceedingly fearful**." So both Hebrew words are essentially the same. They both refer to intentionally causing one to be afraid and in terror as a way of making others do one's bidding, and both refer to causing a desire in others to follow and obey out of the respect and reverence that come from knowing that the one that is leading you is worthy of your respect and reverence. But notice that God in the Old Testament came with fear and trembling and was high above them and separate from them, while in the New Testament, the Son of God came as one of us and lived among us and loved us enough to die for us, resulting in our great respect and reverence for Him.

In the phrase "For God has come to **test you**, and that **His fear** may be before you," we see the purpose of God in all of this. The Hebrew word for "test" is H5254 *nasah*, which means "To **test**; **assay, prove, try**." God is "testing" those in the Old Testament to show how they will react to living under a leadership that rules by trembling and fear of death. In this, God is thereby "proving" that they could only live under His kind of fear—that is, moral respect for God, who has supreme power and yet loves us and cares for us. But not even God can make us respect Him or love Him; that has to be a free-will choice of our hearts and minds.

Whenever there is someone that has much more power than we have, we give that person a certain fear and respect because he or she has the power to make us do what we do not want to do, or even destroy us. And this fear is great when we do not know the person's intentions toward us. If the person's intention is to rule over us out of fear and trembling at that person's greater power to make us do only what is in his or her best interest and not ours, then that person will lose our respect, honor, and reverence, and our heart will desire will be to be free from his or her rule, and we will rebel against that rule and even be willing to risk dying to be free. And there is nothing wrong with wanting to be free to do what is best for all of us, because God, who created us and loves us enough to die for us, wants what is best for us all. But only God, who created us, truly knows what is best for us all, and we have to trust Him and be willing to let Him teach us so that we can know and understand that truth for ourselves.

The way of ruling in the kingdom of God is by love, and the apostle John teaches that "**there is no fear in love**; but **perfect love casts out fear**, because **fear involves torment. But he who fears has not been made perfect in love**" (1 John 4:18). When there is someone who has much more power than we do and loves us and wants what is best for us and uses that great power to protect us and to do what is good for us, we no longer live in fear and trembling but have respect and profound reverence and honor for that person.

The problem we have is *knowing* what is best for us. When we believed the lies of Lucifer in heaven and rejected the ways of God, we believed that his ways were the best for us. The fact that this was not true but was just a lie to trap us is what God is trying to teach us in this temporary life on this temporary earth. There are only two choices here, because there are only two beings who are powerful enough to lead us in two opposite ways of living. We are not powerful enough to be sovereign and live on our own. As Paul teaches, in the end we will either be slaves of Satan or slaves of God Most High:

> Do you not know that to **whom you present yourselves slaves to obey**, you **are that one's slaves whom you obey**, whether of **sin *leading* to death**, or of **obedience *leading* to righteousness**?
>
> [17] But God be thanked that *though* you were **slaves of sin**, yet you **obeyed from the heart** that **form of doctrine** to which you were **delivered**. [18] And having been **set free from sin**, you became **slaves of righteousness**. [19] I speak in **human *terms*** because of the weakness of your flesh. For just as you presented your members *as* **slaves of uncleanness**, and of **lawlessness** *leading* to *more* **lawlessness**, so now present your members *as* **slaves *of* righteousness for holiness**. [20] For when **you were slaves of sin**, you were free in regard to righteousness. [21] What **fruit** did you have then in the things of which you are now ashamed? For **the end of those things *is* death**. [22] But now having been **set free from sin**, and having become **slaves of God**, you have your fruit to holiness, and **the end, everlasting life**. (**Romans 6:16–22**)

In the Old Testament, God teaches us what the ways of Satan are like. When God gave the Israelites **laws in fear and trembling**, the way that Satan would give them laws, they immediately disobeyed those laws. "Then the LORD said to Moses, 'Thus you shall say to the children of Israel: "You have seen that **I have talked with you from heaven**.

²³ You shall not make *anything to be* with Me—gods of silver or gods of gold you shall not make for yourselves. ²⁴ An altar of earth you shall make for Me, and you shall sacrifice on it your burnt offerings and your peace offerings, your sheep and your oxen. In every place where I record My name I will come to you, and I will bless you"""" (**Exodus 20:22–24**).

We see that laws given in fear and trembling to those who believed they could do better on their own did not make them obey but rather made them even more rebellious, and they did just the opposite of what they were told not to do, as we see in **Exodus 32:1–4,** when they thought Moses had died:

> Now when the people saw **that Moses delayed coming down** from the mountain, the people gathered together to Aaron, and said to him, "Come, **make us gods** that shall go before us; for *as for* this Moses, the man who brought us up out of the land of Egypt, **we do not know what has become of him**." ² And Aaron said to them, "Break off the golden earrings which *are* in the ears of your wives, your sons, and your daughters, and bring *them* to me." ³ So all the people broke off the golden earrings which *were* in their ears, and brought *them* to Aaron. ⁴ And **he received *the gold* from their hand**, and he fashioned it with an engraving tool, and **made a molded calf**. Then they said, "**This *is* your god**, O Israel, that **brought you out of the land of Egypt!**"

God had just told them in fear and trembling that they should not build any god of gold or silver. So what did they do when Moses, the one they respected and would listen to, was gone? They build the golden calf and called it their god. These were a stiff-necked people from the time they came out of Egypt, and a "god" who rules by fear and trembling cannot rule a rebellious people. You cannot force people to keep the law using terror, trembling, and fear of punishment and death for very long. And we see that today in Syria, Egypt, and Libya; when people get a taste of freedom and see a chance to be free, they will risk their life to be free from that tyranny. Amazingly, it seems that the scheme of Lucifer, now called Satan, was to deceive us into rebelling against God by breaking

His law of love and then trying to rule over rebellious people who were lawbreakers by using laws given in terror and the fear of death!

In all of this, God also told them and us one thing we all need to do to keep the law in **Deuteronomy 6:4–6**: "Hear, O Israel: The LORD our God, **the LORD *is* one**! [5] You shall **love the LORD your God** with **all your heart**, with **all your soul**, and with **all your strength**. [6] And these words which I command you today shall be **in your heart**." They needed to have a change of heart. They needed to have God's words in their heart! And this is exactly what the author of Hebrews says in the New Testament:

> Because finding fault with them, He says: "*Behold, the days are coming, says the LORD, when I will make a **new covenant** with the house of Israel and with the house of Judah–* [9] ***not according to the covenant*** *that I made with their fathers in the day when I took them by the hand to lead them out of the land of Egypt; because **they did not continue in My covenant**, and I disregarded them, says the LORD.* [10] *For **this is the covenant that I will make** with the house of Israel **after those days**, says the LORD: **I will put My laws in their mind** and **write them on their hearts**; and I will be their God, and they shall be My people.* [11] *None of them shall teach his neighbor, and none his brother, saying, 'Know the LORD,' for all shall know Me, from the least of them to the greatest of them.*" (**Hebrews 8:8–11**).

We will learn other things we need in order to love like Jesus Christ in the church age. And **Deuteronomy 9:6–7** explains why they could not keep the law; they were full of pride and were still believing that they could do better on their own: "Therefore **understand** that the LORD your God is not giving you this good land to possess because of **your righteousness**, for you *are* a **stiff-necked people**. [7] 'Remember. Do not forget how you provoked the LORD your God to wrath in the wilderness. From the day that you departed from the land of Egypt until you came to this place, **you have been rebellious against the LORD**." The righteousness of man is not the righteousness of God. "There is a way *that seems* **right** to a man, But **its end *is* the way of death**" (**Proverbs 16:25**).

WE CANNOT LIVE BY THE LAW

> What shall we say then? *Is the law sin?* Certainly not! On the contrary, **I would not have known sin except through the law**. For I would not have known covetousness unless the law had said, *"You shall not covet."* [8] But sin, **taking opportunity by the commandment, produced in me all** *manner of evil* **desire**. For **apart from the law sin** *was* **dead**. [9] I was alive once without the law, but when the **commandment came**, sin revived and I died. [10] And **the commandment**, which *was* to *bring* **life**, I found to *bring* **death**. [11] For sin, taking occasion by the commandment, **deceived me**, and by **it killed** *me*.
>
> [12] **Therefore the law** *is* **holy**, and the **commandment holy** and **just and good**. [13] Has then what is good become **death** to me? Certainly not! But **sin**, that it **might appear sin**, was **producing death in me** through what is good, so that sin **through the commandment** might become exceedingly sinful. [14] For we know that the law is spiritual, **but I am carnal, sold under sin**. (Romans 7:7–14)

One way to get rid of crime is to make everything legal. However, that does not stop bad things from happening but makes the situation worse, as God proved in the age of anarchy. In the above verse, Paul is saying that even though we may not recognize it, our sin is causing us to die. The law was provided to help us recognize that our sin was killing us. For those who do not want to be told what to do, the law telling them what they must do makes them want to do the opposite all the more. This is why reverse psychology works on children and most adults. The law made us sin more, but the problem was not with the law, the problem was with our sinful nature. The law just intensified the sin that was already there in our hearts and minds, allowing us to recognize it as sin and recognize that it was an offense to life and to a loving God.

Paul continues:

> For what I am doing, **I do not understand**. For what I will to do, that I do not practice; but what I hate, that I do. [16] If, then, I do what I will not to do, **I agree with the law that** *it is* **good**. [17] But now, *it is* no longer I who do it, but **sin that dwells in**

me. **¹⁸** For I know that in me (that is, **in my flesh**) nothing good dwells; for **to will is present with me**, but *how* **to perform what is good** I do not find.

¹⁹ For **the good that I will** *to do,* **I do not do**; but **the evil I will not** *to do,* **that I practice**. **²⁰** Now if I do what I will not *to do,* it is no longer I who do it, but sin that dwells in me. **²¹** I find then a law, that **evil is present with me**, the one who wills to do good. **²²** **For I delight** in the **law of God according** to the **inward man**. **²³** But I see **another law in my members**, warring against the **law of my mind**, and bringing me into captivity to the **law of sin which is in my members**. **²⁴** O **wretched man that I am**! Who will deliver me from this **body of death**? **²⁵** I thank God–through Jesus Christ our Lord! So then, with the **mind I myself serve the law of God**, but with **the flesh the law of sin**. (**Romans 7:15–25**)

The law cannot change hearts and minds. And morality cannot be legislated. When we fell, we had selfish and rebellious hearts and minds. We only cared about ourselves and what would benefit "me, myself, and I." This is worldly thinking, this is carnal thinking, and this is Satan's way of thinking—that we all can do better on our own, with each doing what is in his or her own best interest.

When we think that we are in charge, we do not want anyone telling us what to do. And that is why the law, when it came and told us what we must do, stirred in our hearts the desire to do the opposite, even when the law was in our own best interest. On top of that, we currently live in a body of flesh that is needy, lustful, and sickly, as well as able to experience hunger and pain. And we are surrounded by evil spirits in bodies of flesh and evil spirits without flesh who are demons, along with Satan, who are trying to tempt us to do what is evil.

HAVE CHRISTIANS BEEN SET FREE FROM THE LAW?

But what if someone should ask, **"Did Jesus not say that not one jot or tittle will pass from the law?"** Actually, this is what Jesus said: "Do not think that **I came to destroy the Law** or the Prophets. **I did not come to destroy but to fulfill**. [18] For assuredly, I say to you, **till heaven and earth pass away, one jot or one tittle will by no means pass from the law till all is fulfilled**" (**Matthew 5:18**).

THE LAW OF MOSES

Notice that Jesus said the law will be in effect until "**all is fulfilled**" when "**heaven and earth pass away**." And the apostle Peter tells us that this nuclear meltdown will not happen until the time when Jesus returns to the earth:

> But **the day of the Lord** [the time of Jesus' return] will come as a thief in the night, in which **the heavens will pass away with a great noise**, and the **elements will melt with fervent heat**; both the earth and the works that are in it will be burned up. [11] Therefore, **since all these things will be dissolved**, what manner *of persons* ought you to be in holy conduct and godliness, [12] looking for and hastening the coming of the day of God, because of which **the heavens will be dissolved, being on fire, and the elements will melt with fervent heat?** [13] Nevertheless we, **according to His promise**, look for **new heavens** and **a new earth in which righteousness dwells.** (**2 Peter 3:10–13**)

The phrase "**the heavens**" refers to the first two heavens—the atmosphere around earth, as well as outer space, where the stars and galaxies are—but not the third heaven, where the kingdom of God is. This new heaven and new earth will be revealed to us when God's plan is **fulfilled** in **Revelation 21:1**: "Now I saw a **new heaven** and a **new earth**, for the **first heaven** and the **first earth had passed away**. Also there was no more sea."

When Jesus returns to separate those who love Him and love their brothers and sisters as themselves from those who live in the evil ways of Satan, there will no longer be a need for laws. Doing what is right will be our heart's desire.

But until that time, Christians, even though we have been freed from the law to live by love, are to obey the laws of this world, because we know the truth of what this temporary life on this temporary earth is about, and we put our hope and faith in an eternal life with Christ.

> Therefore **submit yourselves to every ordinance of man for the Lord's sake**, whether to the king as supreme, [14] or to governors, as to **those who are sent by him** for the **punishment of evildoers** and *for the* **praise of those who do good**. [15] For this is the will of God, that **by doing good you may put to silence** the **ignorance of foolish men—** [16] **as free, yet not using liberty** as a **cloak for vice**, but as bondservants of God. [17] **Honor all** *people*. **Love the brotherhood. Fear God. Honor** the **king**. [18] Servants, *be* **submissive to** *your* **masters** with all fear, **not only to the good and gentle**, but **also to the harsh**. [19] For this *is* commendable, **if because of conscience toward God one endures grief, suffering wrongfully**.

[20] For what credit *is it* if, when you are beaten for your faults, you take it patiently? But **when you do good** and **suffer, if you take it patiently**, this *is* **commendable before God**. [21] For **to this you were called**, because **Christ also suffered for us, leaving us an example**, that you should follow His steps: [22] *"Who committed no sin, Nor was deceit found in His mouth";* [23] who, **when He was reviled, did not revile in return; when He suffered, He did not threaten**, but **committed** *Himself* **to Him who judges righteously;** [24] who Himself **bore our sins in His own body on the tree**, that we, having **died to sins**, might **live for righteousness—by whose stripes you were healed**. [25] For you were like sheep going astray, but have now returned to the Shepherd and **Overseer of your souls**. (**1 Peter 2:13–25**)

YOU CANNOT COMMAND SOMEONE TO LOVE YOU

Finally, when God provided the truth of the way to keep the commandments in the Old Testament, He gave it as a commandment, the way Satan would give rules in his kingdom, and we learned in "The Love Branch" that fallen man, with the heart and mind of the lawbreaker, cannot keep the law, and so the law is useless in making people abide by the law. In fact, it makes them want to do just the opposite. This is the heart and mind we all had when we fell from the grace of God by believing the lies of Satan. The commandment is another change in going from the Old Testament to the New Testament, in which Jesus comes to us with knowledge of the truth, understanding, love, and a free-will choice.

These harsh and unloving laws in the Old Testament were provided by God to show us, by having us live according to the ways of Satan, that Satan's ways always lead to corruption, division, misery, sorrow, and death. But in the next age, Jesus comes to show us a better way: "But before **faith** came, we were **kept under guard by the law**, kept for the **faith** which would afterward be revealed. ²⁴ Therefore **the law was our tutor** *to bring us* **to Christ**, that we might be **justified by faith**. ²⁵ But after faith has come, **we are no longer under a tutor**. ²⁶ For **you are all sons of God through faith in Christ Jesus**. ²⁷ For as many of you as were baptized into Christ **have put on Christ**" (**Galatians 3:23–26**). The law was a tutor to teach us that we cannot live by the law.

Loving God above all and loving others as yourself does not make sense to those who believe they can do better on their own and who believe that loving oneself above all is the best way to live: "But the **natural man** does not **receive the things of the Spirit of God**, for **they are foolishness to him**; nor can he know *them*, **because they are spiritually discerned**" (**1 Corinthians 2:14**). So now we know the answer if someone should ask us, **"Why did God give us the law if He knew we could not live righteously by laws?"**

333

These are the ways of Satan; because he cannot see into the hearts of man like God can, strict laws with harsh consequences are the only way he can rule over rebellious people to form the kingdom he is trying to create. God is teaching us that we cannot live by laws. For the pure of heart, the law is not needed. For those with the hearth and mind of the lawbreaker, the law will not work. No one can legislate morality. Wherever there is a need for laws, sin is already present. Keeping the law is a matter of the heart and mind. Love is the only way to keep the law, and no one can force anyone to love him or her, not even God. Love is a free-will matter of the heart.

There is more evidence in the Bible that God never intended for us to live by the law in **Hebrews 10:1–2a, 5–10**:

> For the law, having **a shadow of the good things to come,** *and* **not the very image of the things,** can never with these same sacrifices, which they offer continually year by year, make those who approach perfect. ² For then would they not have ceased to be offered? ... Therefore, when He came into the world, He said: *"**Sacrifice and offering You did not desire,** But a body You have prepared for Me. ⁶ In burnt offerings and sacrifices for sin You had no pleasure. ⁷ Then I said, 'Behold, **I have come**—In the volume of the book it is written of Me— **To do Your will, O God.'"** ⁸ Previously saying, "**Sacrifice and offering, burnt offerings,** and **offerings for sin You did not desire, nor had pleasure in them"** (which are offered according to the law), ⁹ then He said, *"Behold, I have come to do Your will, O God."* He **takes away the first** that **He may establish the second.** ¹⁰ By that will we have been sanctified through the offering of the body of Jesus Christ **once for all.**

Trying to pay for our sins after the fact, over and over again, does not make up for the damage our sins cause and does not make it right with God. That is not what He is looking for. A mind that understands the truth and a heart that loves and only desires to do what is right in the first place are what He seeks.

OUR ONE AND ONLY HOPE

While God knew that fallen man could not keep the law because of the condition of his heart and mind, He gave all of us hope in the words of the prophets that spoke of one who would come and show us all a better way and deliver those who would repent of their ways and believe in God in an age to come. Moses, speaking the inspired words of God, prophesied the coming of Christ:

> The LORD your God **will raise up for you a Prophet like me** from your midst, **from your brethren. Him you shall hear**, [16] according to **all you desired of the LORD your God in Horeb** in the day of the assembly, saying, "Let me not **hear again the voice of the LORD my God**, nor **let me see this great fire anymore, lest I die.**" [17] And the LORD said to me: "**What they have spoken is good.** [18] **I will raise up for them a Prophet like you from among their brethren**, and will put **My words in His mouth**, and He shall speak to them all that I command Him. [19] And it shall be *that* **whoever will not hear My words**, which He speaks in My name, **I will require** *it* **of him.**" (**Deuteronomy 18:15**)

God requires that we listen to the words of Jesus with an open mind and a teachable heart to understand the truth that will make us free.

The prophet Micah prophesies of that future prophet:

> But you, Bethlehem Ephrathah, *Though* you are little among the thousands of Judah, *Yet* **out of you** shall come forth to Me The **One to be Ruler in Israel**, Whose goings forth *are* **from of old, From everlasting.** [3] Therefore **He shall give them up, Until the time** *that* **she who is in labor has given birth**; Then **the remnant of His brethren** Shall **return to the children of Israel.** [4] And He shall stand and **feed** *His flock* In the **strength of the LORD**, In the **majesty** of the **name of the LORD His God**; And **they shall abide**, For now He shall be great To the ends of the earth; [5] And **this** *One* **shall be peace.** (**Micah 5:2–5a**)

Notice that the phrase **"He shall give them up, Until the time** *that* **she who is in labor has given birth"** confirms just what we have been talking about. God has given up His fallen angels in bodies of flesh to be on their own to experience the ways of Satan and to do what they desire in their fallen hearts and minds in the first two ages. He then sends His Son, Jesus, into this world to witness of the truth that will make us free in the third age: "Pilate therefore said to Him, 'Are You a king then?' Jesus answered, 'You say *rightly* that **I am a king. For this cause I was born**, and **for this cause I have come into the world**, that **I should bear witness to the truth.** Everyone who is of the truth hears My voice … And you shall **know the truth**, and **the truth shall make you free'"** (**John 18:37; 8:32**).

Seeking and saving the lost, even if it means suffering and dying for them, is what a king in heaven does. In the phrase "The **remnant of His brethren shall return to the children of Israel**," the "brethren" of Jesus refers to all of us on earth who were with Jesus before the fall from grace in heaven. The "remnant" of Jesus' brethren are God's elect, who are the spiritual descendants of Abram, those who believe God and are in Christ and are saved by the promise of God to Abraham. The remnant of Jesus' brethren will return to the children of Israel in the millennial reign of Jesus Christ. Seeking and saving the lost spiritual sons of Abraham is what Jesus is doing on earth: "And Jesus said to him, 'Today **salvation has come** to this house, because **he also is a son of Abraham**; [10] for the Son of Man has come to **seek and to save that which was lost'"** (**Luke 19:9–10**).

Now that God has shown in the first covenant of the law that the ways of Satan cannot make us righteous, so that we should live, He replaces it with a second covenant, this one a covenant of love, that leads to righteousness and eternal life.

The Third Age of the Church

IN THE CHURCH age Jesus comes to teach us the ways of God that lead to eternal life:

> Owe no one anything **except to love one another**, for **he who loves another has fulfilled the law**. [9] For the commandments, "You shall not commit adultery," "You shall not murder," "You shall not steal," "You shall not bear false witness," "You shall not covet," and if there is any other commandment, are all summed up in this saying, namely, "**You shall love your neighbor as yourself.**" [10] **Love does no harm to a neighbor**; therefore **love is the fulfillment of the law. (Romans 13:8–10)**

Consider all the harsh laws of the Old Testament, the stoning of those who break the law, and repaying like for like: "But if *any* harm follows, then you shall give life for life, [24] eye for eye, tooth for tooth, hand for hand, foot for foot, [25] burn for burn, wound for wound, stripe for stripe" (**Exodus 21:23–25**). Because of the harsh and strict laws in the Old Testament, some think God changed as He went from the Old to the New Testament or that God learned during that time or that Jesus in the New Testament was kinder and gentler than God the Father of the Old Testament. The harshness of the Old Testament has led some Christians to recommend to others to start reading the New Testament first or not to read the Old Testament at all. Even President Obama has publically questioned the harshness of some of the Old Testament laws in the Bible.

In the Old Testament, adultery was punishable by death: "The man who commits adultery with *another* man's wife, *he* who commits adultery with his neighbor's wife, the adulterer and the adulteress, shall surely be put to death" (**Leviticus 20:10**). But in the New Testament, Jesus had mercy on a woman caught in adultery: "Then the scribes and Pharisees brought to Him **a woman caught in adultery**. And when they had set her in the midst, [4] they said to Him, 'Teacher, this woman was caught in adultery, in the very act. [5] Now **Moses, in the law, commanded us that such should be stoned**. But what do You say?' ... [7] So when they continued asking Him, He raised Himself up and said to them, 'He who is without sin among you, let him throw a stone at her first'" (**John 8:3–5, 7**).

And so when someone asks, **"Did God change from the Old Testament to the New Testament? Did God learn? Is Jesus kinder and gentler than God the Father of the Old Testament?"** what should we tell that person?

None of this thinking could be further from the truth. God the Father, speaking through the prophet Malachi, says, "'**For I *am* the LORD, I do not change**; Therefore **you are not consumed**, O sons of Jacob. [7] Yet from the days of your fathers You have gone away from My ordinances And have not kept *them*. **Return to Me**, and **I will return to you**,' Says **the LORD of hosts**" (**Malachi 3:6–7**). We are the ones who chose to leave God.

It is not God who changed; the things God was teaching fallen man changed. For one thing, God the Father and Jesus, His Son, were both working together in the Old Testament and the New. And we learn from Moses, who recorded the first five books of the Old Testament, that Jesus was working with the Father in the Old Testament, for the angel of the Lord that appeared to Moses in the burning bush was the preincarnate Jesus, the Great "I AM":

> Now Moses was tending the flock of Jethro, his father-in-law, the priest of Midian. And he led the flock to the back of the desert, and came to **Horeb**, the **mountain of God**. [2] And **the Angel of the LORD** appeared to him in a **flame of fire from**

the midst of a bush. So he looked, and behold, the bush was burning with fire, but the bush was not consumed. ³ Then Moses said, "I will now turn aside and see this great sight, why the bush does not burn."

⁴ So **when the LORD** saw that he turned aside to look, **God called to him from the midst of the bush** and said, "Moses, Moses!" And he said, "Here I am." ⁵ Then He said, "Do not draw near this place. Take your sandals off your feet, for the place where you stand is holy ground." ⁶ Moreover He said, "**I am** the **God of your father**–the **God of Abraham**, the **God of Isaac**, and the **God of Jacob**." And Moses hid his face, for he was afraid to look upon God. (**Exodus 3:1–6**)

The word "LORD" in all capital letters is translated from the Hebrew word H3068 *yehovah*, which means "The **self Existent** or **eternal**; **Jehovah**, Jewish national name of God." So the **"Angel of the LORD"** is an angel of God the Father, whom the Bible says is in the burning bush. In **Exodus 3:4**, it says that God called to Moses from the midst of the bush. So the **"Angel of the LORD"** is not God the Father but is called God. Who else but Jesus can fulfill that description? So Jesus is identified as the God of Abraham, Isaac, and Jacob! Later, in **Exodus 3:14**, The **"Angel of the LORD"** identifies Himself as **"I AM"**: "And God said to Moses, '**I AM WHO I AM**.' And He said, 'Thus you shall say to the children of Israel, "**I AM has sent me to you**."'"

In the New Testament Jesus reveals that He is the Great I AM of the Old Testament: "'Your father Abraham rejoiced to see My day, and he saw *it* and was glad.' ⁵⁷ Then the Jews said to Him, 'You are not yet fifty years old, and have You seen Abraham?' ⁵⁸ Jesus said to them, 'Most assuredly, I say to you, **before Abraham was, I AM**'" (**John 8:58**). Notice that we see God the Father working together with Jesus in the Old Testament. And in the New Testament we see the same thing: "For this reason the Jews persecuted Jesus, and sought to kill Him, because He had done these things on the Sabbath. ¹⁷ But Jesus answered them, '**My Father has been working until now**, and **I have been working**'" (**John 5:16–17**). Jesus and His Father have been working together to create fallen man in His image from the time of fall in heaven, and they will continue to do so until it is completed in **Revelation 21:6**: "And He said to me, '**It is done**! I am the Alpha and the Omega, the Beginning and the End.'"

We have to understand that the purpose of God in allowing men to live according to the ways of Satan in the Old Testament was to have fallen man experience for himself that God was right and that the words of Satan were a lie and would lead him to his death. If we do not desire with our hearts to keep the law out of the knowledge and understanding of the truth that God's way of love—love for God, our King, above all, and love for our brothers and sisters—is the best way for each individual to live, then the only other way to motivate people keep the law is out of the fear and terror of what will happen to them if they do not keep the law.

As we learned earlier, the apostle John confirms that that the opposite of love is fear, just as the ways of Satan are opposite to the ways of God: "**There is no fear in love**; but **perfect love casts out fear**, because **fear involves torment**. But **he who fears** has not been **made perfect in love**. [19] **We love Him because He first loved us**. [20] If someone says, 'I love God,' and hates his brother, he is a liar; for he who does not love his brother whom he has seen, how can he love God whom he has not seen? [21] And this commandment we have from Him: that **he who loves God *must* love his brother also**" (**1 John 4:18**). And this thought is echoed by the disciple Timothy: "For God has **not given us a spirit of fear**, but of **power and of love** and **of a sound mind**" (**2 Timothy 1:7**). "Therefore, since we are **receiving a kingdom** which **cannot be shaken**, let us have **grace**, by which we may serve God acceptably with **reverence** and **godly fear**" (**Hebrews 12:28**).

The last verse may sound like a contradiction of the first two passages, but unlike what we just learned—that there are two different Hebrew words for "fear" with similar meanings that speak of both fear and terror as well as moral reverence—there are two Greek words translated as "fear" that have different meanings. The Greek word translated as "fear" in the phrase "There is no fear in love" is G5401 *phobos*, which is defined as follows: "From a primary *phobomai* (to be **in fear**); **alarm**

340

or **fright**:- be **afraid +exceedingly, fear, terror**." The Greek word translated as "godly fear" is G2124 *eulabeia*, which means "Properly caution, that is, (**religiously**) reverence (**piety**)." The word "piety" is defined by *Webster's Student Dictionary* as "1. Piousness; specifically a) **Loyal devotion to parents, family**, or **race**. b) **Dutifulness in religion; devoutness**. 2. A pious act or expression." The Greek word *eulabia* refers to the kind of fear God wished the children of Israel had in the Old Testament: "**Oh, that they had such a heart in them** that they would **fear** Me and always keep all My commandments, **that it might be well with them** and with **their children forever!**" (**Deuteronomy 5: 29**).

And now we know what to say if someone should ask, **"Why is the Old Testament is so brutal and harsh?"** It is because God is demonstrating what the ways of living under the reign of Satan would be like in the Old Testament. This teaching is part of our second chance on earth that God granted us that we might understand the truth, change our minds, and chose Him and live forever.

The suffering, misery, fear, and terror of living in Satan's ways causes us to stop and consider that we might be wrong and that we might have made a mistake when we believed in the ways of Satan. And this opens our hearts and minds to consider that God may be right after all. And if we come to God with open minds and teachable hearts, He will teach us the truth that will change us for eternal life.

Looking down from His great perspective in heaven during the first two ages, God lets man find out for himself that living on his own apart from God and His ways leads not to life but to corruption, decay, misery, sorrow, and death. When we were deceived by Satan that we could do better on our own apart from God, we refused to listen to reason, and so God had no choice but to turn us over to walk in our own ways, which were the ways of Satan, and we had to experience good and evil for ourselves to find out *by* ourselves that God was right and understand for ourselves why He was right. Just believing what someone says without reason and facts is not enough. We believed Satan's lies out of blind faith.

In the first age, God taught us that man could not live as a group of independent individuals free to do whatever they wanted, living only for themselves, without any rules or governing leadership; that this way of living only leads to corruption and death; and that freedom is not the complete freedom to do anything one desires. And the result of that age was that "**the LORD was sorry that He had made man on the earth,** and **He was grieved in His heart**" (**Genesis 6:6**).

In the second age, God taught us that fallen man—with the selfish, prideful, heart and mind of the lawbreaker—could not live righteously by laws and a governing leadership alone. Living righteously means living together in a way that is sustainable for eternity. God exposed Lucifer's way of living under laws as a lie; proved that might does not make right; and made clear that living in a way where only the strongest survive ensures only that no one will survive.

All of this is exactly what the apostle Paul explained in this third age:

> But when the apostles Barnabas and Paul heard this, they tore their clothes and ran in among the multitude, crying out [15] and saying, "Men, why are you doing these things? We also are men **with the same nature as you,** and preach to you that **you should turn from these useless things** to the **living God,** who made the heaven, the earth, the sea, and all things that are in them, [16] **who in bygone generations allowed all nations to walk in their own ways** [17] Nevertheless **He did not leave Himself without witness, in that He did good,** gave us rain from heaven and fruitful seasons, filling our hearts with food and gladness." (**Acts 14:14–16**)

In previous ages, God let people walk in their own ways, which were the ways of Satan. When people speak of the harshness of the Old Testament, we need to remember that these were not the ways of God but of Satan, who said we could live better this way. God was proving to all that the ways of Satan were lies and would only lead to their **eternal death**. Even when they tried to be righteous by the law, God knew that people with rebellious hearts focused on what was best for them could not keep the law, which deals in what is best for all.

Most everyone will die once in the flesh (except those who have been and will be raptured), but those who refuse to repent and return to the living God will die in the spirit with Satan in what the Jesus calls the second death: "He who has an ear, let him hear what the **Spirit says to the churches. He who overcomes** shall not be hurt **by the second death**" (**Revelation 2:11**). As the apostle John prophecies, "Then **Death** and **Hades** were cast into the **lake of fire. This is the second death.** [15] And anyone not found written in the Book of Life was cast into the lake of fire" (**Revelation 20:14–25**).

But, no matter how evil things get, God has always kept a "remnant" of believers in the truth of God through the ages:

- In the first age of anarchy: "... when once the **Divine longsuffering** waited in the days of Noah, while *the* **ark was being prepared**, in which a few, that is, **eight souls,** were **saved through water**" (**1 Peter 3:20**).
- In the age of the law: "Isaiah also cries out concerning Israel: *'Though the number of the children of Israel be as the sand of the sea, The remnant will be saved.* [28] *For He will finish the work and cut it short in righteousness, Because the* LORD *will make a short work upon the earth'*" (**Romans 9:27–28**).
- And in the age of the church: "Even so then, at **this present time** there is **a remnant** *according to* **the election of grace**" (**Romans 11:5**).

In the age of the millennium, there will not be just a remnant, but all will be children of God who were saved.

In the Old Testament, Satan blinded their eyes to the truth, and because the kingdom of God is not one of bondage but of free-will choice, God turned them over and let them walk in the ways they chose, in the ways of Satan, so that they and everyone on earth and in heaven could see that the ways of Satan are a lie that leads to corruption, misery, sorrow, and death. In this way they could learn the truth and turn from the lies. God still loved them, and "the Lord is not slack **concerning *His* promise,** as some count slackness, but is **longsuffering** toward us, **not willing**

that any should perish but that all should **come to repentance"** (**2 Peter 3:9**) and seek eternal life. But not even God can make someone love Him, and *agape* love is required of people in order to live with God in His kingdom.

But in the New Testament, Paul explains how Jesus came to bring us the truth that would transform us into the image of God:

> **But their minds were blinded**. For **until this day** the same **veil remains unlifted** in the **reading of the Old Testament**, because **the** *veil* **is taken away in Christ**. [15] But even to this day, **when Moses is read**, a veil lies on their heart. [16] Nevertheless **when one turns to the Lord**, the **veil is taken away**. [17] Now **the Lord is the Spirit**; and **where the Spirit of the Lord** *is*, **there** *is* **liberty**. [18] But we all, with **unveiled face**, beholding **as in a mirror** the glory of the Lord, are being **transformed into the same image** from glory to glory, just as by the **Spirit of the Lord**. (**2 Corinthians 3:14–18**)

Here we see that we were not in the image of God in the beginning, and that the purpose of this temporary life on this temporary earth is to transform us from the image of fallen man (*"adam"* in the Hebrew) into the image of God. And Paul continues in the next chapter:

> But **even if our gospel is veiled**, it is **veiled to those who are perishing**, [4] **whose minds** the **god of this age has blinded**, who **do not believe**, lest the **light of the gospel** of the **glory of Christ**, who is the **image of God**, should **shine on them**. [5] For we do not preach ourselves, but Christ Jesus the Lord, and ourselves your bondservants for Jesus' sake. [6] For it is the **God who commanded light to shine out of darkness**, who has **shone in our hearts** to *give* the **light of the knowledge** of the **glory of God** in the face of Jesus Christ. (**2 Corinthians 4:3–4**)

This **"commanding light to shine out of darkness"** harkens back to the beginning and the notion that the light was the light of knowledge of the ways of life of God (**Genesis 1:1–4**). God divides the light from darkness just as he divides those who belong to Him from those who belong to Satan in the end.

While God let the people live in their own ways in the Old Testament, He did not leave them without a witness but gave them holidays and festivals as foreshadowing of His plan through Christ to save the elect: "So let no one judge you in food or in drink, or regarding **a festival or a new moon or sabbaths,** [17] which **are a shadow of things to come,** but the **substance is of Christ**" (**Colossians 2:16–17**).

LOVING GOD REQUIRES THE UNDERSTANDING OF THE TRUTH OF GOD'S WAYS

In the Old Testament, God reveals that love is the way to keep the law and the way to unite us together as One: "Hear, O Israel: **The LORD our God, the LORD** *is* **one!** [5] You shall **love the LORD your God** with **all your heart,** with **all your soul,** and with **all your strength.** [6] And these words which I command you today shall be **in your heart**" (**Deuteronomy 6:4–6**). But because He gave it to them the way Satan gave his lie to them, without the understanding of this truth with the mind, they thought it was foolishness. God tried to reason with them but they would not listen: "'Come now, and **let us reason together**,' Says the LORD, 'Though your sins are like scarlet, They shall be as white as snow; Though they are red like crimson, They shall be as wool'" (**Isaiah 1:18**).

Truth and reason are what Paul used to do the work Jesus called him to do "to **open their eyes,** *and* to **turn** *them* **from darkness to light,** and *from* the **power of Satan unto God,** that they may receive **forgiveness of sins,** and **inheritance** among them which are sanctified by **faith** that is in me … [Paul] said, 'I am not mad, most noble Festus, but speak the **words of truth** and **reason**'" (**Acts 26:18, 25**). And reason is what Jesus calls believers to use to convince others about salvation: "But sanctify the Lord God in your hearts, and **always** *be* **ready** to *give* a defense to everyone who asks you a **reason** for the hope that is in you, with **meekness** and fear" (**1 Peter 3:15**).

Notice that when Jesus came into this world He added the understanding of the mind to the loving of the LORD from **Deuteronomy 6:4–6**: "Then one of the scribes came, and having heard them **reasoning together**, perceiving that **He had answered them well**, asked Him, 'Which is the first commandment of all?' ²⁹ Jesus answered him, 'The **first of all the commandments** *is:* "**Hear, O Israel**, *the* LORD *our God, the* LORD *is one.* ³⁰ *And you shall* **love the** LORD **your God** *with all your heart, with all your soul, with all your mind, and with all your strength.*" This *is* the **first commandment**. ³¹ And the second, like *it, is* this: "**You shall love your neighbor as yourself.**" There is no other commandment **greater than these**'" (**Mark 12:28–31**). And understanding is exactly what the apostle John says about Jesus' teachings: "And we know that the **Son of God** has **come** and **has given us an understanding**, that we may **know Him who is true**; and **we are in Him who is true**, in His Son **Jesus Christ**. This is the **true God** and **eternal life**" (**1 John 5:20**).

Jesus added "*with **all your mind**"* to the Old Testament version because God knows that we cannot love with the sacrificial, unconditional, agape love of God if we do not understand why God's ways are the right, the best, and the only way to live for eternal life. When Satan deceived us with his ways of living, it was a lie, and so he could not explain with logic and reasoning why his was the best way to live, because it was not. The fact is that Satan could not defend his lie with logic and reasoning, because that requires truth. "… and that **no lie is of the truth**" (**1 John 2:21b**).

God shows us that without the understanding of the truth with the mind, which only the Holy Spirit can give, love is foolishness to those who do not believe, and they do not take it to heart, as Paul teaches: "But the **natural man** does not **receive the things** of the **Spirit of God**, for **they are foolishness to him**; **nor can he know** *them,* because **they are spiritually discerned**" (**1 Corinthians 2:14**). Remember that in this trial going on in the courts of heaven and being carried out on earth, God put us in bodies of flesh so that we could not see or remember our spiritual past and the spiritual realm that was our home, without first turning to God and receiving the truth from the Holy Spirit of God.

In this world of Satan, he is doing all he can to keep us in the dark so that we do not know the truth that will expose his lie and set us free. But in the New Testament, God sends His only begotten Son, Jesus Christ, into Satan's world to help us understand the truth in His Holy Scriptures, which will make us free, as Jesus testifies to Pontius Pilate and us:

> **For this cause I was born**, and for this cause **I have come into the world**, that I should **bear witness to the truth**. Everyone **who is of the truth hears My voice. (John 18:37b)**

> And **you shall know the truth**, and the **truth shall make you free. (John 8:32)**

God leaves us with His Holy Spirit of truth, who will lead us to all truth for those who believe and who diligently seek to know Jesus, as the author of Hebrews describes: "But **without faith** *it is* **impossible to please** *Him,* for he who **comes to God** must **believe that He is**, and *that* **He is a rewarder** of those who **diligently seek Him**" (**Hebrews 11:6**). God wants us to know and understand the truth of His ways and why they lead to eternal life.

IN THE NEW TESTAMENT, JESUS GIVES US A NEW COMMANDMENT

> A **new commandment** I give to you, that you **love one another**; as **I have loved you**, that you also **love one another**. [35] By this all will know that **you are My disciples**, if you have **love for one another. (John 13:34–35)**

Later, John, quoting Jesus, says, "This is **My** commandment, that you **love one another as I have loved you**" (**John 15:12**).

347

But what if someone should ask, **"If God taught us in the Old Testament that man cannot live by the law, why does Jesus give us love as a commandment?"**

The problem in the Old Testament was not that the law was bad; the problem was that because of our fallen nature, what we believed in our minds and desired with our hearts was bad. We were greedy and selfish, full of pride and arrogance, thinking we could live without God. In the New Testament, Jesus teaches us to understand the truth and that truth will lead us into a loving relationship with God. God tells us what His plan is in **Jeremiah 31:33**: "But **this** *is* **the covenant** that I will make **with the house** of Israel **after those days**, says the LORD: **I will put My law in their minds**, and **write it on their hearts**; and I will be their God, and they shall be My people." The phrase **"after those days"** refers to a time after the ages of the Old Testament when God first teaches about the ways of Satan that lead to death.

When You Command Someone to Love You Who Already Does, the Command Becomes Moot

Love must be a free-will choice, but the law is an obligation that must be carried out whether one wants to or not. How is it possible that love fulfills the law? When you want to do with all your heart that which the law says you must do whether you want to or not, the obligation becomes a moot point. You will do it out of love and fulfill the obligation. Love fulfills the law.

My son Nick understood this concept when he was only five years old. I came from a hugging family, and when my own son was born, I loved to hug him all the time. Then one day, with a sly grin on his face, he said, "Dad, I command you to hug me. And with the same sly grin on my face, I said, "Well okay, if I have to," and I gave him a big old bear hug and we both laughed. And that is the point Jesus is making—that love enables us to do with joy what we normally would consider to be work and would not want to do. Come to think of it, even Tom Sawyer, in the whitewashing of a fence, came to understand that there

348

comes a point when work is no longer work but is something that you want to do.

Love Determines Who the Children of God and Children of the Devil Are

> In this the **children of God** and the **children of the devil are manifest** [revealed]: Whoever does not practice righteousness is not of God, nor is he who **does not love his brother**. [11] For **this is the message that you heard from the beginning, that we should love one another**, [12] not as Cain who was **of the wicked one** and murdered his brother. And why did he murder him? Because his works were evil and his brother's righteous. (**1 John 3:10–12**)

The phrase "**This is the message that you heard from the beginning**" refers to "Hear, O Israel: The LORD our God, **the LORD** *is* **one!** [5] You shall **love the LORD your God** with **all your heart**, with **all your soul**, and with **all your strength**. [6] 'And these words which I command you today **shall be in your heart**'" (**Deuteronomy 6:4–6**). When a command or law is something you already desire to do with all your heart, the command becomes a moot point and keeping the law becomes a labor of love.

And this is the free-will choice our ancestors were given: "**I call heaven and earth as witnesses today against you,** *that* **I have set before you life** and **death, blessing** and **cursing**; therefore **choose life**, that both **you and your descendants may live**; [20] that you may **love the LORD your God, that you may obey His voice**, and that you may cling to Him, for **He** *is* **your life** and the length of your days; and that **you may dwell in the land which the LORD swore to your fathers**, to **Abraham, Isaac**, and **Jacob**, to give them" (**Deuteronomy 30:19–20**). Notice what God is saying in this phrase—"that you may **love the LORD your God, that you may obey His voice**." It is when we love the Lord that we will be able to obey His voice, because it is something we already desire to do, and so obeying God becomes a moot point.

But what if someone should ask, **"What is the correct meaning of Communion—the Lord's Supper?"** That is a good question. Let us see what the written Word of God has to teach us about the Lord's Last Supper with His disciples:

THE MEANING OF COMMUNION, THE LORD'S SUPPER

In the following passages, we will see a lot of symbolism between the world of the flesh and the spiritual world: the life of the flesh symbolizing the life of the spirit, the foreshadowing in the flesh of events that will take place in the spiritual realm, and the things that make for the life of the flesh and the life of the spirit.

The Lord's Supper Is Unity and Oneness

> I speak as to wise men; judge for yourselves what I say. [16] The cup of blessing which we bless, is it not the **communion of the blood of Christ**? The bread which we break, is it not the **communion of the body of Christ**? [17] For we, *though* **many**, are **one bread** *and* **one body**; for we all partake of that **one bread. (1 Corinthians 10:15–17)**

It is the sacrifice of the body and blood of Christ, symbolized by the cup of wine and piece of bread, that unites us into One in Him. And, as we will learn, it is the Oneness in Christ that enables Christ to die to save us on the tree that we would have died on, and we live because He lives. We know this is symbolic because this verse also says that we **"are one bread,"** which we know is symbolic. Bread represents that which sustains the life of our body on earth. But man is more than a body of flesh on earth: "But He answered and said, 'It is written, **"Man shall not live by bread alone, but by every word that proceeds from the mouth of God"'"** (**Matthew 4:4**). Jesus is the spiritual bread, the Word

350

of God, who gives us the words from the mouth of God, which sustain our spiritual life:

> And Jesus said to them, "**I am the bread of life**. He who comes to Me **shall never hunger**, and he who believes in Me **shall never thirst** ... **It is the Spirit who gives life**; the **flesh profits nothing**. The **words that I speak to you** are **spirit**, and *they* **are life**." (**John 6:63**)

The manna that came down from heaven to feed God's children of old and save their lives was foreshadowing of Jesus' coming down from heaven to earth to save our lives for eternity by teaching us the meaning of *"every word that proceeds from the mouth of God."* As we have learned, Jesus is known as *the Word*: "In the beginning was **the Word**, and **the Word was with God**, and **the Word was God**. ²The same was in the beginning with God. ³All things were made by him; and without him was not any thing made that was made. ⁴In him was life; and the life was the light of men" (**John 1:1–4**).

We can see the symbolism in Jesus' words in John chapter 6: "**I am the bread of life**. ⁴⁹ Your fathers ate the **manna** in the **wilderness**, and are **dead**. ⁵⁰ This is the **bread which comes down from heaven**, that one may eat of it and **not die**. ⁵¹ I am the **living bread which came down from heaven**. If anyone **eats of this bread**, he will **live forever**; and **the bread that I shall give is My flesh**, which I shall **give** for the **life of the world**" (**John 6:48–50**). And we know that Jesus gave the life of His flesh for the eternal spiritual life of the world.

"Then Jesus said to them, 'Most assuredly, I say to you, unless you **eat the flesh** of the **Son of Man** and **drink His blood**, you have **no life in you**. ⁵⁴ Whoever **eats My flesh** and **drinks My blood** has **eternal life**, and I will raise him up at the last day. ⁵⁵ For My **flesh is food indeed**, and My **blood is drink indeed**. ⁵⁶ He who **eats My flesh** and **drinks My blood abides in Me**, and **I in him**'" (**John 6:53–56**). The breaking of Jesus' flesh and the shedding of His blood on the cross for us was spiritual food and drink for eternal life in **deed**.

The Old Testament speaks of the Passover meal, which foreshadows the Lord's Supper:

> Your **lamb** shall be **without blemish**, a male of the first year ... And they shall **take** *some* **of the blood** and put *it* **on the two doorposts** and on the **lintel of the houses** where they eat it. [8] Then they shall **eat the flesh** on that night; roasted in fire, with **unleavened bread** *and* with **bitter** *herbs* they shall eat it ... For the LORD will pass through to strike the Egyptians; and when He **sees the blood** on the **lintel** and on the **two doorposts**, the LORD will **pass over** the door and **not allow the destroyer to come into your houses to strike** *you*. (**Exodus 12:5, 7–8, 23**)

So considering this background, what did Jesus mean when He said, **"this is My body"** and **"this My blood"** while He was eating the Lord's Last Supper with His disciples? Jesus is our sinless Lamb, the fulfillment of the spotless lamb of old whose flesh they ate so that God would pass over their dwelling places to save them from the Destroyer, Satan. Jesus shows us that He is the fulfillment of the Passover Lamb and the Lord's Supper is the fulfillment of the Passover.

Let us compare two accounts of the Last Supper from Matthew and Luke. Matthew writes, "And as they were eating, **Jesus took bread**, blessed and broke *it,* and gave *it* to the disciples and said, 'Take, eat; **this is My body**.' [27] Then He took the cup, and gave thanks, and gave *it* to them, saying, '**Drink from it, all of you.** [28] For **this is My blood** of the **new covenant, which is shed for many** for the **remission of sins**'" (**Matthew 26:26**). As we learned, the new covenant was a commandment to love, and Jesus is going to show us how much He loves us by being willing to shed His blood on the cross and die for us, who previously rejected Him and chose Satan. **"This is My commandment**, that you **love one another as I have loved you.** [13] **Greater love has no one than this**, than to **lay down one's life for his friends**" (**John 15:12–13**).

Luke writes,

> Then He said to them, "With *fervent* **desire** I have desired to **eat this** Passover with you **before I suffer;** [16] for I say to you, **I will**

352

no longer eat of it until it is fulfilled in the kingdom of God." [17] Then He took the cup, and gave thanks, and said, "Take this and divide *it* among yourselves; [18] for I say to you, **I will not drink of the fruit of the vine until the kingdom of God comes**." [19] And He took bread, gave thanks and broke *it,* and gave *it* to them, saying, "This is **My body which is given for you; do this in remembrance of Me**." [20] Likewise He also *took* the cup after supper, saying, "**This cup *is* the new covenant in My blood**, which is **shed for you**." (Luke 22:15–20)

The suffering and dying that Jesus spoke of at the Last Supper was fulfilled later on the cross:

After this, Jesus, knowing that **all things were now accomplished**, that the **Scripture might be fulfilled**, said, "**I thirst!**" [29] Now a vessel full of **sour wine** was sitting there; and they filled a sponge with **sour wine**, put *it* on hyssop, and **put *it* to His mouth**. [30] So **when Jesus had received the sour wine**, He said, "**It is finished!**" And bowing His head, **He gave up His spirit**. [31] Therefore, because it was the **Preparation *Day,*** that the bodies should not remain on the cross on **the Sabbath** (for **that Sabbath** was a **high day**), the Jews asked Pilate that their legs might be broken, and *that* they might be taken away. (**John 19:28–31**)

Let us notice a few important things from these passages. First, notice that when Jesus and His disciples were celebrating what we now call the Lord's Supper, the Last Supper, or Holy Communion, they were actually eating the last Passover before He died, and that Jesus said, "***With fervent* desire I have desired to eat *this* Passover** with you **before I suffer**." This was perhaps the fourth Passover Jesus had eaten with His disciples, so what made this one so special? Perhaps it was because Jesus knew it was finally the time when He would get to explain the deeper meaning of the Passover.

Perhaps what Jesus meant by these words was something like this: "See this unleavened bread that the Israelites have been breaking and eating as part of the Passover for many generations? This foreshadows My sinless body, which would be broken for you. [In the Bible, leaven is a symbol for sin and pride because it "puffs up," and "God **resists the proud but gives grace to the humble**" (**1 Peter 5:5; Proverbs 3:35**).] See this wine? This represents the **blood** of the **sacrificed lambs,** which the children of Israel originally put over the entrance to their dwelling places and repeated in later years as they sacrificed at the tabernacle and temple for ages as a remembrance of what God did to deliver them from bondage by Pharaoh in Egypt. This was a foreshadowing of My blood that I would freely sacrifice for all of you as an offer of a new covenant of love, which you are able to keep, for those who believe in Me with mind and heart may be freed from bondage by Satan on earth. For the **'life is in the blood,'** and I freely give My life out of My great love for you. And I will lay down My life for you and die on the tree that you would have died on." The tree that we would have died on is the Tree of Knowledge of Good and Evil in the garden of Eden on earth.

Whereas we use the giving of rings to symbolize the unity of two becoming One in marriage, the Jews of that time used wine to seal the marriage covenant. The groom was to provide the wine and offer it to the bride, and her drinking from the cup of wine showed that she consented to the marriage. Jesus' blood is symbolically the offer of a spiritual marriage to all those who accept and drink of it.

And this explains the curious exchange between Jesus and His earthly mother, Mary, at the wedding in Cana: "Now both Jesus and His disciples were invited to the wedding. [3] And when **they ran out of wine**, the mother of Jesus said to Him, '**They have no wine**.' [4] Jesus said to her, 'Woman, **what does your concern have to do with Me? My hour has not yet come**.' … [11] This beginning of **signs** Jesus did in Cana of Galilee, and manifested His glory; and His disciples believed in Him" (**John 2:2–4, 11**). It was the bridegroom's responsibility to provide the wine for the marriage celebration, and it was not yet Jesus' time to be the Bridegroom and provide the wine, symbolically His blood, for His marriage to His bride, the church.

Again, the mysterious John the Baptist, who was filled with the Holy Spirit from his mother's womb (**Luke 1:15**), who leapt in his mother's womb when he heard the voice of Mary when she was carrying Jesus in her womb (**Luke 1:41**), who recognized Jesus as the **Lamb of God** when Jesus came to be baptized (**John 1:29**), and who knew Jesus as the Bridegroom, and he said as much to his followers: "You yourselves bear me witness, that I said, 'I am not the Christ,' but, 'I have been sent before Him.' ²⁹ **He who has the bride is the bridegroom**; but the **friend of the bridegroom**, who stands and hears him, rejoices greatly because of the **bridegroom's voice**. Therefore this joy of mine is fulfilled" (**John 3:28–29**).

Notice also that this Passover was special in that Jesus and His disciples celebrated it early—on Thursday instead of the usual Saturday Sabbath—and that Jesus was killed on Friday, which we call "Good Friday," the day on which the spotless lamb was killed for the Passover, then called the preparation day. God instructed the Jews in the observance of the Passover that they were to kill a lamb without a spot or blemish at twilight, roast and **eat the flesh of the lamb** along with **unleavened bread** (leaven symbolized sin because it puffs up) the next day (a Jewish day is from sunset to sunset), and put the blood of the lamb on the entrance to their dwelling place (**Genesis 12:1–30**).

Jesus is the fulfillment of the Lamb of God without sin that died for **those who believed what God said** and were spared from the Destroyer of the Old Testament when God the Father **passed over** their houses to protect them from the Destroyer (because they were symbolically "under the blood of the Lamb.") This last Passover with His disciples was when Jesus would finally get to reveal that the purpose of the Passover was to foreshadow that Jesus, the Lamb of God, was a fulfillment of the Passover lamb! Also notice that John the Baptist had already recognized Jesus as the Lamb of God when he baptized Jesus in the Jordan River: "The next day **John saw Jesus coming** toward him, and said, '**Behold! The Lamb of God who takes away the sin of the world!**'" (**John 1:29**).

Now notice the words Jesus spoke at the beginning of the Passover: "I will no longer **eat of it until it is fulfilled in the kingdom of God**." The fulfillment of these words will happen when we are all together with Jesus in heaven at the marriage supper of the Lamb.

And I heard, as it were, the voice of a great multitude, as the sound of many waters and as the sound of mighty thunderings, saying, "Alleluia! For the Lord God Omnipotent reigns! [7] Let us be glad and rejoice and give Him glory, for **the marriage of the Lamb has come**, and **His wife has made herself ready**." [8] And to her it was granted to be **arrayed in fine linen**, clean and bright, for **the fine linen** is the **righteous acts of the saints**. [9] Then he said to me, "Write: 'Blessed *are* those who are **called** to the **marriage supper of the Lamb**!'" And he said to me, "These are the true sayings of God." (**Revelation 19:6–9**)

After giving the cup of wine to His disciples to drink, Jesus said, "**I will not drink of the fruit of the vine until the kingdom of God comes**." Notice that Jesus does not mention a fulfillment in heaven, as He did when speaking before the Passover meal. Instead he says "**until the kingdom of God comes**." The kingdom of God is already in heaven, so the only other place the kingdom of God could come to is on earth, where we all were formerly under the rule and reign of the prince of the air, Satan, as Paul describes to the Ephesians: "And you *He made alive,* who were **dead in trespasses and sins**, [2] in which **you once walked according to the course of this world**, according to the **prince** of the **power of the air**, the **spirit who now works** in the **sons of disobedience**, [3] among whom also **we all once conducted ourselves** in the **lusts of our flesh**, fulfilling the **desires of the flesh** and of the mind, and were **by nature children of wrath**, just as the others" (**Ephesians 2:1–3**).

Jesus confirms before He is crucified that Satan is the ruler of this world: "Now is the judgment of this world; **now the ruler of this world will be cast out**. [32] And I, **if I am lifted up from the earth**, will **draw all** *peoples* **to Myself**" (**John 12:31–32**).

Then notice the words of Jesus in **John 19:28–30**, which describe Christ's last moments on the cross before He died: "After this, Jesus, **knowing that all things were now accomplished**, that the **Scripture might be fulfilled**, said, '**I thirst!**' [29] Now a vessel full of **sour wine** was sitting there; and they filled a sponge with **sour wine**, put *it* on hyssop, and put *it* to His mouth. [30] So when **Jesus had**

received the sour wine, He said, '**It is finished!**' And bowing His head, He gave up His **spirit**."

After Jesus refused wine earlier, **Mark 15:23** states that the following occurred: "Then **they gave Him wine** mingled with myrrh to drink, but **He did not take *it*.**" Jesus now, moments before His death, says, "**I thirst!**" Then, after He has drank of the sour wine, Jesus says, "**It is finished!**" and He bows His head in death and gives up His spirit. Jesus did this drinking of wine at the precise moment of His death as a sign to us that the kingdom of God has come to earth and that the kingdom of God is right here, right now. This is the fulfillment of His promise that He made earlier at the Last Supper: "**I will not drink of the fruit of the vine until the kingdom of God comes.**"

The Last Supper promise "I will no longer **eat of it until it is fulfilled in the kingdom of God**" and drinking of the sour wine as Jesus says, "**It is finished!**" is the answer to the earlier prayers of Jesus and His disciples who prayed the Lord's Prayer: "In this manner, therefore, pray: **Our Father in heaven**, Hallowed be Your name. [10] **Your kingdom come**. Your will be done **On earth as *it is* in heaven**. [11] Give us this day our daily **bread**. [12] And forgive us our debts, As we forgive our debtors. [13] And do not lead us into temptation, **But deliver us from the evil one**. For **Yours is the kingdom** and the **power and the glory forever**" [**Matthew 6:9–10**].)

The kingdom of God came to the earth after Jesus' sacrifice on the cross, and His kingdom will be fully established when He returns to earth to conquer His and our enemy forever: "The **devil, who deceived them**, was **cast into the lake of fire and brimstone** where the **beast** and the **false prophet *are*.** And they will be tormented day and night forever and ever ... Then **Death and Hades** were cast into the lake of fire. **This is the second death**. [15] And anyone not found written in **the Book of Life** was cast into the lake of fire" (**Revelation 20:10, 14–15**).

And as a sign that the kingdom of God had come to earth, and that the separation of God and man was over, "Jesus cried out again with a loud voice, and **yielded up His spirit**. [51] Then, **behold**, the **veil of**

the temple was torn in two from top to bottom; and the earth quaked, and the rocks were split, [52] and the graves were opened; and **many bodies of the saints** who had **fallen asleep were raised**" (**Matthew 27:50–52**). The tearing of the temple veil is symbolic for the removal of the veil that kept man from understanding in the Old Testament, which is the truth that Jesus came into the world to teach us and is spoken of in **2 Corinthians 3:14**: "But **their minds were blinded. For until this day** the **same veil remains unlifted** in the **reading of the Old Testament**, because **the** *veil* **is taken away in Christ**. [15] But even to this day, when Moses is read, **a veil lies on their heart**. [16] Nevertheless **when one turns to the Lord**, the **veil is taken away**."

And this coming of the kingdom of God to earth after Jesus' sacrifice on the cross is in agreement with what Jesus said before His transfiguration: "When He had called the people to *Himself,* with His disciples also … And He said to them, 'Assuredly, I say to you that **there are some standing here who will not taste death till they see the kingdom of God present with power'**" (**Mark 8:34a; 9:1**).

Finally, let us all be perfectly clear on the meaning of the breaking and eating of bread in communion and why we continue to do it in celebration of the Lord's Last Supper. As Jesus said, "**This is My body** which is **given for you; do this in remembrance of Me**." It is Jesus' selfless act of unconditional, sacrificial love for us—suffering and dying on a cross in our place and offering a loving, spiritual, marriage-like relationship to those who trust and believe in Him—that has saved us. The eating of the bread and drinking of the wine no more enables us to be united in One with Jesus than putting on rings makes men and women united in marriage on earth. It is the love in the heart and mind that join us together as One on earth or in heaven. Why do we eat this bread and drink this wine? Just like the Jews who previously ate the Passover, we do so to help them remember and not forget what God had done to deliver them from bondage in Egypt; the Lord's Supper is intended to remind us that we may never forget what Jesus the Christ, the Son of God Most High, has done for us to free us from bondage to Satan on earth.

Jesus, who is the Lamb of God, is the fulfillment of the Old Testament sacrificial lamb whose sacrifice saves those who are "under the blood of the lamb" and whose flesh we symbolically eat during the Lord's Supper, which was the last Passover that Jesus ate with His disciples and which was eaten early so that Jesus could be crucified on the exact day that the lamb was killed for the Jewish Passover in the Old Testament.

But what if someone should say, **"How can Jesus die for our sins and save us? After all, God said that if you eat of the fruit of the Tree of Knowledge of Good and Evil, you will surely die, and God's word cannot be broken."**

THE PLAN OF SALVATION

In the third age, known as the church age, God has come into the world He created to tell us of the truth about the ways of the kingdom of God that lead to peace, prosperity, joy inexpressible, and eternal life, after previously showing us that we cannot live for ourselves by ourselves (as Lucifer said, trapping us with his lie). And if we, after suffering under Satan on earth, are willing to listen to God, learn and understand with our minds the truth that will make us free, confess that we were wrong, and with our hearts and minds turn from our ways to the ways of God and be saved, why did Jesus have to suffer and die?

How can God offer forgiveness to some and not others who committed the same offense and still be fair and just? And—a question that divides the church of God—is salvation arrived at by faith or by good works? And how is it that we can be reconciled to God and free from our sentence of death? After all, God said that if we ate of the Tree of Knowledge of Good and Evil—which is a metaphor for believing the ways of Satan, which are evil—we shall surely die. And as we learned in "The Beginning as Seen From Earth," we all ate of the evil fruit of that tree when we believed Satan's lies and followed Satan; the act of eating the fruit symbolically represents our belief in the lies of Lucifer in heaven. We rejected the warning of God that we **"shall surely die."**

And when God speaks a word, what He has said is sure to be done. As God the Father says to the prophet Isaiah, "Remember the former things, those of long ago; **I am God** and **there is no other**; **I am God** and **there is none like Me**. I make known the end from the beginning, from ancient times **what is still to come**. I say: **My purpose will stand**, and **I will do all that I please**. From the east I will summon a bird of prey; from a far off land, a man to **fulfill My purpose**. **What I have said**, **that will I bring about**; **what I have planned**, **that will I do**" (**Isaiah 46:9–11**). And He says again to the prophet Isaiah, "So shall **My word be** that **goes forth from My mouth**; It shall not **return to Me void**, But **it shall accomplish what I please**, And **it shall prosper** *in the thing* **for which I sent it**" (**Isaiah 55:11**). And Jesus, the Son of God, confirms that His Father's word cannot be broken: "Jesus answered them, 'Is it not written in your law, *"I said, 'You are gods"?'* [35] If **He called them gods**, **to whom the word of God came** (and **the Scripture cannot be broken**), [36] do you say of Him whom the Father sanctified and sent into the world, 'You are blaspheming,' because I said, 'I am the Son of God'?" (**John 10:34–36**).

These are all good questions. Let us look to God's Word for the answers:

GOD IS RIGHTEOUS BECAUSE HE CAN SEE INTO THE HEARTS OF MAN

Let us review the situation that fallen man was in on earth. Having believed the lies of Lucifer in heaven that we could do better on our own without God, we rejected our Creator and King and believed and followed Satan, whom God created, in his rebellion against God. So in heaven we were already guilty of committing treason, a crime worthy of death because it destroys the unity and Oneness of the governing kingdom, which as we learned in the chapter "The Tree of Life," is vital to the lives of the citizens.

Thus, rebellion brings death to the kingdom, which brings death to all individuals, and that is why God the Father said that being alone is not good—because we need a loving community united together as One to prosper and live forever.

> And the LORD God said, '*It is* **not good that man should be alone**; I will make him **a helper** comparable to him.' (Genesis 2:18).

> **If a kingdom is divided against itself, that kingdom cannot stand**. (Mark 3:24)

In examining the age of anarchy, we learned how evil things can get when there is no rule and no order, and we also learned that even a bad government is better than no government at all.

In this rebellion in the kingdom of heaven, God could have carried out the death sentence right then and there, and if it had been any other king but God, he would have had to do that to try to keep order and unity in the kingdom. Imagine what would happen in any other kingdom if one-third of its citizens rebelled against their ruler. Well, we do not have to imagine, because human history has seen the collapse of nations over and over again, and we still see it happening today. Man does not know what it takes to create a kingdom that has peace, prosperity, unspeakable joy, and a life that endures forever.

But God, because He can see into the hearts and minds of those He created, can correctly determine their character and nature, and He knows who is speaking the truth. Thus, he can reign by a better set of rules than man and still be fair and just in His judgments. God can offer forgiveness and mercy to those whom He knows can have a change of heart and mind and be reformed, transformed, reconciled, or, as Jesus calls it, "born again." When we believed the lies of Lucifer, we were born of the flesh of Satan's world, but when we believe the truth of God, we are saved to be born again of the Spirit of God's kingdom.

Man can only create laws and try to judge as best as he can. And he can try to create rehabilitation programs for the lawbreakers, but many times justice is not served. And when the righteous are condemned and the guilty are set free, there is no faith in the government of the kingdom and there is dissension and division in the kingdom. And if other kings offer forgiveness without assurance of justice, there is favoritism and partiality, and again there is dissension and division in the kingdom. And we know about division in kingdoms from Jesus: "Every kingdom **divided against itself** is **brought to desolation,** and every city or house **divided against itself will not stand**" (**Matthew 12:25b**). And Paul confirms that God does not play favorites: "For **there is no partiality with God.** [12] For as many as have sinned without law will also **perish without law,** and as many as have sinned in the law will be **judged by the law**" (**Romans 2:11–12**). God is fair and just. And all this is exactly what the apostle Paul teaches:

> But now the **righteousness of God apart from the law is revealed,** being **witnessed** by the **Law and the Prophets,** [22] even the **righteousness of God,** through **faith in Jesus Christ,** to all and on **all who believe.** For there is no difference; [23] for **all have sinned** and **fall short of the glory of God,** [24] being **justified freely by His grace** through the redemption that is in Christ Jesus, [25] whom God set forth *as* a **propitiation by His blood,** through **faith,** to **demonstrate His righteousness,** because in His **forbearance** God had **passed over** the sins that were **previously committed,** [26] to **demonstrate** at the present time **His righteousness,** that He might be **just and the justifier of the one** who has **faith in Jesus.** (**Romans 3:21–26**)

God's righteousness is different from man's righteousness.

> For they being **ignorant of God's righteousness,** and **seeking to establish their own righteousness,** have not **submitted** to the **righteousness of God.** [4] For **Christ** *is* the **end of the law for righteousness** to **everyone who believes.** (**Romans 10:3–4**)

> There is **a way** *that seems* **right to a man,** But **its end** *is* the **way of death.** (**Proverbs 14:12**)

God's righteousness is different from man's righteousness in that He can offer us forgiveness and give us, who were ignorant and had never lived with evil before, a second chance to learn by experience what the result of our bad choice is like. He can also give us an opportunity to change our mind, repent, and ask for forgiveness before God executes final judgment. So God gives those who accept His offer of a second chance a temporary life on a temporary earth, living under the ruler that we chose, the prince of this world, Satan. And God puts us in a body of flesh so that we cannot remember the glorious life we had with God in heaven so that we will not choose God out of selfish reasons. But after we have experienced evil for ourselves and come to understand and believe the ways of God are truth and love leading to unity and oneness, peace, prosperity, unspeakable joy, and eternal life, Jesus can reconcile us to God the Father, our Creator.

The kingdom of God is not one where in which God uses His superior power and might to force people to do what He wants them to do. The kingdom of God is one of freedom and of a free will to choose to live by the ways of God or not. God says,

> See, I have **set before you** today **life and good, death and evil**, [16] in that I command you today to **love the LORD your God**, to **walk in His ways**, and to **keep His commandments, His statutes,** and **His judgments**, that **you may live and multiply**; and the LORD your God will bless you in the land which you go to possess. [17] But **if your heart turns away** so that you **do not hear**, and are **drawn away**, and **worship other gods and serve them**, [18] I **announce** to you today **that you shall surely perish**; you shall **not prolong** *your* **days** in the land which you cross over the Jordan to go in and possess.
>
> [19] **I call heaven and earth as witnesses today against you**, *that* **I have set before you life** and **death, blessing** and **cursing**; therefore **choose life**, that both you and your descendants **may live**; [20] that you may **love the LORD your God**, that you **may obey His voice**, and that you may **cling to Him**, for **He** *is* **your life** and the **length of your days**; and that you may **dwell in the land which the LORD swore to your fathers**, to **Abraham**, Isaac, and Jacob, to give them. (**Deuteronomy 30:19–20**)

As we have learned, when we love to do what we are commanded to do, obeying those commands becomes a moot point. The righteous judgment of God will be to give those who still believe in the ways of Satan exactly what they want—to live with Satan in his ways, under his rule and reign forever.

The book of Revelation describes what that end result of God's judgment will be:

> **The devil, who deceived them**, was **cast into the lake of fire and brimstone where the beast** and the **false prophet** *are*. And they **will be tormented day and night forever and ever**. [11] Then I saw a **great white throne** and Him who sat on it, from whose face the earth and the heaven fled away. And **there was found no place for them**. [12] And I saw **the dead, small and great, standing before God**, and books were opened. And another book was opened, which is *the Book* **of Life**. And **the dead were judged according to their works**, by the things **which were written in the books**. [13] The sea gave up the dead who were in it, and Death and Hades delivered up the dead who were in them. And **they were judged, each one according to his works**. [14] Then **Death and Hades were cast into the lake of fire**. This is **the second death**. [15] And anyone **not found** written in **the Book of Life** was cast into the lake of fire. (**Revelation 20:10**)

So the nature of God to see into the hearts and minds of those He created is what allows Him to offer forgiveness and still be fair and just in His judgment. But how should we answer someone if he or she should ask, **"How can the death of Jesus save us who are condemned to death**?**"**

That we are all still under condemnation on this earth is confirmed by the words of Jesus: "For **God did not send His Son** into **the world to condemn the world**, but that **the world through Him might be saved**. [18] **He who believes in Him is not condemned**; but **he who does not believe is condemned already**, because he **has not believed** in the **name** of the **only begotten Son of God**" (**John 3:17–18**). Jesus' name actually means "God Saves." When we believe in Jesus' name, we are believing that God saves.

Now we have learned that the condemnation stemmed from the rebellion in heaven, when we were spirits or angels in heaven. God had chosen Jesus to be our King, but we rejected God and Jesus, preferring to believe and follow Lucifer. But God did not execute the judgment of death while we were angelic spirits in heaven; He gave us a second chance at life and deferred execution of His judgment until after we live a life on earth in a body of flesh. This is important, because the righteousness of God means loving God above all else and loving our neighbors as ourselves. Love satisfies the law of sin and death, and as we learned in "The Oneness Branch," love is the only thing that can unite us together as One with God. And it is Oneness with Jesus that enables us to be saved.

The apostle Paul compares the Oneness of Christ with the human body:

> "For as **the body is one** and **has many members**, but **all the members** of that **one body, being many, are one body, so also** *is* **Christ**. [13] For **by one Spirit** we were all **baptized into one body** – whether Jews or Greeks, whether slaves or free–and have all been made to **drink into one Spirit**. [14] For in fact **the body is not one member but many** ... And those *members* of the body which we think to be less honorable, on these we bestow greater honor; and our unpresentable *parts* have greater modesty, [24] but our presentable *parts* have no need. But God composed the body, having given greater honor to that *part* which lacks it, [25] **that there should be no schism in the body**, but *that* **the members should have the same care for one another**. [26] And **if one member suffers, all the members suffer with** *it;* or **if one member is honored, all the members rejoice with** *it*. [27] Now **you are the body of Christ, and members individually**." (1 Corinthians 12:12–14, 23–27)

Because God proclaims He will execute the judgment of death of the condemned while we are in the flesh on earth and not while we are spirits in heaven, this allows Jesus to come in the flesh, and by entering into an agape loving relationship with those who understand the truth, He can become One in the flesh with us. And putting on flesh like we did is exactly what the author Hebrews says Jesus did: "Inasmuch then as the **children have partaken of flesh and blood**, He Himself

likewise shared in the same, that **through death** He might destroy him who had the power of death, that is, the **devil**" (**Hebrews 2:14**).

Because we are One with Him and in Him, when He dies, we all die with Him, and in that, we fulfill the commandment of God that we die in the flesh, and His word is not broken. Oneness allows Jesus, out of His great love for us, to figuratively die on the tree that we would have died on, the Tree of Knowledge of Good and Evil! And our loving relationship with Jesus fulfills the law of sin and death because love fulfills the law. It was the loss of Oneness with God in Christ that caused us to be on the path of death in the first place. And it is the restoration of Oneness with God in Christ that saves us and gives us eternal life.

THE GREAT MYSTERY, MARRIAGE, IS LIKE ONENESS IN CHRIST

And as we learned in "The Oneness Branch," this Oneness in the flesh with Jesus is like human marriage:

> Husbands, **love your wives, just as Christ also loved the church** and **gave Himself for her**, [26] that He might **sanctify** and cleanse her with the **washing of water by the word**, [27] that He might present her to Himself a glorious church, not having spot or wrinkle or any such thing, but **that she should be holy** and **without blemish**. [28] So **husbands** ought to **love their own wives as their own bodies**; he who **loves his wife loves himself**. [29] For no one ever **hated his own flesh**, but nourishes and cherishes it, **just as the Lord *does* the church**. [30] For **we are members of His body**, of **His flesh** and of **His bones**. [31] *"For this reason a man shall leave his father and mother and be joined to his wife, and the two shall become **one flesh**."* [32] **This is a great mystery**, but I speak concerning **Christ and the church**." (**Ephesians 5:25–32**)

This Oneness of marriage in the flesh is a depiction and foreshadowing of how those of us who believe are in Christ and are united with Him. In marriage to Christ, we become One with Him. We cease being self-centered and become other centered. Our identity is in Christ and no longer in our self. In Oneness, others become our self. Our sin was a crime worthy of death, and Jesus died to pay that debt. Even in human marriage, when a man and a woman are married they become one legal entity and the debts and assets of each is shared by the other. We are One in good times and in bad, in sickness and in health, for richer or poorer.

When we enter into marriage with Christ, we become One with Him and our debts become His. While we are not able to pay our debt, He can, and He does. As Jesus' bride, we who are submitted to Him also share all that He has, just as all that the Father has also belongs to Jesus: **"All things that the Father has are Mine**. Therefore I said that He will take of Mine and declare *it* to you" (**John 16:15**). Because we are all One in Jesus, when He died, we all died; and because He lives, we all live.

This is why Christ's suffering and dying on the cross did not reconcile everyone to the Father. It can only reconcile those who desire to enter into a loving, marriage-like relationship with Jesus that makes us united as One in Him with us submitting to Him as our spiritual husband and head, as Paul describes to the Colossians:

> And He is the **head of the body**, the **church**, who is the beginning, the **firstborn from the dead**, that in all things He may have the **preeminence**. [19] For it pleased *the Father that* **in Him all the fullness should dwell**, [20] and by Him to **reconcile all things to Himself**, by **Him**, whether **things on earth** or **things in heaven**, having made **peace** through the **blood of His cross**.
>
> [21] And you, who once were **alienated** and **enemies in your mind** by **wicked works**, yet now He has **reconciled** [22] in the **body of His flesh** through **death**, to present you holy, and blameless, and above reproach in His sight– [23] if indeed you **continue in the faith**, grounded and steadfast, and are not moved away from the **hope of the gospel** which you heard. (**Colossians 1:18–23a**)

The hope of the gospel is the hope of eternal life in Christ Jesus.

GOD IS RIGHTEOUS BECAUSE HE CONDEMNED SIN IN THE FLESH

That God did not condemn sin in the spirit but condemned sin in the flesh is exactly what Paul teaches the Romans and us:

> *There is* therefore now **no condemnation to those who are in Christ Jesus,** who do not walk **according to the flesh,** but **according to the Spirit.** [2] For the **law of the Spirit of life in Christ Jesus** has **made me free** from **the law of sin and death.** [3] For what the law could not do in that it was weak through the flesh, God *did* by sending His own Son **in the likeness of sinful flesh,** on account of sin: **He condemned sin in the flesh,** [4] that the **righteous requirement of the law** might be **fulfilled in us who do not walk according to the flesh but according to the Spirit.** [5] For those who live according to the flesh set their minds on the things of the flesh, but **those** *who live* **according to the Spirit,** the **things of the Spirit.**
>
> [6] For to be **carnally minded** *is* **death,** but to be **spiritually minded** *is* **life and peace.** [7] Because **the carnal mind** *is* **enmity against God;** for it is not subject to the **law of God,** nor indeed can be. [8] So then, **those who are in the flesh cannot please God.** [9] But you are not in the flesh but in the Spirit, **if indeed the Spirit of God dwells in you.** Now if anyone **does not have the Spirit of Christ, he is not His.** [10] And **if Christ** *is* **in you, the body** *is* **dead because of sin,** but the **Spirit** *is* **life because of righteousness.** [11] But if the Spirit of Him who raised Jesus from the dead dwells in you, **He who raised Christ from the dead** will also **give life to your mortal bodies** through **His Spirit who dwells in you.** **(Romans 8:1–11)**

Paul teaches us an amazing truth about Oneness in God:

> Now all things *are* of God, who has **reconciled us to Himself through Jesus Christ,** and has given us the ministry of **reconciliation,** [19] that is, that **God was in Christ reconciling the world to Himself,** not imputing their trespasses to them,

and has committed to us the word of reconciliation. [20] Now then, we are ambassadors for Christ, as though **God were pleading through us**: we implore *you* on Christ's behalf, **be reconciled to God**. [21] For **He made Him who knew no sin** *to be* **sin for us**, that we might become **the righteousness of God in Him**. (**2 Corinthians 5:18–21**)

Not only were we in Jesus Christ when He died to save us from our sins, but God the Father was in Christ, suffering with Jesus, reconciling Himself to the world. And we have learned that when we are many in One, "**if one member suffers, all the members suffer with** *it*" (**1 Corinthians 12:26**). Because the Father and Son are One, God the Father suffered with Jesus when He suffered and died to save us. What amazing love God the Father has for us!

And if we are in Christ and died with Him when He died to reconcile us to God the Father, then our lives on earth should reflect this dying to this life in the flesh and living for Christ in the unspeakable joy of the Spirit, as Paul teaches:

For if we are **beside ourselves**, *it is* for God; or if we are of sound mind, *it is* for you. [14] For **the love of Christ compels us**, because we judge thus: that if one **died for all**, then **all died**; [15] and **He died for all**, that **those who live** should **live no longer for themselves**, but **for Him who died for them** and **rose again**. [16] Therefore, from now on, **we regard no one according to the flesh**. Even though we have known Christ according to the flesh, yet **now we know** *Him thus* **no longer**. [17] Therefore, **if anyone** *is* **in Christ**, *he is* **a new creation**; old things have passed away; behold, **all things have become new**. (**2 Corinthians 5:13–17**)

It seems as though Paul is saying that Christians who live with unspeakable joy have to tone it down to be able to relate to those who are still living in misery and sorrow. And that is why Paul cries out to the Romans, saying,

I beseech you therefore, brethren, by the mercies of God, that **you present your bodies a living sacrifice, holy, acceptable to God,** *which is* **your reasonable service**. [2] And **do not**

be conformed to this world, but be **transformed by the renewing of your mind,** that you may **prove** what *is* that good and acceptable and perfect will of God. ³ For I say, through the grace given to me, to everyone who is among you, **not to think** *of himself* **more highly than he ought to think,** but **to think soberly,** as God has dealt to each one a measure of faith. ⁴ For as we have **many members in one body,** but all the members do not have the same function, ⁵ so **we,** *being* **many,** are **one body in Christ,** and individually **members of one another.** **(Romans 12:1–5)**

A living sacrifice is one who has died to the thinking and living by the ways of this world of Satan, is believing and living for eternal life with Christ in heaven, and is willing to sacrifice his or her life in the flesh, if necessary, for faith in Jesus, as He implores us all:

And do not **fear those who kill the body** but cannot **kill the soul.** But rather fear Him who is able to **destroy both soul** and **body in hell.** **(Matthew 10:28)**

When He had called the people to *Himself,* with His disciples also, He said to them, "Whoever desires to come after Me, **let him deny himself,** and **take up his cross,** and **follow Me.** ³⁵ For whoever **desires to save his life will lose it,** but whoever **loses his life for My sake** and the **gospel's will save it.** ³⁶ For **what will it profit a man** if he **gains the whole world,** and **loses his own soul?** ³⁷ Or what will a **man give in exchange for his soul?"** **(Mark 8:34–37)**

ARE WE RECONCILIED WITH GOD BY FAITH OR BY GOOD WORKS?

Let us consider the words of the apostle Peter:

And if you call on the Father, who **without partiality judges according to each one's work,** conduct yourselves throughout **the time of your stay** *here* in fear; ¹⁸ knowing that you were **not redeemed** with corruptible things, *like* **silver or gold,** from your **aimless conduct** *received* by **tradition from your**

fathers, [19] but with the **precious blood of Christ,** as of a **lamb without blemish** and **without spot.** [20] He indeed was **foreordained before the foundation of the world,** but was manifest **in these last times** for you [21] who **through Him believe in God,** who raised Him from the dead and gave Him glory, so that **your faith** and **hope are in God. (1 Peter 1:17–21)**

The issue of whether our reconciliation with God comes by our works or by our faith is an important issue because it divides Jesus' church. Here Peter says that we are being judged by our **works** and in the same passage talks about being redeemed by Jesus' blood for those "who through Him **believe** in God ... so that **your faith** and **hope** are in God." So what if someone should ask, **"Are we reconciled to God the Father by faith in Jesus as our Savior and King or by the good works we do?"**

Indeed we are going to be judged by what we say and do, for Jesus speaks of the day of judgment in many places. But the Bible specifically describes being judged by what we do and say in **2 Corinthians 5:10**: "For we must **all appear before the judgment seat of Christ,** that each one may receive the **things** *done* **in the body,** according to **what he has done, whether good or bad.**" Of course, **"believe"** is the verb, and **"faith"** is the noun of the same concept, and "faith" and "belief" share the same meaning. So how can salvation of our souls be arrived at both by faith and by works? The understanding of this subject is so important to the unity of the church of Jesus Christ that it requires us to look not at just one or two verses but at the full counsel of the Word of God. Let us consider some passages that speak of what is necessary for reconciliation with God.

In the Gospel of Matthew, Jesus teaches that we will be judged by the words we speak: "Brood of vipers! How can you, **being evil, speak good things?** For **out of the abundance of the heart the mouth speaks.** [35] A good man **out of the good treasure of his heart** brings forth **good things,** and an evil man **out of the evil treasure** brings forth **evil things.** [36] But I say to you that **for every idle word men may speak,** they will **give account of it in the day of judgment.**

[37] For **by your words you will be justified**, and **by your words you will be condemned**" (**Matthew 12:34–37**). Here Jesus is saying that the source of good and evil words and deeds is the condition of the mind and heart. In the long run we will do and say what our heart desires, whether good or evil.

In a vision, the apostle John saw what the judgment will be like: "Then I saw a **great white throne** and Him who sat on it, from whose face the earth and the heaven fled away. And there was found no place for them. [12] And I saw the dead, small and great, standing before God, and books were opened. And another book was opened, which is *the Book of Life*. And **the dead were judged according to their works**, by the things which were **written in the books**" (**Revelation 20:12**).

Also, recall that we learned that this life on earth was given to us not only to prove to all of us that the ways of God are eternal life and the ways of Satan lead to corruption, misery, sorrow, and death, as God said; but also to show that God's judgment in heaven of who were good and who were evil—those who are the elect and those who are not—was righteous because He can see into hearts and minds to judge fairly. And to prove to those who cannot see into hearts and minds, He had to repeat the judgment by putting us in bodies of flesh to live a virtual, temporary life on this temporary earth He created so that all could see by their words and deeds that God's judgment is true and fair. In the end, He will have to separate us, because if good and evil remain together, all will die.

Good works are always good, but when it comes to reconciliation with God the Father, the intent of our good works is critical. If we are trying, by our good deeds and by obeying the law, to show that we are righteous all by ourselves—then we are still believing the lies of Satan and not believing the truth of Jesus. The purpose of whole Old Testament is to show us that we cannot live righteously in peace with prosperity, unspeakable joy, and eternal life by living as individuals separated from the loving unity in God. This cannot be accomplished even with many laws, because where there is a need for laws, there are sinful people:

Therefore **by the deeds of the law no flesh will be justified in His sight**, for **by the law** *is* **the knowledge of sin.** ²¹ But now the **righteousness of God apart from the law is revealed**, being witnessed by the Law and the Prophets, ²² even **the righteousness of God**, through **faith in Jesus Christ**, to all and on all **who believe**. For there is no difference;

> ²³ for **all have sinned** and **fall short** of the glory of God, ²⁴ being **justified freely by His grace** through the **redemption** that is in Christ Jesus, ²⁵ whom God set forth *as* a **propitiation** by His blood, through **faith**, to **demonstrate His righteousness**, because in His forbearance God had **passed over** the sins that were previously committed, ²⁶ to **demonstrate** at the **present time His righteousness**, that **He might be just** and the **justifier of the one** who has **faith in Jesus.** ²⁷ Where *is* boasting then? It is excluded. By what law? Of **works**? No, but **by the law of faith.** ²⁸ Therefore we conclude that **a man is justified by faith** apart from the **deeds of the law. (Romans 3:20–28)**

> For if Abraham **was justified by works**, he has *something* **to boast about**, but **not before God.** ³ For what does the Scripture say? *"Abraham believed God, and it was accounted to him for righteousness."* ⁴ Now to **him who works**, the **wages are not counted as grace** but as **debt.** ⁵ But to him who does not work but **believes on Him** who **justifies the ungodly**, his **faith is accounted for righteousness. (Romans 4:2–5)**

Paul teaches that the purpose of God for life on this earth was to create us in His image *for good works*:

> And you *He made alive,* who were **dead in trespasses and sins,** ² in which **you once walked** according to **the course of this world**, according to the **prince of the power of the air**, the **spirit who now works** in the **sons of disobedience,** ³ among whom also **we all once conducted ourselves** in the **lusts of our flesh,** fulfilling **the desires of the flesh** and of the mind, and **were by nature children of wrath, just as the others.**

> ⁴ But God, **who is rich in mercy,** because of **His great love** with which **He loved us,** ⁵ even when we were **dead in trespasses**, made us **alive together with Christ** (by grace

373

you have been saved), **⁶** and **raised us up together**, and made **us sit together** in the **heavenly** *places* **in Christ Jesus**, **⁷** that in the **ages to come** He might show the exceeding riches of **His grace in** *His* **kindness** toward **us in Christ Jesus**. **⁸** For **by grace** you have been **saved through faith**, and that **not of yourselves**; *it is* the **gift of God**, **⁹** not of works, lest anyone should boast. **¹⁰** For we are His workmanship, **created in Christ Jesus for good works**, which God **prepared beforehand** that **we should walk in them**. (Ephesians 2:1–10)

"Even so then, at this present time **there is a remnant** according to the **election of grace**. **⁶** And if **by grace**, then *it is* **no longer of works**; otherwise **grace is no longer grace**. But **if** *it is* **of works**, it is **no longer grace; otherwise work is no longer work**" (Romans 11:6). To work is to earn something good by what you do. A gift or grace is something good that is received without one having done anything to deserve it. God chose us in Him because of who we are, not because of what we have done. But who we are will determine what we do. What we believe in our mind and desire in our heart determines what we say and what we do. God can see what is in our hearts and minds, but the purpose of our words and deeds is to show those who cannot see into our minds and hearts who we are and what our nature is, whether good or evil.

Paul, a Jew himself, challenged other Jews who thought they were not sinners, such as the Gentiles, who did not know God:

We *who are* Jews by nature, and not sinners of the Gentiles, **¹⁶** knowing that **a man is not justified** by the **works of the law** but by **faith in Jesus Christ**, even we have **believed in Christ Jesus**, that we might be **justified by faith in Christ** and **not by the works of the law**; for by the **works of the law no flesh shall be justified**.

¹⁷ But if, while we seek to be **justified by Christ**, we ourselves also **are found sinners**, *is* Christ therefore a minister of sin? Certainly not! **¹⁸** For if I build again those things which I destroyed, I make myself a transgressor. **¹⁹** For **I through the law died to the law** that I **might live to God**. **²⁰** I have been **crucified with Christ**; it is no longer I who live, but **Christ lives in me**; and the *life* which I now live in the flesh **I live by faith in the Son of God**, who **loved me** and **gave Himself for me**. [21] I do not set aside the **grace of God**; for if **righteousness** *comes* **through the law**, then **Christ died in vain**. **(Galatians 2:16)**

This is where we need to distinguish what we mean by "works." If we claim that we can be righteous by doing the things that the law requires, that is self-righteousness and that is claiming that we are justified by our own good works. Then that cuts out the need for the gift of righteousness that comes from unity with Christ and being saved by His death out of His love for us and our love for Him. This is the thinking of Satan, which will lead to our death. As we learned in the second age, when we live by the works of the law, we all die. But if "works" means that we have been saved by understanding and believing in the ways of God and then doing good works out of the desire of our hearts, then that is the evidence of the righteousness of God and the evidence of the kind of "works" that will save us for eternal life.

The letter of Paul written to Titus teaches us how love can change our fallen nature:

For **we ourselves** were also **once foolish, disobedient, deceived**, serving various **lusts and pleasures**, living in **malice** and **envy, hateful** and **hating one another**. [4] But when the **kindness** and the **love of God our Savior** toward man appeared, [5] **not by works of righteousness which we have done**, but **according to His mercy He saved us**, through the washing of regeneration and **renewing of the Holy Spirit**, [6] whom He **poured out on us** abundantly through Jesus Christ our Savior, [7] that having been **justified by His grace** we should become heirs according to the **hope** of **eternal life**. [8] This is a faithful saying, and these things I want you to affirm constantly, that **those who have believed in God** should be careful **to maintain good works**. These things are good and profitable to men. **(Titus 3:3–8)**

Our good works are the evidence of faith that cannot be seen with the human eye.

James, the earthly brother of Christ, teaches us that faith in Jesus means not merely acknowledging who He is. James states that faith comes by diligently seeking to know and understand the truth that can make us free from the lies of Satan that trapped us. And that truth is found in His Holy Word, which God gave to us to know who He is, along with the many miraculous evidences of who He is in His life on earth and in this incredible world He created.

If we will only stop and seek to know Him, all this knowledge and understanding of the truth will produce in us changed minds and hearts that love and care for our brothers and sisters.

> **What *does it* profit**, my brethren, if someone says he **has faith** but **does not have works**? Can faith save him? [15] If a brother or sister is naked and destitute of daily food, [16] and one of you says to them, "Depart in peace, be warmed and filled," but you do not give them the things which are needed for the body, what *does it* profit? [17] Thus also **faith by itself**, if it **does not have works, is dead**. [18] But someone will say, "**You have faith**, and **I have works**." Show me **your faith without your works**, and I will show you **my faith by my works**. [19] You **believe that there is one God**. You do well. **Even the demons believe–and tremble**! (**James 2:14–19**)

Good works are the evidence of the faith in Jesus Christ that a believer already has. Blind faith without any evidence to show that it is based on truth is what we had when we believed the lies of Lucifer and followed him on a path that leads to our death. But Jesus said to Saul, a devout man who believed he was doing the work of God but in reality was persecuting Jesus' church, "I will deliver you from the *Jewish* people, as well as *from* the Gentiles, to whom I now send you, [18] **to open their eyes**, *in order* to **turn *them* from darkness to light**, and *from* the **power of Satan to God**, that they may receive **forgiveness of sins** and **an inheritance** among **those who are sanctified** by **faith in Me**" (**Acts 26:17**). God can use anyone who has a heart and mind for God, even if he or she does not yet understand the truth. God can and will teach anyone who is willing to listen with an open mind and a teachable heart.

James continues:

> [20] But do you **want to** know, O foolish man, that **faith without works is dead**? [21] Was not Abraham our father **justified by works** when **he offered Isaac his son on the altar**? [22] Do you see that **faith was working together with his works**, and **by works faith** was **made perfect**? [23] And the Scripture was fulfilled which says, "*Abraham believed God, and it was accounted to him for righteousness.*" And he was called the friend of God. [24] You see then that **a man is justified by works**, and **not by faith only**. [25] Likewise, was not Rahab the harlot also **justified by works** when she received the messengers and sent *them* out another way? [26] For as the **body without the spirit is dead**, so **faith without works is dead also**. (James 2:13)

Good works is the evidence of faith that is invisible to those who cannot see into the heart and mind like God. And that was one of the reasons God had to put us in bodies of flesh and allow us to live a life on earth—so that all the angels in heaven and on earth could see by our words and deeds that God's judgment was accurate, fair, and just.

THE DIVIDED CHURCH OF CHRIST UNITED AS ONE

The two doctrines of faith and works concerning the Bible divided the Church of Rome in the sixteenth century, when Luther and other Protestants sought to reform the Church of Rome. The biblical doctrine of the Protestants was that justification, or reconciliation, with God could be made "**by grace alone through faith alone because of Christ alone**." This was contrary, or they so both the Protestants and Catholics thought, to the doctrine of the Roman Catholic Church, which taught that we were justified or reconciled to God "**by faith formed by love**," or "**faith and works**." What they did not understand then is that they were both right.

This is how God is going to unite His church in One—by helping us to understand that faith and love and good works are all necessary for reconciliation with God. We cannot truly love someone if we do not have faith in who they are that we may put our full, undivided, trust in them. We do not love someone if we do not help them in the time of their great need.

Faith is the beginning of what we need now on earth to save us, but a loving relationship with God and one another is the goal of our faith after we understand the truth, for we learned that God is a god of Love and God is love: "Beloved, let us love one another, for **love is of God**; and everyone who loves is **born of God** and knows God. [8] He who does not love does not know God, for **God is love**" (**1 John 4:7–8**).

The supremacy of love over faith and works is clearly seen in **1 Corinthians 13:2–3**: "And though I have *the gift of* prophecy, and understand all mysteries and all knowledge, and **though I have all faith**, so that **I could remove mountains**, but **have not love, I am nothing**. [3] And though I bestow all my goods to feed *the poor,* and though I give my body to be burned, but **have not love, it profits me nothing**." And the apostle Paul teaches the Galatians in this way: "For we **through the Spirit** eagerly wait for the **hope** of righteousness by **faith**. [6] For in Christ Jesus neither circumcision nor uncircumcision avails anything, but **faith working through love**" (**Galatians 5:5–6**). Here we see the doctrine of the Roman Catholic Church in the Bible: "**faith working through love**." Faith is believing in God and His ways, but love is actually living by the ways of God!

The Word of God teaches the following:

> **Love never fails**. But whether *there are* prophecies, they will fail; whether *there are* tongues, they will cease; whether *there is* knowledge, it will vanish away. [9] For **we know in part** and we prophesy in part. [10] But when that which is perfect has come, then that which is in part will be done away. [11] When I was a child, I spoke as a child, I understood as a child, I thought as a child; but when I became a man, I put away childish things. [12] For now we see in a mirror, dimly, but then face to face. **Now I know in**

part, but then **I shall know just as I also am known**. [13] And now **abide faith, hope, love**, these three; but **the greatest of these** *is* **love**. (1 Corinthians 13:8–13)

Our limited understanding will become complete in heaven. Faith will become reality, and our hope will be fulfilled, but love will last forever because it is the economy of the kingdom of God.

LOVE IS THE ANSWER

If there still is any confusion, there is a truth that all believers can agree is the way to know that we are reconciled to God. That truth includes both faith and good works, and that truth is love. The apostle John teaches us that agape love produces the desire to do the good deeds for our brothers in need: "Whoever **hates his brother** is a **murderer**, and you know that **no murderer has eternal life** abiding in him. [16] By this **we know love**, because **He laid down His life for us**. And we also ought to **lay down** *our* **lives for the brethren**. [17] But whoever has this world's goods, and sees his brother in need, and **shuts up his heart** from him, how does **the love of God abide in him**? [18] My little children, **let us not love in word or in tongue**, but **in deed** and **in truth**" (1 John 3:10–18).

SOLA SCRIPTURA—THE WORD OF GOD ALONE

Another goal of the Reformation was to remove the traditions of the Roman Catholic Church that were contrary to the teachings of the Bible, but in the end the reformers added traditions of their own. *Sola Scriptura* is a Latin phrase that means "by Scripture alone," and it is the name of the doctrine that states that the Bible alone contains all the knowledge needed for the salvation of fallen man. And the Bible teaches that the Holy Spirit alone provides the understanding of that knowledge of the truth that changes what we think and believe with our minds and what we desire in our hearts.

This change of heart and mind is what makes us free from the lies that trapped us and enslaved us to Satan. The power of the Holy Spirit to open our understanding of the truth of God's Word is what allows both the educated and uneducated alike to understand and enter into a loving relationship with God and be saved. To prove that point, God used an uneducated fisherman, led by the Holy Spirit, to teach the teachers and religious leaders of that day the truth in God's Word that will make us free.

Jesus had some strong words for the religious teachers of His day who rejected the Words of God for the words of man.

> He answered and said to them, "Well did Isaiah prophesy of you hypocrites, as it is written: 'This people honors Me with their lips, But **their heart is far from Me**. [7] And in vain they worship Me, **Teaching as doctrines the commandments of men**.' [8] For **laying aside the commandment of God, you hold the tradition of men** –the washing of pitchers and cups, and many other such things you do." [9] He said to them, "All too well **you reject the commandment of God**, that **you may keep your tradition** … [13] **making the word of God of no effect through your tradition** which you have handed down." (**Mark 7:6–9, 13**)

The apostle Paul warns the Colossians and us: "Beware **lest anyone cheat you** through philosophy and empty deceit, **according to the tradition of men**, according to the **basic principles of the world**, and **not according to Christ**. [9] For in Him dwells all the fullness of the Godhead bodily; [10] and you are complete in Him, who is the head of all principality and power" (**Colossians 2:8**).

THE TRUTH FOUND IN THE WORD OF GOD IS THE ANSWER

Jesus tells us how we can live forever: "But He answered and said, 'It is written, *"Man shall not live by bread alone, but by every word that proceeds from the mouth of God"'"* (**Matthew 4:4**). And Paul teaches us how we can grow in faith, quoting the words of the prophet Isaiah: "So then **faith *comes* by hearing**, and **hearing by the word of God**" (**Romans 10:17**). And this is how God is going to unify His divided church. If we all can agree that an understanding of God's Word is the necessary and sufficient truth that will reconcile us to God through Christ, we will be in Christ and one with God. And anything that is not found in the Bible is just an opinion of fallen man that may or may not be true and good. Only God knows and sees the whole truth.

As man does not understand love without God's help, neither does man understand knowledge of the truth without His help, as we see in a letter of Paul to the Corinthians: "For **we know in part** and we prophesy in part. [10] But when that which is perfect has come, then **that which is in part will be done away**. [11] When I was a child, **I spoke as a child, I understood as a child, I thought as a child**; but when I became a man, **I put away childish things**. [12] For now we see in a mirror, dimly, but then face to face. Now **I know in part**, but then **I shall know** just as I also am known" (**1 Corinthians 13:9–12**).

We do not see the whole truth that God sees. On earth our thinking and understanding is as that of a child compared to that of God our Father by His divine purpose and plan. Let us not divide the church of Christ over a teaching that is not found in the Bible; nor let us say that we belong to some local church before we say we belong to the church of Christ first! This is exactly what the apostle Paul was imploring the church at Corinth to do:

> Now I plead with you, brethren, **by the name of our Lord Jesus Christ**, that **you all speak the same thing**, and *that* **there be no divisions among you**, but *that* you be **perfectly joined together** in the **same mind** and in the **same judgment**. [11] For it has been declared to me concerning you, my brethren, by those of Chloe's *household,* that **there are contentions among you**. [12] Now I say this, that each of you says, "**I am of Paul**," or "**I am of Apollos**," or "**I am of Cephas**," or "I am of Christ." [13] **Is Christ divided**? Was Paul crucified for you? Or were you baptized in the name of Paul? (**1 Corinthians 1:10–13**)

Traditions must be rooted in the Word of God, and different ways of worship are only helpful if they bring us together as one in Christ.

But what if someone should ask, **"What is the meaning and purpose of baptism?"** That is a good question; let us look to the Word of God for answers.

The Meaning and Purpose of Baptism

The first mention of baptism in the New Testament is the baptism of John the Baptist: "In those days John the Baptist came preaching in the wilderness of Judea, ² and saying, '**Repent, for the kingdom of heaven is at hand!**'" (**Matthew 3:1–2**). And John the Baptist describes another baptism:

> And even now **the ax is laid to the root of the trees**. Therefore **every tree which does not bear good fruit is cut down** and **thrown into the fire**.
>
> ¹¹ I indeed **baptize you with water unto repentance**, but He who is coming after me is mightier than I, whose sandals I am not worthy to carry. **He will baptize you with the Holy Spirit** and fire. ¹² His winnowing fan is in His hand, and He will thoroughly clean out His threshing floor, and **gather His wheat into the barn**; but He will **burn up the chaff with unquenchable fire**. (**Matthew 3:10–12**)

Here we see that there are two baptisms: one by water and one by the Holy Spirit. John the Baptist explains that his water baptism is one of repentance. And Mark adds that John's water baptism of repentance was a confession of sins for the remission of sins: "John came baptizing in the wilderness and **preaching a baptism of repentance** for the **remission of sins**. ⁵ Then all the land of Judea, and those from Jerusalem, went out to him and were all baptized by him in the Jordan River, **confessing their sins**" (**Mark 1:4–5**).

Webster's Student Dictionary defines "repent" as "1. To amend or resolve to amend one's life as a result of **contrition** for one's sins. 2. To **change one's mind** with regard to past or future intended action, conduct, etc.

on account of regret. 3. To feel regret **for something one has done** or **failed to do**."

The Matthew passages seem to speak of repentance and the confession of sin as a condition for entry into the kingdom of heaven.

We will see that it is not the water that is necessary in the baptism of water, but the confession of our sins and a repentant heart and mind are required. The apostle John teaches that confession of our sins is necessary for forgiveness by God: "If **we say that we have no sin**, we **deceive ourselves**, and **the truth is not in us**. ⁹ If **we confess our sins**, **He is faithful** and **just to forgive us** *our* **sins** and to cleanse us from all unrighteousness. ¹⁰ If **we say that we have not sinned**, we make Him a liar, and **His word is not in us**" (1 John 1:8–10).

The apostle Peter teaches that a water baptism of true repentance leads to a baptism of the Holy Spirit: "Then Peter said to them, **Repent**, and let every one of you be **baptized in the name of Jesus Christ** for the **remission of sins**; and you **shall receive the gift of the Holy Spirit**" (Acts 2:38).

In **Acts 10:44–47** we see that the baptism of the Holy Spirit can come before baptism by water: "While Peter was still speaking these words, the **Holy Spirit fell upon all those who heard the word**. ⁴⁵ And those of the circumcision who believed were astonished, as many as came with Peter, because **the gift of the Holy Spirit** had been poured out on the Gentiles also. ⁴⁶ For they heard them speak with tongues and magnify God. Then Peter answered, ⁴⁷ '**Can anyone forbid water**, that **these should not be baptized who have received the Holy Spirit** just as we *have?*'"

We can see in the crucifixion of the two criminals beside Jesus that a water baptism is not an absolute requirement for entering the kingdom of heaven but a confession of our sin and a belief in the truth of Jesus is: "Then one of the criminals who were hanged blasphemed Him, saying, 'If You are the Christ, save Yourself and us.' ⁴⁰ But the other, answering, **rebuked him**, saying, 'Do you not even fear God, seeing you are under the same condemnation? ⁴¹ And we indeed justly, for **we receive the**

due reward of our deeds; but this Man has done nothing wrong.' [42] Then he said to Jesus, '**Lord, remember me when You come into Your kingdom.**' [43]And Jesus said to him, '**Assuredly,** I say to you, **today you will be with Me in Paradise**'" (Luke 23:39–43).

So in these passages, perhaps we can conclude that a water baptism does not require water but it does require a confession of sins, a changed heart and mind, and faith in Jesus which lead us to an indwelling of the Holy Spirit. It is the baptism of the Holy Spirit that is our assurance of redemption by Christ. A baptism of water without a heartfelt confession of our sins, a changed heart and mind, and a genuine faith in Christ only assures us of getting wet. We see in the next two passages that an indwelling of the Holy Spirit is our guarantee and assurance of our redemption by Christ and a reconciliation with the God the Father:

> Now He who establishes us with you in Christ and has anointed us *is* God, [22] who also **has sealed us** and **given us the Spirit in our hearts as a guarantee.** (2 Corinthians 1:21–22)

> In Him you also *trusted,* after you **heard the word of truth,** the **gospel of your salvation**; in whom also, **having believed,** you were **sealed with the Holy Spirit of promise,** [14] who is the **guarantee of our inheritance** until the **redemption of the purchased possession,** to the praise of His glory. (**Ephesians 1:13–14**)

And the apostle Paul clearly shows us that and understanding of the truth is most important for the assurance of the Holy Spirit in **1 Corinthians 1:17–21**:

> For **Christ did not send me to baptize,** but **to preach the gospel,** not with wisdom of words, lest the cross of Christ should be made of no effect. [18] For the **message of the cross is foolishness to those who are perishing,** but to us who are being saved it is the power of God. [19] For it is written: "*I will destroy the wisdom of the wise, And bring to nothing the understanding of the prudent.*" [20] Where *is* the wise? Where *is* the scribe? Where *is* the disputer of this age? Has not God made foolish the wisdom of this world? [21] For since, in the wisdom of God, the **world through wisdom did not know God,** it

pleased God through the **foolishness of the message preached to save those who believe**.

Man alone cannot understand the truth that will save him because it is spiritually discerned. Only the Holy Spirit can lead our spirit into all truth.

But what if someone should ask, **"Are infants and young children who are baptized with water not saved?"**

Because children are not old enough to understand, they cannot confess their sins in a heartfelt way. And because they have not heard and understood the teachings of the truth of Jesus that will make them free, they cannot publically profess faith in Jesus with a changed heart and mind. And so they cannot be saved by that baptism. But if that baptism is part of raising them up in faith of Jesus and His words, when they become of the age of understanding they can confirm their faith in Jesus and confess their sins and be baptized with the Holy Spirit as their assurance of belonging to Christ. At that point they are like all of us who were baptized as children. Have we given our life to follow Jesus, forsaking the ways of the world? Until we do, we are still babes who have not grown up in the eyes of God.

And that is exactly what Paul said to the Corinthians. If we have not heard and responded to the gospel so that we understand the spiritual reality of our fall from our home in heaven, died to the ways of the world, and begun to live in a manner deserving of eternal life with Christ in heaven, then our infant baptism has not done any good. "I, brethren, could not speak to you as to **spiritual people** but as to **carnal**, as to **babes in Christ**. ² I fed you with milk and not with solid food; for **until now you were not able to receive it**, and even now **you are still not able**; ³ or you are **still carnal**. For where there are **envy**, **strife**, and **divisions** among you, are you not carnal and behaving like mere men? ⁴ For when one says, '**I am of Paul**,' and another, '**I am of Apollos**,' **are you not carnal?**" (**1 Corinthians 3:1–4**). If the church of Christ today is divided, are we not carnal?

THE PROPHECIES OF JESUS' FIRST COMING

The fulfillment of all of the many prophecies of the Messiah, the Christ, the anointed King who would come to rescue the lost and set the prisoners free, was one of the ways to uniquely identify Jesus as the true Son of God that God the Father had chosen to be King over His children and separate Him from the imposters that claimed to be the Messiah. Let us consider a few of the many Old Testament prophecies that Jesus' first coming fulfills:

- Jesus' birth in **Matthew 1:22**
  So all this was done that it might be **fulfilled** which was spoken by the Lord through the prophet, saying: [23] *"**Behold, the virgin shall be with child**, and **bear a Son**, and they shall **call His name Immanuel**,"* which is translated, "**God with us.**"

This is the **fulfillment** of **Isaiah 7:14**: "Therefore the Lord Himself will **give you a sign**: Behold, the **virgin shall conceive** and **bear a Son**, and shall **call His name Immanuel**."

- That Jesus' earthly father Joseph would bring Him out of Egypt in **Matthew 2:14–15**
  When he arose, **he took the young Child** and His mother by night and **departed for Egypt**, [15] and was there until the death of Herod, that it might be fulfilled which was spoken by the Lord through the prophet, saying, *"**Out of Egypt I called My Son.**"*

This was **prophesied** in **Hosea 11:1**: "When Israel *was* a child, I loved him, And **out of Egypt I called My son**."

- **Matthew 2:16–17**
  Then Herod, when he saw that he was deceived by the wise men, was exceedingly angry; and he sent forth and **put to death all the male children who were in Bethlehem** and in all its districts, from two years old and under, according to the time which he had determined from the wise men. [17] Then was **fulfilled** what was spoken by Jeremiah the prophet, saying: [18] *"A voice was heard in Ramah, Lamentation, weeping, and great mourning, Rachel weeping for her children, Refusing to be comforted, Because they are no more."*

386

This passage in Matthew concerning the time when Herod tries to kill Jesus by killing all of the male children in Bethlehem is the **fulfillment** of **Jeremiah 31:15**: "Thus says the LORD: 'A voice was heard in Ramah, Lamentation *and* bitter weeping, **Rachel weeping for her children, Refusing to be comforted for her children,** Because **they** *are* **no more.**'"

- **Matthew 8: 14–17**

  Now when Jesus had come into Peter's house, He saw his wife's mother lying sick with a fever. [15] So **He touched her hand,** and **the fever left her.** And she arose and served them. [16] When evening had come, they brought to Him many who were demon-possessed. And **He cast out the spirits with a word,** and **healed all who were sick,** [17] that it might be **fulfilled** which was spoken by Isaiah the prophet, saying: *"**He Himself took our infirmities And bore our sicknesses**.*

The words spoken by Isaiah that were **fulfilled** come from **Isaiah 53:4–5**: ""Surely **He has borne our griefs** And **carried our sorrows;** Yet we esteemed Him stricken, Smitten by God, and afflicted. [5] But He *was* **wounded for our transgressions,** *He was* **bruised for our iniquities;** The chastisement for our peace *was* upon Him, And **by His stripes we are healed.**"

- **Matthew 13:10–15**

  And the disciples came and said to Him, "Why do You speak to them in parables?" [11] He answered and said to them, "Because **it has been given to you to know the mysteries** of the **kingdom of heaven,** but to them **it has not been given.** [12] For **whoever has, to him more will be given, and he will have abundance;** but **whoever does not have, even what he has will be taken away from him.** [13] Therefore I speak to them in parables, because **seeing they do not see,** and **hearing they do not hear, nor do they understand.** [14] "And in them the **prophecy of Isaiah is fulfilled,** which says: '**Hearing you will hear and shall not understand,** And **seeing you will see and not perceive;** [15] For the hearts of this people have grown dull. Their ears are hard of hearing, And their eyes they have closed, **Lest they should see with their eyes** and **hear with** their ears, Lest they should understand with their hearts and turn, So that I should heal them.'"

The words spoken by Isaiah that were **fulfilled** come from **Isaiah 6: 9–10** "And He said, "Go, and tell this people: **'Keep on hearing**, but **do not understand**; **Keep on seeing**, but **do not perceive.'** [10] Make the heart of this people dull, And **their ears heavy**, And **shut their eyes**; Lest they **see with their eyes**, And **hear with their ears**, And **understand with their heart**, And **return and be healed.**"

- **Matthew 13:34–35**
  All these things Jesus **spoke to the multitude in parables**; and without a parable He did not speak to them, [35] that **it might be fulfilled** which was spoken by the prophet, saying: "*I will open My mouth in parables; I will utter things kept secret from the foundation of the world.*"

These words of the Old Testament prophet are found in **Psalm 78:2**: "**I will open my mouth in a parable**; I will **utter dark sayings of old.**"

- **Matthew 21:1–7**
  Now when they drew near Jerusalem, and came to Bethphage, at the Mount of Olives, then Jesus sent two disciples, [2] saying to them, "Go into the village opposite you, and immediately you will find **a donkey tied**, and **a colt with her**. Loose *them* and bring *them* to Me. [3] And if anyone says anything to you, you shall say, '**The Lord has need of them**,' and immediately he will send them." [4] All this was done that it **might be fulfilled** which was spoken by the prophet, saying: [5] "*Tell the daughter of Zion, 'Behold, your King is coming to you, Lowly, and sitting on a donkey, A colt, the foal of a donkey.'*" [6] So the disciples went and did as Jesus commanded them. [7] They brought the donkey and the colt, laid their clothes on them, and set *Him* on them.

The Old Testament prophet that spoke these words is Zechariah: "Rejoice greatly, O daughter of Zion! Shout, O daughter of Jerusalem! Behold, **your King** is coming to you; He *is* just and having salvation, **Lowly and riding on a donkey**, A colt, **the foal of a donkey.**" (**Zechariah 9:9**)

- **Matthew 26: 30–32**

  And when they had sung a hymn, they went out to the Mount of Olives. [31] Then Jesus said to them, "All of you will be made to stumble because of Me this night, for **it is written**: *'I will strike the Shepherd, And the sheep of the flock will be scattered.'* [32] But after I have been raised, I will go before you to Galilee."

These words of Jesus are the fulfillment of the prophet Zechariah: "Awake, O sword, against My Shepherd, Against the Man who is My Companion," Says the LORD of hosts. "Strike the Shepherd, And the sheep will be scattered." (**Zechariah 13:7a**)

- **Matthew 27:35**

  Then they crucified Him, and **divided His garments**, **casting lots**, that it might be **fulfilled** which was spoken by the prophet: *"They divided My garments among them, And for My clothing they cast lots."*

This verse is the fulfillment of **Psalm 22:14–18**: "I am poured out like water, And **all My bones are out of joint**; My heart is like wax; It has melted within Me. [15] My strength is dried up like a potsherd, And **My tongue clings to My jaws**; You have brought Me to the dust of death. [16] For dogs have surrounded Me; The congregation of the wicked has enclosed Me. They **pierced My hands and My feet**; [17] **I can count all My bones**. They look *and* stare at Me. [18] They **divide My garments among them**, And **for My clothing they cast lot**s."

RECOGNIZING THE SIGNS OF JESUS' SECOND COMING

While God the Father spoke through the prophets, giving signs to our fathers so that they would recognize the Messiah's first coming, Jesus speaks to His disciples and us to help us recognize the signs of Christ's return to earth:

Now as He sat on the Mount of Olives, the disciples came to Him privately, saying, "Tell us, **when will these things be**? And **what will be the sign of Your coming**, and of **the end of the age**?"

> [4] And Jesus answered and said to them: "Take heed that no one deceives you. [5] For many will come in My name, saying, 'I am the Christ,' and will deceive many. [6] And you will **hear of wars and rumors of wars**. See that you are not troubled; for all *these things* must come to pass, but **the end is not yet**. [7] **For nation will rise against nation**, and kingdom against kingdom. And there will be **famines**, **pestilences**, and **earthquakes** in various places. [8] All these *are* the **beginning of sorrows**.
>
> [9] "Then they will **deliver you up to tribulation** and **kill you**, and **you will be hated by all nations** for **My name's sake**. [10] And then **many will be offended**, will **betray one another**, and will **hate one another**. [11] Then **many false prophets** will rise up and deceive many. [12] And because **lawlessness will abound**, the **love of many will grow cold**. [13] But he who endures to the end shall be saved. [14] And **this gospel of the kingdom will be preached in all the world** as a witness to all the nations, and **then the end will come**." (**Matthew 24:3–14**)

While we cannot know the day or hour of Jesus' second coming, there are prophesies of the general "time" of His return so that those who believe in God can be prepared. "But **of that day and hour no one knows, not even the angels of heaven**, but **My Father only**. [37] **But as the days of Noah** *were,* so also will the coming of the Son of Man be. [38] For as in the days before the flood, they were eating and drinking, marrying and giving in marriage, until the day that Noah entered the ark, [39] and **did not know until the flood came** and **took them all away**, so also will the coming of the Son of Man be" (**Matthew 24:36–39**). Notice that God gave Noah, the only righteous man, a warning of His plans to destroy the world with a flood so that he could prepare an ark and save himself and his family.

The prophet Isaiah prophesies about a nation being born in one day: "'Who has heard such a thing? Who has seen such things? **Shall the earth be made to give birth in one day?** *Or* **shall a nation be born at once?** For as soon **as Zion was in labor**, She gave **birth to her children**. [9] Shall I bring to **the time of birth**, and not cause delivery?' says the LORD. 'Shall I who cause delivery shut up *the womb?'* says your God" (**Isaiah 66:8–9**).

Jesus instructs us to watch for the birth of the nation of Israel—symbolically, as the fig tree coming back to life—as a sign that the end times are here: "Now **learn this parable from the fig tree**: When its **branch has already become tender** and **puts forth leaves**, you know that **summer** *is* **near**. ³³ So you also, when you see all these things, **know that it is near–at the doors**! ³⁴ Assuredly, I say to you, **this generation will by no means pass away till all these things take place**. ³⁵ **Heaven and earth will pass away**, but **My words will by no means pass away**" (Matthew 24:32–35).

When Jesus first came to earth, His people, Israel, did not recognize Him and believe in Him as the Messiah, their anointed King from God, and they rejected Him. And so God rejected them for a time and went to teach the truth of the gospel to the Gentiles. This is symbolically represented by "Jesus finding no fruit on the fig tree" in this passage in the gospel of Matthew: "Now in the morning, as He returned to the city [Jerusalem], He was hungry. ¹⁹ And seeing **a fig tree** by the road, He **came to it** and **found nothing on it but leaves**, and said to it, 'Let no fruit grow on you *ever again*.' Immediately **the fig tree withered away**" (Matthew 21:18–19).

But the Greek word for the phrase "**ever again**" in Jesus' phrase "Let no fruit grow on you **ever again**" is G165 *aion* (pronounced ahee-onh'), which means "From the same as G104; **properly an age**; by extension perpetuity (also past); by implication the world; **specifically (Jewish)** a **Messianic period** (present or future)." So, properly rendered, this verse says, "Let no fruit grow on you until the end of this age." The age that Jesus was present in was the third age, the age of the Messiah coming to earth, the age of the church of Jesus the Messiah. This is the age that we are in. We are two thousand years or so in the future relative to the time of Jesus, but we are still in the messianic period!

So what Jesus is teaching by this "**parable from the fig tree**" is that when Jesus came to the Jews the first time, He found that they were not bearing any **fruit** for the kingdom of God (believers who have faith in God). That the fig tree had leaves on it meant that it should have had figs on it, which figuratively signifies that the Jews were a godly nation in appearance only. And so Jesus said that they would not bear any fruit for the time of the messianic age. But at the end of that age, when Israel would come back to life as nation, they would bear fruit during the tribulation, as the apostle John describes: "And I heard the number of **those who were sealed.** one **hundred** *and* **forty-four thousand of all the tribes** of the **children of Israel** *were* sealed" (**Revelation 7:4**).

In fulfillment of Isaiah's prophecy and Jesus' words, Israel came back to life as a nation on May 14, 1948, after nearly two thousand years during which they were not a nation but were scattered among other nations. This is a date that I will never forget, because I was born on May 14 exactly eight years later, in 1956. All of us who are alive today are part of that generation that will not pass away until we see "**all these things take place!**"

The prophet Amos speaks of a time when Israel would return to their own land: "'**I will bring back the captives of My people Israel**; They shall build the waste cities and inhabit *them;* They shall plant vineyards and drink wine from them; They shall also make gardens and eat fruit from them. ^{15} I will **plant them in their land,** And **no longer shall they be pulled up** From the **land I have given them,**' Says the LORD your God" (**Amos 9:14–15**).

The prophet Jeremiah prophesies of the return of Israel: "'Therefore behold, the days are coming,' says the LORD, 'that it shall no more be said, "The LORD lives who brought up the children of Israel from the land of Egypt," ^{15} but, "The LORD lives who brought up the children of Israel **from the land of the north** and from **all the lands where He had driven them.**" For I will **bring them back** into **their land which I gave to their fathers**'" (**Jeremiah 16:14–15**).

Ezekiel prophesies of the gathering of Israel out of the nations to their own land: "Then say to them, 'Thus says the Lord GOD: "Surely I will **take the children of Israel from among the nations,** wherever they have gone, and will gather them from every side and **bring them into their own land**; ^{22} and I will make them one nation in the land, **on the mountains of Israel**; and **one king** shall be king over them all;

they shall no longer be two nations, nor shall they ever be divided into two kingdoms again"""" (**Ezekiel 37:21–22**). As we shall see, the phrase "and **one king** shall be king over them all" will be fulfilled by Jesus in the millennium. Amazingly, we who are alive today are standing right in the middle of this prophesy being fulfilled!

Then I stumbled across a website that claimed that the date Israel became a nation, on **May 14** evening to **May 15** evening (the Jewish day was from sunset to sunset) was the fulfillment of prophecy of **Ezekiel 39:27–29,** to the very day: "'When I have **brought them back** from the peoples and **gathered them out of their enemies' lands**, and I am hallowed in them in the sight of many nations, [28] then they shall know that I *am* the LORD their God, who **sent them into captivity among the nations**, but also **brought them back to their land**, and left none of them captive any longer. [29] And I will not hide My face from them anymore; for I shall have **poured out My Spirit** on the **house of Israel**,' says the Lord GOD." The date of that prophecy was calculated from information in **Ezekiel 40:1–4** to be the Jewish month of Nisan 10, 573 BC. From this date they calculated 1,260 years + 1,260 years = AD 1948, in the fourteenth day of May at the feast of Pentecost. It is interesting to note that we do not have to adjust for the number of years in this calculation due to the difference in the number of days in the twelve Jewish months compared to our twelve months, because the Jews had a method to adjust their twelve-month year to the 365.25-day solar year, just as we have leap years that add a day to our calendar every four years. The Jewish months stayed fixed to the four seasons just as ours do.

So when I took 1,260 + 1,260 = 2,520 years − 573 years, I got 1,947. And because there is no year numbered 0, that made it 1948! I do not know where the two numbers 1,260 came from, but the significance of these numbers to me is that at the end of the church age there will be the tribulation, which will last for seven years, but at the midpoint, after 3½ years, or forty-two months of 30 days, or 1,260 days, there will be the great tribulation, which will last another 1,260 days, as we will discuss in the chapter "The Tribulation."

The most amazing thing that I learned is that the day Israel became a nation was on the day of Pentecost, the anniversary day of when the Holy Spirit indwelt the disciples of Christ. And we see from the **Ezekiel 39:27–29** prophecy that God said He would pour out His Spirit on the house of Israel: "'I will not hide My face from them anymore; for **I shall have poured out My Spirit** on the **house of Israel**,' says the Lord GOD." Understanding mysteries in the Bible is exciting as well as illuminating. I present this now that perhaps someone may find a deeper understanding of this. There are Jewish scholars who have calculated biblical prophecies to be exact to the very day. But we will focus on understanding the meaning and purpose of life on planet earth.

GOOD AND EVIL CANNOT LIVE TOGETHER

In this third age, God has witnessed the truth through His Son, Jesus, to fallen man who have experienced evil for themselves and are now ready and willing to listen to God and reason with Him to learn and understand why God's ways are the only ways that lead to eternal life, power, prosperity, peace, and unspeakable joy. We learned that God's ways are totally opposite to the ways of Satan and that good and evil cannot coexist, for Jesus Himself testifies by saying, **"He who is not with Me is against Me**, and **he who does not gather with Me scatters"** (**Luke 11:23**). He also reveals the truth: "Jesus said to him, 'I am the way, the truth, and the life. No one comes to the Father except through Me'" (**John 14:6**).

We have also learned that God separating good from evil is a common theme throughout the Bible and will culminate in the rapture before the tribulation, where those who are alive and believe in Jesus will be gathered together in the clouds with Jesus and those who have died in Jesus (**1 Thessalonians 4:13–18**). And these are joined with the saints that come out of the tribulation, in which God will use suffering, trials, and tribulation to glean the last of the harvest of mankind who commit their lives to God and His Christ, to separate them from those who still believe in Satan and his Antichrist. And as the apostle John asks and answers, "Who is a liar but he who **denies** that **Jesus is the Christ? He is antichrist** who **denies the Father and the Son**" (**1 John 2:22**).

There are only two choices here. In the end we all will be either sons of God or sons of Satan. "Whoever has been **born of God** does not sin, for His seed remains in him; and he cannot sin, because he has been **born of God**. [10] In this the **children of God** and the **children of the devil** are manifest: Whoever **does not practice righteousness is not of God**, nor *is* he who **does not love his brother**" (**1 John 3:10**).

In the next age to come, the millennium, God, who alone has the power, sovereignty, knowledge, understanding, and wisdom to establish justice in His kingdom, will separate those who chose the ways of Satan and evil from those who chose the ways of God and goodness (**Deuteronomy 30:19–20**). When those who are evil, whether in bodies of flesh or not, have been removed from the earth, Jesus will demonstrate to all who are in the heavens and on the earth that God's ways are righteous and true and that they are life. In this God shows that love is unity is life is the truth!

The Rapture

LET US CONSIDER the words of the prophet Daniel: "And many of those who **sleep in the dust of the earth** shall awake, **Some to everlasting life, Some to shame *and* everlasting contempt.** ³ Those who are wise shall shine Like the brightness of the firmament, And **those who turn many to righteousness Like the stars forever and ever**" (**Daniel 12:2–3**). Daniel lived in the age of the Old Testament, when those "who sleep" (died in the flesh) were kept as captives by Satan in hell, or hades, with him, and we learned that hell was in the earth. It was not until Jesus died on the cross and first descended into hell that he took those who believed in God captive to be with Him in paradise. "Therefore He says: '*When He ascended on high, He led captivity captive, And gave gifts to men.*' ⁹ (Now this, '*He ascended*'—what does it mean but that He also **first descended** into the **lower parts of the earth**? ¹⁰ He who descended is also the one who **ascended far above all the heavens**, that He might fill all things.)" (**Ephesians 4:8–10**). By these words of the Bible we know that all those in the Old Testament who died believing in God are already with Jesus in heaven.

At the end of this age, the church age, most every Bible scholar agrees that there will be what is called the rapture. This event will involve the believers who are alive and in Jesus—the church, the saints of Jesus Christ—as Paul teaches us, having been taught by Jesus: "But I do not want you to be **ignorant**, brethren, concerning those who have fallen asleep, lest you **sorrow as others who have no hope.** ¹⁴ For if we believe that Jesus died and rose again, **even so God will bring with Him** those who **sleep in Jesus**" (**1 Thessalonians 4:13–14**).

This is confirmation that those who died believing in Christ from the beginning until the time of the tribulation are already with Jesus in heaven. And when Jesus raptures those who are still alive, He will bring those who have died with Him.

Paul continues in his letter to the Thessalonians:

> For this we say to you by the **word of the Lord**, that **we who are alive** *and* **remain** until **the coming of the Lord** will **by no means precede those who are asleep**. [16] For the Lord Himself will descend from heaven with a shout, with the voice of an archangel, and with **the trumpet of God**. And the **dead in Christ** will rise first. [17] Then **we who are alive** *and* **remain** shall be **caught up together** with **them in the clouds** to **meet the Lord in the air**. And thus we shall always be with the Lord. [18] Therefore comfort one another with these words. (**1 Thessalonians 4:15–18**)

Notice that this passage says that the dead will already be with God in heaven before those who are alive are raptured. The comfort that Paul wants to give to "survivors" of those who have died is that they are already with the Lord Jesus.

The word "rapture," which is not found in the Bible, comes from the phrase "caught up," which is translated from the Greek word G726 *harpazo* (pronounced har-pad'-zo), and means "To **seize** (in various applications): – **to catch** (**away, up**), **pluck, pull, take** (by **force**)." *Webster's Student Dictionary* defines the English word "rapture" as "**Spiritual or emotional ecstasy**; also, an expression or indication of this **ecstasy**." This going home to be with Christ will be an exciting time for Christians, because this is what Jesus suffered and died for, and it is what we have figuratively taken up our cross and suffered and died to this life in the flesh for. As Jesus said, "If anyone **desires to come after Me**, let him **deny himself**, and **take up his cross**, and follow Me. [25] For whoever **desires to save his life** will **lose it**, but whoever **loses his life for My sake** will **find it**" (**Matthew 16:24–25**).

JESUS DESCRIBES THE RAPTURE

Now when He was asked by the Pharisees when the kingdom of God would come, He answered them and said, "The kingdom of God **does not come with observation**; ²¹ nor will they say, 'See here!' or 'See there!' **For indeed, the kingdom of God is within you**." ²² Then He said to the disciples, "The days will come when you will desire to see one of the days of the Son of Man, and you will not see *it*. ²³ And they will say to you, 'Look here!' or 'Look there!' **Do not go after** *them* **or follow** *them*. ²⁴ For as the **lightning that flashes** out of one *part* under heaven shines to the other *part* under heaven, **so also the Son of Man will be in His day**.

²⁵ "But first He must **suffer many things** and **be rejected by this generation**. ²⁶ And as it was in the **days of Noah**, so it will be also in the days of the Son of Man: ²⁷ They **ate**, they **drank**, they **married wives**, they were given in marriage, until the day that Noah entered the ark, and the flood came and destroyed them all. ²⁸ Likewise as it was also in the **days of Lot**: They **ate**, they **drank**, they **bought**, they **sold**, they **planted**, they **built**; ²⁹ but on the day that Lot went out of Sodom it rained fire and brimstone from heaven and destroyed *them* all. ³⁰ Even so will it be in **the day when the Son of Man is revealed**.

³¹ "In **that day**, he who is on the housetop, and his **goods** *are* **in the house**, let him not come down to take them away. And likewise the one who is in the field, **let him not turn back**. ³² **Remember Lot's wife**. ³³ **Whoever seeks to save his life will lose it**, and **whoever loses his life will preserve it**. ³⁴ I tell you, **in that night** there will be two *men* in one bed: the **one will be taken** and the **other will be left**. ³⁵ Two *women* will be grinding together: the **one will be taken** and the **other left**. ³⁶ Two *men* will be in the field: the **one will be taken** and the **other left**." ³⁷ And they answered and said to Him, "Where, Lord?" So He said to them, "Wherever the **body is**, there the **eagles will be gathered together**." (Luke 17:20–37).

The phrase "Wherever the **body is**, there the **eagles will be gathered together**" may indicate that when we are raptured our body is left behind for the birds of prey, but there could be another meaning, because the word "eagle" is translated from the Greek word G105 *aetos,* which means "From the same as G109; an eagle (**from its wind like flight**)." And the phrase "gathered together" is translated from the Greek word G4863 *sunago*, which means "**To lead together**, that is, to **collect and convene**; **assemble (selves, together)**, **come together**, **gather (selves together, up, together)**, **lead into**, resort, **take in**." So this seems to indicate that we are gathered together in our bodies of flesh and taken up as on the wings of eagles in a wind-like flight to be with Christ, and our corruptible bodies are made incorruptible during the flight, because nothing corruptible will be in heaven. "For **this corruptible** must put on **incorruption**, and **this mortal** *must* put on **immortality**" (**1 Corinthians 15:53**).

While most everyone who has studied the Bible believes in the rapture of the saints, there is a lot of disagreement about when the rapture will occur. Let us now consider what the Bible says about the rapture of the church, when believers of Jesus Christ leave this world of Satan and are reunited in unspeakable joy and spiritual ecstasy with Christ in heaven—that which should be the desire and goal of every believer.

EVIDENCE FOR THE RAPTURE BEFORE THE TRIBULATION

THE PRETRIBULATION RAPTURE CHAPTER

Now, brethren, concerning the **coming of our Lord Jesus Christ** and our **gathering together to Him**, we ask you, [2] not to be soon shaken in mind or troubled, either by spirit or by word or by letter, as if from us, **as though** the **day of Christ had come**. [3] Let no one deceive you by any means; for *that Day will not come* **unless the falling away comes first**, and the **man of sin is revealed**, the **son of perdition**, [4] who opposes and exalts himself above all that is called God or that is worshiped, so that **he sits as God in the temple of God, showing himself that he is God.**

⁵ Do you not remember that when I was still with you I told you these things? ⁶ And now you know what is restraining, that he may be revealed **in his own time**. ⁷ For **the mystery of lawlessness** is already at work; only **He who now restrains** *will do so* **until He is taken out of the way**. ⁸ And **then the lawless one will be revealed**, whom the Lord will consume with the breath of His mouth and destroy with the brightness of His coming. ⁹ The coming of the *lawless one* **is according to the working of Satan**, with all power, signs, and **lying wonders**, ¹⁰ and with **all unrighteous deception among those who perish**, because **they did not receive** the **love of the truth**, that they **might be saved**.

¹¹ And for this reason **God will send them strong delusion**, that they should **believe the lie**, ¹² that they all may be condemned **who did not believe the truth but had pleasure in unrighteousness**. ¹³ But we are bound to give thanks to God always for you, brethren beloved by the Lord, because **God from the beginning chose you for salvation** through **sanctification by the Spirit** and **belief in the truth**, ¹⁴ to which **He called you** by our gospel, for the obtaining of the glory of our Lord Jesus Christ. (**2 Thessalonians 2:1–14**)

Especially notice that this passage speaks of God's elect, those of us that believe in the truth, whom "**God from the beginning chose you for salvation**." The "**day of Christ**," when Jesus returns at the end of the tribulation, will not occur until after the "falling away" happens and the man of sin—the son of perdition, the lawless one, the Antichrist—is revealed. The "**gathering together to Him**" speaks of a pretribulation rapture, and the phrase "only **He who now restrains** *will do so* **until He is taken out of the way**" is taken by many Bible scholars to refer to the rapture of Christians with the indwelling of the Holy Spirit, the body of Christ, who is resisting the advancement of evil. The verse that speaks of the lawless one is a reference to the abomination of desolation, when the antichrist "**sits as God in the temple of God, showing himself that he is God**," which we will see happens at the midpoint of the tribulation.

PRETRIBULATION RAPTURE EVIDENCE

> So that we ourselves boast of you among the churches of God for your **patience and faith** in all your **persecutions** and **tribulations that you endure,** [5] *which is* manifest **evidence** of the **righteous judgment of God,** that you may be counted **worthy of the kingdom of God,** for which you also suffer; [6] since *it is* **a righteous thing with God to repay** with **tribulation** those **who trouble you,**
>
> [7] and to *give* **you who are troubled rest with us** when the **Lord Jesus is revealed from heaven with His mighty angels,** [8] in flaming fire taking vengeance on those **who do not know God,** and on those who do not obey the gospel of our Lord Jesus Christ. [9] These **shall be punished** with **everlasting destruction** from the **presence of the Lord** and **from the glory of His power,** [10] when He comes, **in that Day,** to be glorified in His saints and to be admired among **all those who believe,** because our testimony among you was believed. (**2 Thessalonians 1:4–10**).

This verse shows us that the everlasting destruction comes by being separated from the power of the Lord. This passage seems to say that the godly believers will not partake of the tribulation that those who persecuted the godly will suffer. And that the punishment of "those **who do not know God**" will be the everlasting destruction that occurs when they are separated from the presence of the Lord and His power.

PRETRIBULATION RAPTURE—WE ARE NOT APPOINTED TO WRATH

> But let us who are of the day be sober, putting on the breastplate of faith and love, and *as* a helmet the hope of salvation. [9] For **God did not appoint us to wrath,** but to obtain **salvation through our Lord Jesus Christ,** [10] who died for us, that **whether we wake or sleep,** we should **live together with Him.** [11] Therefore comfort each other and edify one another, just as you also are doing. (**1 Thessalonians 5:8–11**)

This passage seems to speak of a pretribulation rapture of the saints who have not died; with "wrath" referring to the tribulation that we, the believers in Christ, will miss.

EVIDENCE FOR THE RAPTURE IN THE MIDDLE OF THE TRIBULATION

MIDTRIBULATION RAPTURE

There is a rapture that occurs in the middle of the seven-year tribulation that is described in the book of Revelation as being on wings of an eagle: "Now when the **dragon saw that he had been cast to the earth**, he persecuted the woman who gave birth to the male *Child*. ¹⁴ But the woman **was given two wings of a great eagle**, that she might fly into the wilderness **to her place, where she is nourished for a time and times and half a time**, from the presence of the serpent ... And the dragon was enraged with the woman, and he went to make war with **the rest of her offspring**, who **keep the commandments of God** and have the **testimony of Jesus Christ**" **(Revelation 12:13–14, 17)**.

The phrase "**for a time and times and half a time**" may refer to three and a half years, which makes this at the midpoint of the tribulation. And "the woman" refers to those of fallen mankind, those that used to follow and belong to Satan, the Dragon, but now believe the truth of God and belong to Christ and are raptured to a place where they are now free to be with Christ and safe from Satan. Here we see that they are given a wind-like flight as on the wings of an eagle to be with Christ Jesus.

The phrase "**the rest of her offspring**" indicates that this "woman" is more than one person and refers to the elect or chosen part of the woman of **Genesis 2:23**: "And Adam said: 'This *is* now bone of my bones And flesh of my flesh; She shall be called **Woman**, Because **she was taken out of Man**.'" As we learned, the Woman was taken from

Adam, the leader of fallen mankind. And Eve is the first woman, who is the mother of all mankind. "And Adam called his wife's name Eve, because **she was the mother of all living**" (**Genesis 3:20**).

MIDTRIBULATION RAPTURE

"So when you see the *'abomination of desolation,'* spoken of by **Daniel the prophet, standing where it ought not**" (let the reader understand), "then let those who are in Judea flee to the mountains. [15] Let him who is on the housetop not go down into the house, nor enter to take anything out of his house. [16] And let him who is in the field not go back to get his clothes. [17] But woe to those who are pregnant and to those who are nursing babies in those days! [18] And pray that your **flight** may not be in winter. [19] For *in those days* there will be **tribulation**, such as has not been since the beginning of the creation which God created until this time, nor ever shall be. [20] And **unless the Lord had shortened** those **days, no flesh would be saved**; but for the **elect's sake, whom He chose, He shortened the days**." (**Mark 13:14–20**)

Perhaps the shortening of days is a reference to the shortening of suffering in the days of the tribulation, which is brought about by God rapturing the elect to be with Him after that suffering causes them to realize that we are not in control and cannot live without God. God does not let us suffer more than is necessary to bring us to faith. These who came to faith in the first half of the tribulation did not need to suffer more in the great tribulation. For it is during the times in which we suffer that we are drawn closer to God, as many who have suffered greatly give witness to. My suffering with cancer is the wakeup call that drew me back to God, and the evil disaster that occurred on September 11, 2001, brought our country back to God for a time.

403

MIDTRIBULATION RAPTURE

Matthew's version of this event adds the words **"great tribulation,"** referring to the event that begins at the midpoint of the seven-year tribulation:

> "Therefore when you see the *'abomination of desolation,'* spoken of by Daniel the prophet, standing in the holy place" (whoever reads, let him understand), [16] "then let those who are in Judea flee to the mountains. [17] Let him who is on the housetop not go down to take anything out of his house. [18] And let him who is in the field not go back to get his clothes. [19] But woe to those who are pregnant and to those who are nursing babies in those days! [20] And pray that your flight may not be in winter or on the Sabbath. [21] For then there will be **great tribulation**, such as has not been since the beginning of the world until this time, no, nor ever shall be. [22] And **unless those days were shortened**, no flesh would be saved; but **for the elect's sake those days will be shortened**." (Matthew 24:15–22)

Mark and Matthew are saying almost the same thing—that the abomination of desolation occurs at the midpoint of the tribulation. And if those days were not shortened, no flesh would be saved. It seems that this means there will be those who become believers in the first three and a half years of tribulation but they would later receive temptation beyond what they were able to withstand if they went through the next three and a half years of the great tribulation. And so Christ will raptured them to be faithful to His believers by making a way of escape for them: "No temptation has overtaken you except such as is common to man; but God *is* faithful, who will not allow you **to be tempted beyond what you are able**, but with the temptation will also **make the way of escape**, that you may be able to bear *it*" (**1 Corinthians 10:13**).

EVIDENCE FOR THE RAPTURE AT THE END OF THE TRIBULATION

POSTTRIBULATION RAPTURE EVIDENCE

There is one glory of the sun, another glory of the moon, and another glory of the stars; for *one* star differs from *another* star in glory. [42] So also *is* the resurrection of the dead. **The body** is sown in corruption, it is raised in incorruption. [43] It is sown in dishonor, it is raised in glory. It is sown **in weakness, it is raised in power**. [44] It is **sown a natural body**, it is **raised a spiritual body**. There is a natural body, and there is a spiritual body. [45] And so it is written, *"The first man Adam became a living being."* The **last Adam** *became* a **life-giving spirit**.

[46] However, the spiritual is not first, but the natural, and afterward the spiritual. [47] The first man *was* of the earth, *made of dust*; the second Man *is* the Lord from heaven. [48] As *was* **the man of dust**, so also *are* **those who are made of dust**; and as *is* the **heavenly Man**, so also *are* those *who* are **heavenly**. [49] And as **we have borne the image of the man of dust**, we shall **also bear the image of the heavenly Man**. [50] Now this I say, brethren, that **flesh and blood cannot inherit the kingdom of God**; nor does corruption inherit incorruption.

[51] Behold, **I tell you a mystery**: We shall **not all sleep**, but we shall **all be changed**– [52] in a moment, in the **twinkling of an eye**, at the **last trumpet**. For the **trumpet will sound**, and the dead **will be raised** incorruptible, and we shall be changed. [53] For this **corruptible must put on incorruption**, and this **mortal *must* put on immortality**. [54] So when this corruptible has put on incorruption, and this mortal has put on immortality, then shall be brought to pass the saying that is written: *"Death is swallowed up in victory."*

[55] *"O Death, where is your sting? O Hades, where is your victory?"* [56] **The sting of death *is* sin, and the strength of sin *is* the law**. [57] But thanks *be* to God, who gives us the victory through our Lord Jesus Christ. [58] Therefore, my beloved brethren, be

steadfast, immovable, always abounding in the work of the Lord, knowing that your labor is not in vain in the Lord. (**1 Corinthians 15:41–58**)

This description of the rapture of the dead and the living in Christ is said to occur at the "**last trumpet**." If this is a reference to the last of the seven trumpets that are sounded in the tribulation, then this "rapture" occurs at the end of the tribulation and with the second coming of the Lord with a shout—the voice of an archangel—to do battle with the Antichrist called the Beast and his followers. "Then the **seventh angel sounded**: And there were loud voices in heaven, saying, 'The **kingdoms of this world have become** *the kingdoms* **of our Lord** and of **His Christ**, and He shall reign forever and ever!'" (**Revelation 11:15**).

POSTTRIBULATION RAPTURE

Then if anyone says to you, "Look, here *is* the Christ!" or, "Look, *He is* there!" do not believe it. ²² For false christs and false prophets will rise and **show signs and wonders to deceive, if possible, even the elect**. ²³ But take heed; see, I have told you all things beforehand. ²⁴ But in those days, **after that tribulation**, the sun will be darkened, and the moon will not give its light; ²⁵ the **stars of heaven will fall**, and the powers in the heavens will be shaken. ²⁶ Then **they will see the Son of Man coming in the clouds** with great power and glory. ²⁷ And then **He will send His angels**, and **gather together His elect** from the **four winds**, from the **farthest part of earth to the farthest part of heaven**. (**Mark 13:21–27**)

So, as the tribulation ends, Jesus will still gather His elect from earth.

POSTTRIBULATION RAPTURE

In Matthew's version of this same discourse of Jesus, he adds the words "with **a great sound of a trumpet**," which helps us identify this as occurring after the great tribulation:

Then if anyone says to you, "Look, here *is* the Christ!" or "There!" do not believe *it*. ²⁴ For false christs and false prophets will rise and show great signs and wonders to deceive, if possible, even the elect. ²⁵ See, I have told you beforehand. ²⁶ Therefore if they say to you, "Look, He is in the desert!" do not go out; *or* "Look, *He is* in the inner rooms!" do not believe *it*. ²⁷ For as the **lightning comes from the east and flashes to the west,** so also will the **coming of the Son of Man be**. ²⁸ For wherever the carcass is, there the eagles will be gathered together.

²⁹ **Immediately after the tribulation of those days** the sun will be darkened, and the moon will not give its light; the stars will fall from heaven, and the powers of the heavens will be shaken. ³⁰ Then **the sign of the Son of Man will appear in heaven,** and then **all the tribes of the earth will mourn,** and they will **see the Son of Man coming on the clouds of heaven** with power and great glory. ³¹ And He will send His angels **with a great sound of a trumpet,** and they will gather together **His elect from the four winds, from one end of heaven to the other. (Matthew 24:23–31)**

Notice that in the end, Jesus is gathering His elect—those on earth who were chosen before the world began, who were previously raptured and are now in heaven—together with those elect who are still on earth, **"His elect from the four winds, from one end of heaven to the other,"** to be with Him forever.

Now that we have explored some of the verses that refer to some kind of "catching up" of those who are still alive to be with Jesus and other believers, we can see how there can be disagreement as to when the rapture occurs. In the book of Revelation, we will see that in addition to the pretribulation rapture, there will be saints that come out of the tribulation alive and who are caught up to heaven at the halfway point, three and one half years into the tribulation, and at the end of the great tribulation, which lends support for both the midtribulation and posttribulation views. So now we can answer the question, when does the rapture occur? by saying there are three raptures: one at the beginning, one at the midpoint, and one at the end of the tribulation.

And then there are those who are martyred for their belief in Christ Jesus during the tribulation, which leads to the question, but what if someone should ask, **"But what about the dead in Christ—those that died in the flesh while believing in Christ—are they not raptured too?"**

THE RAISING OF THOSE CHRISTIANS WHOSE BODY OF FLESH HAS DIED

In order to answer the question posed at the end of the last section, we first we need to define what a "rapture" is. Looking back to the ages of time before Jesus won our freedom from the bondage of Satan by suffering and dying for us on the cross, when people died, their spirit was separated from their body of flesh and went to hades—called sheol, hell, the deep, and the abyss—which is the dwelling place of Satan and his fallen angels, which we all once were. Nevertheless, Jesus informs us in the parable of Lazarus the beggar and the rich man that those who believed in the ways of God were separated from those who did not: "But Abraham said, 'Son, remember that in your lifetime you received your good things, and likewise Lazarus evil things; but now he is comforted and you are tormented. ²⁶ And besides all this, between us and you there is a great gulf fixed, so that those who want to pass from here to you cannot, nor can those from there pass to us.' And besides all this, between us and you **there is a great gulf fixed**, so that **those who want to pass from here to you cannot**, nor can **those from there pass to us**" (**Luke 16:25–26**).

But when Jesus died and rose and ascended to heaven in victory over sin, death, and Satan, He first descended into hell and took those who had been captives and now belonged to Him and brought them to paradise to be with Him. Paradise is in heaven, where Jesus is, as we read of when Jesus is on the cross with another who was being crucified: "And Jesus said to him, 'Assuredly, I say to you, **today** you will be **with Me** in **Paradise'**" (**Luke 23:43**). And as we learned earlier, "paradise" is another word for the true garden of Eden, which is in heaven. The word "paradise" is translated from the Greek word G3857 *paradeisos*, which means "Of Oriental origin; **a park**, that is, (specifically) **an Eden (place of future happiness, "paradise") - paradise.**"

Jesus speaks of the raising of the dead from two distinctly different time periods:

> Most assuredly, I say to you, **he who hears My word** and **believes in Him who sent Me** has **everlasting life**, and **shall not come into judgment**, but has passed from **death into life.** [25] Most assuredly, I say to you, the **hour is coming,** and **now is,** when the **dead will hear** the **voice of the Son of God;** and **those who hear will live.** [26] For as the Father has **life in Himself,** so He has granted the Son to have **life in Himself,** [27] and has given Him authority to execute judgment also, because He is the Son of Man. [28] Do not marvel at this; for the **hour is coming** in which **all who are in the graves** will **hear His voice** [29] and **come forth—those who have done good**, to the **resurrection of life,** and **those who have done evil**, to the **resurrection of condemnation.** (John 5:24–29)

The first half of this passage seems to be speaking about the time "that **now is**," the current time of the narrative, when Jesus is about to suffer and die and arise from the dead but first descends into hell to release those who "**hear My word** and **believes in Him** who sent Me" and were held captive by Satan before Jesus redeems them and takes them back to live with Him in paradise, as Paul teaches to the Ephesians and us: "Therefore He says: '*When He ascended on high, He led captivity captive, And gave gifts to men.*' [9] (Now this, '*He ascended*'—what does it mean but that He also **first descended into the lower parts of the earth?** [10] He who descended is also the one who ascended far above all the heavens, that He might fill all things.)" (**Ephesians 4:8–10**).

These are the elect of God, the saints that believed in God in the Old Testament. The Greek word for "ascended" in the phrase "***When He ascended on high***" is G305 *anabaino*, (pronounced an-ab-ah'ee-no), which means "To go up (literally or figuratively): **arise, ascend** (up), climb (go, grow, **rise**, spring) up, **come (up).**" This sounds a lot like the rapture but is for those who have already died in the flesh and ascend with Christ in a group.

The second half of this passage seems to refer to a time ("the **hour is coming**")—the time after Christ's ascension until the tribulation and the time at the end when Christ returns—and applies to both the good and evil "**who are in the graves.**" This includes those who will be martyred for their faith in Christ and die in the flesh during tribulation.

In the end, **those who have done good** through the ages will experience the **resurrection of life**, but those who have done evil and are condemned will not experience spiritual ecstasy or "joy inexpressible"; rather, they will experience wailing and the gnashing of teeth. This is when those who belong to Christ will be separated from those who belong to Satan, as Jesus describes: "So it will be at the **end of the age**. The angels will come forth, **separate the wicked from among the just**, [50] and cast them into the **furnace of fire**. There will be **wailing** and **gnashing of teeth**" (**Matthew 13:49–50**).

So in all of this we see that those who believe and die in the flesh will not be "raptured" but upon their death will separate from their body of flesh and ascend (or, in the Greek, *anabaino*) to be with Christ in the paradise that is in heaven. The word "rapture," or the Greek word G726 *harpazo*, can only apply to those who are good, believe in Jesus, and are alive; they will ascend to be with Christ *in the clouds.*

So with this understanding let us take a new look at **1 Thessalonians 4:14–17**, which describes the "catching up together in the clouds" that we call the rapture:

> For if we believe that Jesus died and rose again, even so **God will bring with Him** those who **sleep in Jesus**. [15] For this we say to you by the word of the Lord, that we who are **alive *and* remain** until the coming of the Lord **will by no means precede those who are asleep**. [16] For the Lord Himself will **descend from heaven** with a shout, with the voice of an archangel, and **with the trumpet** of God. And **the dead in Christ will rise first**. [7] Then we who are **alive *and* remain shall be caught up**

together with **them in the clouds** to meet the Lord in the air. And thus we shall always be with the Lord.

Perhaps the "**dead in Christ**" will "rise" first because upon their death they have already made the trip to heaven to be with Christ in paradise. And perhaps that is what Paul is saying in the phrase "**God will bring with Him** those who **sleep in Jesus**." And those who believe and are still alive on earth at the end of the messianic age will be caught up to meet "**them in the clouds**" because Jesus and the risen dead have descended from heaven and are already together in the clouds.

The Greek word for "**rise**" in the phrase "**the dead in Christ will rise first**" is G450 *anistimi*, which can mean "To **arise** or **stand up**," as one would do when called to attention at the sound of a trumpet. So if the dead who are already with Jesus **descend from heaven** to meet in the clouds with those who are alive and are raptured, with the emphasis on a gathering together with Jesus, then this is the reason the "**dead in Christ will rise first**."

Being alive in the flesh when you meet Jesus in the air must be extremely exciting, even ecstatic. But those who have died in the flesh believing in Jesus during the church age before the rapture, and the saints who are martyred for their faith in Jesus during the tribulation, have to make the same trip to heaven to be with Jesus, which has to be terribly exciting as well. Is the only difference between the two that most believers will have to suffer the death of the flesh and make the journey to heaven alone rather than in a group?

It is interesting to note that there were two raptures in the Old Testament. Two godly men were taken up to meet Jesus while they are still alive, one in the age of the anarchy, and one in the age of the law. The first was Enoch, whose rapture is described in **Genesis 5:24**: "And Enoch walked with God; and **he *was* not**, for God **took him**." And there was Elijah in **2 Kings 2:11**: "Then it happened, as they continued on and talked, that suddenly a chariot of fire *appeared* with horses of fire, and **separated the two of them**; and Elijah **went up** by a **whirlwind into heaven**."

The word in the Hebrew translated as "God **took him**" in the Genesis passage is H3947 *laqach*, which means "Accept, **carry away, fetch**, get, receive, **seize, send for**, take **(away, up)**"; and the Hebrew word translated as "**went up** by a **whirlwind**" is H5927 *alah*, which means "Arise, **ascend up, at once**, (cause to make) **come up, fetch up, take away (up)**." Both are very much like the definition of the rapture in the Greek, and both apply to those still alive.

There were two raptures in the New Testament as well. There was the time when the apostle Paul was raptured up to paradise to be taught by Jesus. Paul, speaking of himself, said,

> It is doubtless not profitable for me to boast. I will come to **visions** and **revelations of the Lord**: [2] I know a man in Christ who fourteen years ago—whether **in the body I do not know**, or whether **out of the body I do not know**, God knows—such a one was **caught up to the third heaven**. [3] And I know such a man—whether in the body or out of the body I do not know, God knows— [4] how **he was caught up into Paradise** and **heard inexpressible words**, which it is not lawful for a man to utter. (**2 Corinthians 12:1–4**)

The Greek word translated as "caught up" in this passage is G726 *harpazo*, the same Greek word that is used for the rapture.

And then, of course, there was Jesus: "Now it came to pass, while He blessed them, that **He was parted from them** and **carried up into heaven**" (**Luke 24:51**). The Greek word for the ascension of Jesus Christ is G399 *anaphero*, which means "**To take up** (literally or figuratively) bear, **bring** (carry, lead) **up, offer up**." This has a slightly different meaning, perhaps, because He was an offering—a sacrifice of Himself to His Father in heaven for our sins.

These raptures give hope for us who believe in Christ now and even for those who have not yet received Jesus and His truth. For even if they miss the first rapture, when they see these amazing things happening that were foretold in the Bible, they might receive redemption by faith in Jesus in the midtribulation rapture, or they might be martyred for their faith. Only those who are enjoying the evil ways of this world under Satan and are taking pleasure in unrighteousness that will not be saved in the tribulation: "And **for this reason God will send them strong delusion**, that they should **believe the lie**, [12] that they all may be **condemned** who **did not believe the truth** but had **pleasure in unrighteousness**" (**2 Thessalonians 2:11–12**).

The book of the Revelation (of Jesus Christ) shows us that there will be saints who come out of the tribulation and the great tribulation. This should not encourage anyone to delay seeking Jesus our Lord now, because in the tribulation there will truly be great suffering, and many saints will be beheaded for their faith in Jesus. To receive redemption by faith in Jesus Christ as your Lord and Savior now is to avoid the terror and great suffering on earth and rather to watch the tribulation from the peace and comfort of heaven with Jesus.

These three-tiered raptures seem to be the way with God; He is loving and merciful and does not want us to suffer any more than we need to. He first tries to get our attention and turn us around with as little pain and suffering as possible and continues with ever-increasing trials until He does finally get our attention. By doing this He shows us that He did try to get our attention with less tribulation, and we know that we did not respond with lesser trials. That is the way it happened with me. I know that God gave me a number of gentler wake-up calls that I ignored. I am just very thankful that He kept trying and did not give up on me.

And that is what He will be doing in the tribulation. Some have already received His call and responded. They do not need any more trials to get their attention; these are the ones who are raptured before the tribulation. Some, who have not yet received Him, need to go through the first half of the tribulation before they wake up and come to Him. And then there are those who are slow learners, as I was, and are still focused on themselves, thinking they can live apart from God's grace. But they will realize how much they need God and His ways that lead to eternal life in the great tribulation. Then there are those whose hearts are so hardened that they are beyond hope of change and are given up to remain with Satan in hell forever.

The Tribulation

THE DAY OF THE LORD

THE DAY OF the Lord is when the trial in heaven that is being carried out on earth is wrapped up, and the Bible speaks of the things that must occur first:

> But this is what was spoken by the **prophet Joel**: [17] "And **it shall come to pass in the last days**, says God, That I will **pour out of My Spirit on all flesh**; Your sons and your daughters **shall prophesy**, Your young men **shall see visions**, Your old men **shall dream dreams**. [18] And on My menservants and on My maidservants I **will pour out My Spirit in those days**; And they shall **prophesy**. [19] I will show wonders in heaven above And signs in the earth beneath: Blood and fire and vapor of smoke. [20] The **sun shall be turned into darkness**, And the **moon into blood**, **Before** the coming of the great and awesome **day of the LORD**. [21] And it shall come to pass That **whoever calls on the name of the LORD Shall be saved**." (Acts 2:16–21)

THE DAY OF THE LORD

> Deliver such a one to Satan for **the destruction of the flesh**, that **his spirit may be saved** in the **day of the Lord Jesus**. [6] **Your glorying is not good**. Do you not know that **a little leaven leavens the whole lump**? [7] Therefore purge out the old leaven, that you may be a new lump, since you truly are

unleavened. For indeed **Christ**, our **Passover**, was **sacrificed for us**. [8] Therefore let us **keep the feast**, not with old leaven, nor with the **leaven of malice and wickedness**, but with the **unleavened** *bread* **of sincerity and truth**. (1 **Corinthians 5:5–8**)

As mentioned previously, leaven metaphorically represents pride because it "puffs up." Here God is confirming what we learned in the third age of the church—that good and evil cannot coexist. A little evil makes the whole kingdom evil. Sin is like cancer. I, for one, know that a little cancer makes the whole body cancerous and causes the whole body to die—good cells, cancer cells, and all.

THE DAY OF THE LORD

For you yourselves know perfectly that the **day of the Lord** so comes as a thief in the night. [3] For when they say, "**Peace and safety**!" then sudden destruction comes upon them, as **labor pains** upon a pregnant woman. And they shall not escape. [4] But you, brethren, are **not in darkness**, so that **this Day** should overtake you as a thief. [5] **You are all sons of light** and **sons of the day**. We are not **of the night** nor of **darkness**. (1 **Thessalonians 5:2–5**)

THE DAY OF GOD

But the day of the Lord will come as a thief in the night, in which the heavens will pass away with a great noise, and the elements will melt with fervent heat; both the earth and the works that are in it will be burned up. [11] Therefore, **since all these things will be dissolved, what manner** *of persons* **ought you to be** in holy conduct and godliness, [12] looking for and hastening the coming of the **day of God**, because of which the heavens will be dissolved, being on fire, and the elements will melt with fervent heat? [13] Nevertheless **we, according to His promise, look for new heavens** and a **new earth** in which **righteousness dwells**. (2 **Peter 3:10**)

415

THE REVELATION OF JESUS CHRIST

It is important to note that the revelation in the Book of Revelation is from Jesus. Jesus is doing the revealing, and it is the apostle John who is doing the writing.

> The Revelation of Jesus Christ, which **God gave Him to show His servants**–things which must **shortly take place**. And He sent and signified *it* by His angel to His servant John, ² who bore witness to the word of God, and to the testimony of Jesus Christ, to all things that he saw. ³ **Blessed** *is* **he who reads** and **those who hear the words of this prophecy**, and **keep those things which are written in it**; for the time *is* near. **(Revelation 1:1–3)**

John, to the seven churches which are in Asia: Grace to you and peace from Him who is and who was and who is to come, and from the **seven Spirits** who are before His throne, ⁵ and from Jesus Christ, the faithful witness, the **firstborn from the dead**, and the **ruler over the kings of the earth**. To Him who **loved** us and washed us from our sins **in His own blood**, ⁶ and has **made us kings** and **priests to His God and Father**, to Him *be* glory and dominion forever and ever. Amen.

⁷ Behold, **He is coming with clouds**, and **every eye will see Him**, even **they who pierced Him**. And all the **tribes** of the earth will mourn because of Him. Even so, Amen. ⁸ "**I am** the **Alpha and the Omega**, *the* **Beginning and** *the* **End**," says the Lord, "who is and who was and who is to come, the Almighty." ⁹ I, John, both your brother and companion in the tribulation and kingdom and patience of Jesus Christ, was on the island that is called Patmos for the word of God and for the testimony of Jesus Christ. ¹⁰ I was **in the Spirit** on the **Lord's Day**, and I heard behind me a loud voice, as of a trumpet, ¹¹ saying, "I am the Alpha and the Omega, the First and the Last," and, "What you see, **write in a book** and send *it* to the seven churches which are in Asia: to Ephesus, to Smyrna, to Pergamos, to Thyatira, to Sardis, to Philadelphia, and to Laodicea."

¹² Then I turned to see the voice that spoke with me. And having turned I saw **seven golden lampstands**, ¹³ and in the midst of

the **seven lampstands** one like the Son of Man, clothed with a garment down to the feet and girded about the chest with a golden band. [14] His head and hair *were* white like wool, as white as snow, and His eyes like a flame of fire; [15] His feet *were* like fine brass, as if refined in a furnace, and His voice as the sound of many waters; [16] **He had in His right hand seven stars**, out of His mouth went a sharp two-edged sword, and His countenance *was* like the sun shining in its strength.

[17] And when I saw Him, **I fell at His feet as dead**. But He laid His right hand on me, saying to me, "Do not be afraid; I am the First and the Last. [18] I *am* He who lives, and was dead, and behold, I am alive forevermore. Amen. And **I have the keys of Hades and of Death**. [19] Write the things which you have seen, and the things **which are**, and the things **which will take place after this**. [20] The **mystery of the seven stars which you saw in My right hand**, and the **seven golden lampstands**: The **seven stars** are the **angels** of the **seven churches**, and the **seven lampstands** which you saw are the **seven churches.** (**Revelation 1:4–20**)

There are some things in this passage that are very intriguing, such as where it states that when He comes to earth, **"every eye will see Him, even they who pierced Him."** Is this passage saying that all the dead will be alive again, good and evil? Also notice that God is revealing a mystery that Jews might appreciate. The lampstands and lamps were furnishings in the temple of God on earth in which the Jewish priests served, but it had ten lamps and lampstands: "the lampstands of pure gold, five on the right *side* and five on the left in front of the inner sanctuary, with the flowers and the lamps and the wick-trimmers of gold" (**1 Kings 7:49**).

Hebrews 8:1–13 says that Jesus is serving as the High Priest in the true temple in heaven, of which the inner sanctuary on earth is an inferior copy:

Now *this is* the main point of the things we are saying: We have such a High Priest, who is **seated at the right hand** of the **throne of the Majesty in the heavens**, [2] a Minister of the sanctuary and of the **true tabernacle which the Lord erected**, and **not man**. [3] For every high priest is appointed to offer both gifts and sacrifices. Therefore *it is* necessary that this one also have something to offer.

[4] For if He were on earth, He would not be a priest, since there are priests who **offer the gifts according to the law**; [5] who **serve the copy** and **shadow of the heavenly things**, as Moses was divinely instructed when he was about to make the tabernacle. For He said, *"See that you make all things according to the pattern shown you on the mountain."* [6] But now **He has obtained a more excellent ministry**, inasmuch as He is also **Mediator of a better covenant**, which was **established on better promises**.

[7] For if that **first *covenant* had been faultless**, then no place would have been sought for a second. [8] Because finding fault with them, He says: *"Behold, the days are coming, says the* LORD, *when I will make a new covenant with the house of Israel and with the house of Judah—* [9] *not according to the covenant that I made with their fathers in the day when I took them by the hand to lead them out of the land of Egypt; because they did not continue in My covenant, and I disregarded them, says the* LORD.

[10] *"For this is the* **covenant** *that I will make with the house of Israel* **after those days***, says the* LORD: *I will* **put My laws in their mind** *and* **write them on their hearts**; *and I will be their God, and they shall be My people.* [11] *None of them shall teach his neighbor, and none his brother, saying, 'Know the* LORD,' *for all shall know Me, from the least of them to the greatest of them.* [12] *For I will be merciful to their* **unrighteousness***, and their sins and their lawless deeds* **I will remember no more.**" [13] *In that He says,* "A **new covenant**," **He has made the first obsolete**. Now what is becoming obsolete and growing old is ready to vanish away.

The phrase "**after those days**" refers to the time after the age of anarchy and the age of the law.

Perhaps there were ten lamps in the tabernacle that Moses was instructed to make because the old covenant was based on the law, the Ten Commandments. Jesus reveals here that the **number of lamps** in the

true tabernacle in heaven is seven, symbolizing the **"angels,"** or **pastors**, of the **seven churches** that have been given a **new covenant** based on **truth and love**—the **belief and understanding** in the **mind that love of the heart fulfills the law and unites us as One in Christ**. The word translated as "angel" in the phrase "The **seven stars are the angels** of the **seven churches**" is the Greek word G32 *aggelos*, which means "A messenger; especially an 'angel'; by implication **a pastor**:- angel, messenger."

Chapters 2 and 3 of Revelations contain the letters from Jesus describing what the seven churches have done well and what they need to correct in themselves. The Bible scholar David Jeremiah indicates that these seven churches of Asia also represent the nature of the church through the years. I have not studied the history of the church since its beginnings to know that this so, but if this is so, and if the end is near (and I think it is), then the church of this present time is like the church of Laodicea.

Listen to what Jesus says to the church of Laodicea:

> And to the angel of the church of the Laodiceans write, 'These things says the Amen, the Faithful and True Witness, the Beginning of the creation of God: [15] **I know your works**, that you are **neither cold nor hot**. I could wish **you were cold or hot**. [16] So then, because **you are lukewarm**, and neither cold nor hot, **I will vomit you out of My mouth**. [17] Because you say, '**I am rich**, have become **wealthy**, and have **need of nothing**'—and do not know that you are **wretched, miserable, poor, blind**, and **naked**— [18] I counsel you to buy from Me gold refined in the fire, that you may be rich; and white garments, that you may be clothed, *that* the **shame of your nakedness may not be revealed**; and anoint your eyes with eye salve, **that you may see**.
>
> [19] "**As many as I love, I rebuke and chasten**. Therefore be **zealous** and **repent**. [20] Behold, **I stand at the door and knock**. If anyone hears My voice and opens the door, I will come in to him and **dine with him**, and **he with Me**. [21] To him **who overcomes** I will grant to **sit with Me on My throne**, as I also overcame and sat down with My Father on His throne.

²² He **who has an ear, let him hear** what the Spirit says to the churches." (**Revelation 3:14–21**)

This accurately describes the lukewarm church of today. To be hot is to be "on fire for the Lord." Being cold for God is like being an atheist. But an atheist has at least used reasoning to come to the conclusion that there is no God. The atheist has come to the wrong conclusion, but at least God can reason with him. And many atheists have come to faith by reasoning, such as C. S. Lewis and Lee Strobel. Those who are lukewarm are indifferent to God and will not even bother to think about whether there is a God or not; they just do not care, and so God cannot even reason with them, and so He spits them out. We can definitely see that in the church today. Perhaps we are seeing the "falling away" spoken of in **2 Thessalonians 2:3**.

Seven Lamps Are the Seven Spirits of God

> And from the throne proceeded lightnings, thunderings, and voices. **Seven lamps of fire** *were* **burning before the throne**, which are the **seven Spirits of God**. (**Revelation 4:5**)

Here we can see confirmation of what we have already learned. The seven lamps and lampstands are the seven churches on earth, the body of Christ which is righteous and will be part of the Holy Spirit of Christ when we are again in our home in heaven and shed our earthly bodies of flesh.

WORTHY IS THE LAMB

> And I saw in the right *hand* of Him who sat on the throne **a scroll written inside** and **on the back**, sealed with seven seals. ² Then I saw a strong angel proclaiming with a loud voice, "Who is worthy to open the scroll and to loose its seals?" ³ And no one in heaven or on the earth or under the earth was able to open the scroll, or to look at it. ⁴ So I wept much, because no one was found worthy to open and read the scroll, or to look at it. (**Revelation 5:1–4**)

Jesus Is the Only One Who Can Open the Seven Seals

> But one of the elders said to me, "Do not weep. Behold, the **Lion** of the **tribe of Judah**, the **Root of David**, has prevailed to open the scroll and to loose its seven seals." **(Revelation 5:5)**

The Lamb Who Was Slain Has Seven Horns, Seven Eyes, Which Are the Seven Spirits of God

> And I looked, and behold, in the midst of the throne and of the four living creatures, and in the midst of the elders, stood a Lamb as though it had been slain, having **seven horns** and **seven eyes**, which are the **seven Spirits of God** sent out into all the earth. **(Revelation 5:6)**

This verse seems to be self-explanatory; the seven horns and eyes represent the seven spirits of God in heaven or the seven churches on earth.

The Golden Bowls Are the Prayers of the Saints

> Then He came and took the scroll out of the right hand of Him who sat on the throne. ⁸ Now when He had taken the scroll, the four living creatures and the twenty-four elders fell down before the Lamb, each having a harp, and golden bowls full of incense, which are the **prayers of the saints. (Revelation 5:7–8)**

Every Knee Shall Bow—Every Tongue Confess

> And they sang a new song, saying: "You are worthy to take the scroll, And to open its seals; For You were slain, And have **redeemed us to God by Your blood** Out of **every tribe** and **tongue** and **people** and **nation**, ¹⁰ And have made us **kings** and **priests** to our God; And **we shall reign on the earth**." ¹¹ Then I looked, and I heard the voice of many angels around the throne, the living creatures, and the elders; and the number of them was ten thousand times ten thousand, and thousands of thousands, ¹² saying with a loud voice: "**Worthy is the Lamb who was slain** To receive power and riches and wisdom, And strength and honor and glory and blessing!" ¹³ And every creature which is in heaven and **on the earth** and **under the earth** and **such**

as are in the sea, and all that are in them, I heard saying: "Blessing and honor and glory and power *Be* to Him who sits on the throne, And to the Lamb, forever and ever!" [14] Then the four living creatures said, "Amen!" And the twenty-four elders fell down and worshiped Him who lives forever and ever. (**Revelation 5:9–14**)

This passage seems to be a future fulfillment of what Paul said in **Philippians 2:9–11**: "Therefore God also has highly exalted Him and given Him the name which is above every name, [10] that **at the name of Jesus every knee should bow**, of those **in heaven**, and of those **on earth**, and of those **under the earth**, [11] and *that* every tongue should confess that Jesus Christ *is* Lord, to the glory of God the Father."

THE SEVEN SEALS

THE FIRST SEAL—THE RIDER OF THE WHITE HORSE WAS GIVEN A CROWN

Now I saw when **the Lamb opened one of the seals**; and I heard one of the four living creatures saying with a voice like thunder, "Come and see." [2] And I looked, and behold, a white horse. He who sat on it **had a bow**; and **a crown** was **given to him**, and he went out conquering and to conquer. (**Revelation 6:1–2**)

This seems to be a reference to the Antichrist. The crown symbolizes that he is given authority to try to make a kingdom for himself while Jesus' saints, who were raptured before the tribulation, are resting peacefully with Him in heaven. The white horse symbolizes that he is first appearing as a white knight to save the world as though he were Jesus the Christ, the anointed King. When Jesus the real Christ does return as our conquering King and Savior after the tribulation, He will be riding a white horse: "Now I saw heaven opened, and behold, a **white horse**. And He who sat on him *was* called **Faithful and True**, and **in righteousness** He judges and makes war" (**Revelation 19:11**).

Jesus warned us about imposters: "For such *are* **false apostles**, deceitful workers, transforming themselves into apostles of Christ. [14] And no wonder! For **Satan himself transforms himself** into an **angel of light**. [15] Therefore *it is* no great thing **if his ministers** also **transform themselves** into **ministers of righteousness**, whose end will be according to their works" (**2 Corinthians 11:13–15**). Remember that Satan is the one who wants his kingdom to be higher than Jesus' kingdom and wants to be like God Most High. And so Satan, the "counterfeiter," needs to have one like Jesus the Christ under him, and so he sets up his Antichrist on earth.

The Second Seal—The Rider of the Red Horse Was Given a Sword

> When He opened the second seal, I heard the second living creature saying, "Come and see." [4] Another horse, fiery red, went out. And it was granted to the one who sat on it to **take peace from the earth**, and that *people* should **kill one another**; and there was given to him a great sword. (**Revelation 6:3–4**)

This foreshadows the time when the Antichrist will reveal his true nature and purpose and go out to destroy everything that is of God and kill those who were left behind. The Antichrist's harsh rule causes division and hatred, and there will be many wars and murders of all nations and people.

The Third Seal—The Rider of the Black Horse Had a Pair of Scales in his Hand

> When He opened the third seal, I heard the third living creature say, "Come and see." So I looked, and behold, a black horse, and he who sat on it had a pair of scales in his hand. [6] And I heard a voice in the midst of the four living creatures saying, "A **quart of wheat for a denarius**, and **three quarts of barley for a denarius**; and do not harm the oil and the wine. (**Revelation 6:5–6**)

The scales are a metaphor for commerce, because in those days silver, gold, and copper were measured with scales. The Antichrist's harsh rule on earth by fear of death has squelched productivity and has caused the prices of commodities to necessarily skyrocket.

The Fourth Seal—The Rider of the Pale Horse Was Death

> When He opened the fourth seal, I heard the voice of the fourth living creature saying, "Come and see." [8] So I looked, and behold, **a pale horse**. And the name of him who sat on it was **Death**, and **Hades** followed with him. And power was given to them over a fourth of the earth, to **kill with sword**, with **hunger**, with **death**, and by the **beasts of the earth**. (**Revelation 6:7–8**)

Now it appears that the demonic spiritual world symbolized by hades, or hell, is getting involved in the battle, and the one that the demons are following is perhaps the Antichrist, but possibly Satan, the leader of the underworld. And they are allowed to kill those who are resisting him and his rule, even whole nations, but the suffering of this time causes many of the elect to believe in God, and many are beheaded for their faith.

The Fifth Seal—The Tribulation Saints under the Altar

> When He opened the fifth seal, I saw **under the altar the souls** of those who had been **slain for the word of God** and for the **testimony which they held**. [10] And they cried with a loud voice, saying, "How long, O Lord, holy and true, until You judge and avenge our blood on those who dwell on the earth?" [11] Then **a white robe was given to each of them**; and it was said to them that they should rest a little while longer, **until** both *the number of* their **fellow servants** and their **brethren**, who would **be killed as they** *were*, **was completed**. (**Revelation 6:9–11**)

This passage shows that there were those who become believers during the first half of the tribulation who were willing to die for their faith in Jesus. These are the **tribulation saints,** who were **martyred for their faith in Jesus** during the **first three and a half years of the tribulation**. This passage also predicts that some will be martyred for their faith in Jesus in the second three and one-half years of the tribulation, a period called the great tribulation. The white robes that were given them were to cover their nakedness and represent the righteousness of God and harken back to the time when we all were naked by having rejected the righteousness of God and instead believed in the ways of evil and darkness by believing the lies of Satan: "Then the LORD God called to Adam and said to him, 'Where *are* you?' [10] So he said, 'I heard Your voice in the garden, and **I was afraid because I was naked**; and I hid myself.' [11] And He said, '**Who told you that you** *were* **naked**? Have you eaten from the tree of which I commanded you that you should not eat?'" (**Genesis 3:9–11**).

The Sixth Seal—The Great Day of the Wrath of the Lamb— The Great Tribulation Has Come

> I looked when He opened the sixth seal, and behold, there was a **great earthquake**; and the **sun became black** as sackcloth of hair, and the **moon became like blood**. [13] And the **stars of heaven fell to the earth**, as a fig tree drops its late figs when it is shaken by a mighty wind. [14] Then the **sky receded as a scroll when it is rolled up**, and **every mountain and island was moved out of its place**. [15] And the kings of the earth, the great men, the rich men, the commanders, the mighty men, every slave and every free man, hid themselves in the caves and in the rocks of the mountains, [16] and said to the mountains and rocks, "Fall on us and hide us from the face of Him who sits on the throne and from the **wrath of the Lamb**! [17] For the **great day of His wrath has come**, and who is able to stand?" (**Revelation 6:12–17**)

In this passage, the "**stars of heaven [that] fell to the earth**" symbolize not angels but actual meteors falling from outer space to the earth, causing great earthquakes. The resulting dust in the air is darkening the sun and causing the moon to appear red, as when smoke from a great forest fire or ash from a volcano will make the sun appear orange or red. And this passage signals that we are at the midway point of the tribulation and the "**great day of His wrath**"; the great tribulation is about to begin.

144, 000 Servants of God Sealed

> After these things I saw four angels standing at the four corners of the earth, holding the four winds of the earth, that the wind should not blow on the earth, on the sea, or on any tree. ² Then I saw another angel ascending from the east, having the **seal of the living God**. And he cried with a loud voice to the four angels to whom it was granted to harm the earth and the sea, ³ saying, "Do not harm the earth, the sea, or the trees till we have **sealed** the **servants of our God on their foreheads**." ⁴ And I heard the number of those who were sealed. one **hundred** *and* **forty-four thousand** of all the **tribes of the children of Israel** *were* **sealed**:
>
> ⁵ of the tribe of Judah twelve thousand *were* sealed;
> of the tribe of Reuben twelve thousand *were* sealed;
> of the tribe of Gad twelve thousand *were* sealed;
> ⁶ of the tribe of Asher twelve thousand *were* sealed;
> of the tribe of Naphtali twelve thousand *were* sealed;
> of the tribe of Manasseh twelve thousand *were* sealed;
> ⁷ of the tribe of Simeon twelve thousand *were* sealed;
> of the tribe of Levi twelve thousand *were* sealed;
> of the tribe of Issachar twelve thousand *were* sealed;
> ⁸ of the tribe of Zebulun twelve thousand *were* sealed;
> of the tribe of Joseph twelve thousand *were* sealed;
> of the tribe of Benjamin twelve thousand *were* sealed. (**Revelation 7:1–8**)

In **Revelation chapter 14**, when we view the tribulation a second time from the perspective of earth, we will see that these are taken up to be with Christ before the throne of God. This is evidence of the **midtribulation rapture**. Notice that the tribe of Dan is not listed among the twelve tribes. They are the tribe that rejected the true God and worshipped their own god, a golden calf: "Those who swear by the sin of Samaria, Who say, 'As your god lives, O Dan!' And, 'As the way of Beersheba lives!' They shall fall and never rise again" (**Amos 8:14**).

The Great Tribulation Saints

> **After these things** I looked, and behold, a great multitude which no one could number, **of all nations, tribes, peoples,** and **tongues**, standing before the throne and before the Lamb, clothed with white robes, with **palm branches in their hands,** [10] and crying out with a loud voice, saying, "**Salvation *belongs* to our God who sits** on the **throne**, and to the **Lamb**!"
>
> [11] All the angels stood around the throne and the elders and the four living creatures, and fell on their faces before the throne and worshiped God, [12] saying: "Amen! Blessing and glory and wisdom, Thanksgiving and honor and power and might, *Be* to our God forever and ever. Amen." [13] Then one of the elders answered, saying to me, "**Who are these arrayed in white robes, and where did they come from?**" [14] And I said to him, "Sir, you know." So he said to me, "**These are the ones who come out** of the **great tribulation,** and **washed their robes** and **made them white in the blood of the Lamb.**
>
> [15] "Therefore **they are before the throne of God,** and serve Him day and night in His temple. And He who sits on the throne **will dwell among them.** [16] They shall neither hunger anymore nor thirst anymore; the sun shall not strike them, nor any heat; [17] for **the Lamb who** is in the **midst of the throne will shepherd them** and **lead them to living fountains of waters**. And God will wipe away every tear from their eyes." (**Revelation 7:9–17**)

The figures in white robes in the above passage are the great tribulation saints, those who will be raptured and martyred for their faith in Jesus during the last three and a half years of the tribulation, called the great tribulation. We are not told at this point when in the great tribulation the last rapture occurs, but when we view the tribulation a second time from the perspective of earth, we will see that these saints are taken up to be with Christ in Revelation 18 at the fall of Babylon the Great.

I can relate to these great tribulation saints because they are slow learners, just as I was. When God gave me my cancer wake-up call by having a doctor tell me I would go blind and die from a cancerous brain tumor, God miraculously saved my life. That should have been enough to get my attention, but instead I had the mind that I was going to go back to work and do my best to forget that this cancer crisis ever happened.

Well, God gave me a personal "great tribulation" of hydrocephalus, and a second brain surgery that brought me to my knees, crying out to God for help. The result is that I am so thankful that God did not give up on me and loved me enough to let me suffer more, that through my momentary suffering I might be saved for eternity. When the great tribulation saints realize how close they came to losing eternal life and living in eternal damnation, they will be exceedingly grateful.

This is exactly what the apostle Paul described in **2 Corinthians 4:16–18:** "Therefore we do not lose heart. Even though our **outward man is perishing**, yet the **inward** *man* is being renewed day by day. [17] For our **light affliction**, which is but for **a moment**, is **working for us a far more exceeding** *and* **eternal weight of glory**, [18] while we do not look at the things which are seen, but at the things which are not seen. For the **things which are seen** *are* **temporary**, but the things **which are not seen** *are* **eternal**." Recall what I wrote earlier about God needing to cover our spirits with bodies of flesh so that we could not see and remember the spiritual reality, but only what our five senses allowed us to perceive—the things of this world.

The Seventh Seal—Seven Angels Given Seven Trumpets

> When He opened the **seventh seal**, there was silence in heaven for about half an hour. [2] And I saw the seven angels who stand before God, and to them were given **seven trumpets**. [3] Then another angel, having a golden censer, came and stood at the altar. He was given much incense, that he should offer *it* with the prayers of all the saints upon the golden altar which was before the throne. [4] And the smoke of the incense, with the prayers of

the saints, ascended before God from the angel's hand. [5] Then the angel took the censer, filled it with fire from the altar, and threw *it* to the earth. And there were noises, thunderings, lightnings, and an earthquake. [6] So the seven angels who had the seven trumpets prepared themselves to sound. (**Revelation 8:1–6**)

The seventh seal appears to be the preparation for the seven trumpets to come.

THE SEVEN TRUMPETS

The First Trumpet—Hail and Fire Mixed with Blood

The **first angel sounded**: And hail and fire followed, mingled with blood, and they were thrown to the earth. And a third of the trees were burned up, and all green grass was burned up. (**Revelation 8:7**)

The Second Trumpet—Fiery Mountain Thrown into the Sea

Then the second angel sounded: And *something* like **a great mountain burning with fire** was thrown into the sea, and **a third of the sea became blood**. [9] And a third of the living creatures in the sea died, and a third of the ships were destroyed. (**Revelation 8:8–9**)

This sounds like it might be a huge meteor hitting the earth.

The Third Trumpet—A Great Star from Heaven Fell on the Rivers

Then the third angel sounded: And a great star fell from heaven, burning like a torch, and it fell on a third of the rivers and on the springs of water. [11] The name of the star is Wormwood. A third of the waters became wormwood, and **many men died from the water**, because **it was made bitter**. (**Revelation 8:10–11**)

The Fourth Trumpet—Sun and the Moon Darkened

Then the fourth angel sounded: And a third of the sun was struck, a third of the moon, and a third of the stars, so that a third of them were darkened. A third of the day did not shine, and likewise the night. [13] And I looked, and I heard an angel flying through the midst of heaven, saying with a loud voice, "**Woe, woe, woe** to the inhabitants of the earth, because of the remaining blasts of the trumpet of the three angels who are about to sound!" (**Revelation 8:12–13**)

The next three trumpets are so woefully horrific that they are called "the three woes."

The Fifth Trumpet—A Star Fallen from Heaven with Keys to the Bottomless Pit

Then the fifth angel sounded: And I saw **a star fallen from heaven to the earth**. To him **was given the key to the bottomless pit**. [2] And he opened the bottomless pit, and smoke arose out of the pit like the smoke of a great furnace. So **the sun** and the **air were darkened** because of the **smoke of the pit**. [3] Then out of the smoke **locusts came upon the earth**. And to them was given power, as the scorpions of the earth have power.

[4] They were commanded **not to harm the grass of the earth**, or any green thing, or any tree, but only **those men who do not have the seal of God on their foreheads**. [5] And they were not given *authority* to kill them, **but to torment them *for* five months**. Their torment *was* like the torment of a scorpion when it strikes a man. [6] In those days **men will seek death** and **will not find it**; they will **desire to die**, and **death will flee from them**. [7] The shape of the locusts was like horses prepared for battle. On their heads were crowns of something like gold, and **their faces *were* like the faces of men**. [8] They had hair like women's hair, and their teeth were like lions' *teeth*.

[9] And they had breastplates like breastplates of iron, and the sound of their wings *was* like the sound of chariots with many horses running into battle. [10] They **had tails like scorpions**,

and there were stings in their tails. Their power *was* to hurt men five months. **[11]** And they had as **king over them** the **angel of the bottomless pit**, whose name in Hebrew *is* **Abaddon**, but in Greek he has the name **Apollyon**. **[12] One woe is past**. Behold, **still two more woes are coming after these things**. **(Revelation 9:1–12)**

The phrase regarding the locusts being allowed to harm "only **those men who do not have the seal of God on their foreheads**" implies that there must be some still on earth who have or are going to have the seal of God on their foreheads.

The "star" mentioned in verse one of this passage is an angel, and the phrase "**a star fallen from heaven to the earth**" reminds us of the words of Jesus speaking about the fall of Satan: "And He said to them, "**I saw Satan fall like lightning from heaven**" (**Luke 10:18**). This king of the demonic angels is identified by his names. The Greek word G3 *Abaddon* is defined as follows: "Of Hebrew origin[H11]; **a destroying angel**: Abaddon." The Hebrew word H11 *abbaddon* is defined as follows: "Intensively from H6; abstractly **a perishing**; concretely **Hades**:- **destruction**." The Hebrew word H6 *abad* is defined as "**To wander away,** that is **lose oneself**; by implication **to perish (causatively to destroy) destruction with no escape, fail, lose, be void of, have no way to flee**." And the word "Appolyon" is translated from the Greek word G623 *Apolluon*, which means "**A destroyer** (that is, **Satan**): **Appolyon**."

We might wonder how the demons from the pit can be "commanded **not to harm the grass of the earth**, or any green thing, or any tree" when "all green grass was burned up" in the first trumpet in **Revelation 8:7**. But we know that after a fire grass can rather quickly regrow from its roots, and only one-third of the trees were burned in the first trumpet.

The Sixth Trumpet—At the Euphrates River, a Two-Hundred-Million-Man Army on the Move

Then the sixth angel sounded: And I heard a voice from the **four horns** of the golden altar which is before God, ¹⁴ saying to the **sixth angel who had the trumpet**, "Release the four angels who are **bound at the great river Euphrates**." ¹⁵ So the four angels, who had been **prepared for** the **hour** and **day** and **month** and **year**, were released to **kill a third of mankind**.

¹⁶ Now the number of the army of the horsemen *was* **two hundred million**; I heard the number of them. ¹⁷ And thus I saw the horses in the vision: those who sat on them had **breastplates of fiery red, hyacinth blue**, and **sulfur yellow**; and the heads of the horses *were* like the heads of lions; and out of their mouths came fire, smoke, and brimstone. ¹⁸ By these three *plagues* **a third of mankind was killed**–by the fire and the smoke and the brimstone which came out of their mouths. ¹⁹ For their power is in their **mouth** and **in their tails**; for their **tails** *are* **like serpents**, having heads; and with them they do harm.

²⁰ **But the rest of mankind, who were not killed by these plagues, did not repent of the works of their hand**s, that they should not worship demons, and idols of gold, silver, brass, stone, and wood, which can neither see nor hear nor walk. ²¹ And **they did not repent of their murders** or their **sorceries** or their **sexual immorality** or their **thefts**. (**Revelation 9:13–21**)

At this point all of God's elect, those who would believe in Jesus Christ, have been martyred for their faith or raptured from the earth to be with God forever. And these last plagues demonstrate how hardened the hearts and minds of the remaining people on earth are against God and the truth.

The Seven Thunderings

I saw still another mighty angel coming down from heaven, clothed with a cloud. And **a rainbow** *was* **on his head, his face** *was* **like the sun**, and **his feet like pillars of fire**. ² He had **a little book** open in his hand. And he set his right foot on the

432

sea and *his* left *foot* on the land, [3] and cried with a **loud voice,
as *when* a lion roars**. When he cried out, **seven thunders
uttered their voices**. [4] Now when the seven thunders uttered
their voices, I was about to write; but I heard a voice from heaven
saying to me, "**Seal up the things which the seven thunders
uttered**, and **do not write them**."

[5] The angel whom I saw standing on the sea and on the land
raised up his hand to heaven [6] and swore by Him who lives
forever and ever, who created heaven and the things that are in it,
the earth and the things that are in it, and the sea and the things
that are in it, that **there should be delay no longer,** [7] but **in
the days of the sounding of the seventh angel, when he
is about to sound**, the **mystery of God** would **be finished,
as He declared to His servants the prophets. (Revelation
10:1–7)**

The mighty angel that came down from heaven, by His description, is
Jesus Christ. The seven thunderous utterings that John was not allowed
to write are to be revealed in the days when the seventh angel actually
sounds his trumpet. For now these words are a mystery to us.

The Little Book—You Must Prophesy Again

Then the voice which I heard from heaven spoke to me again and
said, "Go, **take the little book** which **is open** in the hand of
the angel who stands on the sea and **on the earth**." [9] So I
went to the angel and said to him, "**Give me the little book**."
And he said to me, "**Take and eat it**; and it will make your
stomach bitter, but it will be as sweet as honey in your mouth."
[10] Then I took the little book out of the angel's hand and ate it,
and it was as sweet as honey in my mouth. But when I had eaten
it, my stomach became bitter. [11] And he said to me, "**You must
prophesy again** about **many peoples, nations, tongues**, and
kings." **(Revelation 10:8–11)**

Perhaps the sweet taste in the passage above is from reading about those
who have understood and accepted the truth and know that God is
good, "Oh, **taste and see that the LORD *is* good**; Blessed *is* the man

433

who trusts in Him! ⁹ Oh, fear the LORD, you His saints! *There is* **no want** to those who fear Him" (**Psalm 34:89**).

Perhaps the bitter taste might be the knowledge of those who will not accept the truth and remain in the lies of Satan: "And I say to you that many will come from east and west, and **sit down with Abraham, Isaac,** and **Jacob in the kingdom of heaven.** ¹² But **the sons of the kingdom** will be **cast out into outer darkness.** There will be **weeping** and **gnashing of teeth**" (**Matthew 8:11–12**). Notice that there are two kingdoms: the kingdom of God in heaven and the kingdom of Satan on earth.

It is not clear whether the phrase "**You must prophesy again**" is speaking of the "big book," the scroll that contains the revelation of the future that John has been witnessing of until now, or if it is speaking of the "little book" that John was just given. Perhaps it applies to both, because they each speak of **many peoples, nations, tongues,** and **kings.** We will see how the little book is the whole story of the Bible in condensed form; it is "about **many peoples, nations, tongues,** and **kings**," concerning the kingdom of heaven that has come to earth, and the kingdom of earth. First, in **Chapter 12** of **Revelation,** John will prophesy from the little book concerning the kingdom of God on earth. And later, in **Chapter 17** of **Revelation,** John will prophesy from the little book concerning the kingdom of Satan on earth.

But first we will see how the seventh trumpet wraps up the tribulation from God's perspective in heaven. And then John will show us the tribulation a second time, as seen from man's perspective on earth. And so we will end up seeing the tribulation story twice. Perhaps this is the significance of the scroll being written on both sides: "And I saw in the **right** *hand* **of Him** who sat on the throne a scroll **written inside** and **on the back,** sealed with seven seals" (**Revelation 5:1**). The side facing heaven was read first, and the side facing the earth was read last.

Notice that until Chapter 10, the apostle John has been in the Spirit in heaven: "After these things **I looked,** and behold, a **door** *standing* **open in heaven.** And the first voice which I heard *was* like a trumpet speaking with me, saying, '**Come up here,** and **I will show you**

things which **must take place after this.**' ² Immediately **I was in the Spirit**; and behold, **a throne set in heaven**, and one sat on the throne" (**Revelation 4:1–2**).

But when the little book in Jesus' hand is given to John, Jesus is standing on earth: "He had a **little book open** in his hand. And he set **his right foot on the sea** and *his* **left** *foot* **on the land**" (**Revelation 10:2**). And that John's perspective in this vision is now from earth is seen in the beginning of chapter 11, when John is asked to measure the temple on earth: "Then I was given a reed like a measuring rod. And the angel stood, saying, 'Rise and **measure the temple of God**, the altar, and those who worship there. ² But **leave out the court** which is **outside the temple**, and **do not measure it**, for it has been **given to the Gentiles**'" (**Revelation 11:1–2**). And we know this is the temple on earth because the one in heaven does not have a Gentile court, because there are no Gentiles (nonbelievers) in heaven.

THE TWO WITNESSES

Then I was given a reed like a measuring rod. And the angel stood, saying, "Rise and measure the temple of God, the altar, and those who worship there. ² But leave out the court which is outside the temple, and do not measure it, for it has been given to the Gentiles. And they will tread the holy city underfoot *for* **forty-two months**. ³ And **I will give** *power* **to my two witnesses, and they will prophesy one thousand two hundred and sixty days**, clothed in sackcloth." ⁴ These are the **two olive trees** and the **two lampstands standing before the God of the earth**.

⁵ And if anyone wants to harm them, **fire proceeds from their mouth** and devours their enemies. And if anyone wants to harm them, he must be killed in this manner. ⁶ These have **power to shut heaven**, so that **no rain falls** in the **days of their prophecy**; and they **have power over waters to turn them to blood, and to strike the earth with all plagues**, as often as they desire. ⁷ When they finish their testimony, **the beast that ascends out of the bottomless pit** will make war against

them, overcome them, and kill them. **⁸** And their dead bodies *will lie* in the street of **the great city which spiritually is called Sodom** and **Egypt, where also our Lord was crucified**.

⁹ Then *those* from **the peoples, tribes, tongues,** and **nations** will see their dead bodies **three-and-a-half days**, and not allow their dead bodies to be put into graves. **¹⁰** And those who dwell on the earth will rejoice over them, make merry, and send gifts to one another, because these two prophets tormented those who dwell on the earth. **¹¹** Now **after the three-and-a-half days** the **breath of life** from God entered them, and they stood on their feet, and great fear fell on those who saw them.

¹² And they heard a loud voice from heaven saying to them, "**Come up here**." And **they ascended to heaven in a cloud**, and their enemies saw them. **¹³** In the same hour there was **a great earthquake**, and a tenth of the city fell. In the earthquake seven thousand people were killed, and **the rest were afraid** and **gave glory to the God of heaven**. **¹⁴** The **second woe is past**. Behold, the **third woe is coming**. (**Revelation 11:1–14**)

These two witnesses who will prophesy during the great tribulation; they will start to prophesy after forty-two months, which is three and one-half years, and they will prophecy 1,260 days, which is also three and one-half years of 360 days. The witnesses are the fulfillment of the prophecy of Zechariah:

Now the angel who talked with me came back and wakened me, as a man who is wakened out of his sleep. **²** And he said to me, "What do you see?" So I said, "I am looking, and there *is* a **lampstand of solid gold** with a bowl on top of it, and on the *stand* **seven lamps with seven pipes** to the **seven lamps**. **³ Two olive trees** *are* by it, one at the right of the bowl and the other at its left." **⁴** So I answered and spoke to the angel who talked with me, saying, "What *are* these, my lord?" … And I further answered and said to him, "**What *are these* two olive branches** that *drip* into the receptacles of the **two gold pipes** from which the **golden *oil* drains**?" **¹³** Then he answered me and said, "Do you not know what these *are?*" And I said, "No, my lord." **¹⁴** So he said, "**These *are* the two anointed ones**, who **stand beside the Lord of the whole earth.**" (**Zechariah 4:1–4, 12–14**)

The identity of these two witnesses is the subject of much speculation, but the two names that seem to make the most sense are Moses and Elijah. Moses and Elijah were the two that appeared to Jesus and "who **stand beside the Lord of the whole earth**" when He was transfigured, not long before He was crucified: "Now after six days Jesus took Peter, James, and John his brother, led them up on a high mountain by themselves; ² and **He was transfigured** before them. His face shone like the sun, and His clothes became as white as the light. ³ And behold, **Moses and Elijah** appeared to them, **talking with Him**" (**Matthew 17:1–3**).

Not only this, but Moses was the lawgiver whom God used to show that people with the hearts and minds of lawbreakers cannot be made righteous by the law and thus are doomed to death. Elijah represents the prophets who all together prophesied of the coming of Jesus, who would show that love alone enables us to unite in the oneness that is essential for eternal life. And Jesus taught us that love fulfills the law and prophets: "Jesus said to him, '"You shall **love the LORD your God with all your heart, with all your soul, and with all your mind.**"³⁸ This is *the* first and great commandment. ³⁹ And *the* second *is* like it: *"You shall love your neighbor as yourself."* ⁴⁰ On these two commandments **hang all the Law and the Prophets**'" (**Matthew 22:37–40**).

On top of that, these two witnesses are said to "have **power to shut heaven,** so that **no rain falls** in the **days of their prophecy**; and they **have power over waters to turn them to blood,** and to **strike the earth with all plagues,** as often as they desire." Moses was given the power to turn water into blood and to unleash nine other plagues when he delivered the children of Israel out of bondage in Egypt (**Exodus 4–12**). And Elijah was given the power to stop the rain: "And **Elijah** the Tishbite, of the inhabitants of Gilead, said to Ahab, *'As the LORD God of Israel lives,* before whom I stand, **there shall not be dew nor rain these years, except at my word**'" (**1 Kings 17:1**).

The Seventh Trumpet—The Kingdoms of the World Become the Kingdoms of Our Lord and of His Christ

Then the **seventh angel sounded**: And there were loud voices in heaven, saying, "The **kingdoms of this world** have become *the kingdoms* **of our Lord and of His Christ**, and **He shall reign forever and ever!**" [16] And the twenty-four elders who sat before God on their thrones fell on their faces and worshiped God, [17] saying: "We give You thanks, O Lord God Almighty, The One who is and who was and who is to come, Because You have taken Your great power and reigned.

[18] "The nations were angry, and Your wrath has come, And **the time of the dead**, that they **should be judged**, And that You should **reward Your servants** the **prophets and the saints**, And those who fear Your name, small and great, And should **destroy those** who **destroy the earth**." [19] Then the **temple of God was opened in heaven**, and the ark of His covenant was seen in His temple. And there were lightnings, noises, thunderings, an earthquake, and great hail. (**Revelation 11:15–19**)

Here we are at the end of the tribulation from the perspective of God in heaven, when the kingdom of God has victory over the kingdom of Satan and the nations of the earth will be judged by the lives they lived, whether good or bad.

THE WOMAN, THE CHILD, AND THE DRAGON

Chapter 12 of Revelation is a short summary of the whole story from the time of the fall from grace in heaven, when we all on earth were those "who **exchanged the truth of God** for the **lie**, and **worshiped** and **served** the **creature** rather than the **Creator**, who is blessed forever. Amen" (**Romans 1:25**), to the time of the end of God's plan to reconcile those who would have a change of heart and mind by learning and understanding the truth of God. It seems that this short story is the "little book" Jesus gave John to figuratively "digest," saying to him, "**You must prophesy again** about **many peoples, nations, tongues, and kings.**"

THE WOMAN

> Now a **great sign** appeared **in heaven: a woman** clothed with **the sun**, with **the moon under her feet**, and on her head a garland of **twelve stars**. ² Then being with child, she cried out in labor and in pain to give birth. (**Revelation 12:1–2**)

A "sign" in the Bible always points to some greater meaning than the word or thing doing the pointing. In this case the word "woman" refers to something other than just a single person. And we see that is the case in the rest of the chapter, such as in **Revelation 12:15**: "And the dragon was enraged with **the woman**, and he went to make war with the **rest of her offspring**, who keep the commandments of God and have the testimony of Jesus Christ."

What we have already learned in the "The Meaning and Purpose of Life on Earth" and the "The Beginning as Seen from Earth" will help us understand this prophecy. The woman, it seems, is the "Woman" described in **Genesis 2: 23b**: "She shall be called **Woman**, Because she [mankind], was taken out of **Man** [indicating the separation of Mankind from their head and leader, "*Adam,*" which is a Hebrew word that describes the fallen nature of the one we believed in and followed – Satan]." (See also the discussion concerning the "Wife" and the "Husband," or H802 **ishshah nashym** and H376 **ysh** in the Hebrew, in the chapter "The Beginning as Seen from Earth.")

Notice that the "Woman" in this prophecy is described as having a garland of twelve stars on her head, which represents the angels in heaven. As we have learned, in the Bible, stars often represent angels. Notice also that the phrase "Now a **great sign** appeared **in heaven: a**

woman clothed with **the sun**" says that the Woman is "**in heaven**," which is confirmed by the stars and the moon, all of creation, being *under* her feet.

Revelation 12:2 says that the woman in heaven was already pregnant and about to give birth. This birth seems to be that of a kingdom because we know that Jesus was the angel chosen and anointed by God the Father to be King over the angels in heaven. But the "birth" of that kingdom was delayed because it was interrupted by Lucifer, represented as a red dragon, later called Satan, who deceived one-third of these angels with a lie.

THE DRAGON

> And **another sign** appeared **in heaven**: behold, a great, **fiery red dragon** having seven heads and ten horns, and seven diadems on his heads. ⁴ **His tail drew a third** of the **stars of heaven** and **threw them to the earth**. And the dragon stood before the **woman** who was ready to give birth, to **devour her Child** as soon as it was born. (**Revelation 12:3–4**)

Notice that the "**fiery red dragon**" is in heaven, where he is called Lucifer, but after his rebellion resulting from the deception of one-third of heaven's angels, he is cast down to the earth with his fallen angels, where he is now called Satan. So all of the angels in heaven that believed the lies followed Lucifer and were cast to the earth, where they are called Mankind, or in the Hebrew *Adam*, or as in this passage, "**the woman**." Also notice that the woman that is now on earth was part of the woman in heaven—all the angels of heaven that were going to be in the kingdom of Christ, the chosen and anointed angel of God, Jesus the Christ, before the rebellion of Lucifer.

The fact that there was an earth to cast Satan and his followers down to was because God had a plan to reconcile those He knew were ignorant of the truth because they had never experienced evil before, but would have a change of heart and mind once they knew and understood the truth that Satan's ways would lead to corruption, misery, sorrow, and their death and that the ways of God are the only path to peace, prosperity, unspeakable joy, and everlasting life.

Part of God's plan was the creation of the universe, the heavens, and the earth as a place for the fallen angels to experience good and evil for themselves. The other part of the plan was to send His anointed Son, Jesus, into the world to witness of the truth that would make us free and then suffer and die to pay the penalty for the sins of those who would enter into a loving relationship with Him, making them One in Him.

Satan did not know or understand the plan of God. All he knew was that the birth of Jesus the Christ was the key for God to free His children, but to Satan it meant losing his best and brightest slaves, and so he did everything he could to stop that from happening.

THE CHILD

She bore a male **Child** who was to **rule all nations** with a rod of iron. And her Child was **caught up** to **God** and **His throne.** (**Revelation 12:5**)The Greek word for the phrase "caught up" is the same Greek word G726 *harpazo* used for the rapture of Christ's Church. The "Child" is Jesus the Christ, the chosen and anointed Son of God whom God chose to be our King and sent into the world to witness of the truth in order to reconcile the fallen angels in flesh, which are God's elect, chosen by God before the heavens and the earth were created. Jesus rescued those that belonged to Him by drawing them to Him by His great love for them. Jesus would suffer and die out of love for us even though we had rejected Him and His truth and believed the lies of Satan and followed him. That Jesus was "caught up" to heaven means that He first died to this world on the cross and was resurrected and ascended into heaven. Jesus, the first fruit of many who would follow, showed us the way. By dying to self and this world of Satan and committing our lives to God and His Christ as our King, we are free to live in peace, productivity, and joy inexpressible forever.

The "She" in this verse has a double meaning. In the big picture, "She" refers to all mankind, because Jesus' lineage is traced all the way back

441

to the first man, Adam, the patriarchal father of all humans on earth. And Jesus is called the Son of Man as well as the Son of God. In the small picture, she is the one, Mary, who gave birth to Jesus in the flesh.

THE FIRST RAPTURE

"Then **the woman** fled into the wilderness, where she has a place prepared by God, that they should feed her there **one thousand two hundred** and **sixty days**." (**Revelation 12:6**)

This is the first rapture of the Church of Christ—those who knew they made a mistake and were wrong when they believed and chose Satan, and who repented and asked for forgiveness and wanted to come back home as prodigal sons and daughters of God. The place prepared by God is paradise in heaven, which we learned is the true garden of Eden, of which the one on earth is but a copy.

SATAN CAST OUT OF HEAVEN—VICTORY IS DECLARED

> And **war broke out in heaven: Michael** and **his angels fought** with the **dragon**; and the **dragon** and **his angels fought**, [8] but they did not prevail, nor was a place found for them in heaven any longer. [9] So the **great dragon was cast out**, that **serpent of old**, called the **Devil** and **Satan, who deceives the whole world**; he was cast to the earth, and his angels were cast out with him. [10] Then I heard a loud voice saying in heaven, "Now salvation, and strength, and the kingdom of our God, and the power of His Christ have come, for **the accuser of our brethren**, who **accused them before our God day and night**, has been **cast down**. [11] And they overcame him by the **blood** of the **Lamb** and by the **word of their testimony**, and they **did not love their lives** to the **death**." (**Revelation 12:7–11**)

We might be tempted to think that this passage is speaking of the beginning, when we all were cast out with Satan, but the phrase "**that**

serpent of old, called **the Devil and Satan, who deceives the whole world**; he was cast to the earth, and his angels were cast out with him" indicates that the previous casting out of us with Satan took place long ago. This casting out of heaven is of Satan alone. The reason for the delay in casting out Satan forever is that Satan accused God's judgment of the elect of being unjust. And so God had to convene the courts of heaven and have a trial to prove that He was telling the truth and that His choosing of the elect was fair and just. The trial in heaven is between Satan and his followers, and Jesus and His followers. This trial was conducted on earth, but it has now concluded, and Satan has been found guilty and permanently cast out of heaven and down to hell on earth. Satan is now on earth to provide the evil to test the faith of the rest God's chosen elect on earth in the tribulation.

THE WRATH OF SATAN

"Therefore **rejoice, O heavens**, and you who dwell in them! **Woe to the inhabitants** of the **earth** and the **sea**! For the **devil has come down to you**, having great wrath, because he knows that he has a short time." [13] Now when the **dragon** saw that he had been **cast to the earth**, he persecuted **the woman** who gave birth to **the male** *Child*. (**Revelation 12:12–13**)

THE SECOND "RAPTURE" OF THE TRIBULATION SAINTS

But **the woman** was given two **wings of a great eagle**, that she might fly into the wilderness **to her place**, where she is nourished for **a time** and **times** and **half a time**, from the presence of the serpent. [15] So the serpent spewed water out of his mouth like a flood after the **woman**, that he might cause her to be carried away by the flood. [16] But the earth helped the woman, and the earth opened its mouth and swallowed up the flood which the dragon had spewed out of his mouth. (**Revelation 12:14–16**)

443

THE THIRD RAPTURE OF THE GREAT TRIBULATION SAINTS

> And the dragon was enraged with **the woman**, and he went to make war with **the rest of her offspring**, who **keep the commandments of God** and **have the testimony of Jesus Christ**. (**Revelation 12:17**)

This now leaves us at the midpoint of the tribulation. The last of the elect, the believers, referred to as "**the rest of her offspring**, who keep the commandments of God and have the testimony of Jesus Christ," who will come out of the second half of the tribulation, are called the great tribulation saints.

Chapter 12 is the summary of the whole story in the Bible, which perhaps is the prophecy by John contained in the little book. It is the story of the angels who believed the lies of Lucifer and fell from the grace of God in heaven to earth; the birth of Jesus the Christ, who came to the earth, took on flesh, witnessed of the truth that will make us free, and died for us on cross to reconcile those who believe in Him to God; His ascension into heaven; the rapture of the church, the body of Christ, being taken up in three separate "harvests" to be with Him forever as citizens in His Kingdom in heaven. And now, after this little book, we are again at the beginning of the tribulation from the standpoint of man on earth.

THE TRIBULATION AS VIEWED FROM EARTH

THE BEAST FROM THE SEA

Now we will see the tribulation story unfold again, but this time from John's perspective on earth:

> Then I stood on the sand of the sea. And I saw **a beast** rising up out of the **sea**, having **seven heads** and **ten horns**, and on

his horns ten crowns, and on his heads a blasphemous name.
² Now the beast which I saw was **like a leopard**, his feet were
like *the feet of* a bear, and his mouth **like the mouth of a
lion**. The **dragon gave him his power, his throne**, and
great authority. ³ And *I saw* **one of his heads** as if it had been
mortally wounded, and his **deadly wound was healed**.

And all the world marveled and **followed the beast**. ⁴ So **they
worshiped the dragon** who gave authority to **the beast**;
and they worshiped the beast, saying, "Who *is* like the beast?
Who is able to make war with him?" ⁵ And he was given a
mouth speaking great things and blasphemies, and he was given
authority to continue for **forty-two months**. ⁶ Then he opened
his mouth in blasphemy against God, to blaspheme His name,
His tabernacle, and **those who dwell in heaven**.

⁷ **It was granted to him** to make **war with the saints** and to
overcome them. And authority was given him over every tribe,
tongue, and nation. ⁸ All who dwell on the earth will worship
him, **whose names** have not been **written** in the **Book of
Life of the Lamb** slain from the **foundation of the world**. ⁹ If
anyone has an ear, let him hear. ¹⁰ He who **leads into captivity
shall go into captivity**; he who **kills with the sword** must
be **killed with the sword**. Here is the **patience** and the **faith
of the saints**. (**Revelation 13:1–10**)

The Beast from the sea is the Antichrist, who will try to deceive all
mankind but especially the elect of God—those whose names were
written in the Book of Life from the foundation of the world—in an
attempt to make them worship him. This is exactly what Jesus warned
us about: "For **false christs** and **false prophets** will rise and **show
signs and wonders to deceive, if possible, even the elect**. ²³ But
take heed; see, I have **told you all things beforehand**" (**Mark
13:22–23**). Notice that this first Beast is in the image and likeness of
the Dragon, who is called Lucifer or Satan: "And another **sign** appeared
in heaven: behold, a great, **fiery red dragon** having **seven heads** and
ten horns, and **seven diadems on his heads**" (**Revelation 12:3**).

This first beast of the sea is Satan's Antichrist, who as we have learned
is Satan the counterfeiter's attempt to be like God. And so he has to

have a counterfeit christ, the so-called Antichrist, so that he can show himself as God. The prophet Daniel describes this beast of the sea as the fourth and last of the beasts that come out of the sea. These four beasts are the four kings of the four great kingdoms of the earth. As we have already learned, the Bible uses horns to represent kings of nations, and a diadem is a crown.

THE PROPHECIES OF DANIEL

In **chapter 7** of the book of **Daniel**, the prophet Daniel has a dream of four **beasts** that come out of the sea. The first was like a lion, the second was like a bear, the third was like a leopard, and the fourth beast was unlike the other **beasts**.

> After this I saw in the night visions, and behold, **a fourth beast, dreadful and terrible, exceedingly strong**. It had huge iron teeth; it was devouring, breaking in pieces, and trampling the residue with its feet. **It *was* different from** all the **beasts that *were* before it**, and it had **ten horns**. [8] I was considering the horns, and there was **another horn, a little one**, coming up among them, **before whom three of the first horns were plucked out by the roots**. And there, **in this horn**, *were* eyes like the **eyes of a man**, and a **mouth speaking pompous words**. (**Daniel 7:7–8**)

> Then I wished to **know the truth** about the **fourth beast**, which was **different from all the others**, exceedingly dreadful, *with* its **teeth of iron** and its **nails of bronze**, *which* devoured, broke in pieces, and trampled the residue with its feet … Thus he said: "The **fourth beast** shall be **A fourth kingdom on earth**, Which shall be different from all *other* kingdoms, And shall **devour the whole earth**, Trample it and break it in pieces. [24] The **ten horns *are* ten kings** *Who* shall **arise from this kingdom**. And **another shall rise after them**; He shall be different from the first *ones*, And **shall subdue three kings**.

> [25] "He shall **speak *pompous* words** against **the Most High**, Shall **persecute** the **saints** of the **Most High**, And shall intend to **change times and law**. Then *the* **saints shall be given**

into his hand For **a time and times and half a time**. [26] 'But the **court shall be seated**, And they shall **take away his dominion**, To consume and destroy *it* forever. [27] Then the kingdom and dominion, And the greatness of the kingdoms under the whole heaven, Shall be given to the people, the saints of the Most High. His kingdom *is* an everlasting kingdom, And all dominions shall serve and obey Him." (**Daniel 7:19, 23–27**)

This prophecy of Daniel agrees with an earlier prophecy in which God has Daniel interpret the dream of Nebuchadnezzar, king of Babylon, which is the first mighty kingdom of the world and the first beast to come out of the sea.

As for you, O king, thoughts came *to* your *mind while* on your bed, *about* **what would come to pass after this**; and **He who reveals secrets** has made known to you what will be. [30] But as for me, **this secret** has **not** been **revealed to me** because **I have more wisdom** than anyone living, but **for** *our* **sakes** who make known the interpretation to the king, and that you may know the thoughts of your heart.

[31] You, O king, were watching; and behold, **a great image!** This great image, whose splendor *was* excellent, stood before you; and its form *was* awesome. [32] This **image's head** *was* **of fine gold**, its **chest** and **arms of silver**, its **belly** and **thighs of bronze**, [33] its **legs of iron, its feet partly of iron** and **partly of clay**. [34] You watched while a **stone was cut out without hands**, which struck the image on its feet of iron and clay, and broke them in pieces. [35] Then the iron, the clay, the bronze, the silver, and the gold were **crushed together**, and became **like chaff** from the summer threshing floors; the wind carried them away so that **no trace of them was found**. And the **stone that struck the image** became a great mountain and **filled the whole earth.**

[36] This *is* **the dream.** Now we will tell **the interpretation of it** before the king. [37] You, O king, *are* a king of kings. For the God of heaven has given you a kingdom, power, strength, and glory; [38] and wherever the children of men dwell, or the beasts of the field and the birds of the heaven, He has given *them* into your hand, and has made you ruler over them all– **you** *are* **this**

head of gold. [39] But after you shall arise **another kingdom** inferior to yours; then **another**, a **third kingdom of bronze**, which shall rule over all the earth. [40] And the **fourth kingdom shall be as strong as iron**, inasmuch as iron breaks in pieces and shatters everything; and like iron that crushes, *that kingdom* will break in pieces and crush all the others.

[41] Whereas you saw the **feet** and **toes, partly of potter's clay** and **partly of iron**, the **kingdom shall be divided**; yet the **strength of the iron shall be in it**, just as you saw the **iron mixed with ceramic clay**. [42] And *as* the toes of the feet *were* partly of iron and partly of clay, *so* **the kingdom shall be partly strong** and **partly fragile**. [43] As you saw iron mixed with ceramic clay, they will mingle with the **seed of men**; but **they will not adhere to one another**, just as **iron does not mix with clay**.

[44] And **in the days of these kings** the God of heaven will **set up a kingdom which shall never be destroyed**; and the kingdom shall not be left to other people; it shall break in pieces and consume all these kingdoms, and it shall stand forever. [45] Inasmuch as you saw that the stone was cut out of the mountain without hands, and that it broke in pieces the iron, the bronze, the clay, the silver, and the gold—the great God has made known to the king what will come to pass after this. The **dream is certain**, and **its interpretation is sure**. (**Daniel 2:29–45**)

In these prophesies of Daniel, we see the end of man's kingdoms will become the kingdom of God, as we saw at the end of the tribulation as seen from God's perspective in heaven: "Then the seventh angel sounded: And there were loud voices in heaven, saying, 'The **kingdoms of this world** have become *the kingdoms* **of our Lord and of His Christ**, and He shall reign forever and ever!'" (**Revelation 11:15**). We see from the history contained in the Bible that the first kingdom of gold is Babylon. The great kingdom that follows is Persia, the kingdom of silver. The following kingdom, the kingdom of bronze, is the Grecian empire of Alexander the Great. The next great kingdom, the kingdom of iron, is the kingdom of Jesus' time, the Roman Empire. And finally, the fifth kingdom is to be made up of ten kings and kingdoms loosely connected together with part of it strong and part of it weak; this is the kingdom of clay and iron.

We know that this fifth kingdom will make up the final worldwide kingdom of the earth and will be led by the Antichrist. And we also know that this "little horn, that speaks pompous words against the Most High" is the Antichrist, who will come out of this kingdom of ten horns. We also have learned that the revelation of the Antichrist will not happen until the rapture of God's church, the believers of Jesus that are taken out of the way: "For the **mystery of lawlessness** is already at work; only **He who now restrains** *will do so* until **He is taken out of the way**. [8] And then **the lawless one will be revealed**, whom the Lord will **consume with the breath** of His mouth and **destroy** with the **brightness of His coming**. [9] The coming of **the** *lawless one* is according to the **working of Satan**, with **all power**, **signs**, and lying wonders, [10] and with all **unrighteous deception** among those who perish, because they did not receive the **love of the truth**, that they **might be saved**" (**2 Thessalonians 2:7–10**).

We have learned that we who see the people of Israel become a nation again after almost two thousand years of being scattered in other nations will be the generation that will not pass away until all this takes place, as Jesus had assured us: "Assuredly, I say to you, **this generation will by no means pass away till all these things take place**" (**Matthew 24:34**). Putting all these things together, is it any wonder that many think that these ancient prophesies are speaking of the time in which we live and that the Beast, the Antichrist, is alive today and is preparing himself for what will be the last great kingdom of man on earth? Many think that the ten horns refer to the ten leaders of the ten major nations of the European Union and that the Antichrist will try to restore the old Roman Empire to conquer the world. Now let us continue in the book of Revelation to see what it will shortly be like on earth.

THE BEAST FROM THE LAND

> Then I saw **another beast** coming up **out of the earth**, and he
> had **two horns like a lamb** and spoke like **a dragon**. [12] And
> he exercises all the authority of the first beast in his presence,
> and causes the earth and those who dwell in it to **worship** the
> **first beast**, whose **deadly wound was healed**. [13] He **performs
> great signs**, so that he **even makes fire come down from
> heaven** on the earth in the sight of men. [14] And he deceives those
> who dwell on the earth by those **signs which he was granted
> to do** in the sight of the beast, telling those who dwell on the
> earth to **make an image** to the **beast** who was **wounded** by
> the **sword** and **lived**.
>
> [15] He was **granted** *power* to give breath to the image of the
> beast, that the **image of the beast** should both **speak** and cause
> as many as **would not worship** the **image** of the **beast** to be
> killed. [16] He causes all, both small and great, rich and poor, free
> and slave, to **receive a mark** on their **right hand** or on their
> **foreheads**, [17] and that **no one** may **buy or sell** except **one who
> has the mark** or the **name of the beast**, or the **number of
> his name**. [18] Here is wisdom. Let him who has understanding
> calculate the number of the beast, for it is the **number of a man**:
> **His number** *is* **666. (Revelation 13:11–18)**

The beast from the land is the False Prophet and he could be considered
an antichrist but not *the* Antichrist, for even in Christ's time Jesus said,
"Little children, it is the last hour; and as you have heard that the
Antichrist is coming, **even now many antichrists have come**, by
which we know that it is the last hour" (**1 John 2:18**). The Bible does
not say much about who the False Prophet is other than that he is given
authority to do great signs to deceive men into worshipping the image
of the Beast that came out of the sea, and to receive the mark of the
Beast on their forehead or hand. As we will see, this mark will identify
those that belong to Satan.

Many people have speculated on what the number 666 refers to, and
we will also. In the King James Version of **Revelation 13:18**, there
is a whole phrase that is translated from the Ancient Greek. "Here is

wisdom. Let him that hath understanding count the **number of the beast**: for it is the number of a man; and his number *is* **Six hundred threescore *and* six**." The whole phrase "**Six hundred threescore *and* six**" is translated from the ancient Greek G5516 *chi xi stigma* (pronounced khee xee stig'-ma) and is defined as "the 22nd, 14th, and an obsolete letter (G4742 **as a cross**) of the Greek alphabet (intermediate between the 5th and 6th), used as numbers; denoting respectively 600, 60, 6; as a numeral:- six hundred three score and six."

Strong's number G4742 corresponds to the Greek word *stigma* (pronounced stig'-mah), which is defined as follows: "From a primary word *stizo* (to stick, that is, to prick); **a mark incised or punched (for recognition of ownership)**, that is (figuratively) **scar of service:- mark**." Could this possibly mean that the letters representing the Beast's name, *chi* and *xi*, along with the obsolete letter G472 **as a cross**, when put together, make a symbol that includes a cross for a *stigma*—a tattoo or brand that marks a person as belonging to the Beast who is the Antichrist? And can these letters also be used as numbers in the Ancient Greek that total 666? After all, the Antichrist pretends to be the Christ to deceive many. For now we will let others ponder the meaning of the number of the beast and focus on the meaning and purpose of life on planet earth.

The 144, 000 and the Teaching of the Gospel

Then I looked, and behold, **a Lamb standing on Mount Zion**, and with Him one hundred *and* forty-four thousand, having **His Father's name written on their foreheads**. [2] And I heard a voice from heaven, like the voice of many waters, and like the voice of loud thunder. And I heard the sound of harpists playing their harps. [3] They sang as it were a new song before the throne, before the four living creatures, and the elders; and no one could learn that song except the **hundred *and* forty-four thousand** who were **redeemed from the earth**. [4] These are the ones who were not defiled with women, for they are virgins. These are the ones who follow the Lamb wherever He goes. These were **redeemed** from *among* men, *being* **firstfruits to God** and **to the Lamb**. [5] And in their mouth was found no deceit, for they are without fault before the throne of God. (**Revelation 14:1–5**)

This passage specifically speaks of the firstfruits of Israel—those of the tribes of Israel who were "sealed" in chapter 6 of Revelation who are in Jerusalem on Mount Zion with Jesus and are raptured at the midpoint of the tribulation.

THE HARVEST OF THE TRIBULATION SAINTS

Then I saw another angel flying in the midst of heaven, having the **everlasting gospel** to **preach** to **those who dwell** on the **earth**–to every nation, tribe, tongue, and people– [7] saying with a loud voice, "Fear God and give glory to Him, for the **hour of His judgment** has come; and worship Him who made heaven and earth, the sea and springs of water." [8] And another angel followed, saying, "**Babylon is fallen**, is fallen, that great city, because she has made all nations drink of the wine of the wrath of her fornication." (**Revelation 14:6–8**)

Because the first angel in heaven said, "The **hour of His judgment** has come," the words of the second angel, "**Babylon is fallen,**" are a prediction of the coming fall of Babylon, which happens in (**Revelation 18:2**). This also implies that the fall of Babylon is part of God's final judgment.

[9] Then a third angel followed them, saying with a loud voice, "If anyone worships the beast and his image, and **receives** *his* **mark on his forehead or on his hand**, [10] he himself shall also drink of the wine of the wrath of God, which is poured out full strength into the cup of His indignation. He shall be tormented with fire and brimstone in the presence of the holy angels and in the presence of the Lamb. [11] And the smoke of their torment ascends forever and ever; and they have no rest day or night, who

worship the beast and **his image**, and whoever **receives the mark of his name**."

¹² Here is the patience of the saints; here *are* those who keep the commandments of God and the faith of Jesus. ¹³ Then I heard a voice from heaven saying to me, "Write: '**Blessed *are* the dead who die in the Lord from now on**.'" "Yes," says the Spirit, "that they may rest from their labors, and their works follow them." ¹⁴ Then I looked, and behold, **a white cloud**, and on the **cloud sat one like the Son of Man**, having on His head a golden crown, and in His hand a sharp sickle. ¹⁵ And another angel came out of the temple, crying with **a loud voice to Him who sat on the cloud**, "Thrust in Your sickle and reap, for the time has come for You to reap, for the harvest of the earth is ripe." ¹⁶ So **He who sat** on the **cloud thrust in His sickle on the earth**, and the **earth was reaped**. (Revelation 14:9–16)

This is the harvest of the **tribulation saints**, which includes the 144,000 of Israel and the rest of the believers in Christ. This harvest is evidence of a **midtribulation rapture**, involving those from every nation who are being gathered together to meet Jesus in a cloud. We know these are not the great tribulation saints because of the voice from heaven saying, "**Blessed *are* the dead who die** in the **Lord from now on**," which tells us that there are still those in the future who would rather die for their faith in God than take the mark of the Beast showing they belong to the Antichrist.

THE HARVEST OF SATAN'S FOLLOWERS FOR GOD'S WRATH

Then another angel came out of the temple which is in heaven, he also having a sharp sickle. ¹⁸ And another angel came out from the altar, who had power over fire, and he cried with a loud cry to him who had the sharp sickle, saying, "Thrust in your sharp sickle and gather the clusters of the vine of the earth, for her grapes are fully ripe." ¹⁹ So the angel thrust his sickle into the earth and gathered the vine of the earth, and threw *it* into the great winepress of the wrath of God. ²⁰ And the winepress was trampled outside the city, and blood came out of the winepress, up to the horses' bridles, for one thousand six hundred furlong. (**Revelation 14:17–20**)

This passage may be referring to the removal of those that are making war against Israel to destroy her before God's plan to teach the truth to the remnant of His elect, who will be prodded by the great suffering and evil in the last half of the tribulation and hear the testimony of God's two witnesses and will understand the truth and become the great tribulation saints.

PREPARATION FOR THE SEVEN BOWL JUDGMENTS

Then I saw another sign in heaven, great and marvelous: seven angels having the seven last plagues, for in them the wrath of God is complete. [2] And I saw *something* like a **sea of glass mingled with fire**, and **those who have the victory over the beast**, over his image and over **his mark** *and* over **the number of his name**, standing on the sea of glass, having harps of God.

[3] They sing the **song of Moses**, the servant of God, and the **song of the Lamb**, saying: "Great and marvelous *are* Your works, Lord God Almighty! **Just and true *are* Your ways**, O King of the saints! [4] Who shall not fear You, O Lord, and glorify Your name? For *You* alone *are* holy. For all nations shall come and worship before You, For **Your judgments have been manifested**."

[5] After these things I looked, and behold, the temple of the **tabernacle of the testimony in heaven** was opened. [6] And out of the temple came the seven angels having the seven plagues, clothed in pure bright linen, and having their chests girded with golden bands. [7] Then one of the four living creatures gave to the seven angels seven golden bowls full of the wrath of God who lives forever and ever. [8] The temple was **filled with smoke from the glory of God** and from His power, and no one was able to enter the temple till the seven plagues of the seven angels were completed. (**Revelation 15:1–8**)

THE SEVEN BOWL JUDGMENTS

The First Bowl—Foul and Loathsome Sores on Men

Then I heard a loud voice from the temple saying to the seven angels, "Go and pour out the bowls of the wrath of God on the earth." ² So the first went and poured out his bowl upon the earth, and a foul and loathsome sore came **upon the men** who had the **mark of the beast** and those **who worshiped his image. (Revelation 16:1–2)**

The Second Bowl—The Sea Becomes Blood

Then the second angel poured out his bowl on the sea, and it became blood as of a dead *man;* and every living creature in the sea died. **(Revelation 16:3)**

The Third Bowl—Rivers Becomes Blood

Then the third angel poured out his bowl on the rivers and springs of water, and they became blood. ⁵ And I heard the angel of the waters saying: "You are righteous, O Lord, The One who is and who was and who is to be, Because You have judged these things. ⁶ For they have shed the blood of saints and prophets, And You have given them blood to drink. For it is their just due." ⁷ And I heard another from the altar saying, "Even so, Lord God Almighty, true and righteous *are* Your judgments." **(Revelation 16:4–7)**

The Fourth Bowl—The Sun Scorched Men with Fire

Then the fourth angel poured out his bowl on the sun, and power was given to him to scorch men with fire. ⁹ And men were scorched with great heat, and they blasphemed the name of God who has power over these plagues; and **they did not repent and give Him glory. (Revelation 16:8–9)**

The Fifth Bowl—The Kingdom Is Full of Darkness

Then the fifth angel poured out his bowl on the **throne of the beast**, and his kingdom became full of darkness; and they gnawed their tongues because of the pain. [11] They blasphemed the God of heaven because of their pains and their sores, and **did not repent of their deeds**. (**Revelation 16:10–11**)

The Sixth Bowl—The Demons Gather the Kings to Battle

Then the sixth angel poured out his bowl on the great river Euphrates, and its water was dried up, so that the **way of the kings from the east might be prepared**. [13] And I saw three **unclean spirits** like frogs *coming* out of the mouth of the **dragon**, out of the mouth of the **beast**, and out of the mouth of the **false prophet**. [14] For they are **spirits of demons**, performing signs, *which* go out to the kings of the earth and of the whole world, **to gather them to the battle** of that **great day of God Almighty**. [15] "Behold, I am coming as a thief. **Blessed** *is* **he who watches**, and keeps his garments, lest he walk naked and they see his shame." [16] And they **gathered them together** to the **place called in Hebrew, Armageddon**. (**Revelation 16:12–16**)

The Seventh Bowl—The Battle of Armageddon

Then the seventh angel poured out his bowl into the air, and a **loud voice** came out of the **temple of heaven**, from the throne, saying, "**It is done!**" [18] And there were noises and thunderings and lightnings; and there was **a great earthquake**, such a mighty and great earthquake as had not occurred since men were on the earth. [19] Now **the great city was divided into three parts**, and the cities of the nations fell. And great Babylon was remembered before God, to give her the cup of the wine of the fierceness of His wrath. [20] Then **every island fled away**, and **the mountains were not found**. [21] And **great hail from heaven** fell upon men, *each hailstone* about the weight of a talent. Men blasphemed God because of the plague of the hail, since that plague was exceedingly great. (**Revelation 16:17–21**)

THE SCARLET WOMAN AND THE BEAST

Just as chapter 12 spoke of the "Woman" who represented mankind and spoke of those who belonged to Christ and were raptured out of this world of Satan in three different harvests, chapter 17 speaks of those of the "Woman," who represents those who belong to Satan and remain in his kingdom on earth. And just as Jerusalem, the city of peace, represents the kingdom of God on earth, Babylon, the city of tyranny, represents the kingdom of Satan. Perhaps chapter 17 is the second half of the little book, and when John ate the first half, dealing with those in the kingdom of God, it was sweet, and when he got to the end of the little book, dealing with the kingdom of Satan, it was bitter.

BABYLON THE GREAT, THE MOTHER OF HARLOTS

Then one of the seven angels who had the seven bowls came and talked with me, saying to me, "Come, I will show you the **judgment** of the **great harlot who sits on many waters**, [2] with whom the kings of the earth committed fornication, and the inhabitants of the earth were made drunk with the wine of her fornication." [3] So he **carried me away in the Spirit** into the wilderness. And I saw **a woman sitting on a scarlet beast** *which was* full of names of blasphemy, having **seven heads and ten horns**.

[4] The **woman** was arrayed in purple and scarlet, and adorned with gold and precious stones and pearls, having in her hand a golden cup full of abominations and the filthiness of her fornication. [5] And **on her forehead** a name *was* written: MYSTERY, BABYLON THE GREAT, THE MOTHER OF HARLOTS AND OF THE ABOMINATIONS OF THE EARTH. [6] I saw **the woman, drunk** with the **blood of the saints** and with the **blood of the martyrs of Jesus**. And when I saw her, I marveled with great amazement. [7] But the angel said to me, "Why did you marvel? I will tell you the **mystery** of the **woman** and of the **beast that carries her**, which has the **seven heads** and the **ten horns**.

457

8 "**The beast that you saw was**, and **is not**, and **will ascend** out of the **bottomless pit** and go to **perdition**. And those who dwell on the earth will marvel, whose names **are not written** in the **Book of Life** from the **foundation of the world**, when they see the **beast that was**, and **is not**, and **yet is**. 9 **Here** *is* **the mind which has wisdom**: The **seven heads** are **seven mountains** on which the **woman sits**. 10 There are also **seven kings**. Five have fallen, one is, *and* the other has not yet come. And when he comes, he must continue a short time. 11 And **the beast that was**, and **is not, is himself also the eighth**, and **is of the seven**, and is going to **perdition**. 12 The **ten horns** which you saw are **ten kings** who have received no kingdom as yet, but they receive authority for one hour as kings with the beast.

13 "These are of **one mind**, and they will **give their power** and **authority to the beast**. 14 These will **make war with the Lamb**, and the **Lamb will overcome them**, for **He is Lord of lords** and **King of kings**; and those *who are* **with Him** *are* **called, chosen**, and **faithful**." 15 Then he said to me, "The **waters which you saw**, where the harlot sits, are **peoples, multitudes, nations**, and **tongues**. 16 And the **ten horns** which you saw **on the beast**, these will **hate the harlot**, make her **desolate and naked**, eat her flesh and burn her with fire. 17 For **God has put it into their hearts to fulfill His purpose**, to be of **one mind**, and to **give their kingdom to the beast**, until the **words of God are fulfilled**. 18 And the **woman** whom you saw is that **great city** which **reigns over** the **kings of the earth**." (**Revelation 17:1–18**)

The word "**perdition**" in the phrase "**will ascend** out of the **bottomless pit** and go to **perdition**" comes from the Greek word G684 *apoleia* (pronounced ap-o'-li-a), which means "From presumed derivative of G622; **ruin** or **loss** (**physical, spiritual** or **eternal**):- **damnable** (-nation), **destruction, die, perdition, pernicious ways, waste**." The phrase "bottomless pit" is translated from the Greek word G12 *abussos*, which means "From G1 (as a negative particle) and a variation of G1037; **depthless**, that is, (specifically), (**infernal**) "abyss":- **deep, (bottomless) pit** [which we learned means the same as hell and hades]".

And so we see that "the **beast that was**, and **is not**, and **yet is**," is speaking of the Antichrist, the Beast that came out of the sea (the deep, the abyss, the bottomless pit) who was mortally wounded and miraculously lived again. This is Satan's (the Dragon's) evil counterfeit version of Christ who died and rose again. And he is the one who will be going from his place in hell or the deep on earth that he came out of and into the infernal abyss that is the second death, the lake of fire spoken of in **Revelation 20:14**. This is the total and final separation from the life that is found only in God and is not the result of what God has done, but what people have done to themselves, for "The Lord is not slack concerning *His* **promise**, as some count slackness, but is **longsuffering toward us, not willing that any should perish** but that all should come to repentance. [10] But the **day of the Lord** will come as a thief in the night, in which the **heavens will pass away with a great noise**, and the elements will melt with **fervent heat**; both the **earth** and the **works that are in it** will be **burned up**" (2 **Peter 3:9–10**).

Now consider the following passage: "**The seven heads are seven mountains on which the woman sits**. [10] There are also **seven kings. Five have fallen, one is,** *and* **the other has not yet come**. And when he comes, he must continue a short time. [11] And **the beast that was, and is not, is himself also the eighth, and is of the seven**, and is going to **perdition**." Remember that the woman on the scarlet beast, arrayed in scarlet and purple, is the evil counterpart of the woman in chapter 12 who represented the part of fallen mankind that were the elect of God—those written in the Lamb's book of life from the foundation of the world whom God raptured or snatched out of Satan's kingdom to be with Jesus in heaven. On the other hand, the scarlet woman represents those of fallen mankind who are not written in the Lamb's book of life and who belong to Satan throughout the ages of time on earth.

Also consider that the angel is giving us the answer to the mystery of the woman and the beast that has seven heads and ten horns. The angel tells us that the "seven heads" are "seven mountains" and there are also "seven kings." So right away we know that these are not literal mountains but are symbolic. The Bible uses mountains as symbols of kingdoms, perhaps because mountain fortresses are not easily conquered. And in the following two passages, we see two mountain kingdoms. David says, "LORD, by Your favor **You have made my mountain stand strong**" (**Psalm 30:7**). David's mountain is the mountain that Jerusalem sits on. "'And I will repay **Babylon** And all the inhabitants of **Chaldea** For **all the evil they have done In Zion** in your sight,' says the LORD. ²⁵ 'Behold, I *am* against you, **O destroying mountain**, Who destroys all the earth,' says the LORD. "And I will stretch out My hand against you, Roll you down from the rocks, And **make you a burnt mountain**" (**Jeremiah 51:24–25**).

And so we might consider that the mountains and seven kings represent the seven kingdoms on earth throughout the ages. Egypt, Assyria, Babylon, Medo-Persia, and Greece would be five world empires that have fallen at the time of the apostle John's writing. The Roman Empire is the one that "is" at John's time, and the reconstituted Roman empire of ten prominent kings, that is weaker than the first, is the one future to John and current to us, the European Economic Union.

The Greek word translated as "mountains" in the passage "Here *is* the mind which has wisdom: The seven heads are seven **mountains** on which the woman sits" is G3735 *oros*, which is defined as follows: "Probably from an obsolete word oro (**to rise** or "**rear**": perhaps akin G142: compare G3733): a mountain (**as lifting itself above the plain**): hill, mount (ain)." **Revelation 17:15** also tells us that the waters on which the harlot sits "are peoples, multitudes, nations, and tongues," and so the seven mountains represent the seven kings that "rise" above the peoples and nations to conquer and create those seven world empires. The fact that the harlot is drunk with the blood of the saints indicates that she opposes the kingdom of God through the ages and opposes the ways of God.

So the Antichrist, the Beast that comes out of the sea, is to be king of the eighth empire on earth, and he is of the seven because he is part of Satan's plan to show the world that he can rule the world apart from God and the ways of God and still be prosperous and powerful like God. But instead, God is proving to the world that the ways of Satan will always lead to the collapse of the kingdom, and the unity of the kingdom is what we have learned is necessary for the life of the individual subjects of that kingdom, and a divided kingdom will always lead to their death.

THE FALL OF BABYLON THE GREAT

Babylon Is Fallen, Is Fallen

> After these things I saw another angel coming down from heaven, having great authority, and the earth was illuminated with his glory. ² And he cried mightily with a loud voice, saying, **"Babylon the great is fallen, is fallen**, and has become **a dwelling place of demons, a prison for every foul spirit**, and a **cage** for every unclean and **hated bird!** ³ For all the nations have drunk of the wine of the wrath of her fornication, the kings of the earth have committed fornication with her, and the merchants of the earth have become rich through the abundance of her." **(Revelation 18:1–3)**

THE RAPTURE OF THE GREAT TRIBULATION SAINTS

> And I heard another **voice from heaven** saying, **"Come out of her, my people**, lest you share in her sins, and lest you receive of her plagues." **(Revelation 18:4)**

So, as we can see in the above passage, even at the end of the great tribulation we find saints who are raptured to be with Jesus in heaven, just as we saw great tribulation saints in the first version of the tribulation seen from the perspective in heaven.

BABYLON'S GREAT RICHES COME TO NOTHING

> For her sins have reached to heaven, and **God has remembered her iniquities**. ⁶ Render to her just as she rendered to you, and repay her double according to her works; in the cup which

461

she has mixed, mix double for her. [7] In the measure that **she glorified herself** and **lived luxuriously**, in the same measure give her **torment and sorrow**; for she says in her heart, "I sit *as* queen, and am no widow, and **will not see sorrow**." [8] Therefore her plagues will come in one day–**death and mourning and famine**. And **she will be utterly burned with fire**, for strong *is* the Lord God who judges her.

[9] The **kings of the earth** who committed fornication and lived luxuriously with her will weep and lament for her, when they see the smoke of her burning, [10] standing at a distance for fear of her torment, saying, "Alas, alas, that **great city Babylon**, that mighty city! For **in one hour your judgment has come**." [11] And the merchants of the earth will weep and mourn over her, for no one buys their merchandise anymore: [12] merchandise of gold and silver, precious stones and pearls, fine linen and purple, silk and scarlet, every kind of citron wood, every kind of object of ivory, every kind of object of most precious wood, bronze, iron, and marble; [13] and cinnamon and incense, fragrant oil and frankincense, wine and **oil**, fine flour and wheat, cattle and sheep, horses and chariots, and **bodies and souls of men**.

[14] The **fruit** that **your soul longed for has gone from you**, and all the things which are rich and splendid **have gone from you**, and you shall find them no more at all. [15] The merchants of these things, who became rich by her, will stand at a distance for fear of her torment, weeping and wailing, [16] and saying, "Alas, alas, that great city that was clothed in fine linen, purple, and scarlet, and adorned with gold and precious stones and pearls! [17] For **in one hour such great riches came to nothing**."

Every shipmaster, all who travel by ship, sailors, and as many as trade on the sea, stood at a distance [18] and cried out when **they saw the smoke of her burning**, saying, "What *is* like this great city?" [19] They threw dust on their heads and cried out, weeping and wailing, and saying, "Alas, alas, that great city, in which all who had ships on the sea became rich by her wealth! For **in one hour she is made desolate**." [20] Rejoice over her, **O heaven**, and *you* **holy apostles and prophets**, for **God has avenged you on her**! (**Revelation 18:5–20**)

462

A GREAT STONE THROWN INTO THE SEA

Then a mighty angel took up a stone like a **great millstone** and **threw** *it* **into the sea**, saying, "Thus with violence **the great city Babylon shall be thrown down**, and shall not be found anymore. ²² The sound of harpists, musicians, flutists, and trumpeters shall not be heard in you anymore. No craftsman of any craft shall be found in you anymore, and the sound of a millstone shall not be heard in you anymore. ²³ The light of a lamp shall not shine in you anymore, and **the voice of bridegroom** and **bride** shall not **be heard in you anymore**. For your merchants were the great men of the earth, for **by your sorcery all the nations were deceived**. ²⁴ And **in her was found** the **blood of prophets and saints**, and of all who were slain on the earth. (**Revelation 18:21–24**)

THE MARRIAGE OF THE LAMB

After these things I heard a loud voice of a great multitude in heaven, saying, "Alleluia! Salvation and glory and honor and power *belong* to the Lord our God! ² For true and righteous *are* His judgments, because He **has judged the great harlot** who **corrupted the earth** with her fornication; and He has avenged on her the blood of His servants *shed* by her." ³ Again they said, "Alleluia! **Her smoke rises up forever and ever!**" ⁴ And the **twenty-four elders** and the four living creatures fell down and worshiped God who sat on the throne, saying, "Amen! Alleluia!"

⁵ Then a voice came from the throne, saying, "Praise our God, all you His servants and those who fear Him, both small and great!" ⁶ And I heard, as it were, the voice of a great multitude, as the sound of many waters and as the sound of mighty thunderings, saying, "Alleluia! For the Lord God Omnipotent reigns! ⁷ Let us be glad and rejoice and give Him glory, for **the marriage of the Lamb has come**, and **His wife has made herself ready**." ⁸ And to her it was granted to be arrayed in fine linen, clean and bright, for the **fine linen** is the **righteous acts of the saints**.

⁹ Then he said to me, "Write: 'Blessed *are* those who are called to **the marriage supper of the Lamb!**'" And he said to me,

"These are the true sayings of God." [10] And I fell at his feet to worship him. But he said to me, "**See *that you do* not *do that!* I am your fellow servant**, and of **your brethren** who have the **testimony of Jesus**. Worship God! For the **testimony of Jesus** is the **spirit of prophecy**." (**Revelation 19:1–10**)

Notice that all believers in Christ are His Bride and are spiritually "married" to Jesus, or are like subjects in His kingdom, just as He said: "'Therefore, in the resurrection, whose wife of the seven will she be? For they all had her.' [29] Jesus answered and said to them, '**You are mistaken, not knowing the Scriptures** nor the **power of God.** [30] For in the resurrection they neither marry nor are given in marriage, but are like angels of God in heaven'" (**Matthew 22:28–30**). In heaven we will be angels, fellow servants of each other and God the Father and Jesus, His Son. The power of God is in the unity of Oneness like a marriage in which Jesus is the Bridegroom and we, His church, are His Bride.

THE KING OF KINGS AND THE LORD OF LORDS IN BATTLE

Now I saw heaven opened, and behold, a **white horse**. And He who sat on him *was* called **Faithful and True**, and in righteousness He judges and makes war. [12] His eyes *were* like a flame of fire, and on His head *were* many crowns. He had a name written that no one knew except Himself. [13] He *was* clothed with a robe dipped in blood, and **His name is called The Word of God**. [14] And the armies in heaven, clothed in fine linen, white and clean, followed Him on white horses.

[15] Now out of His mouth goes a sharp sword, that with it He should strike the nations. And He Himself will rule them with a rod of iron. He Himself treads the winepress of the fierceness and wrath of Almighty God. [16] And He has on *His* robe and on His thigh a name written: **KING OF KINGS AND LORD OF LORDS.** [17] Then I saw an angel standing in the sun; and he cried with a loud voice, **saying to all the birds** that fly in the midst of heaven, "**Come and gather together** for the **supper**

of the great God, [18] that **you may eat** the **flesh of kings**, the **flesh of captains**, the **flesh of mighty men**, the flesh of horses and of those who sit on them, and the flesh of all *people,* free and slave, both small and great." (**Revelation 19:11–18**)

THE CAPTURE OF THE BEAST AND THE FALSE PROPHET

And I saw the **beast**, the **kings of the earth**, and **their armies**, gathered together to **make war against Him** who sat on the horse and against His army. [20] Then the **beast was captured**, and with him the **false prophet** who worked signs in his presence, by which **he deceived those who received** the **mark of the beast** and those who **worshiped his image**. These two were **cast alive into the lake of fire** burning with brimstone. [21] And the rest were killed with the sword which proceeded from the mouth of Him who sat on the horse. And **all the birds were filled with their flesh**. (Revelation 19:19–21)

The Millennium

SATAN BOUND FOR A THOUSAND YEARS

> Then I saw an angel coming down from heaven, having the **key to the bottomless pit** and a great chain in his hand. ² He laid hold of the **dragon**, that **serpent of old**, who is *the* **Devil** and **Satan**, and **bound him for a thousand years**; ³ and he cast him into the **bottomless pit**, and shut him up, and set a seal on him, so that he should **deceive the nations no more** till the **thousand years were finished**. But after these things he must be **released** for **a little while**. (**Revelation 20:1–3**)

AT THE TIME of the end of the tribulation, all the elect, the saints that were on the earth, have all been raptured or died in faith and are together in heaven with God. The Dragon, the Beast and the False Prophet have gathered together the kings and nations of the whole world to battle on that great day of God Almighty at a place called Armageddon. Babylon the Great is fallen. Jesus, as the Bridegroom, is married to His Bride, the congregation of the saints. Jesus, the Lord of Lords and the King of Kings, has gone to battle with His army to battle the Beast and the kings of the earth and their armies. The Beast and the False Prophet have been captured and thrown alive into the lake of fire, and the rest have been killed. Satan, that Serpent of old, has been bound with a chain and thrown into the bottomless pit for a thousand years, and a seal has been put on him that he shall deceive no more until the thousand years are up.

Someone might ask, "**What is the purpose of the millennial reign with Christ?**" We were raptured to be with Christ in heaven. Are we not supposed to live with Jesus and the Father as fellow angels, sons of God, and spirits as part of the Holy Spirit of God *in heaven*? For Jesus said, "And if I go and **prepare a place for you**, I will come again and **receive you to Myself**; that **where I am**, *there* **you may be**" (**John 14:3**). Are we not supposed to judge angels? As Paul said, "Do you not know that **we shall judge angels**?" (**1 Corinthians 6:3**).

These are all good questions, but remember that part of the plan of God in the trial going on in the Courts of heaven was to show fallen man the truth that the ways of Satan—being separated from God and on our own—are a lie that leads to death and that the ways of God are the only ways of eternal life. Because we refused to listen, God had to turn us over to Satan and allow us to discover for ourselves, by experiencing good and evil, that God was right. In the first two ages God showed us that anarchy did not work and that lawless people who are focused on themselves cannot live by the law. In the third age, the church age, Jesus came to show us the truth that will make us free, and He suffered and died out of His amazing love for us, to reconcile us by faith and love to God the Father, and to teach us that the righteous cannot live in a world together with the evil ways of Satan and his demons.

So God has shown us the ways to live together that do not work; the ways that do not lead to peace, prosperity, unspeakable joy, and eternal life. But that does not show us that God has a better way that does work; a way that does lead to peace, prosperity, love, joy inexpressible, and life. In order to do that, the evil influence of Satan must be removed, and then God is able to show all in heaven and on earth a better way:

> For now we **know in part** and we **prophesy in part**. [10] But **when** that which **is perfect has come**, then that which **is in part** will be done away. [11] When I was a child, I spoke as a child, **I understood as a child, I thought as a child**; but when I became a man, I put away childish things. [12] For now **we see in**

467

> a mirror, **dimly**, but then **face-to-face**. Now I **know in part**, but **then** I shall **know just as I also am known**. [13] And now abide **faith**, **hope**, **love**, these three; but **the greatest of these** *is* **love**. (**1 Corinthians 13:12–13**)

The "**when**" in the phrase "**when** that which **is perfect is come**" and the "then" in the phrase "**then** I shall **know just as I also am known**" refer to the time of the millennium and forever thereafter.

THE MILLENNIAL REIGN OF CHRIST AND HIS SAINTS

> And I saw **thrones**, and **they** sat on them, and **judgment was committed to them**. Then *I saw* **the souls** of those who had been **beheaded for their witness to Jesus** and **for the word of God**, who had not worshiped the **beast or his image**, and had **not received** *his* **mark on their foreheads** or on **their hands**. And they lived and **reigned with Christ for a thousand years**. [5] But the **rest of the dead did not live again until** the **thousand years were finished**. This *is* the **first resurrection**. [6] Blessed and holy *is* he who has part in the first resurrection. Over such **the second death** has no power, but they shall be **priests of God** and **of Christ**, and shall reign with Him **a thousand years**. (**Revelation 20:4–6**)

In the millennium, the last age, with Satan bound so that he cannot interfere, Jesus proves to us, His elect; to Satan and his demons; and to the angels in heaven, by demonstration in the lives of man, that God is right and His ways are righteous. In the millennial reign of Christ there will be peace, prosperity, and unspeakable joy such as the world has never known. Notice the words "This *is* the **first resurrection**." Perhaps this refers to a resurrection of life in the flesh, because the ways of Satan were shown to lead to death in the flesh and so God had to prove that His ways lead to eternal life in the flesh. The second resurrection would then be when Jesus takes us to heaven to live with Him forevermore.

Satan Is Released to Try to Deceive the Nations

> Now **when the thousand years have expired**, Satan will be released from his prison [8] and will go out to **deceive the nations** which are in the four corners of the earth, **Gog and Magog**, to gather them together to battle, **whose number *is* as the sand of the sea**. [9] They went up on the breadth of the earth and surrounded the camp of the saints and the beloved city. And **fire came down from God out of heaven** and **devoured them**. [10] The **devil**, who **deceived them**, was **cast into the lake of fire and brimstone** where the **beast** and the **false prophet** *are*. And they will be tormented day and night forever and ever. (**Revelation 20:7–10**)

We may wonder where the evil people that Satan led came from after the tribulation. The answer is found in **Revelation 20:5**, which tells us that unbelieving dead do not take part in the millennium but do live again after the one-thousand-year reign: "But the **rest of the dead did not live again until the thousand years were finished**." That is exactly the period of time we are now looking at in the book of the Revelation. "When the **thousand years** have expired, **Satan will be released** from his prison" (**Revelation 20:7b**).

The word "Gog" comes from the Greek word G1136 *Gog*, which means "Of Hebrew origin [H1463]; Gog, a symbolic name for some **future Antichrist** – Gog." Similarly, the word "Magog" comes from the Greek word G3098 *Magog*, which means "Of Hebrew origin [H4031]; Magog, **a foreign nation**, that is, (figuratively) **an Antichristian party** – Magog." The Hebrew word H1463 *gog* means "Of uncertain derivation; Gog, **the name of an Israelite**, also of some **northern nation**:- Gog."

So not only will Satan be released, but so will the dead who were his followers—Magog, "**A foreign nation**, an **Antichristian party**." And that includes the Beast called in the Hebrew, Greek, and English "Gog," which is the symbolic name of the future Antichrist. **Revelation 20:8** tells us that they "will **go out to deceive the nations** [the saints, the elect of God] which are in the four corners of the earth." The Bible does not say whether Satan and his evil hordes were able to deceive anyone, but I personally do not think it needs to.

Once we who believe have experienced a lifetime of good and evil, corruption, misery, sorrow, and death in this world of Satan, and then have experienced living a thousand years in peace, love, prosperity, and unspeakable joy with Christ on earth, knowing that heaven with Jesus will be unimaginably better, the choice is a no-brainer, and we cannot be deceived again. At this point Satan's only choice is to try to take us by force. For these are the ways of Satan—deception first, and then force. Satan originally deceived us in heaven when we had never experienced evil. But now that we have experienced evil for ourselves on earth and know what it is like, we won't be fooled again.

This evil horde is gathered together to surround the city of Jerusalem, where Jesus and His saints have been ruling and reigning for a thousand years. It does not seem that there is much of any kind of battle, but fire comes down from God in heaven and consumes them: "They went up on the breadth of the earth and **surrounded the camp** of the **saints** and the **beloved city. And fire came down from God out of heaven and devoured them.** [10] The **devil**, who **deceived them**, was cast into the **lake of fire and brimstone** where the **beast** and the **false prophet** *are*. And they will be tormented day and night forever and ever" (**Revelation 20:9–10**).

The trial going on in heaven is now over, with evidence of God's truths being exhibited on this temporary earth in the lives of man, fallen angelic spirits in bodies of flesh, their faith tested and tried as they live out their lives to see how they respond when the going gets rough, to determine what is in their hearts and minds. The saints have already been judged by what they have done with their lives, whether good or bad, and have been rewarded accordingly: "The nations were angry, and Your wrath has come, And the time of the dead, that **they should be judged**, And **that You should reward Your servants** the **prophets** and the **saints**, And **those who fear Your name, small and great**, And should destroy those who destroy the earth" (**Revelation 11:18**).

THE WHITE THRONE JUDGMENT

Now the works of Satan's followers are judged and those followers are punished for their deeds by being forced to live the way they chose with Satan forever:

> Then I saw a **great white throne** and Him who sat on it, from whose face **the earth** and the **heaven fled away**. And **there was found no place for them**. [12] And I saw the dead, small and great, standing before God, and **books were opened**. And **another book was opened**, which is *the Book* **of Life**. And the dead **were judged according to their works**, by the **things which were written in the books**. [13] **The sea** gave up the dead who were in it, and **Death** and **Hades** delivered up the dead who were in them. And they were judged, **each one according to his works**. [14] Then **Death** and **Hades** were cast into **the lake of fire**. This is the **second death**. [15] And anyone not found written in the **Book of Life** was cast into the **lake of fire. (Revelation 20:11–15)**

The word "written" in the phrase "by the **things which were written in the books**" is translated from the Greek word G1125 *grapho*, which is defined as follows: "A primary verb; to "grave," especially to **write**; figuratively to **describe, write**." If man can record a man's words and actions in a video to convict people on earth, perhaps God can record what we are thinking in our minds and desiring in our hearts? And God speaks of this time through Jeremiah the prophet, "But **this** *is* **the covenant** that I will make with the house of Israel after those days, says the LORD: **I will put My law in their minds**, and **write it on their hearts**; and **I will be their God**, and **they shall be My people**" **(Jeremiah 31:33)**.

This is the end that Jesus talked about while He was on earth:

> Then Jesus said to His disciples, "If anyone desires to come after Me, let him deny himself, and take up his cross, and follow Me. [25] For whoever **desires to save his life will lose it**, but whoever **loses his life for My sake will find it**. [26] For what profit is it to a man if he **gains the whole world**, and **loses his own soul**?

Or what will a man give in exchange for his soul? [27] For the Son of Man will come in the glory of His Father with **His angels**, and then **He will reward each according to his works.**" **(Matthew 16:25–27)**.

Notice that Jesus is speaking of man, God's fallen angels, who are now His angels, who will be rewarded for what they have done on earth.

Jesus lays it on the line: this world is temporary, and this life on earth is not the main event. We **are no fools** if we should **choose**, to **give what we cannot keep; to gain what we can never lose** (adapted from a song by Kathy Troccoli to apply to all of us who understand the truth). How foolish are they that spend a lifetime on earth, trying to make a kingdom for themselves on this temporary planet and by their own choice being left out of the kingdom of peace, prosperity, unspeakable joy, and love that lasts forever.

THE NEW JERUSALEM

THE BRIDE OF THE LAMB

Now I saw a **new heaven** and a **new earth**, for the **first heaven** and the **first earth had passed away**. Also there was **no more sea**. [2] Then I, John, saw the **holy city**, **New Jerusalem**, coming down out of heaven from God, **prepared as a bride adorned for her husband**. [3] And I heard a loud voice from heaven saying, "Behold, the **tabernacle of God** *is* **with men, and He will dwell with them**, and they shall be His people. **God Himself will be with them** *and be* their God. [4] And God will **wipe away every tear from their eyes**; there shall be **no more death, nor sorrow, nor crying**. There shall be **no more pain**, for the former things have passed away."

[5] Then He who sat on the throne said, "Behold, **I make all things new**." And He said to me, "Write, for these words are true and faithful." [6] And He said to me, "**It is done!** I am the Alpha and the Omega, **the Beginning** and the **End**. I will give of the fountain of the **water of life** freely to him who thirsts.

⁷ He who overcomes shall **inherit all things**, and I will be his God and **he shall be My son**.

⁸ "But the cowardly, unbelieving, abominable, murderers, sexually immoral, sorcerers, idolaters, and all liars **shall have their part** in the **lake which burns with fire and brimstone**, which is the **second death**." ⁹ Then one of the seven angels who had the seven bowls filled with the seven last plagues came to me and talked with me, saying, "Come, I will show you the **bride, the Lamb's wife**."

¹⁰ And he **carried me away in the Spirit** to a great and **high mountain**, and **showed me the great city**, the holy Jerusalem, descending out of heaven from God, ¹¹ having the **glory of God**. Her light *was* like a most precious stone, like a jasper stone, clear as crystal. ¹² Also she had a great and high wall with twelve gates, and **twelve angels at the gates**, and names written on them, which are *the names* **of the twelve tribes** of the **children of Israel**: ¹³ three gates on the east, three gates on the north, three gates on the south, and three gates on the west. ¹⁴ Now the wall of the city **had twelve foundations**, and **on them were the names** of the **twelve apostles of the Lamb**.

¹⁵ And he who talked with me had a gold reed to measure the city, its gates, and its wall. ¹⁶ The city is laid out as a square; its length is as great as its breadth. And he measured the city with the reed: **twelve thousand furlongs**. Its length, breadth, and height are equal. ¹⁷ Then he measured its wall: one hundred *and* forty-four cubits, *according* to the **measure of a man**, that is, **of an angel**. ¹⁸ The construction of its wall was *of* jasper; and **the city *was* pure gold, like clear glass**.

Again notice that man is spoken of as angels!

¹⁹ The foundations of the wall of the city *were* adorned with all kinds of precious stones: the first foundation *was* jasper, the second sapphire, the third chalcedony, the fourth emerald, ²⁰ the fifth sardonyx, the sixth sardius, the seventh chrysolite, the eighth beryl, the ninth topaz, the tenth chrysoprase, the eleventh jacinth, and the twelfth amethyst. ²¹ The twelve gates *were* twelve pearls: each individual gate was of one pearl. And the street of the

city *was* pure gold, like transparent glass. ²² But I saw no temple in it, for the **Lord God Almighty** and the **Lamb are its temple**.

²³ The city had no need of the sun or of the moon to shine in it, **for the glory of God illuminated it. The Lamb** *is* **its light**. ²⁴ And the nations of those who are saved shall walk in its light, and the kings of the earth bring their glory and honor into it. ²⁵ Its gates shall not be shut at all by day (**there shall be no night there**). ²⁶ And they shall bring the glory and the honor of the nations into it. ²⁷ But **there shall by no means enter it anything that defiles**, or causes **an abomination or a lie**, but only **those who are written in the Lamb's Book of Life**. (**Revelation 21:1–27**)

Our New Dwelling Place Is with God in Heaven

And he showed me a pure river of **water of life**, clear as crystal, proceeding from the throne of God and of the Lamb. ² In the middle of its street, and on either side of the river, *was* the **tree of life**, which bore twelve fruits, **each** *tree* yielding its fruit every month. The **leaves of the tree** *were* for the healing of the nations. ³ And there shall be no more curse, but the **throne of God** and of **the Lamb shall be in it**, and His servants shall serve Him. ⁴ They shall see His face, and **His name** *shall be* **on their foreheads**. ⁵ There shall be no night there: They need no lamp nor light of the sun, for the Lord God gives them light. And **they shall reign forever and ever**. ⁶ Then he said to me, "These words *are* faithful and true." And the Lord God of the holy prophets **sent His angel to show His servants** the **things which must shortly take place**. (**Revelation 22:1–6**)

JESUS IS COMING QUICKLY

"Behold, **I am coming quickly**! Blessed *is* he who **keeps the words** of the **prophecy of this book**." ⁸ Now I, John, saw and heard these things. And when I heard and saw, I fell down to worship before the feet of the angel who showed me these things. ⁹ Then he said to me, "See *that you do* not *do that*. For I am your fellow servant, and **of your brethren the prophets**, and of those **who keep the words of this book**. Worship God."

[10] And he said to me, "Do not seal the words of the prophecy of this book, for the **time is at hand**. [11] **He who is unjust, let him be unjust still**; he who is filthy, let him be filthy still; **he who is righteous, let him be righteous still; he who is holy, let him be holy still**. [12] And behold, **I am coming quickly**, and **My reward** *is* **with Me**, to give to **every one according to his work**. [13] I am the Alpha and the Omega, *the* Beginning and *the* End, the First and the Last." [14] Blessed *are* those who do His commandments, that **they may have the right** to the **tree of life**, and may enter through the gates into the city. [15] But outside *are* dogs and sorcerers and sexually immoral and murderers and idolaters, and **whoever loves and practices a lie**. [16] "I, Jesus, have sent My angel to testify to you these things in the churches. I am the Root and the Offspring of David, the **Bright and Morning Star**." [17] And the Spirit and the bride say, "Come!" And let him who hears say, "Come!" And let him who thirsts come.

Whoever desires, let him take the **water of life** freely. [18] For I testify to everyone **who hears the words** of the **prophecy of this book**: If anyone **adds to these things**, God will add to him the plagues that are written in this book; [19] and **if anyone takes away** from the **words of the book of this prophecy**, God shall take away his part from the **Book of Life**, from the holy city, and *from* the things which are written in this book. [20] He who testifies to these things says, "Surely I am coming quickly." Amen. Even so, **come, Lord Jesus!** [21] The grace of our Lord Jesus Christ *be* with you all. Amen. (**Revelation 22:7–21**)

THE TRIAL IS OVER

By the end of the Holy Scriptures we find that the trial in the courts of heaven is over concerning the truth about the ways that lead to death and the ways that lead to everlasting life and concerning God's judgment about which of the fallen angels who were deceived and believed the lies of Lucifer and rejected the truth of God would have a change of heart and mind and believe in the ways of God once they experienced the truth about evil and therefore would belong to Him.

God proved in the Old Testament, during the ages of anarchy and the law, by having His fallen children walk in their own ways, that the ways of Satan always lead to corruption, misery, sorrow, and death, whether man lives by laws or not. In the New Testament, during the church age and the millennial reign, God proved that good and evil cannot exist together and that the ways of God lead to peace, prosperity, joy inexpressible, and eternal life.

And God has proven that his election of those written in the Lamb's Book of Life from the foundation of the world—the ones he elected in the beginning, while we were still in heaven—was just, fair, and righteous. He has done so by the way we lived our lives, by our deeds, and by the words we spoke, all of which have been recorded in the books of heaven. And we who believe are His prodigal children. We are reconciled to Him, restored as citizens in the kingdom of God. We are free from the captivity of Satan; spiritually married to Jesus, the Son of God; and safely under His rule and reign to enjoy freedom, love, peace, prosperity, unspeakable joy, and eternal life, with all of the following having been accomplished:

THE SONS OF GOD AND THE SONS OF SATAN HAVE BEEN REVEALED

Little children, let no one deceive you. He who practices righteousness is righteous, just as He is righteous. **8 He who sins is of the devil, for the devil has sinned from the beginning**. For this **purpose the Son of God** was manifested, that He might **destroy the works of the devil**. 9 Whoever has been **born of God does not sin**, for His seed remains in him; and he cannot sin, because he has been **born of God**. 10 In this the **children of God** and the **children of the devil** are manifest: Whoever does not **practice righteousness** is not of God, nor *is* he who does not love his brother.

[11] For this is **the message** that you **heard from the beginning,** that we should **love one another,** [12] not as Cain *who* **was of the wicked one** and murdered his brother. And why did he murder him? Because **his works were evil** and **his brother's righteous.** [13] Do not marvel, my brethren, if the **world hates you.** [14] We know that **we have passed from death to life,** because **we love the brethren.** He who **does not love** *his* **brother abides in death.** [15] Whoever hates his brother is a murderer, and you know that no murderer has eternal life abiding in him. [16] By this **we know love,** because **He laid down His life for us.** And we also ought to **lay down** *our* **lives for the brethren.** [17] But whoever has this world's goods, and sees his brother in need, and shuts up his heart from him, how does the love of God abide in him? [18] My little children, **let us not love in word or in tongue,** but in **deed and in truth.** [19] And by this we know that **we are of the truth,** and shall assure our hearts before Him. (**1 John 3:7–19**)

JUDGMENT AND SEPARATION OF ALL THE FALLEN ANGELS HAS BEEN COMPLETED

"'For to everyone who has, **more will be given,** and he will have abundance; but from him who does not have, even what he has will be taken away. [30] And **cast** the **unprofitable servant** into the **outer darkness.** There will be **weeping** and **gnashing of teeth.**' [31] "When the Son of Man comes in His glory, and **all the holy angels with Him,** then He will sit on the throne of His glory.

[32] All the nations will be gathered before Him, and **He will separate them one from another, as a shepherd divides** *his* **sheep from the goats.** [33] And He will set the sheep on His right hand, but the goats on the left. [34] Then the King will say to those on His right hand, '**Come, you blessed of My Father, inherit the kingdom prepared for you** from the **foundation of the world.**'" (**Matthew 25:29–34**)

THE PROCESS OF CREATING FALLEN MAN INTO THE IMAGE OF GOD IS COMPLETE FOR BELIEVERS

In Genesis we find the plan for fallen mankind, called "*Adam*" in the Hebrew. This is the beginning of the trial on earth: "Then God said, **'Let Us make man in Our image, according to Our likeness'**" (**Genesis 1:26a**). To accomplish this plan in a process that involves a lifetime on planet earth, God begins by creating man and woman with different skills, talents, and abilities so that they need each other and love each other and become One in a family setting, which is a taste and foreshadowing of the ways of the "Oneness in heaven. "So God **created** man **in His *own* image**; in the **image of God** He **created** him; **male and female** He **created** them … Therefore a man shall leave his father and mother and be **joined to his wife**, and they shall become **one flesh**"(Genesis1:27; 2:24).

As we learned in the chapter "The Beginning as Seen From Earth," the word "**created**" is translated from the Hebrew word "*bara*," which indicates that creating us in His image is **a process**. And this process continues in **Genesis chapter 2** when God puts flesh on the first two of many human beings in **Genesis 2:7, 21–22** which is also spoken of in **Genesis 3:21**: "Also for Adam and his wife the LORD **God made tunics of skin, and clothed them**." That man did not begin in the image of God is clearly seen in the birth of the third son of Adam: "And Adam lived one hundred and thirty years, and **begot *a son* in his own likeness, after his image**, and named him Seth" (**Genesis 5:3**), from **Psalm 51:5**: "Behold, I was brought forth in iniquity, And in sin my mother conceived me," and from the doctrine of Original Sin.

The process of experiencing good and evil for ourselves and choosing which way we want to live is the subject and purpose of both the Bible and this book that I was called by God to write. In the Old Testament, Satan blinded their eyes to the truth, and because the kingdom of God is not one of bondage but of free-will choice, God turned us over and let us walk in the ways we chose, in the ways of Satan, so that we and everyone in heaven could see that the ways of Satan are a lie that leads to corruption, misery, sorrow, and death. He did so that we could learn the truth and turn from the lies. God still loved us, and His heart's desire was that none of us would perish but that all would come to repentance and seek eternal life.

But in the New Testament, Paul explains how Jesus came to bring us the truth that would transform us into the image of God:

> **But their minds were blinded.** For **until this day** the same **veil remains unlifted** in the **reading of the Old Testament**, because **the *veil* is taken away in Christ**. [15] But even to this day, **when Moses is read**, a **veil lies on their heart**. [16] Nevertheless **when one turns to the Lord**, the **veil is taken away**. [17] Now **the Lord is the Spirit**; and **where the Spirit of the Lord *is*, there *is* liberty**. [18] But we all, with **unveiled face**, beholding **as in a mirror** the glory of the Lord, are being **transformed into the same image** from glory to glory, just as by the **Spirit of the Lord**. (**2 Corinthians 3:14–18**)

And we learned that "**the Spirit of the Lord**" is the many spirits who are believers in Christ and are united in One with His Spirit which is holy, forming the Holy Spirit of Christ.

Paul continues in the next chapter:

> But **even if our gospel is veiled**, it is **veiled to those who are perishing**, [4] **whose minds** the **god of this age has blinded**, who **do not believe**, lest the **light of the gospel** of the **glory of Christ**, who is the **image of God**, should **shine on them**. [5] For we do not preach ourselves, but Christ Jesus the Lord, and ourselves your bondservants for Jesus' sake. [6] For it is the **God who commanded light to shine out of darkness**, who has **shone in our hearts** to *give* the **light of the knowledge** of the **glory of God** in the face of Jesus Christ. (**2 Corinthians 4:3–4**)

This "**commanding light to shine out of darkness**" harkens back to the beginning and the light that was the light of the knowledge of the ways of life of God: "**In the beginning** God created the heavens and the earth. [2] The earth was without form, and void; and **darkness *was* on the face of the deep**. And the **Spirit of God** was hovering over the face of the waters. [3] Then God said, '**Let there be light**'; and there **was light**. ⁴ And **God saw the light**, that *it was* **good**; and God divided the **light from the darkness**" (**Genesis 1:1–4**). Just as God divides the light from the darkness in the beginning, He divides those who belong to Him from those who belong to Satan in the beginning and in the end.

The apostle John confirms this as he speaks of Jesus, the Word, who was there in the beginning: "In the beginning was the Word, and the Word was with God, and **the Word was God.** ² **He was in the beginning with God.** ³ All things were made through Him, and without Him nothing was made that was made. ⁴ **In Him was life**, and **the life** was the **light of men.** ⁵ And the **light shines in the darkness**, and the **darkness did not comprehend it**" (**John 1:1–4**). But there were some who recognized that they were lied to and came to the light to seek understanding of the truth. These are the ones that were separated from the darkness.

The apostle Paul confirms that God foreknew, before the foundation of the world, who would belong to Him: "For whom He **foreknew**, He also **predestined** *to be* **conformed** to the **image of His Son**, that He might be the firstborn among many brethren" (**Romans 8:29**). And Paul also confirms that we all were in the image of the leader of this world, Satan, and that those who believe the truth will be transformed into the image of Christ: "The **first man** *was* **of the earth**, *made* **of dust**; the **second Man** *is* the Lord from heaven. ⁴⁸ As *was* the **man of dust**, **so also** *are* **those** *who are made* **of dust**; and as *is* the heavenly *Man*, so also *are* those *who are* heavenly. ⁴⁹ And as **we have borne the image** of the *man* **of dust, we shall also bear the image** of the **heavenly** *Man*" (**1 Corinthians 15:49**).

And now that we who believe in God and are in the image of Christ Jesus, the Son of God, Paul says to us,

> **Set your mind on things above**, not on **things on the earth**.
> ³ For **you died**, and **your life is hidden with Christ in God**.
> ⁴ When Christ *who is* our life appears, then you also will appear with Him in glory. ⁵ Therefore **put to death** your members which are on the earth: **fornication, uncleanness, passion,**

evil desire, and **covetousness, which is idolatry.** ⁶ Because of these things the wrath of God is coming upon the sons of disobedience, ⁷ **in which you yourselves once walked** when you lived in them. ⁸ But now you yourselves are to **put off all these: anger, wrath, malice, blasphemy, filthy language** out of your mouth. ⁹ **Do not lie to one another,** since you have **put off the old man** with his deeds, ¹⁰ and have **put on the new man** who is **renewed in knowledge** according to **the image of Him** who created him. (**Colossians 3:8–10**)

WHERE SHOULD YOU GO FROM HERE?

And now that we know the truth that will save our lives, if we truly have the love of God in us, then there will be a fervent desire in our hearts to share this life-giving truth in a spirit of love with our family, our friends, our neighbors, and even our enemies. We have to remember that our battle is not against each other on earth, for we are all in the same boat, having been deceived, but we are in a spiritual battle for what we know and understand to be true with our minds and believe with all our hearts, "for **we do not wrestle against flesh and blood**, but against principalities, against powers, against the **rulers of the darkness of this age**, against **spiritual** *hosts* **of wickedness** in the **heavenly** *places*" (**Ephesians 6:12**).

Jesus has called us to "go therefore and **make disciples of all the nations, baptizing** them in the name of the **Father** and of the **Son** and of the **Holy Spirit**" (**Matthew 28:19**). "And a servant of the Lord **must not quarrel** but **be gentle to all**, able to **teach, patient,** ²⁵ **in humility** correcting those who are in opposition, if God perhaps will grant them repentance, so that they **may know the truth,** ²⁶ and *that* they may **come to their senses** *and escape* the snare of the devil, having been **taken captive by him** to *do* **his will**" (**2 Timothy 2:24–26**).

Those who now know the truth—that agape love, loving God our creator above all and loving each other as much as we love ourselves, unites us as One in Christ Jesus and saves us from eternal death and gives us eternal life—should be walking around with the knowledge that we have a priceless gift more valuable than any amount of gold, silver, diamonds, and rubies. And this is a gift we may freely share with others! We have to be humble, though, remembering that this is a free gift that God has shared with us that we might share it with others.

We have to remember that if we do not share this truth in a way that will make others want to know and understand this truth, it will not do them any good. We have to remember that it is only God who can give a person the Holy Spirit of Truth that can open their hearts and minds to the truth that will make them free. For it is God alone who knows who will respond to the truth and who will not. Our job is not to pick and choose, but to share it with everyone.

When you begin to share the truth with others, you will be confronted with the lies of this world, often in the form of bad science. Because God is a god of truth, and because one truth never conflicts with other truths, then we would expect the Word of God to be consistent with science properly done. But be careful what some people call science, because it may be far from the truth, as the apostle Paul warns in a letter to Timothy: "O Timothy, keep that which is committed to thy trust, **avoiding profane *and* vain babblings**, and oppositions of **science falsely so called**: [21] Which some professing have erred concerning the faith. Grace *be* with thee. Amen" (**1 Timothy 6:20–21 KJV**).

So to grow in faith and to be prepared to respond to the lies of the world, you should check out the many books and videos that document the many evidences in all branches of science that you can find at your local Christian bookstore or online. I can personally recommend six video products and books that are a good place to start:

- The Truth Project is a video series by Dell Tackett that your church can use as a Bible study. For more information, go to thetruthproject.org. Study guides can be purchased through the Focus on the Family website at focusonthefamily.com.

- The book: In Six Days – Why 50 scientists choose to believe in creation. Edited by John F. Ashton PhD
- FaithSearch is a series of books and videos by Dr. Don Bierle available at Christian bookstores or by phone at (800) 964-1447 or (952) 401-4501, or online at www.faithsearch.org.
- The video series I Don't Have Enough Faith to Be an Atheist by Frank Turek and the book of the same name by Norman L. Geisler and Frank Turek are available at Christian bookstores and at crossexamined.org.
- TrueU is an excellent DVD series available at www.trueu.org and focusonthefamily.org.
- And an excellent resource to teach the deep Christian faith of our founding fathers: The DVD Training Course & Study Guide: "Monumental" – Restoring America As The Land Of Liberty. Presented by Kirk Cameron & Stephen Mc Dowell

May God bless you, and may the Spirit of God be with you, my brothers and sisters in the Lord.

And now let us pray together the prayer of the prodigal, which we all are.

THE PRAYER OF THE PRODIGAL

Heavenly Father, this is your son Rick, the one that You love, the one that loves You more and more every day as I get to know who You are and Your Holy nature, as I get to know who I am and my fallen nature, and the fact that at some time in my past I rejected You, Your Truth and Your Ways, and believed the lies of Satan and his ways.

And yet, You still love me and want me back. What amazing love You have for me Father. And so I stand before You now, having experienced good and evil in this temporary life on this temporary earth, and confess to You and to heaven above, that I was so very wrong and You were so very right. You have the ways of eternal life. The ways of Satan are corruption, misery, sorrow, and death.

Father, I pray that You would forgive me for I want to come home. I don't deserve to be called Your son, but make me Your servant that I might live with You forever. In Jesus name I pray. Amen.

A LAST WORD FROM THE AUTHOR:

I hope that this book has helped you to understand the meaning and purpose that God has for our lives on planet earth and that you have learned things that you never knew were in the Bible. I have worked very hard these last twenty years to make this book the best I can with God's help. And now, I would very much like your feedback on how I could make the next version of this book better. Let me know which parts were hard to understand, but first make sure that you were on your knees praying for the help of the Holy Spirit because the words of God are spiritually discerned! If you believe that I have erred in my interpretation of the Word of God, please include Bible references. Send your comments to feedback@truthandlove.us and may God bless you on your faith journey.

Your Brother in the Lord,

Rick Schramm